THE HOLY SPIRIT
IN THE
MEDIAEVAL CHURCH

THE HOLY SPIRIT
IN THE
MEDIAEVAL CHURCH

A STUDY OF CHRISTIAN TEACHING
CONCERNING THE HOLY SPIRIT
AND HIS PLACE IN THE TRINITY
FROM THE POST-PATRISTIC AGE
TO THE COUNTER-REFORMATION

BY

HOWARD WATKIN-JONES, M.A.

'*Historia est fundamentum doctrinae.*'—FLACIUS.

WIPF & STOCK · Eugene, Oregon

Wipf and Stock Publishers
199 W 8th Ave, Suite 3
Eugene, OR 97401

The Holy Spirit in the Mediaeval Church
A Study of the Christian Teaching Concerning the Holy Spirit
and His Place in the Trinity from the Post-Patristic Age
to the Counter-Reformation
By Watkin-Jones, Howard
Softcover ISBN-13: 978-1-6667-3521-5
Hardcover ISBN-13: 978-1-6667-9206-5
eBook ISBN-13: 978-1-6667-9207-2
Publication date 9/23/2021
Previously published by The Epworth Press, 1922

This edition is a scanned facsimile of
the original edition published in 1922.

To

MY FATHER AND MOTHER,
WHO FIRST LED ME INTO THE WAYS OF
THE SPIRIT;

AND TO THE MEMORY OF

HENRY BARCLAY SWETE, D.D.,
LATE REGIUS PROFESSOR OF DIVINITY IN THE
UNIVERSITY OF CAMBRIDGE,

WHOSE WORK CONCERNING THE SPIRIT
I AM HONOURED IN CONTINUING.

PREFACE

THIS book is the result of a request made to me in 1911 by the late Professor Swete to continue his work on the development of the Doctrine of the Holy Spirit which, as he remarked at the time and implied later in his preface to *The Holy Spirit in the Ancient Church*, he felt he would not live to undertake beyond the Age of the Fathers. Being engaged then in reading round the subject in the mediaeval period, I consented to this request, little thinking that, owing to the comparative newness of the ground, it would involve a task covering the space of eleven years. Even so, this book makes no pretensions to being exhaustive, but simply seeks, by surveying the thousand years which separate the Ancient Church from the Modern, to show in as true a light as may be possible what is the foundation of modern thought concerning the Person and work of the Holy Spirit and His place in the Triune Life of God.

Since this is a continuation of Professor Swete's work it naturally follows his method, which, with certain variations, is probably the best for an historical study of mediaeval doctrine as for one of patristic. I am myself responsible for the translations, and have given full references throughout to assist any who may desire to consult the originals for themselves. References are given in each case to modern authorities, of which three have been especially valuable—Erdmann's *History of Philosophy*, Fisher's *History of Christian Doctrine*, and Herzog's *Religious Encyclopaedia*.

My sincere thanks are due to the President of the Wesleyan Methodist Conference (the Rev. J. Alfred Sharp) and the officers of the Epworth Press for their kindness and interest; to the Rev. Dr. H. Maldwyn Hughes, Principal of Wesley House, Cambridge, for reading most of the MS. and making several suggestions; and to the Rev. R. Newton Flew, M.A., for compiling the Index of Subjects.

H. W.-J

LONDON,
May, 1922

'A man who does not know what has been thought by those who have gone before him is sure to set an undue value upon his own ideas.'—MARK PATTISON (quoted by LORD ACTON).

'Every religious and moral faith clothes itself in an intellectual form as a means of self-manifestation and propagation. But every such intellectual form is fatally inadequate to its object and to that extent simply symbolical; with the process of time it undergoes various interpretations or becomes profoundly modified . . . This is why we have a history of dogma '—AUGUSTE SABATIER.

'Orate pro nobis, ut Spiritus Sanctus Paraclitus inspiret animas servorum suorum ad defendendam catholicae fidei veritatem.'—ALCUIN.

CONTENTS

CHAP		PAGE
	INTRODUCTION	11

PART I

FROM THE BEGINNING OF THE SEVENTH CENTURY TO THE CLOSE OF THE ELEVENTH CENTURY: THE CARLOVINGIAN RENAISSANCE AND THE PREPARATORY PERIOD OF SCHOLASTICISM

I.	FOREWORD	21
II	ISIDORE, HILDEFONSUS, BEDE	23
III	ADOPTIONISTS AND ANTI-ADOPTIONISTS	31
IV	ALCUIN, LEO III, AND THE 'FILIOQUE'	41
V	THE EASTERN CHURCH	51
VI	LATER CARLOVINGIANS	55
VII	SCOTUS ERIGENA	63
VIII	FORERUNNERS OF SCHOLASTICISM	68

PART II

FROM THE CLOSE OF THE ELEVENTH CENTURY TO THE CLOSE OF THE THIRTEENTH CENTURY · THE FLOURISHING PERIOD OF SCHOLASTICISM

I	FOREWORD	79
II	THE FATHER OF SCHOLASTICISM	83
III	THE SCHOLASTIC 'RATIONALISTS'	89
IV	HILDEBERT AND THE SUMMISTS	105
V	THE FOURTH LATERAN COUNCIL	121
VI	THE SCHOLASTIC MYSTICS	125
VII	THE EASTERN CHURCH	142
VIII	ALEXANDER OF HALES AND ALBERTUS MAGNUS	146
IX	THOMAS AQUINAS	154

PART III

FROM THE CLOSE OF THE THIRTEENTH CENTURY TO THE BEGINNING OF THE SIXTEENTH CENTURY. THE PRE-REFORMATION PERIOD

I	FOREWORD	173
II	DECADENT SCHOLASTICISM	176
III	THE SCHOLASTIC REVIVAL	195
IV	THE ANTI-SCHOLASTIC MYSTICS	214
V	THE EASTERN CHURCH	223
VI	THE PRE-REFORMATION REFORMERS	227
VII	THE HUMANISTS	240

CONTENTS

PART IV

FROM THE BEGINNING OF THE SIXTEENTH CENTURY TO THE BEGINNING OF THE SEVENTEENTH CENTURY. THE REFORMATION AND ITS IMMEDIATE RESULTS

I.	FOREWORD	249
II.	THE THEOLOGY OF LUTHER AND MELANCHTHON	252
III.	THE REFORMED THEOLOGY OF ZWINGLI	262
IV	THE REFORMED THEOLOGY OF CALVIN	269
V.	THE THEOLOGY OF ENGLISH PROTESTANTISM	281
VI.	LATER LUTHERANS AND THE PHILIPPISTS	288
VII.	EARLY SOCINIANISM	297
VIII.	THE COUNTER-REFORMATION	304

PART V

SUMMARY OF THE DOCTRINE OF THE HOLY SPIRIT IN THE MEDIAEVAL CHURCH

I.	THE GODHEAD OF THE SPIRIT	317
II.	THE RELATION OF THE HOLY SPIRIT TO THE FATHER AND THE SON	320
III.	THE PERSONAL LIFE OF THE SPIRIT	329
IV.	THE WORK OF THE SPIRIT IN CREATION	332
V.	THE WORK OF THE SPIRIT IN INSPIRATION	334
VI.	THE WORK OF THE SPIRIT IN THE INCARNATION	337
VII.	THE MISSION OF THE SPIRIT	339
VIII.	THE WORK OF THE SPIRIT IN THE SACRAMENTS	343
IX.	THE WORK OF THE SPIRIT IN JUSTIFICATION AND SANCTIFICATION	347
X.	THE WITNESS OF THE SPIRIT	352
	INDICES	355

INTRODUCTION

'It is not the duty and part of any Christian, under pretence of the Holy Ghost, to bring in his own dreams and fantasies into the Church; but he must diligently provide that his doctrine and decrees be agreeable to Christ's Holy Testament, otherwise, in making the Holy Ghost the Author thereof, he doth blaspheme and belie the Holy Ghost to his own condemnation '—*Homily on Whitsunday.*

'Quicunque communicat Spiritui Sancto, statim communicat Patri et Filio. In omnibus enim approbatur eamdem operationem esse Patris, et Filii, et Spiritus sancti. Quorum autem una est operatio, una est et substantia '—HIERONYMUS.

INTRODUCTION

It can be no matter for surprise that great stress should be laid by modern thought on the Doctrine of the Holy Spirit, a doctrine which is being realized with such certainty in the movements of the modern world. Modern thought, however, is itself the result of growth, and present views concerning the Person and work of the Holy Spirit are necessarily incomplete without some knowledge of the process of their growth. The so-called cosmic view of the operations of the Spirit is the outcome of a gradual broadening of the individual view which took place to a great extent during the centuries of the mediaeval period. Thus, by way of development, it came to be perceived that 'not only is the human body the temple of the Holy Spirit, but also the body of humanity.' Modernism must not be a new Montanism which finds its glory in superseding law and gospel together with the incontestible facts of experience. Professor Swete has remarked: 'There is a special importance in portraying the relation of the Holy Spirit to modern thought, and in bringing such modern thought into line with historical development. Modern thought on this subject is surely wrong when it discards as a basis all attempt at historicity.'[1] One could go even farther, in asserting that the very idea of the existence of a Holy Spirit, and therefore of an eternal Inspirer and Teacher, postulates the inevitability of doctrinal development.

'The Christianity of the present day has not been evolved directly out of the New Testament.'[2] The New Testament is not a theological treatise.[3] The revelation of the Holy Spirit therein contained was principally that of a new Power, and the content of the Apostolic Age was fundamentally experimental. But the Patristics inevitably began to explore

[1] In conversation at Cambridge, June 15, 1911.
[2] H. B Swete, *The Holy Spirit in the Ancient Church*, p. 4.
[3] See Origen on the intentional apostolic ambiguity, *De Princ.*, preface 3; quoted by Bethune-Baker, *Early Christian Doctrine*, p 201n

the realm of this content, and endeavoured to fit into the mind what had already been fitted into the heart. Dogmatic definition had to be given to the revered mysteries of revealed truth.[1] Moreover, the Early Church and the Church of the Middle Ages developed their inward experience of the Holy Spirit as well as their intellectual conceptions of Him. These are not mutually exclusive in theory, though they were so occasionally in practice. So this development of experience, in its very nature progressive, has added to the earlier deposits of truth valuable increments which can be traced only to the Spirit of God as their Source. In spite of the hesitancy of the post-Apostolic Age to speculate concerning the hypostasis of the Spirit, and of the constant acknowledgement of writers in the later centuries of the mystery which ever defies certain types of such speculation, the Church Catholic has been developing this doctrine under the guidance of that self-same Spirit who should lead her into all the truth, and impart revelations unto the later disciples such as their earliest forerunners were unable to bear.[2] And so the modern age will learn more by entering thankfully into the labours of others than by endeavouring to enter upon an independent novitiate of its own. In the words of Sabatier: ' We should fall to the level of the brute if each one had to begin for himself the work of the ages.'

At times in the course of this study it may seem that inner spiritual realities are enshrouded by a maze of the perceptions and the blindnesses, the controversies, and the invectives of the human side of such a development; and in the attempt to do justice to variations and eccentricities the historian of a doctrine, as Professor Moberly has remarked, seems often to be setting forth an account which is more perplexing than edifying.[3] This may well be the case if an unwarranted separation is made between the general and the special history of doctrine.[4] But in this continuation of Dr. Swete's work

---

[1] W. P. Paterson, *The Rule of Faith*, p 215 · 'It would be a serious blemish on the perfect religion if, in making provision for our spiritual needs, it left us in a condition of intellectual oppression and dissatisfaction '

[2] Auguste Sabatier, in *The Religions of Authority and the Religion of the Spirit*, quotes Lessing as saying ' If God were to offer me in one hand the immutable truth and in the other the search for truth, I should say in all humility, " Lord, keep the absolute truth ; it is not suited to me Leave to me only the power and the desire to seek for it, though I never find it wholly and definitively." '

[3] R C Moberly, *Atonement and Personality.*

[4] See G. P. Fisher, *History of Christian Doctrine*, p. 17.

his method will be followed, namely that of presenting in its unity the system of each theologian as a step towards ascertaining the distinct contribution of each period, and then summarizing the various teachings of the whole with a view to correct historical perspective, therefore to a real spiritual result. In all history of doctrine the methods of synthesis and analysis together demonstrate a real progress arising from the witness of Scripture, the witness of spiritual experience, and deepening thought concerning both. In revealed religion as in natural science there is an evolution which is unfolding a richer knowledge of the Holy Spirit, for He Himself is the Cause of the progressive witness of Christendom to Christ.[1] The world can discover more about the Unseen as it discovers more about Jesus and the reality of the new life in His Spirit.

After the patristic period there was a gradual building up of the edifice of literary achievement. But this improvement was only gradual. In the style of the writers of the early mediaeval period there is little that is really attractive, partly because it is more ponderous than that of their predecessors of the third to the seventh centuries, partly because the theologians themselves exhibit more politeness towards their opponents! A slight falling off in the habit of constant Scripture quotation can be observed, a habit which was a feature of the post-apostolic divines, and in its stead a greater desire to depend on philosophy and logic for the establishing of argumentative positions. From the fourteenth century onwards the commentary method gained a firmer hold, commentaries being issued not only on books of the Bible, but also on works of previous writers, as, for example, the many treatises on the *Sentences* of Petrus Lombardus. The later scholastic commentators on the *Sentences* also freely used the method of the *conclusio* or the syllogism, by which the negative and positive sides of a question were thoroughly examined, and then a decision made upon them.[2] Allusions to the classics occur more frequently, while the ancient love of amassing and marshalling proof-texts noticeably cools ; and the nearer the student approaches the modern period the more he finds literary styles which may be termed sermonic, institutional, and confessional.

[1] Swete, *The Holy Spirit in the New Testament*, p. 314.
[2] Also noted by Fisher, *ibid*, p 215

Further, in the consideration of a subject which must involve to a degree that of the whole Trinity, it is interesting to see how the practice of analogizing the Trinity with reference to nature and to man is carried on with greater frequency since that practice was popularized by Augustine. This 'indication by suggestion' was regarded by the Schoolmen as the most valuable outside of direct scriptural evidence, as any kind of mathematical proof (according to Roger Bacon) is utterly impossible. The common practice of seeking for analogies of the Trinity gradually centred upon psychology as the most fruitful field for its purpose, and the truth that man is created in the Image of God may yet carry more significance than that of which we are now aware.[1] After all, the analogical method is only one of those many legitimate methods which may easily be perverted or unduly forced.

In the progress from the patristic to the mediaeval period there is a distinct change in the character of theological presentation. After the days of the Ancient Church, when the Being of God and the Person of Christ were thoroughly discussed and the doctrines of the Trinity and of the Holy Spirit were in process of formation, the Mediaeval Church comes with its compilers and their codification of dogmas, with its philosophers who gave to the Church for the first time a real philosophy of the Spirit, and with its scientific theologians who regarded theology not only as a science in itself but as queen of the sciences, to which almost every other science should do homage by means of illustration. A new impulse is seen to be given to the unfolding of the Doctrine of the Holy Spirit in East and West, and consequently to the controversy concerning the interior relations of the Godhead. The question of the procession of the Spirit from the Father only, or from the Son as well as from the Father, continued to be a battle-ground for the two sections of the Church, while the less debatable subject of the operations of the Spirit was naturally treated more harmoniously. The *Filioque* controversy was to the

---

[1] Moberly attaches little value to analogies Referring to their use in pre-modern times, he writes. 'Neither any one of them, nor (still less) all together, go far towards enabling uni-personal man to enter into the consciousness of Tri-personality. No analogy drawn from an imperfect personality can truly mirror the Trinity of God' (*ibid*, pp 172, 176) So Gregory of Nazianzus, cf Swete, *The Holy Spirit in the Ancient Church*, p 244 On the other hand, Dean Inge remarks 'One might almost dare to say that all conclusions about the world above us which are *not* based on the analogy of our own mental experiences are either false or meaningless' (*Christian Mysticism*, p 34).

Doctrine of the Holy Spirit largely what the Adoptionist controversy was to the Doctrine of the Person of Christ.

The Greek contribution to the sum of mediaeval thought is small indeed in proportion to that of the West, owing to the comparative unprogressiveness of the Greek theology and to the Greek writers themselves being in a decided minority. Certain also of the Eastern divines appeared to surrender an important element of distinction in their theology, as some of the Western debaters were not slow in pointing out.[1] Harnack states that 'the Greek Church has no history of dogma after the seven great Councils,' and adds: 'It is incomparably more important to recognize this fact than to register the theologoumena which were later on introduced by individual bishops and scholars in the East, who were partly influenced by the West.'[2] In other words, the dogmatic development of the Eastern Church ceases with John of Damascus, who died in the same year as the meeting of the seventh Ecumenical Council. Yet there is a doctrinal interest attaching even to individual Greek authors, particularly to those who incline to the Western opinions. Accordingly selections from the theologians of the East will be taken and viewed apart from those of the West in order to preserve in the course of the present study continuity of thought in each of the great Churches of Christendom.

In the West, according to Harnack,[3] one complete development stretches from Augustine to the Reformation. Augustine (cf. *De Trinitate* and *De fide et Symbolo*) was the pioneer in the use of the human analogy for the purpose of illustrating the Divine Triunity. He is, however, most important as being the originator of the formal statement of the twofold and timeless procession of the Holy Spirit from the Father and the Son as from one Source. The *Filioque*, then definitely promulgated, continued to provoke heated controversy between East and West during the early years of the Mediaeval Church. The overwhelming majority in the West followed the lead of Augustine from the uninspiring dialectics of the Schoolmen, through the more spiritually powerful teachings of the Mystics, to the stirring messages of Luther and the Reformers. The

---

[1] On the contrary, certain Western theologians favoured the Eastern view of the Procession, though the Greeks attached no such importance to that as did the Latins to the favouring of the Western view by certain Eastern theologians

[2] Harnack, *Hist of Dogma* (E. Trans), 1 19   [3] *Ibid*, v 8.

Reformation, being both Protestant and Trinitarian, gave rise in turn to the two opposites of the revived Catholicism of Trent and the rationalism of Socinus.

The scope of the present study extends from Gregory the Great and John of Damascus, who close the Age of the Fathers in the West and East, to the earliest years of the seventeenth century. It thus embraces the Reformation and its immediate results, in accordance with the view of Schaff that the Middle Ages cradle the Protestant Reformation as well as the papal Counter-Reformation. Thus Harnack asserts, on the one hand, the essentially mediaeval character of post-Tridentine Catholicism and Socinianism, and, on the other, the essentially modern character of the Reformation, which therefore forbids, within the limits of a mediaeval survey, any consideration of Protestant theology as far as the Formula of Concord (1577) and the Dort Decrees (1619).[1] To this view the scope of this work is adapted. Meanwhile it is of interest to note that the thought of the West remained pre-eminently theological until well into the seventeenth century.

While the first main period, taken by itself, lays its greatest stress upon the Divine Unity, the chief interest throughout the first two main periods lies in the gradual working out of the *Filioque* controversy, and it is principally owing to this that the Doctrine of the Holy Spirit again comes to the fore with such prominence in the twelfth century. Most authors of treatises on this subject wrote, as has been indicated, from the Latin standpoint; hence the preponderance of opinion in favour of adding *Filioque* to the Creeds. The Church of the West has never gone back on the advance made during this second period in the matter of the Spirit's procession from the Son. Striking arguments for the existence of the Trinity are also seen to be developed by the Schoolmen with increasing penetration of reasoning, but statements of belief touching the Holy Spirit outside the debatable area of the procession do not undergo severe changes, while the few changes themselves are usually not of outstanding importance. These earlier writers lay the emphasis upon the Being rather than upon the work of the Spirit, though the latter side of the doctrine has profound significance in the teachings of Alcuin, Bernard,

---

[1] *Ibid*, vii 169, the Formula and the Dort Decrees being regarded not as the classic expression of the Reformation but as marks of transition to the modern period

and the Mystics, as also in Thomas Aquinas, the greatest of the Schoolmen. The channels of the Spirit's operations in the soul of man were, moreover, not so rigidly sacramentarian.

A glimpse at the last two main periods suggests that one or two avenues of controversy have received a final closure, while others have obviously been opened. The West more than ever continues to emphasize the *Filioque*, though any serious debate concerning the Spirit's procession from the Son has practically ceased to exist. The West asserts that the East has had the worst of the argument, and Huss goes so far as to say that the Greeks really agree with the truth of the *Filioque*, even though they are constantly professing to disagree. Indeed, Georgios Scholarios, the Eastern Patriarch, appears none too decided on the point—to people who do not reckon with his political motives. Together with the Eastern Church, which receives the condemnation of the Western as being heretical and schismatic, there are heretics in the West also, who treat the *Filioque* along with other subjects with marked scepticism; such are Faustus Socinus, John of Wesel, and Michael Servetus. Again, the work of the Holy Spirit is gradually brought forward, while His Being gradually retires, for a time, into the background. Unceasing insistence upon the operations of the Spirit in the soul in response to faith is found in the Reformers, and to them justification by faith apart from any action of the Spirit is unthinkable. In the words of Nitzsch: ' The dogmatic theology of the Reformation attended at first solely to the point of justification by faith, and developed the idea of faith still farther, along with those who are essentially connected with it, the Holy Spirit, repentance, works, love.'[1] The movement which is responsible for such a development is worthily represented by Zwingli, Tyndale, Bugenhagen, Calvin, and Brenz. In these two periods, again, there is manifestly a recognition of the danger of loose thinking, and, accordingly, an unusual readiness to define terms. The word ' person,' for example, receives most careful attention, being defined philosophically, and also studiously compared with the terminology employed by the Greeks. The Doctrine of the Trinity is more frequently

---

[1] *System of Christian Doctrine*, §140, quoted by Hare (*Mission of the Comforter*, ed 1876, Note AB p 441)

explained by means of the 'love argument,' to the effect that, as it is the nature of God to love, He must have had from eternity some Object of love, namely the Son, the Holy Spirit being the mutual love of the Two, and therefore the Bond of the Three. Roger Bacon fully illustrates this attitude.

PART I

FROM THE BEGINNING OF THE SEVENTH CENTURY TO THE CLOSE OF THE ELEVENTH CENTURY

THE CARLOVINGIAN RENAISSANCE AND THE PREPARATORY PERIOD OF SCHOLASTICISM

    I. FOREWORD
   II. ISIDORE, HILDEFONSUS, BEDE
  III. ADOPTIONISTS AND ANTI-ADOPTIONISTS
  IV. ALCUIN, LEO III., AND THE 'FILIOQUE'
    V. THE EASTERN CHURCH
  VI. LATER CARLOVINGIANS
 VII. SCOTUS ERIGENA
VIII. FORERUNNERS OF SCHOLASTICISM

ὁ δὲ Σωτὴρ..., τοῦ τε Πνεύματος τοῦ ἁγίου χορηγὸς ὢν αὐτός, ὅμως δὲ λέγεται νῦν χρίεσθαι ἵνα πάλιν, ὡς ἄνθρωπος λεγόμενος τῷ Πνεύματι χρίεσθαι, ἡμῖν τοῖς ἀνθρώποις, καθάπερ τὸ ὑψωθῆναι καὶ τὸ ἀναστῆναι, οὕτως καὶ τὴν τοῦ Πνεύματος ἐνοίκησιν καὶ οἰκειότητα κατασκευάσῃ —ATHANASIUS.

I

FOREWORD

THE first main period of the Mediaeval Church covers the years from the beginning of the seventh century to the close of the eleventh, the darkest period of the Middle Ages. It was 'in the middle of the eleventh century' that 'the rupture between the Churches of the East and the West was completed.'[1] This period closes with the forerunners of Scholasticism who precede Anselm, the real founder of Scholasticism. During these years the faith of the Church gradually received a rational setting. Consequently, in preparation for the systematizing labours of the Schoolmen, the majority of these earlier theologians are seen to be stupendous compilers of the material handed on by the Fathers.

Within the limits of this period there are at least twenty-two writers of repute on the Doctrine of the Holy Spirit. In addition to the two representatives of the Eastern Church, chosen from the ninth century, who will require separate consideration, the Western representatives may be roughly apportioned to their several centuries thus . two to the seventh, eight to the eighth, six to the ninth, none to the tenth, and four to the eleventh. This apportionment will suffice to show that the interest in this doctrine, which had ebbed and flowed according to the theological emphasis of the day since the time of Ignatius, was destined still to be subject to considerable variation, the absence, for example, of any important references to the Holy Spirit in the tenth century being due mainly to the shifting of controversy to the Doctrine of the Person of Christ. This is reminiscent of a similar postponement of the Doctrine of the Spirit in the Nicene period, necessitated by a defence of the Deity of Christ against Arian attacks.[2] Similarly, again, when the tenth century concluded, increased

---

[1] Fisher, *ibid*, p 201   [2] Swete, *Holy Spirit in the Ancient Church*, p 6

attention was given to the Doctrine of the Spirit, just as after the settlement of the earlier Arian questionings concerning the Son. No doubt the years of the tenth century suffered a slight reaction after the intense theological activity of the Carlovingian Renaissance, and they were also marked by a lowering of spiritual tone in Europe ; yet they saw the revival of monastic religion in the celebrated foundation of Clugny (910) and also the continuance of theological debate on other topics.

II

ISIDORE: HILDEFONSUS: BEDE

THE seventh century had not long begun when Mohammedanism arose, with its stern monotheism, at the very time when the Eastern Church had degenerated in spiritual influence and was disturbed with the monophysite and monothelite controversy concerning the Person of Christ. During this century the Saracens poured Westward, though it would appear that their beliefs were not so much anti-trinitarian as anti-tritheistic.[1] Contemporary with this movement were changes in the West, where the Roman Empire was being hard pressed by the Lombards and the Slavs, and where the Franks and the Visigoths were the dominant peoples. Thus there was all the greater need for the unity and authoritative strictness of the Western Church.

Gregory the Great had left valuable legacies to the Church. Not only had he been a great reformer and ecclesiastical statesman, but he had also been mainly responsible for the conversion of Visigothic Spain, Britain, and the Lombards to the Catholic faith. These legacies were made the most of in the Carlovingian Renaissance, a fertile period in the midst of the barren post-patristic age, when the Church revived her missionary labours beside producing noted theologians and compilers. An instance of this is visible in the steadfast manner in which the Church of the Franks held to the *Filioque* in face of the Eastern view, Alcuin being one of her champions in this respect, and Theodulf of Orleans even receiving an imperial command to write a defensive exposition of this addition to the Creed.

ISIDORE

The beginnings of this strengthening of the Church of the West are seen in connexion with Isidore (*c.* 560–636),

---

[1] 'Videtur Mahumet contra sanctissimam trinitatem nihil voluisse scribere, solum pluralitatem deorum damnans '—Nicolas of Cusa, *Cribratio Alchoran, lib* 1 The Christianity with which Mahomet was acquainted was a corrupt type of Christianity and Judaism combined, and its theology would be none of the purest   But Nicolas was of the opinion that the Mohammedans ought openly to confess the Trinity, seeing that the Koran contains so many statements which accord with that belief !

Archbishop of Seville, a conspicuous representative of an active Catholicism in Spain.[1] His spiritual leadership was invaluable to the Church of his age, while his powers of compilation are exhibited in his *Etymologies*, which have been termed an encyclopaedia of all the sciences, and also in his three books of *Sentences*, a most important theological work embodying the accepted thought of the Western Church upon the foundation of Augustine. Both of these works show something of his views on the Person and work of the Holy Spirit. He lays the emphasis where the Spanish Church laid it, namely, on the twofold procession of the Spirit, and he regards the *Filioque* as a strengthening of belief in the Trinity and in the Godhead of the Spirit. 'Every incorporeal nature,' he remarks, ' is called " spirit " in the Holy Scriptures . . . therefore the Spirit of God is called " holy." ' The Spirit he holds to be ' the co-essential and consubstantial Holiness of Both.' He is not called ' begotten,' lest two Sons should be suspected in the Trinity. For that reason, too, He is not predicated ' unbegotten,' lest two Fathers should be supposed to be in the Trinity.'[2] 'The Holy Spirit alone proceeds from the Father and the Son, therefore He alone is pronounced the Spirit of Them Both.'[3] So Isidore, along with his assertion of the Spirit's Deity, presses for the *Filioque*, as did the many Spanish Councils of the seventh century, when the Church in Spain was the citadel of the dogma against the heresy of Arius. In fact, it was Isidore's elder brother, Leander, whom he succeeded in the archbishopric of Seville, who presided at the third Council of Toledo in 589, when the *Filioque* was first made part of the Creed as used in the West.[4]

Isidore asserts that the Trinity is so named because one Whole is caused by Three (*fiat totum unum ex quibusdam tribus*), as it were a Triunity, as memory (*memoria*), understanding (*intelligentia*), and will (*voluntas*), ' in which the mind (*mens*) contains in itself some likeness of the Divine Trinity. For while they may be three, they are one.' This analogy pointing

---

[1] Professor Swete has dealt briefly with Isidore, *ibid*, p 346 (q v), but Isidore is here referred to again as he doubtless stands at the threshold of the new Renaissance
[2] *Etymol* vii 3 (ed Migne, and usually so unless otherwise stated) Another sentence from the same chapter, which Swete translates, reads ' Hoc autem interest inter nascentem Filium et procedentem Spiritum sanctum, quod Filius ex uno nascitur, Spiritus sanctus ex utroque procedit '
[3] *Ibid*, 4   [4] Swete (*ibid*, pp 344ff) notes the various Councils of Toledo, the third of which is the most important

to the Deity as 'One in Nature and Three in Persons' was previously used by Augustine. During the controversy on the Procession, however, misunderstanding was apt to arise from confusion of the Latin and Greek terminologies. ' Belief among the Greeks concerning the Trinity is expressed,' he states, ' in this way : one οὐσία, as much as if one Essence or Nature is spoken of ; three " hypostases," which to a Latin sounds like three " Persons " or three " Subsistences." '[1] These verbal explanations, which had for some time been necessary in the Ancient Church, continued so to be in the Mediaeval Church as East and West sought to retain common ground for discussion. Beatus and others after him followed Isidore in having still to insist on the right equations amid various interpretations of theological formulae.[2]

Isidore wrote little on the work of the Spirit, as His own Church was engaged in making her contribution more especially in other ways. He cites John xvi. 12, 13, remarking, ' Here, moreover, He [the Holy Spirit] proceeds not only by Nature, but always for the purpose of completing the works of the Trinity does He proceed unceasingly.'[3] So the procession of the Spirit is seen to have an external as well as an internal impulse, namely that of being the Completer of the operations of the Triune God as also that of the unity of the three Divine Persons. The Holy Spirit, who is the Spirit of the Father and the Son, 'is Creator just as the Father and the Word.' His participation in the Advent of Christ is mentioned in addition to His creatorship. ' Christ declared that He was sent not only by the Father but also by the Holy Spirit,' while ' the coming of Christ was from time to time proclaimed by the holy prophets, secretly instructed through the Holy Spirit.'[4] Thus the information concerning the Mission of the Son could naturally be supplied by One who had co-operated in that Mission with the Father.

Hildefonsus

The work of Isidore was carried on in Spain by his pupil Hildefonsus († 669), Archbishop of Toledo. Among his many literary labours there is a contribution to dogmatic theology

---
[1] *Ibid*, 4
[2] For the ' one hypostasis ' of the Western Church and the ' three hypostases ' of the Eastern Church, with their reconciliation, see Swete, *ibid*, p 173
[3] *Ibid*, 3   [4] *Sent*, 1 15

entitled *Annotationes de Cognitione Baptismi*. The preface to this work contains the statement that 'the Spirit Himself has inspired Scripture with a view to the salvation of men.' The work proper contains at its outset a definition of God, as do so many of the treatises of mediaeval theologians. 'God,' he writes, 'is one, indivisible, incomprehensible, inestimable (*inaestimabilis*), immortal, omnipotent, perfect, and eternal. . . . He is before all things, over all things, within all things, without all things.'[1] He is immanent and transcendent Spirit. 'This God is Father, Son, and Holy Spirit. But the Father is from no one (*a nullo*) but Himself (*ex se*), and He alone is Father. The Son is begotten from the Father, and is therefore co-eternal with the Father; and He alone is Son. The Holy Spirit proceeds inseparably from (*ex*) the Father and the Son; and He alone is Holy Spirit. The whole Trinity is one God,'[2] whose unity is strongly emphasized throughout the book. Baptism is administered in the Name of the Trinity,[3] and the actions of the undivided Trinity are constantly mentioned.

With the Divine Unity as a background, Hildefonsus deals at some length with the inter-relations of the three Persons when treating of the Incarnation. 'The whole Trinity was engaged in the fact of the Incarnation, since the operations of the Trinity are inseparable; yet the Person of the Son alone submitted to this, for all things that relate to the Person of Christ through this dispensation could not in any way relate to the Persons either of the Father or of the Holy Spirit. For it is not right to speak of the Father and the Spirit as born of the Virgin or as hung on the Cross (*cruci suspensos*).'[4] In that human sense, therefore, the Son underwent an experience which was not shared in every particular by the Father and the Holy Spirit, being born of (*natus de*) the Holy Spirit and the Virgin Mary, and thus partaking of a human as well as of a Divine substance.

Questions naturally arose in the pursuit of any such line of thought. 'How,' he asks, 'do we speak of Christ as born of the Holy Spirit if the Holy Spirit did not beget Him?' Special mention of the Holy Spirit in this connexion seems at first

---

[1] 'Hic est ante omnia, super omnia, intra omnia, extra omnia'
[2] *Annotat*, 3   He adds 'non aliud habens, et aliud subsistens.'
[3] *Ibid*, 31, 112, &c.   [4] *Ibid*, 9

somewhat unwarranted, ' as the entire Trinity produced that
" Creature " which the Virgin conceived and brought forth
(though belonging to the Person of the Son alone), and the
operations of the Trinity are indeed inseparable.'[1] At least
there is the testimony of Scripture, already noticed, as to the
part taken by the Spirit in reference to the Incarnation, though
Hildefonsus readily admits that the actual difference between
the relation of the Son to the Father and that of the Son to
the Spirit is difficult to explain. Yet he insists that though
the Son is begotten of the Spirit He is not called the Spirit's
Son [2] ' Assuredly no one has ever spoken of those who are
born of water and the Holy Spirit as sons of water, but clearly
they are spoken of as sons of God the Father and of their
mother the Church. Even so, therefore, He who is begotten
of the Holy Spirit is the Son of God the Father, not of the
Holy Spirit.'[3] The customary terminology in use with
regard to those who are received into the Church by baptism
is an important guide to correctness of thought as touching
the unique Sonship of Christ ; such is the drift of an unusual
form of argument. As to the warning against the confusion
of two Sons or of two Fathers in the Trinity, consequent on
the assertion of the Spirit as either begotten or unbegotten,
Hildefonsus follows the teaching of Isidore almost word for
word.[4] He does likewise in describing the difference between
the generation of the Son and the procession of the Spirit,
' because the Son is begotten of One, while the Holy Spirit
proceeds from Both.'[5] The Spanish approval of the *Filioque*
is often set forth.

This treatise also contains little regarding the work of the
Spirit. The unity of the Trinity in external action is resumed
where Isidore left it, and is stressed even more forcibly by his
pupil. The whole Trinity is evidenced in the work of creation[6]
as also in the Incarnation of the Son, though the special task
of the Spirit in the second instance is also asserted. The New
Birth of the Spirit is declared to accompany baptism, bringing with it a filial relation to God and the Church. The Holy
Spirit is given by means of the imposition of hands, yet even
then He is bestowed not by men but by God.[7]

---

[1] See *ibid*, 40   [2] *Ibid*, 41   [3] *Ibid*, 42   [4] *Ibid*, 58   [5] *Ibid*, 59
[6] *Ibid*, 4   [7] *Ibid*, 129, 130

BEDE

This period, preparatory to the greater activity of thought under the patronage of Charlemagne, may once more be exemplified by a notable representative of early English culture. The Venerable Bede (673–735), the learned Anglo-Saxon presbyter renowned for his versatility and industry in scholarship, was one of the most illustrious of the academic and ecclesiastical authorities of the West. He may be considered, with some assurance, to embody the main outlook of the whole of Saxon theology. Erdmann suggests that his work *De rerum naturae* is an instance of his regard for Isidore of Seville,[1] and certainly there is a similarity of scheme between this work of Bede's and the *Etymologies* of Isidore. Thus it may be allowable also to expect a general similarity of theological standpoint between the Churches of England and of Spain at this period, drawing, as they did, upon the common heritage which they had received from the Western Patristics.

Neither as Church historian nor as spiritual teacher does Bede appear to have been appreciated to the full by the religious world of his day.[2] Those who lay foundations are more highly estimated when the building rises fair upon their work, and when others enter into their labours. But Bede's theology must have exercised a definite influence upon the thought of the West during his lifetime, for he makes a real contribution to contemporary discussions, throwing his weight into the scale in emphasis of the views of the Occidental Fathers which had already found, and were yet to find, strong defenders in the orthodox writers of the Spanish and Frankish Churches.

His opinions on the Doctrine of the Holy Spirit can be seen in his *Commentaries*, and, among these, that upon the Gospel of St. John will suffice for the immediate purpose. In this work Bede confines himself almost entirely to the consideration of the Being of God, and within those limits he emphasizes most the unity of the Trinity, the complete oneness of the Persons. It is possible that he laid such stress upon this truth in view of the continued spread of Mohammedanism with its plausible advantage over the supposed tritheism of the

---

[1] Erdmann *History of Philosophy* (tr Hough), 1 290 f , where he also regards Bede as the pioneer of Scholastic philosophy

[2] Milman *Latin Christianity*, ii 276 · ' The works of Bede were written for a very small intellectual aristocracy '

Christian creed, for it was not until three years before Bede's death that this movement received its final check in the West at the hands of Charles Martel. He thereupon begins with the assertion that 'The Spirit is God,'[1] but this must not be understood as in any way implying a plurality of Gods. 'The Holy Spirit, proceeding from the Father and the Son, is also Himself God; just as the Father is God and the Son is God, even so the Holy Spirit is also God; not three gods, but one God, one glory (*lumen*), one Substance, one Nature, one majesty, one eternity, one greatness (*magnitudo*), one power, one goodness.'[2] So, again, Bede speaks of the Holy Spirit as the 'first principle' (*principium*), but he hastens to add that there are not three first principles, corresponding to the three Persons of the Trinity, but only one first principle; for he repeats, 'There are not three gods, but one God; . . . not three " omnipotents," but one Omnipotent.' The Spirit is the Spirit of the Father and of the Son, proceeding from Them Both, and therefore is of one Substance, power, and majesty along with Them.[3] The fact of there being three Persons in the Trinity does not preclude us from having our relationship with the Trinity as such.[4] 'In nothing must the Father be believed to be without the Son and the Holy Spirit.' The presence of any One of the Persons means the presence of the inseparable Three. Yet in stressing the unity of the Godhead, Bede guards against Mohammedanism without and Sabellianism within. 'Often, indeed, have we said that the operations of the Trinity are inseparable, but we have said too that the Persons should be praised singly, so that both the Unity and the Trinity may be understood to be not only without separation but also without confusion.'[5] And in his comments on the seventeenth chapter, throughout which the Divine unity is especially to the fore, he continues the trinitarian safeguard expressed in the previous sentence. 'The Father, Son, and Holy Spirit are not three gods, but the Trinity Itself is one only true God (*unus solus verus Deus*). The Father, however, is not the same as the Son, nor the Son the same as the Father, nor the Holy Spirit the same as the Father or the Son, because They are three, Father, Son, and Holy Spirit. Here is a definition of the triunity of the Deity which, while steadfastly upholding His oneness or μοναρχία,

[1] Cap 4   [2] *Ibid*, 7   [3] *Ibid*, 8   [4] *Ibid*, 14   [5] *Ibid*, 16

laid down the distinctive belief of the Church as against Mohammed or Sabellius.

The above extracts from Bede which show his attitude to the doctrine of the Trinity also contain proof of his adherence to the Western view of the Procession. He does not add the *Filioque* in every mention of the Spirit's procession from the Father—which is not surprising, as this addition had not altogether passed its liquid stage in the West—but in many instances he does state his belief in the procession of the Spirit from the Son also.[1] In this connexion, too, he instances the Lord's words to the disciples in chapter xx., 'Receive the Holy Spirit,' with the remark that 'by breathing upon them He indicated that the Holy Spirit is not the Spirit of the Father alone, but also His own '—an echo of Augustine. The Godhead of the Holy Spirit, and His equality to the other Persons in the Trinity, are both set forth as being largely consequent upon His procession from the Father and the Son.

The little that this writer asserts with reference to the work of the Spirit follows, for the most part, his line of thought on the Being of the Trinity. 'Inseparable are the works not only of the Father and of the Son, but also of the Holy Spirit.'[2] Nevertheless, baptism especially is administered ' in the Holy Spirit,' and is accompanied by the cleansing from sins ' through the grace of the Holy Spirit.' It is not the outward rite, but the Divine mercy working through it, which is the source of such spiritual efficacy.[3]

Bede and the two Spanish divines, Isidore and Hildefonsus, were particularly insistent on handing on from the earlier age a theology of the Holy Spirit and of the Trinity, along with the Western conception of the Procession, which was to strengthen the foundation of the Latin position against that of the Greeks during the ninth and succeeding centuries.

---

[1] ' De Patre et Filio procedens ' (7) , ' Ex Patre et Filio procedens ' (8), &c
[2] *Ibid* , 17.
[3] *Ibid* , 1 This is reminiscent of the attitude of Cyril of Jerusalem (Swete, *ibid* , p. 206).

III

ADOPTIONISTS AND ANTI-ADOPTIONISTS

THE ADOPTIONISTS

THE Carlovingian Renaissance brought with it a revived faculty for discussion which is apparent in a controversy that did not primarily concern the Doctrine of the Holy Spirit, but which nevertheless deeply affected the peaceful trend of Western thought. Adoptionism,[1] as an attempt to uphold the Monarchian theory, exemplifies the case of heresy arising out of heresy, and that almost unwittingly; for intellectual activity in doctrinal development seemed so far ahead of fitting phraseology in which it might be contained and safeguarded, that the distance between the two was responsible for much misunderstanding. The Moorish Spaniard Migetius, who upheld the very anthropomorphic view of a corporeal existence of the three Persons in the Godhead, drew upon himself the condemnation of one of the leading divines of the country, ELIPANDUS (*fl.* 790–800), Archbishop of Toledo. Elipandus was eager to dismiss any suggestion of material corporeality from the conception of the Trinity, and, in his eagerness, he alluded to the Son, in the days of His flesh, as *filius adoptivus*—an assertion which raised the controversy from the side of the orthodox theologians in Spain and in France. It might have been that the Archbishop was unconsciously influenced by the tenets of Islam concerning the solitary oneness of God to put forward this defence of the Divine monarchy. Certain it is that Mohammedanism, with its Eastern and Western Caliphates, had a strong grip upon the civilized world at the time; and also that this religion and Judaism were the two principal 'heresies' attacked by Western churchmen of the eighth and ninth centuries. But, whatever be the origin of the idea in the mind of Elipandus, the idea itself was held to undermine the Doctrine of the Trinity as

[1] Adoptionism regarded Christ as adopted as to His humanity though not as to His Divinity See Fisher's note on p 205 (*Hist of Christian Doc*)

taught by the Church, and it is natural that during the controversy the discussions should converge upon the Second Person rather than upon the Third.

Though, however, the Doctrine of the Person of Christ was uppermost in the Adoptionist debates, the writers involved also dealt with the Doctrines of the Trinity and of the Holy Spirit with equal definiteness if not at equal length. Further, the protagonists of the *filius adoptivus*, although decidedly unorthodox on that account, seem to have been generally in line with the *fides catholica* when they had to consider truths relating to the Spirit. Elipandus adheres to the pronounced verdict of the Church of Spain in emphasizing the procession of the Holy Spirit from the Father and also from the Son.[1] Then follows a trinitarian formula which is typically Occidental: 'Behold the three Persons of the Father, the Son, and the Holy Spirit, spiritual, incorporeal, undivided, unconfused, co-essential, consubstantial, co-eternal in one Divinity and power and majesty: without beginning, without end, always abiding ... a Trinity of Persons subsisting in one Deity.'[2] Again, in another of his letters, Elipandus makes a statement concerning the Son to which none of his opponents would object when he remarks that 'the Son of God is co-eternal and consubstantial with the Holy Spirit.'[3] This setting of the Doctrine of the Trinity would appear quite orthodox from these extracts alone, though, if he 'lower' the essence of the Son, he would, according to his own symbol of faith, also 'lower' the essence of the Father and of the Spirit. It will be seen how Beatus and Etherius were not slow in pointing this out to him. The *Symbolum Fidei* of Elipandus, as quoted by these two ecclesiastics, is too traditional to yield any 'newness' in his doctrine of the Spirit, while the very part which he played in the Adoptionist Controversy accounts for the fact that he wrote comparatively little on the theology of the Holy Spirit, and nothing on His work.

Felix of Urgel

While in the midst of his Spanish critics Elipandus found a supporter in Felix, Bishop of Urgel, who proved to be the chief debater in the defence of Adoptionism, and who, in

---

[1] *Ad Migetium Haereticum*, Epist 1 5   [2] *Ibid*, 1 9
[3] Epist iv   *Ad Albinum* 11

ADOPTIONISTS AND ANTI-ADOPTIONISTS

consequence, confined his attention almost entirely to the Person of the Son. The same might be said of the orthodoxy of his trinitarian profession as has already been said with reference to that of his co-sectarian Elipandus. In his *Confession of Faith* he speaks of the Son 'for whom, with the Father, in the unity of the Holy Spirit, there is a like and co-equal glory before all ages, now, and for the days of eternity.' It is probable, however, that these words formed part of the orthodox *Confession* which Pope Adrian compelled him to draw up while in captivity at Rome in 793, and which he repudiated on regaining his liberty. Nevertheless, the controversy was brought to an end on the withdrawal of his Adoptionist statements in 800; hence it may be safely assumed that his views on the Doctrine of the Holy Spirit were substantially in harmony with those of the Western Church.

THE ANTI-ADOPTIONISTS

Almost immediately after its declaration by the Archbishop of Toledo the Adoptionist position began to be assailed by certain leaders of the Church of the day. The orthodox clergy in Spain at once regarded the *filius adoptivus* as a dangerous innovation in the accepted teaching concerning the inner Life of God, and BEATUS (*c.* 730–798), Abbot of Libana, and ETHERIUS (*fl.* 790), Bishop of Osma, addressed a joint letter of protest to Elipandus before he was championed by Felix. That the Son of God in His human nature was infinitely higher than a Divinely adopted man is clear from a study of the Gospels. 'Since the Holy Spirit proceeds from the Father and the Son, He [the Son] breathed (*insufflans*) the Holy Spirit Himself upon the Apostles, that it might the more plainly be shown that He pre-existed as—because He Himself was—the Son of God, from whom the Holy Spirit proceeds.'[1]

The procession of the Spirit from the Son, a belief to which the Spanish Church, including Elipandus, rigidly adhered, *ipso facto* makes the position of Adoptionism utterly untenable. Such appears to be the line of argument taken by these two joint authors. They thereupon offer to the erring prelate a trinitarian *Confession* of their own: 'Alone in His own Person the Holy Spirit exists only as Holy Spirit. ... And thereupon there really exists a Trinity, since neither the

[1] *Ad Elipandum Epistola*, 1. 10.

Father, nor the Holy Spirit, was begotten, but only the Son. Neither did the Son, nor the Holy Spirit, beget, but only the Father. Neither did the Father, or the Son, proceed from Two, but only the Holy Spirit. ... The Holy Spirit is also God, just as the Father and the Son, but He is God from the Father and the Son, not from Himself ... and there are not three Gods but one God. ... Also the Holy Spirit is God omnipotent, and alone self-sufficient (*sibi sufficiens*) in His own Person. And these Three are not three omnipotent Gods, but one omnipotent God, Father, Son, and Holy Spirit ; ... and for that reason the Holy Spirit is alone self-sufficient, because the Three are together one God.'[1] Thus in conjunction with the assertion of the *Filioque*, which would naturally be expected from such a quarter of the theological world, these writers confess the full Personality and omnipotence of the Holy Spirit, together with the Spirit's Deity as derived from the Father and the Son, and also the perfect oneness of the Godhead, in which, nevertheless, each Person preserves His characteristic relationship and function.

Beatus and Etherius think fit to enlarge upon certain implications contained in the acceptance of the unity of God. Apparently they do not doubt their opponent's sincerity in his use of orthodox phrases in reference to the Holy Spirit, but they administer a grave warning as to the logical consequences of his heresy. Orthodoxy concerning any two Persons in the Trinity is, of necessity, seriously impaired by heterodoxy concerning the Third, and it is possible for people to use unimpeachable terminology in respect of the Holy Spirit, which would, in point of fact, disguise real error concerning Him, so long as they hold wrong beliefs as touching the Father and the Son.[2] Distortion of one aspect of revealed religion undermines the whole fabric.

Lastly, brief reference is made to the terms ' Substance ' and ' Person,' and to their mutual relation from the Latin standpoint. ' The Son with the Father and the Holy Spirit is one Substance, and not one Person ; but They are three Persons.'[3]

---

[1] *Ibid*, i 19   The unity of the Trinity is also emphasized in i 47 and ii 53, 55, 71

[2] *Ibid*, i 98   ' Qui recte credit de Patre et de Filio, et de Spiritu sancto non recte credit, iam nec de Patre recte credit   Qui recte credit de Filio et de Patre, et de Spiritu non recte credit, iam nec de Filio recte credit   Qui recte credit de Spiritu sancto, et de Patre et Filio non recte credit, iam nec de Spiritu sancto recte credit '

[3] *Ibid*, ii 70

ADOPTIONISTS AND ANTI-ADOPTIONISTS

Beatus and Etherius had good reason to see the necessity of following the example of their countryman, Isidore, in emphasizing the importance of clarity of language as well as of thought.

When Felix of Urgel joined Elipandus the area of the controversy was at once widened. Urgel lies at the foot of the Pyrenees, and thus the cause of Adoptionism passed through a door from Spain into the kingdom of the Franks. It is not to the present purpose to treat of Anti-Adoptionism as such in this its second period, but merely to examine the theology of the Spirit contained in the works of certain champions of the Catholic faith who proceeded against Felix and his followers. In the nature of the case these writers deal at length with the Doctrine of the Son, yet their views on the Trinity in general and on the Holy Spirit in particular are clearly set forth.

Paulinus of Aquileia

The outstanding opponent of Felix was Alcuin, though, as he became even more prominent in the *Filioque* Controversy, he can more usefully be considered at length in that connexion. The majority of his great writings relate to that question, while, on the other hand, most of his purely Anti-Adoptionist arguments are not of such immediate interest. But Alcuin stemmed the tide of the Adoptionist errors not simply by polemic but also by the stimulus of personal example. He was the soul of the counter-movement, and thus he infused the spirit of resistance into those who thought deeply as he did. One of the first to catch this spirit was Paulinus of Aquileia (†c. 802), an intimate friend of Alcuin, and an influential and able character. Like his friend, Paulinus enjoyed the favour of Charlemagne, and, as Patriarch of Aquileia, beside becoming a redoubtable antagonist of the Greek view of the Procession, he joined Alcuin in exposing the heresy of Felix, against whom he wrote three books. It is natural, again, to expect that, in this work, Paulinus should deal principally with the Doctrine of the Son, yet, in his zeal for the full Deity of the Son, he includes the Holy Spirit in the same defence: 'If then you deny that Christ Jesus is true God and true Son of God because He is our Advocate and intercedes for the sins of wrong-doers, I ask why you presume to assert differently concerning the Holy Spirit, who also is our Advocate, and was not incarnate, in reference to whether He is true God, or not? ... For just as it is in no way a hindrance to the Holy Spirit, because He is called Advocate and is asserted to plead for us, that He should be true God; so also it is in no way denied to God, our Saviour Christ Jesus, who was deemed worthy to become Advocate and Mediator on our behalf, that He should be true God and very own Son of God. Therefore, as the Holy Spirit is true God,' &c.[1] Paulinus is here inferring the full Divinity of the Son from the fact of the full Divinity of the Spirit, which Felix, along with Elipandus, apparently grants; so that the present argument of Paulinus is a temporary converse of the reasoning of the earlier Fathers, which inferred the Deity of the Spirit from that of the Son. Moreover, this writer pursues his aim against Felix in the form of his doxologies, as, for instance: 'Jesus ... who with the Father and the Holy Spirit lives and reigns, God in a perfect Trinity, both now and always, through all unending ages of ages, Amen.'[2]

In the second book the work of the Holy Spirit is mentioned in connexion with the birth of Jesus, and with the preparation for the coming to earth of the Son of God. The Spirit is also termed 'the Spirit of Sanctification.'[3] The third book contains the assertion that the Father, Son, and Holy Spirit are neither two nor three 'first principles,' but one 'first principle' (*principium*),[4] while chapter xvii. begins with a prayer addressed to the Holy Spirit separately. Thus, in the attentions of Paulinus, the theology of the Spirit predominated over the operations of the Spirit as being more to the matter in hand in relation to the Being of the Son, whose Divinity he was enforcing in his argument with Felix.

LEIDRADUS

If the Anti-Adoptionists already noted were the writers of this counter-movement, Leidradus and Benedict of Aniane were its preachers, and these continued the campaign on behalf of the Church in a more public sense. Both of them, however, were also authors, and Leidradus, Archbishop of Lyons, in his book *On the Sacrament of Baptism*, upholds the orthodox

---

[1] *Contra Felicem Urgellitanum Episcopum*, i. 24 [2] *Ibid*, i 53
[3] *Ibid*, ii 1 [4] *Ibid*, iii 7

view of the Trinity in Unity in face of the damaging theories of the heretics. He attaches deep importance to the witness of the traditions of the Church, as contrasted with Elipandus and Felix and their followers, who were so vigorously setting it at nought. 'After the Apostolic Creed,' he writes, 'most sure is the faith which the teachers of the churches have handed down, namely, that it is confessed that the Father, Son, and Holy Spirit are one invisible God, of one Essence and power and eternity; so that, while distinctive character (*proprietas*) is preserved for Each of the Persons, neither must the Trinity be divided in Substance (*substantialiter*), nor be confused at all in Persons (*personaliter*). Moreover, it must be confessed that the Father is unbegotten (*ingenitum*), the Son begotten (*genitum*), yet that the Holy Spirit is neither begotten nor unbegotten, but proceeding from (*ex*) the Father and the Son. It must be confessed that the Son proceeds from the Father by generation, and that the Holy Spirit, in proceeding, is certainly not generated.'[1] Leidradus, though he safeguards the distinction between these two processions, allows himself to combine terms which nearly all the theologians of the West strove to keep apart. The usual mode of explaining the derivations of the Son and of the Spirit from the Father was by generation and procession respectively; whereas Leidradus speaks of the Son as 'proceeding by generation'—an overlapping expression of thought which would hardly be characteristic of Alcuin, a more practised writer. Yet, like Alcuin, he puts forth a carefully balanced view of trinitarian doctrine, stressing the union, without confusion, of the Divine Persons, and regarding the *Filioque* as contributing to the *proprietas* as well as to the *substantia*. There is, at any rate, no doubt as to the place assigned by him to the Holy Spirit, both as to His Personality and His Divine attributes. We are therefore prepared to read that when Leidradus touches upon the subject of his book he links the Sacrament of Baptism to the Trinity, stating that the former is administered in the Name of the latter,[2] and that in this holy rite spiritual blessings are bestowed. 'It must be understood,' however, 'that the Holy Spirit is given in many ways, not only in baptism, but also after baptism,' so that, even in a sacramental treatise, Leidradus appears to take a wider view of the bestowal of the

[1] *Liber de Sacramento Baptismi*, 5 [2] *Ibid*, 6

Spirit than Alcuin, who specially mentions the Gift of the Spirit by manual imposition after baptism. Moreover, Leidradus warns his readers against regarding the Holy Spirit as a Gift from any human hands. ' Since we can receive the Holy Spirit,' he asserts, ' we cannot give Him ; but we beseech the Lord that He may be given.'[1] This statement is a reminder of Alcuin's words concerning the Holy Spirit's voluntary bestowal of Himself. This Divine Gift is of Divine grace and not of human merit.

It was fortunate for the Catholic Church that, on his death, Leidradus was succeeded in his Archbishopric by Agobard, another Carlovingian Renaissance leader, who carried on his Anti-Adoptionist labours.

BENEDICT OF ANIANE

The colleague of Leidradus and of Alcuin in this part of the campaign was a monastic statesman of noble ancestry and of considerable ability, who also figures prominently in the revival of culture and of religious thought connected with the name of Charlemagne. Benedict (750–821), Abbot of Aniane, in his *Little Works*, concentrates his attention principally upon the Being of the Holy Spirit, thus leaving to his contemporaries the exposition of that comparatively narrow view of the Spirit's work which they thought necessary for their immediate purpose. He expresses his belief in ' an inseparable Trinity, united without confusion (*permixtione*), distinct without separation ; for the Father, Son, and Holy Spirit are true God, complete and one.' This very unity makes impossible any consideration of before or after, superiority or inferiority, comparison or separation, addition or subtraction, within this complete and perfect Oneness.[2] It was the foundation of the vital truth that God is One which Benedict saw was being injured by the teachings of the Adoptionists. ' So,' he urges, ' let three Persons be believed in, but not three Substances ; three distinct Personalities (*proprietates*), but not three distinct powers (*potestates*).' God is ' one Eternity without beginning, even as one Majesty without ending.'[3] Benedict

[1] *Ibid*, 7
[2] ' Ipsa enim per se ratio docet quia unus nec posteriorem recipit nec priorem, comparationem vel separationem nescit habere qui solus est, minor non potest esse qui plenus est , quia perfectioni nec addi quidquam nec minui post '
[3] With this enlargement : Sine auctore Pater, sine tempore Filius, sine majore Spiritus sanctus '

has much of Alcuin's respect for the evidence of Christian tradition. ' For if you ask the Catholic Church about the Father—what He is—it says " God " ; if about the Son, it says " God " ; if about the Holy Spirit, it says " God " . . . Observe, then, how we may believe in Three and One. Equality causes a Unity of perfections, distinctive character causes a Trinity of Persons.' This argument is borne out by reference to the trinitarian formula used at the rite of baptism, and numerous quotations from Scripture are made in support of the full Deity of the Holy Spirit.[1] In the course of his writings Benedict continues to keep the subject of the Unity of God in the forefront of his theology. ' Again, this is the Catholic Faith, that we adore one God in Trinity and a Trinity in Unity, neither confounding the Persons, nor dividing the Substance. For indeed there is one Person of the Father, another of the Son, another of the Holy Spirit. But the Deity of the Father, Son, and Holy Spirit is one. Their glory equal, and Their majesty co-eternal.' God, then, is not ' threefold,' or a triad of different Beings, but one Being of tripersonal life, whose attributes also are the attributes of One.[2] Further, this unity of Essence, power, and eternity is alluded to in an orthodox Confession of the conventionally Western type contained in *Opusculum* 4, as is also the assertion of the procession of the Spirit from the Son as well as from the Father.[3]

A strong emphasis on the perfect unity of God is thus the main contribution of Benedict to the theology of the Church. This meant ascribing to the Holy Spirit everything—in Being, attribute, and operation—which is ascribed to God. Not that Benedict excelled in originality of thought in connexion with doctrinal development, but he certainly knew where to place the emphasis, which is decidedly a quality of a strong mind.

Though the Adoptionists were active and determined in the dissemination of their views, they soon gave way before the cumulative force of the writings and sermons of the defenders of the Faith, who in turn were supported by Leo III. Anti-Adoptionist theology placed foremost the Catholic

[1] *Opusculum* 1.
[2] *Opusculum* 3 . ' Non coaeternae majestes, non aequales gloriae, non trina, aut triplex divinitas, id est, unum , sed una est divinitas, una deitas, aequalis gloria, coaeterna majestas Identidem nec etiam trinus Deus, sed Trinitas Deus est unus '
[3] Benedict preferred *essentia* to *substantia*, Alcuin *natura*

belief in the one inseparable Triunity of God, whose oneness is enhanced by the perfection of harmony in His inner relations, and by the unifying quality of the procession from the Father and the Son of the Holy Spirit, who is Their common Life in infinite co-equality. In conjunction with this, assertions have been made upholding the Godhead and Personality of the Holy Spirit, His function as the Gift of God to men—whether through the sacraments or otherwise—and His mission of sanctifying grace to the human heart. It was the insistence upon these truths that greatly assisted the conservation of Catholic doctrine at the close of the eighth century and the beginning of the ninth.

IV

ALCUIN, LEO III, AND THE 'FILIOQUE'

AMONG the statements of belief concerning the Holy Spirit recorded by the Western Church during the seventh and eighth centuries, one has been conspicuous, namely His Procession from the Son as well as from the Father ; and this Latin view of the Procession is the outstanding feature of theological debate during the ninth century. The Nicene Creed had expressed its belief simply in the Holy Spirit (καὶ ἐν τῷ Πνεύματι τῷ ‘Αγίῳ), an assertion made in the absence of controversy on the subject, and therefore sufficient for the immediate purpose. An enlarged form of the Nicene Symbol, known as the Creed of Constantinople, added the belief in the procession of the Spirit from the Father (καὶ εἰς τὸ Πνεῦμα τὸ ἅγιον ... τὸ ἐκ τοῦ πατρὸς ἐκπορευόμενον). So far Catholic Christendom was united. But after the year 381 discussion began to arise with reference to the relation of the Holy Spirit to the Son, in which the Western theologians, for the most part, adhered to the Augustinian view of the Procession which, while maintaining the Divine Monarchy, held the procession of the Spirit to be from the Father and the Son by one spiration. 'All things whatsoever the Father hath are mine' was the text which formed the Scriptural basis of the Western reasoning, and continued so to be in the later centuries of the Mediaeval Church. But whatever be the right or the wrong of the argument, this discussion developed into controversy when the Eastern Church discovered that the Western divines had quietly taken upon themselves to add *Filioque* (' and from the Son ') to the Latin form of the Catholic Creed. To this addition the Greeks rigidly refused to adhere, while the breach between them and the Latins over this question became widened by the eagerness with which the Latin standpoint was emphasized by the Spanish theologians, who made the debatable insertion in the creed of their famous third Toletan Council.[1] The union of Catholic forces in Spain and France against the Adoptionists helped to cement their union in the matter of the *Filioque*, so that the Frankish Church joined in supporting the Augustinian teaching, adopted as it was by Charlemagne himself.

ALCUIN

At the Court of Charlemagne, this teaching concerning the Procession of the Holy Spirit found a great defender in Alcuin (c. 735-804), the English monk and ecclesiastical statesman who had been honoured with a place in the imperial circle, and who used it successfully for the advancement of true learning. Though Alcuin has already been noted as one of the supreme causes of the suppression of Adoptionism, he is still more important, from the standpoint of doctrinal development, in relation to the present discussions concerning the *Filioque* in particular, and to the subject of the Trinity in general. In his insistence upon theology as the greatest science it is not difficult to perceive his decided veneration for tradition; and his writings are masterpieces of systematized rather than of independent thought.

In his many *Letters*, as well as in his large works, his comprehensive outlook upon the whole Doctrine of the Holy Spirit can be clearly ascertained. Persons are baptized in the Name of the Father, the Son, and the Holy Spirit, whose Deity and Name are one, and whose donation (*largitio*) is therefore one.[2] And we are not baptized in the Names of the Father, of the Son, and of the Holy Spirit, but in one Name, which is comprehended as God.[3] A form repeated at baptism reads, 'Blessed be the Holy Trinity, one God omnipotent, Father, Son, and Holy Spirit.' 'And then, especially, while the white vestments are being removed from the baptized persons, it is fitting for those, who in baptism have received remission of all sins, to receive the Holy Spirit from the bishop (*pontifex*) by imposition of hands (*per manus impositionem*).'[4] So the consideration of baptism in the Triune Name also introduces the subject of the Trinity in Alcuin's letters. 'Against the poison of Arian perfidy we are accustomed to

---

[1] 'There is no evidence to show that the addition was intentional'—Bethune-Baker, *Christian Doctrine*, p 216n
[2] Ep 33 (A D 796).   [3] Ep 90 (798)   [4] Ep 80 (798).

affirm that the Father, Son, and Holy Spirit are of one Substance,' although, he adds, ' one Nature ' is the term more frequently used by the Fathers. Moreover, this ' Nature ' is the self-determining factor of the individual characteristics of the Persons of the Trinity, beside being the unifying possession of the Three, ' just as the Essence is one, the omnipotence is one, and the Godhead is one.'[1] This Spirit Himself, the Paraclete, was sent by the Father and the Son,[2] His Mission including the inspiration of the human mind as instanced by the prophets,[3] and His invisible working in the soul by faith. This inner working of the Spirit is the proof by which ' you may understand that the Holy Trinity uniformly (*aequaliter*) works for the salvation of man.'[4] Indeed, here and there, throughout these letters, the statement is frequently made that the Holy Spirit dwells in pure hearts and inspires them. In point of fact, most of the references to the Holy Spirit made by him up to this point occur in prayers, as he seems to have reserved for his other works the more formal and weighty exposition of this doctrine.

In his *Commentary on St. John's Gospel* Alcuin begins to expound his pneumatology with greater precision. ' Undoubtedly,' he says, ' the Father is rightly called the " first principle " (*principium*), and the Son the " first principle " ; yet there are not two first principles. Just as the Father is God and the Son is God, there are yet not two Gods, but one God must be affirmed ; so the Father is the first principle, and the Son the first principle, yet there are not two first principles, but one first principle must be confessed. Therefore the Holy Spirit also is the first principle, yet there are not three first principles, Father, Son, and Holy Spirit, but one first principle.' He enlarges upon this unity in the First Cause by referring to the unity of the one omnipotent God without plurality of Essences ; but he would, at the same time, point out that this very unity is emphasized by the perfection of inner relationship. ' The Holy Spirit, because He self-exists, is God ; because He is from the Father and the Son, He is Holy Spirit ; since the Spirit is of the Father and of the

[1] Ep 161 (*anno-incerto*) ' Quia Pater, et Filius, et Spiritus sanctus una est substantia, nam substantia dicitur, quia subsistit   quod saepius in libris catholicorum Patrum invenitur, Patrem, et Filium, et Spiritum sanctum unius est naturae   Igitur Deus natura est Deus, et Filius natura est Filius, et Spiritus sanctus natura est Spiritus sanctus, et est una natura horum trium '
[2] Ep 111 (*anno-incerto*)   [3] Ep 7 (793) and 34 (796)   [4] Ep 36 (796)

Son, proceeding out of the Father and the Son, of one Substance, power, majesty, along with the Father and the Son.'[1] Again, this perfection of relationship within the Trinity carries with it a perfection of equality. 'The Holy Spirit receives from the Father, since He proceeds from the Father, from whom also the Son is begotten. . . . In which words the Holy Spirit also is equal to the Father and the Son, since there is one Substance, one Nature, one majesty, one glory, one eternity of the Father, Son, and Holy Spirit, and there is one God omnipotent, invisible, incomprehensible to every creature, Father, Son, and Holy Spirit.'[2] The principle of the equality of the Third Person to the First and Second is next extended to the " equality " of the procession and of the mission of the Third from the First and the Second. In commenting upon xv. 26, Alcuin remarks : ' It shows that the same Holy Spirit proceeds equally from the Father and the Son, and is sent equally by the Father and the Son ; but on account of the distinction of the Persons He is here said to proceed from the Father, and to be sent by the Son. . . . And further, He comes of His own accord (*sua sponte*), since He is co-equal with the Father and the Son, that it may be recognized that there is one will and one operation of the Holy Trinity.'[3]

Alcuin's exegesis of passages in this Gospel which relate to the operations of the Spirit reveals the considerable interest which he took in the subject. The meaning of Christ's gift of the Spirit to the disciples before Pentecost was explored by many writers in the Mediaeval Church, and Alcuin discusses it at some length. ' We must inquire why it is that our Lord at one time, while He was yet on earth, gave the Holy Spirit, and also at another time, when He was ruling in heaven. For neither in any other place is the Holy Spirit clearly represented as having been given, save now when He is taken possession of by being breathed upon them (*per insufflationem*), and afterwards when He is described as coming from heaven in different tongues. Why then is He given beforehand to the disciples on earth, and afterwards is sent from heaven, unless there are two precepts of love (*charitatis*)—love (*dilectio*), namely, of God and of neighbour ? The Spirit is given on

---

[1] *Comment in Joan* (on viii 25) 'Spiritus sanctus, quod ad se est, Deus est; quod a Patre et Filio, Spiritus sanctus est'
[2] On xvi 14, 15   [3] On xv 26 (chap xxxvii)

earth that our neighbour may be loved; the Spirit is given from heaven that God may be loved. As therefore there is one love and there are two precepts, so there is one Spirit and there are two gifts. . . . That is to say, " when He had said this, He breathed on them and saith to them : ' Receive the Holy Spirit ' "—by breathing upon them He indicated that the Holy Spirit is not the Father's Spirit only, but also His own.'[1] Alcuin, however, labours to remove any misconceptions which might easily be attached to the yet mightier bestowal of the Holy Spirit at Pentecost. ' Not that aforetime the Holy Spirit was not in the hearts of the disciples, or even in the hearts of the Saints of old (*antiquorum sanctorum*), but He was never given with such evident fullness, as on the tenth day after the Ascension He is observed to be sent upon a hundred and twenty people.'[2] A note on the Spirit's work in baptism may complete the present survey of this Commentary : ' The Lord baptizes in the Holy Spirit by forgiving sins through the grace of the Holy Spirit,'[3] a statement reminiscent of Bede's view of the Spirit as the Source of sacramental efficacy.

Alcuin was a strong supporter of the *Filioque*, and, as such, he addressed a pamphlet, *On the Procession of the Holy Spirit*, to Charles the Great, who held views similar to his own. This little work, wholly given to this subject, was meant to explain more fully the orthodox Latin view to the Christian monarch, his friend and correspondent. ' For, in the words of the Holy Gospel and in the synodal letters of the blessed Fathers and in many books of men learned in spiritual knowledge, it is plainly declared—the Holy Spirit, who is of one and the same Substance with the Father and the Son, because He proceeds from, and is sent by, Both.' This preliminary statement is followed by exposition and supported by liberal quotation.[4] The second chapter opens with a declaration which may contain a side-thrust at the Adoptionists as well as a frontal blow at the opponents of the *Filioque*. ' The Holy

---

[1] On xx. 22 ; which exposition is found almost word for word also in *De Fide Sanct. Trin*, ii 21.
[2] On xvi 7 : ' sed manifesta plenitudine ante sic non fuit datus quomodo,' &c
[3] Chap ii 33.
[4] *Libellus de Proc Sp s* (*Alcuinus ad Carolum Magnum*) i. Quotations are made from St Luke, St John, Pope Leo, the Cappadocian Gregorys, Hieronymus, Augustine, Cyril of Alexandria, Pope Gelasius, Athanasius, Hilary, Pope Ambrosius, Gennadius, Isidore, Boethius, and Paschasius.

Spirit, who is co-equal and co-eternal with the Father and the Son, is, in some parts of Scripture, called the Spirit of the Father; yet in others, by reason of the unity of will, power, eternity, and of the Substance of the Holy Trinity, He is called the Spirit of Christ.' The remainder of this chapter is filled with supporting references.[1] In the third chapter he asserts: ' Our Saviour testifies that He sends the Holy Spirit, and that, in His [the Saviour's] own name, He is sent by the Father.'[2] A statement as to the equality of the Persons in the Trinity constitutes his conclusion : ' As is the Father . . . so is the Son, so also the Holy Spirit ; for in this Trinity nothing is before (*prius*) or after (*posterius*), nothing greater (*majus*) or less (*minus*), but all three Persons are co-eternal and co-equal with Each Other.'

There is little doubt but that the greatest contribution to Trinitarian Doctrine made by Alcuin is his work entitled *On the Faith of the Holy Trinity*, which is a summing-up of his views on the subject of the Being of the Spirit rather than a fresh presentation of them.[3] ' All Scripture,' he remarks, ' implies that the Father, Son, and Holy Spirit are one God, of the same Substance, and of one Essence, and of inseparable Unity in the Godhead.' The Spirit of the Father and of the Son must not be confused with the Father and the Son, though He is co-equal with Them and completes Their Unity (*ad Trinitatis pertinens unitatem*). There was no confusion of Persons in the Creation story, ' for if that one Essence of the Father, Son, and Holy Spirit were one Person, it would not read (*non diceretur*) " in Our Image," but " in My Image." Yet the attributes of the Father and of the Son in Their Deity are also the attributes of God the Holy Spirit,[4] and this in turn does not deny that the Spirit possesses His own peculiar relationship to the Father and the Son.[5] The Holy Spirit, then, is the Gift of God, who proceeds equally from the Father

---

[1] From St Peter, St Paul, Pope Leo, Augustine, Ambrosius, and Fulgentius.
[2] Citations follow from St John, St. Luke, Acts, Gregory of Nazianzus, Augustine, and Athanasius
[3] 'The treatise *De Fide Sanctae Trinitatis*, the last of Alcuin's dogmatic writings, and perhaps in his eyes the most important of them all, was not controversial in tone   The basis of the entire work is Augustinian '—C J B Gaskoin, *Alcuin* (Camb , 1904), p 159
[4] *De Fide S Trin*, lib 1. 2.
[5] *Ibid*, 4   ' Prorsus et Spiritus sanctus relative dicitur ad Patrem et Filium, sed non eodem modo quo inter se Pater et Filius . . Non dicimus Patrem Spiritus sancti . . . Filium Spiritus sancti.'

and the Son, and who is 'the ineffable Communion' of Them Both,[1] for He Himself is perfect God. The procession of the Spirit equally from the Father and the Son is especially emphasized by Alcuin,[2] as is also the perfection of the unity of the Trinity.[3] 'The unity of inseparable Nature cannot contain separable Persons.'[4]

Before Alcuin leaves his subject, he follows the example of Isidore and Hildefonsus in guarding against loose terminology in reference to the internal relations of the Persons and particularly to the subject of the Incarnation. 'The Holy Spirit, at least, is neither unbegotten, nor is He anywhere called begotten : lest if He should be called unbegotten, as the Father, two Fathers would be understood to be in the Holy Trinity ; or if He should be called begotten, as the Son, in like manner two Sons would be reckoned to be in the same Holy Trinity. But He must, without violation of faith, be said only to proceed from the Father and the Son.'[5] This line of reasoning is developed in the third Book, with particular reference to the Incarnation, and the author becomes somewhat original, but even here in part he follows Hildefonsus almost word for word. He asks the question 'how it may be asserted that Christ was born of (*de*) the Holy Spirit and the Virgin Mary, when the Son is in no sense the Son of the Holy Spirit ? . . . Take those who are born of (*ex*) water and the Holy Spirit. Why! no one would rightly call them sons of water, or of the Holy Spirit, but they are distinctly called sons of God the Father and of their mother the Church. So then, He who was born of the Holy Spirit is the Son of God the Father, and not of the Holy Spirit. For if Christ were called the Son of the Holy Spirit according to His humanity, there would be two Fathers in the Holy Trinity, and the God-Man would have had two Fathers, the one of Deity, the other of humanity.'[6] Another warning is deemed necessary in the same connexion : 'Though the Nature of the Holy Trinity is one, yet not the whole Trinity became incarnate, but only the Person of the Son.'[7] A lengthy confession of the Trinitarian Faith is found at the

---

[1] *Ibid*, 5   [2] *Ibid*, 5, 11, and iii 8, &c
[3] *Ibid*, 5, 8, 10, 11, *lib* ii (prologue), and 19   'Haec Trinitas unus est Deus . non tamen tres dii, sed unus Deus plenus et perfectus   Perfectus Deus Pater, et Filius, et Spiritus sanctus . ideo Trinitas potius quam triplex dicenda est'
[4] *Ibid*, i 13   [5] *Ibid*, 14; also ii 9   [6] *Ibid*, iii 3   [7] *Ibid*, 10.

close of the third Book, but it merely covers the same ground.

The specifically Western view of systematic theology, of which Alcuin was so notable an exponent, found strong support in a political event of profound significance which took place during Alcuin's closing years, also during the pontificate of Leo III. In A.D. 800 Charlemagne, King of the Franks, was crowned Emperor of the West by the Pope in the Church of St. Peter at Rome, an incident to which Lord Bryce refers as ' the central event of the Middle Ages ' and ' the starting-point of modern history.'[1] The remaining authority of Eastern imperial power in the West was now broken, and there came into being the Holy Roman Empire, which had already been prepared for by constant Frankish intervention in Italy in defence of papal Rome against the Lombards. The proclamation of the revival of the old Roman imperialism gave further security to the power of Charles, established the temporal sovereignty of the Pope in Rome, and also raised the status of Christendom in Europe, though this very situation meant the unnatural creation of an imperial theocracy which nursed the forces of disintegration in its own bosom. But now that Charlemagne wore the imperial crown, he was in a stronger position to further the cause of the *Filioque*, one of his doctrinal tenets, so that the Council of Aix, summoned by him in 809, was influenced by him to make this insertion in the Creed of the Church. Leo, however, took exception to this high-handed action on the part of the Emperor. If East and West were now separate imperially they were not yet so ecclesiastically, and the Pope saw that the latter situation also would follow upon any formal adoption of the *Filioque* by the whole of the Church of the West. The relationship between the two great sections of the Catholic Church, already strained by this adoption in Spain and France, would be completely severed by any similar action on the part of Rome; accordingly the pontiff refused to sanction any tampering with the Creed either at Aix or on any later occasion.[2] So the theological enthusiasm of the temporal head of the West became a source of considerable embarrassment to his spiritual colleague.

[1] *Holy Roman Empire*, 49, 50   Cf Gibbon, *Rome*, v 403
[2] The *Encycl Brit* mentions another synod in 810 at which this question was again raised

Leo III

In taking part in the *Filioque* controversy, Pope Leo III († 816) was thus in the very difficult position of a temporizing medium between East and West, seeing that these two sections of the Catholic Church were still theoretically united. For this reason, then, while the Pope personally agreed with the Western view of the procession of the Spirit,[1] he resolutely condemned any insertion of it in the Creeds of Christendom. He had helped the Spanish and Frankish Churches against Elipandus and Felix, but he refused to countenance their 'official' approval of the *Filioque*, which approval, in that it was 'official,' would completely alienate the Eastern Church. There was thus ample reason for his dislike of any symbolic embodiment of his private opinions, and this dislike has already been instanced by his firm refusal to ratify the *Filioque* addition which the Council at Aix had sanctioned.[2] But, while he felt compelled to restrain the ardour of the upholders of the *Filioque* from considerations of ecclesiastical diplomacy, he nevertheless attempted to explain the attitude of the Western mind and of his private reasoning to the Churches of the Orient. If open disagreement necessitated careful management, it also provided the greater opportunity for explanation, and, with this in view, Leo addressed a letter on the Procession question *To All the Eastern Churches*. In this, the fifteenth of his letters, his beliefs are found in confessional form. 'We believe,' he writes, 'in the Holy Trinity, that is to say, the Father, Son, and Holy Spirit, one God omnipotent, of one Substance, of one Essence, of one power, the Creator of all creatures, from whom are all things, through whom all things, in whom all things: the

---

[1] Dr Swete remarks that it was probably Gregory the Great who bent Leo's persona inclinations to the 'correctness' of the *Filioque* (*H Sp in A C*, p 349). Cf also Harnack, *History of Dogma*, v 304

[2] Cf Bishop Pearson, *On the Creed*. 'The matter [of the use of the *Filioque* in the Creed] being referred to Leo III, he absolutely concluded that no such addition ought to be tolerated; for in the Acts of the Synod held at Aquisgranum [Aix] we find it so determined by the Pope, upon the conference with the legates   Beside, lest the Roman Church might be accused to join with the Spanish and French Churches in this addition, the same Pope caused the Creed publicly to be set forth in the Church, graven in silver plates, one in Latin and another in Greek, in the same words in which the Council of Constantinople had first penned it' Durandus, in the Introduction to *Distinction II* of his *Commentary on the Sentences of Lombard*, mentions the Greek denial of the *Filioque*, and also its omission 'in Symbolo Leonis papae III', with the comment, 'Spiritus sanctus dicitur a Patre procedere, et nulla fit mentio de Filio, ideo nolunt concedere quod a Filio procedat, imo dicunt nos excommunicatos, quia Leo papa aliter docentes excommunicavit'

Father from Himself, not from Another, the Son begotten by the Father, true God from true God, true Light from true Light, not, however, two Lights but one Light; the Holy Spirit proceeding equally from the Father and the Son, consubstantial, co-eternal with the Father and the Son. The Father is perfect God (*plenus Deus*) in Himself, the Son is perfect God begotten by the Father, the Holy Spirit is perfect God proceeding from the Father and the Son. Yet we do not speak of three Gods, but of one God omnipotent, eternal, invisible, unchangeable, who is wholly present everywhere, not divided into parts, but wholly in all things, not locally, but personally. . . . And these Three are one God, since there is one Substance—Father, Son, and Holy Spirit. . . . In the Father there is eternity, in the Son equality, in the Holy Spirit the combination (*connexio*) of eternity and equality. They are all one in Substance and Essence, in omnipotence and Deity.'[1] Leo, indeed, has much the same ideas as Alcuin, and it is worthy of note that he is at heart thoroughly Western, whatever his official attitude to contemporary controversy. While asserting the unity of God, he speaks of the perfect and complete Deity of each Person of the Trinity, and of the universal presence in the world of the entire Godhead. His view of the Holy Spirit as the Completer, the Bond, or the common Life of the Trinity is reminiscent both of Alcuin and of Isidore.

In attempting a compromise between his private and his official attitude to the dogma of the Procession, Leo, according to Gibbon,[2] doubtless assumed the liberality of a statesman, but, equally without doubt, his position of liberality was inherently weak, and therefore practically useless as a means of stemming the tide of Westernism which flowed upon Rome from Spain and France. True, Leo and others after him succeeded in postponing for two centuries formal adherence to the *Filioque* on the part of the papacy, but when, in the eleventh century, the ecclesiastical severance of East from West followed the earlier imperial severance, there was no further call for such diplomatic compromise, and from that time onwards the Roman Church has openly taught the procession of the Spirit from the Son as well as from the Father

---

[1] *Epistola* 15, 'Omnibus orientalibus Ecclesiis'   [2] *Rome*, vi, p 524.

V

THE EASTERN CHURCH

It is during this main period that the Church Catholic emerged from the Graeco-Latin age of the Fathers, and became more and more distinctly Eastern and Western as the early Mediaeval Age advanced. Hellenism afforded the Eastern Church a principle of unity such as was lacking in the West, and which largely accounted for the stability of its system amid controversies within and attacks without. This very stability, aided by the versatility of the Greek genius, was the foundation of an active thought which is seen to be in constant conflict with the theological presentation of the West. The beginnings of the schism between these two great branches of the Church are evident in the fury of the Iconoclastic controversy which was set on foot in 726 by the edict of the Eastern Emperor, Leo the Isaurian, condemning as idolatrous the worship of sacred images and ordering their removal. In 787 the Second Council of Nicaea reversed the imperial decision by upholding image worship, as its members claimed, ' under the guidance of the Holy Spirit.' ' We, who adore the Trinity, worship images.'[1] But in 794 Charlemagne and the Council of Frankfort signified the Frankish repudiation of the standpoint of the Nicene Council, and the separatist movement in the Christian Church was encouraged by the revival of the Western Empire in the year 800.

The coming division between the Churches of the Orient and the Occident, which became an accomplished fact two centuries later, was already made certain by the addition of heated theological controversy to their various political and ecclesiastical disagreements. Ever since the *Filioque* had been incorporated in the Creed at the third Council of Toledo, the Doctrine of the Procession of the Holy Spirit had been, and still was, the main subject of contention. The last representative of the Greek Patristic Age, John of Damascus,

[1] Milman, *Latin Christianity*, ii, pp. 391, 392.

had summed up the teaching of Eastern orthodoxy in the statement that the Holy Spirit proceeds 'from' the Father 'through' the Son,[1] but this *via media* did not appeal to the majority of Western churchmen, whose view of the Doctrine of the Procession was confessedly Augustinian. Moreover, the temporizing policy of Leo III would in no way remove the Oriental suspicion of Roman inclination toward the open course which the Spanish and Frankish divines had pursued. Leo had taken pains to explain his own position to the Eastern Churches, and now NICEPHORUS (756–828), Patriarch of Constantinople, addressed a letter to him, containing a confession of his own faith, from which the Western addition to the Creed is naturally omitted. Concerning the Holy Spirit he wrote : ' I confess that I believe in the Holy Spirit, life-giving (*vivificum*) and most holy. I believe in a Trinity of one Essence (*homousiam*) . . . inseparable, unalterable, eternal . . . potent with the same honour, with the same Deity.' Nicephorus speaks of the Holy Spirit as ' having His Substance from the Father, not by any newness of relation (*novitate*), but by procession, He having shared the same eternity along with the Father and the Son ; being indeed eternal, yet not without source (*absque principio*), as He it is who proceeds from the Father.' The head of the Eastern Church was as anxious as the head of the Western to emphasize the unity of God, and in that unity he regards the Holy Spirit as possessing an inseparable subsistence ; but as for the doctrine of the Procession, the patriarch recognized only the First Person of the Trinity as the one Source of the Holy Spirit, and his position would not be at all obscure to Leo, his correspondent.

Nicephorus was but the forerunner of a more notable patriarch of Constantinople, who made use of the *Filioque* addition to widen considerably the existing breach between the Latin and Greek Churches. The controversy which now opened up was a tangle of politics and theology. After Ignatius had been wrongfully deposed from the patriarchal see, his successor was found in an able layman named PHOTIUS (*c.* 805–891), an ex-military courtier who was a wide reader,

---

[1] Banks, *Development of Doc*, p 101, accuses John of subordinationism, which the Westerns considered could be avoided by the implications of the *Filioque* But was Dr Banks entirely accurate in terming this attitude of John of Damascus a ' retrograde step ' ? It may have been so, chronologically , but John was, in Dr Swete's language, ' a redactor of antiquity rather than a theologian of constructive power '

a clever writer, and an outstanding exponent of contemporary ecclesiastical scholarship. He was, however, deposed and excommunicated by a decree of Pope Nicholas I, and the papal mandate ordered the reinstatement of Ignatius. The danger of the feud becoming more than personal was realized when Photius replied, in 866, by an encyclical letter, charging the Roman Church with sundry corruptions and doctrinal innovations, one of which was the addition of the *Filioque* to the Creed of Constantinople. Two Councils held at Constantinople in 867 and 879 ratified these charges of Western heresy and condemned the *Filioque* as a deliberate falsification of the Creed. Certainly the diplomatic stand once taken by Leo III made no pretence of permanence, and the use of the *Filioque* had evidently crept into the Roman Church after his death. At any rate, the action of Photius ushered in a very bitter stage in the mutual disagreements of East and West, and the patriarch of Constantinople promoted the cleavage still further by a publication on the Doctrine of the Holy Spirit which was distinctly anti-Western.

His book *On the Mystagogy of the Holy Spirit*[1] is an example of his dialectical powers and also of the faculty for plausible presentation which he seemed to possess in other spheres than that of theological debate alone. The *Mystagogy* is devoted almost entirely to the question of the Procession, its lack of reference to the work of the Spirit being typical of Greek theology. In part, it may be briefly summarized thus : The Spirit proceeds from the Father and not from the Son ; for, if He proceeds from the Son, He would proceed from the humanity of the Son, which is absurd ; and if He proceeds from Both, there would be a double procession ; while if His procession is from the Father and the Son as from one Source, it is a case of Sabellianism. There is a sense, certainly, in which the Spirit is said to be the Spirit of the Son, but He is principally the Spirit of the Father. As to the *Filioque* (καὶ ἐκ τοῦ Υἱοῦ), it is upheld neither by Scripture nor by the Fathers; in fact, it is not ' natural ' that the Spirit should proceed from the Son, but only from the Father. This epitome of the reasoning of Photius may be regarded as generally representative of the Eastern mind with reference to this keen theological issue.

[1] Λόγος περὶ τῆς τοῦ Ἁγίου Πνεύματος μυσταγωγίας

Greek theology recognized the mediatorial work of the Son in the procession of the Holy Spirit from the Father, but declined to regard the Son as the Source (*principium* or αἴτιον) of the Spirit in the same sense as the Father. When Augustine laid the foundation in the West of a definite theology of the *Filioque*, he spoke of the Spirit's procession from the Father and the Son as from one Source only, and not from two Sources —which the Greeks constantly asserted to be the Western belief. This is a position which may not differ seriously from the Eastern view of the procession of the Spirit from the Father through the Son, as Dr. Swete has suggested.[1] But Photius branded the Augustinian standpoint as Sabellian, and doubtless the Eastern Church was influenced against taking any steps toward mutual understanding by the manner in which the Spanish and Frankish Churches together had adopted the *Filioque*, a manner which, from the Greek point of view, was anything but mutual. Moreover, the quarrel between Photius and Nicholas engendered such anti-Roman bitterness in the East that political differences at times loomed larger than theological[2]; so the schism which Photius had encouraged became gradually more complete, until its abrupt climax in the eleventh century, when Michael Caerularius, a successor of Photius in the patriarchate, was excommunicated by the papal legates in his own church at Constantinople.

[1] *Holy Spirit in the Ancient Church*, p. 370   [2] Cf Gibbon, *Rome*, vi , p. 527.

VI

LATER CARLOVINGIANS

AFTER the death of Charlemagne, his unwieldy Empire, itself divided into varied races, and enduring constant attacks from the Northmen, became partitioned among incapable sons, who, in turn, found themselves confronted by the increasing aggression of the papacy. In the midst of this political decline the later masters of the Carlovingian Renaissance continued to serve the Church with their wide scholarship by consolidating the Western system of theology handed on to them principally by Alcuin. The action of Photius, so far from weakening the case for the *Filioque*, had actually strengthened Western adherence to it, so much so that, in Harnack's language, 'the *Filioque* became the symbolic watchword in the whole of the West.'[1] A series of brilliant writers now took up this watchword, and, at the hands of Theodulf of Orleans, Ratramnus of Corbie, Aeneas of Paris, Hincmar of Rheims, and others of their school, the Frankish view of the Doctrine of the Holy Spirit received an able presentation. This view may be exemplified by reference to two of these names, which may be regarded as representative of the attitude of them all. Paschasius Radbertus of Corbie will also be noticed as making a contribution somewhat different in character from that of the others.

THEODULF OF ORLEANS

Theodulf († 821, probably from poison[2]), Bishop of Orleans, who came to the Court of Charlemagne to assist the revival of learning in the Frankish kingdom, was a strong defender of the standpoint of Western orthodoxy in reference to the Holy Spirit. In response to an imperial demand for a treatise in substantiation of the *Filioque* he produced his *De Spiritu Sancto*, with the supplementary title of *Veterum Patrum sententiae, quod a Patre Filioque procedat*, and the dedication

[1] *Hist of Dogma*, v, p 304   [2] *Encycl Brit*

'to Charles the Great, Emperor.' The supplementary title itself reveals the scheme of his work, which is, in effect, a compendium of certain teachings of the Fathers, of whom the majority are Western, with a commentary thereon which binds his authorities together into an apologetic system.[1] These authorities, notably Augustine, are quoted principally as upholding the procession of the Holy Spirit from both the Father and the Son, though they are also brought in to illustrate and to endorse a general exposition of the Doctrine of the Trinity. Accordingly, Theodulf begins his treatise by expressing his belief in the Unity of God : ' I believe that the Son is in the Father and the Father in the Son, that the Spirit, who is also the Paraclete, who proceeds from the Father, is both of the Son and of the Father, because He also proceeds from the Son . . . and therefore I confess an inseparable Trinity.' Again : ' Concerning the Holy Spirit, there is no doubt at all that He is ignorant of nothing . . . and that He wholly abides in the Son ; and, just as He proceeds from God the Father, so He proceeds from the Son, in order that the whole Trinity may be believed to be one God. . . . And when any one worships the Son, in Him he worships the Father, also the Holy Spirit.' The procession of the Spirit from the Son is asserted to show that He is the Spirit of the Son, and thereby to emphasize the oneness of the Deity, a use of the *Filioque* already found in the earlier Carlovingian writers.

Having laid the foundation of his argument in establishing the Divine Unity by Western reasoning, Theodulf discusses the inter-relations of the inner Life of God. ' Hence,' he resumes, ' it is proved by the clearest evidences that the Holy Spirit, the Spirit who is the Paraclete, the Spirit who proceeds from the Father, is the Spirit of the Son, the Spirit of Christ, the Spirit of Jesus. For the whole Trinity exists inseparably in one Substance, Godhead, and power.' Thus the absolute oneness of the Divine Life presupposes no difference in relation between the Spirit and the Father on the one hand, and the Spirit and the Son on the other.[2] The writer's mind appears to be very similar to that of Benedict of Aniane in

---

[1] His authorities comprise such names as Ambrose, Hieronymus, Augustine, Gregory of Rome, Isidore, Vigilius of Africa, Proclus of Constantinople, Agnellus, Cassiodorus, and Prudentius

[2] ' Spiritus appellatus est veritatis, et veritas Christus est, unde et ab isto similiter sicut ex Deo Patre procedit '

laying hold of the great truth of the unity of God, and in perceiving, at the same time, that the *Filioque* of the Western Church tends to strengthen this truth while guarding against the heretical position of Sabellius. It is in accordance with such reasoning that he adds the remark that this Holy Spirit is neither the Father nor the Son ; for while ' They are One (*unum*) in Deity, They are also Three in personal Names (*in nominibus personarum*). . . . Hence one Person is the Father who begat, and Another the Son who is only-begotten from Him, and Another the Spirit, the Paraclete, who proceeds from one Nature,'[1] all these distinct mysteries of relationship being revealed within the one Divine Substance.[2] ' The Father was made by no one, nor is He created, nor begotten The Son is from the Father alone, not created, but begotten. The Holy Spirit was not made by the Father and the Son, neither is He created, nor begotten, but proceeding ' ; and this Trinity of co-equal and unconfused Persons in the one adorable Godhead is confessed by Theodulf in phraseology similar to that employed by Alcuin.[3] ' Therefore,' pronounces the bishop, ' he who wants to be saved, let him think thus about the Trinity.'

Before the book is concluded, varied references are made to the Fathers which further illustrate the views of the author. Ambrose reminds him that the procession of the Holy Spirit from the Father and the Son does not involve any separation from Them, but rather the opposite. On no account are the Father, Son, and Holy Spirit to be regarded as three Gods, nor, on the other hand, is the Holy Spirit to be thought of as a part of either the Father or the Son. Nothing, in fact, must be admitted which would in any way undermine the trinitarian teaching of Augustine.[4] Finally, he is led to consider the subject of the Mission of the Spirit by certain extracts from

[1] ' Itaque alter est Pater in persona qui genuit, et alius Filius qui unigenitus ab ipso est, et alius Spiritus paraclitus, qui de una natura procedit,'—which is definitely Augustinian

[2] ' quam Graeci dicunt ὁμούσιον ' (for ὁμοούσιον, a contraction common in mediaeval Latin writers)

[3] ' Unus ergo Pater non tres patres, unus Filius non tres filii, unus Spiritus sanctus non tres spiritus sancti Et in hac Trinitate nihil prius aut posterius, nihil majus aut minus, sed totae tres personae coaeternae sibi sunt et coaequales Ita ut per omnia, sicut iam supra dictum est, et Trinitas in unitate, et unitas in Trinitate veneranda sit '

[4] '   Spiritum quoque sanctum, non ingenitum, neque genitum, sed ex Patre Filioque procedentem, eo quod Patris et Filii sit Spiritus, et ipse consubstantialis et coaeternus ambobus '

the *De Spiritu Sancto* of Ambrose and from a commentary by Hieronymus upon the *De Spiritu Sancto* of Didymus. One truth is clear to him here, namely, that the Son, as well as the Father, sends the Holy Spirit upon the Church and upon the human race ; and, if the Son and the Spirit are the Sources of Each Other's mission, They are so not from any injustice of subservience (*subjectionis injuria*) but from one joint exercise of authority (*communitas potestatis*). Moreover, ' this Spirit, the Comforter, is sent by the Son, not in accordance with the ministry of angels, prophets, and apostles, but as it seems good to the Spirit of God, by His wisdom and truth, to be sent, seeing that the Spirit Himself possesses an undivided Substance along with the Father and the Son, and with the same wisdom and truth.' Thus the mission of the Spirit by the Son implies no inferiority on the part of the Spirit, as neither does the fact that He is called ' the Spirit of God ' and ' the Spirit of Christ.' Nor is the Holy Spirit tied to any rite or office performed by human ministry, as if His operations could be directed, for instance, by the prophets whom He Himself inspires. He who is God can be sent only by the will of God, namely His own.

Theodulf's contribution to the theology of the ninth century is based on such a plan as to recall the fact that he lived in the age of the ' compilers,' and yet the character of his work justifies its being regarded as a contribution. If comparatively little is found in his writings concerning the work of the Spirit, that, in the main, was not their purpose. The imperial request made to him was to set forth a defensive exposition of the Western development of the Creed, and, within the limits, thus involved, of the Nature of the Spirit and of the Trinity he worked out ideas which declare him to be by no means devoid of a mind of his own. His high conceptions of the Unity of the Trinity and of the Being of the Holy Spirit within the Trinity were especially needed in the Church of his time, and he presented these interpenetrating truths with that careful thought which could have been the outcome only of real spiritual scholarship.

PASCHASIUS RADBERTUS.

Another celebrated theologian of the later Carlovingian period is Paschasius Radbertus († *c.* 855), who, for seven years, was Abbot of Corbie, in Picardy. Of his profound knowledge and capacity for deep thought there is no doubt, and good reason exists for endorsing Harnack's opinion that he was perhaps the most learned and able theologian after Alcuin.[1] He makes, however, but a small contribution to the development of the Doctrine of the Holy Spirit, partly on account of his mind being diverted in other directions, as witness his championship of the transubstantiation view of the Lord's Supper, and partly because, when he does speak of it, he brings to this, as to other subjects, a type of mystic expression which is fantastic and often obscure. This method of treatment is exemplified by the second book of his *Commentary on St. Matthew's Gospel*, a work which covered a period of years. In reference to the descent of the Holy Spirit in the form of a dove, he remarks: ' Moreover, the same Holy Spirit had not been able to appear to mortal eyes unless in bodily form (*corporali specie*). Wherefore, indeed, we suppose that the body was fashioned more probably out of air or out of water than generated from any other body. Accordingly we say that He appeared in a Divine mystery (*in mysterium*), and, further, as He who had fashioned it wished, and at such time as He wished.'[2] This speculation reveals at least that same insistence upon the sovereignty of the Divine will of the Spirit of God which had characterized the writings of the more dogmatic Theodulf: but when Radbertus proceeds to draw several conclusions from the figure of a dove, he becomes altogether too fanciful for serious consideration. This figure then gives place to another, in which the Spirit is regarded as a fire of virtue-giving power, and, as such, must not be quenched. 'Also,' he writes, 'in the Acts of the Apostles the Holy Spirit is therefore recorded to have appeared in fire, that it might be a symbol, for those whom He had filled He had made all aglow (*ardentes*).' So may the Holy Spirit be fittingly spoken of as fire, ' since God is a consuming fire.' And yet this fire is ' the fire of perfect love,' so much so that the Holy Spirit 'intercedes on our behalf with unutterable groanings.'

Though Radbertus was possessed of an unusual imagination, he has something to give to doctrinal history, and it is by no

[1] *Ibid*, v 312
[2] *'Comm in Matth Evang*, *lib* ii, *cap* 3, pp 180-184 (ed 1618)

means his fancy alone which comprises his freshness. In an age when theologians tended to follow not only each other's ideas but also, to some extent, each other's verbal setting, this writer reveals real ability by breaking away from many of the conventional methods of his time, and by causing his poetic spirit to seize upon Divine truths which certain of his contemporaries, through the very rigidity of their outlook, were unconsciously missing. To Radbertus the Holy Spirit is Some One near, Some One vitally concerned in human life, Whose perfect love can be ignored in face of the supremacy of His will; and, at the same time, whose love is capable of so filling men as to make them ministers of living flame. The above emphasis laid on spiritual passion was a striking addition to the literature of the Church, and thus formed a useful complement to the more systematic type of theological treatise represented by the majority of the works of Western contemporaries.

HINCMAR

A brief survey of the writings of a third representative of the later Carlovingian age reveals him to be a reversion to the systematic type. Like Radbertus, Hincmar (c. 806–882), Archbishop of Rheims, was too deeply engrossed in other theological subjects, as well as in affairs of ecclesiastical state, to be of outstanding importance for the purpose of this present study. Radbertus had gained from him support in his stand on behalf of transubstantiation, while the Archbishop himself drew the fire of many Frankish devotees of Augustine by his unexpected and successful attack upon the severe dogma of double predestination which was being affirmed by Gottschalk. Accordingly, while Hincmar cannot by any means be accused of lacking independence of thought, when he approaches the Doctrine of God he is almost devoid of any such independence, and his work *On One and not a Triple Godhead* simply reveals his adherence to the Catholic faith as interpreted by the Western Church. But in doctrinal development the wise use of a writer's faculty of emphasis is as needful as 'independence,' and the title of Hincmar's work shows that particular part of the Catholic faith which he regarded as requiring most careful attention from Christian believers.

Any definition of the Trinity which safeguards the Unity

of God must eradicate any notion of a created origin of the Spirit. ' For,' he asserts, ' the Holy Spirit was not to receive from any creature which is subject to the Father and the Son . . . but undoubtedly from the Father, from whom the Spirit proceeds, from whom the Son is begotten. Thus the Nature, that is the Deity, of the Father, is the Nature of the Son, is the Nature of the Holy Spirit, who proceeds equally from the Father and the Son, and who is inexpressible (*ineffabilis*) as the common Life of the Father and the Son, who wholly (*totus*) proceeds from the Father, and wholly from the Son.'[1] Accordingly there is but one Nature in God, and the very oneness of that Nature is sealed by the unifying Life of the Spirit. Here, again, the *Filioque* is regarded as ministering to the Unity of the Deity, while the ' equality ' of procession from the first and second Persons is due, not to the evenness of two shares in an operation, but to the immeasurableness of two infinities, where the one complete function is described as from Each. The whole is equal to the whole, and there Hincmar leaves the mystery as not admitting of further human description ; though he would no doubt concur with the common Western view which resolved the equality of procession into oneness of source, a view summarily condemned as Sabellian by Photius and the Easterns. At least, Hincmar confesses his belief in the highest possible position of the Holy Spirit within the one Deity. ' And so,' he resumes, ' just as the Father, also the Son, is complete and perfect God, by all means is He one God together with the Father and the Son, and also one Substance, one Deity, one Godhead, one Essence, one Nature which cannot be parted asunder among the Persons. . . . Therefore there is no threefold Nature, or threefold Deity, but one Nature, and one Deity of the Father, Son, and Holy Spirit, and this Trinity is one God alone, good, great, eternal, omnipotent.'

These sentences, with their insistence upon the oneness of God, pointed then, and still point, to that as the profound truth underlying every consideration of the mysterious personal relationships or eternal 'modes' of Life revealed within that Holy Oneness. It is impossible that the Divine Nature should rightly be regarded as divided into three separate Entities. Trinitarian Doctrine is infinitely removed from tritheism,

De una et non trina Divinitate

so that Hincmar and his Western contemporaries, like their immediate predecessors, regarded the perfect co-inherence of the Persons within God as itself an emphasis and also a de-isolation of the Divine Unity. At the same time, the Archbishop's teaching is free from any confounding of the Divine Persons. His denial of Their mutual separation is the affirmation, not the negation, of the existence of interior personal communion in the Deity. This is apparent when he proceeds, after the manner of other exponents of orthodoxy, to uphold the Godhead, co-Essence, and personality of the Persons in the Trinity, together with the individual character (*proprietas*) of Each. The third Person, indeed, is the Source of this communion. 'The Holy Spirit alone,' adds Hincmar, 'proceeds from the Father and the Son, therefore He alone is called the Spirit of Both.' In accordance with the custom of the period, the rest of the book consists of a series of quotations and comments thereon, which do not yield any new interest, but merely uphold the main thesis.

The chief stress of later Carlovingian theology appears, then, to be laid on the Unity of God, which Unity is principally supported by two doctrines, namely (i.) the procession of the Holy Spirit from the Son as well as from the Father, and (ii.) the perfect equality of the Holy Spirit to the Father and the Son. As touching the *Filioque*, now in official use in Spain and France, there was no doctrinal disagreement between the Churches of these countries and the Roman Church. Bishop Pearson (*On the Creed*) truly states that 'in the time of Pope John VIII [who died in the same year as Hincmar] it was declared that the addition of *Filioque*, made in the Creed, should be taken away,' but this declaration has no theological significance, for Pope John was a clever statesman who did not scruple to employ the theological process for grinding his own political axe. In fact, the *Filioque* is known to have been upheld as well as abandoned for reasons of policy. Thus there arises all the greater necessity for care in sifting the chaff of statecraft from the grain of theology, and for declining to regard as 'development' any doctrinal position at all traceable to state motives. When, indeed, such motives are eliminated, the assertion can be made with confidence that the *Filioque* gained ground steadily in Rome in spite of any apparent setback.

VII

SCOTUS ERIGENA

JOHANNES SCOTUS ERIGENA (c. 813–891) stands at the junction of the Carlovingian Renaissance and the introductory period of Scholasticism, and in him the former glides into the latter. Born and educated in Ireland, he came to the Court of Charles the Bald, probably at the same time as Paschasius Radbertus, and flourished there for many years, participating in the two controversies concerning transubstantiation and predestination against Radbertus and Gottschalk. With Erigena the age of the compilers, which had been necessary for the conservation of theology in a turbulent period, comes to an end, and the amazing freshness of his mind was responsible for the marked differences between his own ideas and those of his contemporaries. He is, indeed, the first writer on the Trinity of outstanding interest within the limits of this volume. Himself a later Carlovingian, he nevertheless broke away from the system of later Carlovingian theology, so much so that he drew upon himself the violent opposition of the forces of Western orthodoxy. He caught the Carlovingian emphasis on the unity of God, but he rejected the interrelations of hypostases as usually presented by the Church, while his doctrine of the Procession is Greek rather than Latin. He was not the only writer to discover that 'originality' was quickly construed as heresy by the majority of the representatives of Mediaevalism.

Erigena was a *bête noir* to so many theologians on account of his alliance with Neo-Platonism, the latest philosophic system of the Greek genius. In this system the Absolute Cause—the Cause of all love and of all good—is the Source of the World-Idea, which, again, is the origin of the World-Soul. The World-Soul, in its component parts in the souls of men, finds itself divided in devotion to God on the one hand, and to the material universe on the other; but its absorption into God can nevertheless be obtained through reverent contemplation. Neo-Platonism was thus an attempt to form a unifying basis for thought, a common denominator to which the workings of the infinite and the finite could be resolved. As such it had previously attracted Augustine, whose mind was ever open to the appeal of the speculative, and who held the opinion that philosophy was a necessity to Christian dogmatics if Scriptural witness were ever to have a reasoned exposition. To this end Augustine had employed a method of human analogy which, incidentally, had doomed any merely dyadic conception of God; and Erigena, in his use of the analogical method, followed the lead of Augustine. But if he thought for one moment that his Augustinian credit would enable him to draw without limit upon Western credulity, he was wide of the mark. There was in Augustine, as Erdmann states,[1] a distinct tendency toward pantheism, with a consequent tendency toward belief in the unreality of evil; but when Neo-Platonism, with its far stronger tendencies in the same direction, came as an additional influence upon Erigena, it so captivated his dialectical mind as to place him out of sympathy with the authoritative teaching of the Western Church.

Scotus, however, was the originator of the mediaeval doctrine of the essential oneness of philosophy and religion, a oneness which was at the heart of the Neo-Platonic system, and which was to become the basis of the philosophy of the Schoolmen.[2] He had thus seized upon the valuable truth, often overlooked, that theology, philosophy, and science possess a fundamental unity, though the Scholastics hammered this unity into a system of iron dogmatism which definitely discouraged independence or individuality of thought. In course of time authority transgressed its proper limits, and theology came to be represented as so inelastic that its alliance with philosophy and science was ultimately broken. But the beginnings of this alliance are visible in Erigena's principal work *De Divisione Naturae*, in which he attempts a reduction of Christian revelation and human reason to one philosophic level. This course leads him on to a pantheistic terminus, in which God is actually

---

[1] *Hist of Philosophy*, 1. 277

[2] Harnack, *Hist of Dogma*, v 274n 'The most learned and perhaps, also, the wisest man of his age, he maintained the complete identity of *religio vera* and *philosophia vera*, and thus restored to its central place the fundamental thought of ancient philosophy'

and literally the all-in-all, in which the immaterial appears to be the material and the material the immaterial. In this portrayal of what was, in essence, the Neo-Platonic position, it is not surprising to find that evil is asserted to have no real existence, and thus one might naturally expect no such belief in the regenerative operations of the Holy Spirit as that which characterizes the theology of Alcuin. Moreover, his Neo-Platonic leanings affected his presentation of trinitarian doctrine. The human mind is composed of rational soul, the faculty of reason, and the faculty of feeling, which is an analogy of a similar triplicity in the Divine Mind ; but to Erigena this is a nominal triad, with no near affinity to the Doctrine of the Trinity as taught by the Church.[1] Yet, with all his liking for Greek speculation, much of his linguistic style resembles the forms in general use. In this book he upholds ' the co-essential eternity of Father, Son, and Holy Spirit.'[2] ' For,' he adds, ' the Spirit Himself is co-essential with the Father and the Son as touching His Godhead (*secundum divinitatem*). . . . The Trinity subsists in Essence (*substantialiter*) through Himself, and is not created by (*ex*) any Cause.'[3] But, having laid down the Unity and Eternity of God, he refers to the procession of the Holy Spirit in terms which are Eastern rather than Western. ' The Spirit,' he remarks, ' proceeds from (*ex*) the Father through (*per*) the begotten Son.' The Father is the One from whom the Spirit proceeds, the Son the One ' by whom and through whom He proceeds.'[4] Later in the book (§ 32) he again speaks of the Spirit as *from* the Father, *through* the Son, thus revealing another point of divergence from the systematic theology of his partners in the Carlovingian Renaissance.

Neo-Platonism made a strong appeal to the Church through a certain Greek Christian, probably of Alexandria, who is known to doctrinal history as pseudo-Dionysius ; and Scotus, in writing his *Expositions of the pseudo-Dionysian Epistles*, helped them to become the groundwork of much of early scholastic reasoning. The very nature of his undertaking accounts for a tendency toward inexactitude in theological

---

[1] Cf. Alice Gardner, *Studies in John the Scot* (1900), p 40 ' The Cause of all may be regarded as Being, Wisdom, and Life, Each of which is to be associated with one of the names of the Trinity ' [2] *De Div Nat*, ii 20.
[3] *Ibid*, 28. Erdmann (*ibid*, i, p 295) instances from this work Erigena's idea of the one creative energy of the Divine Triunity by the quotation : ' Pater vult, Filius facit, Spiritus perficit ' [4] *Ibid.* 22.

terminology which is noticeable in his *Expositions of the Heavenly Hierarchy*. The Holy Spirit is, he writes, ' the Spirit of the Father and the Son, in whom and through whom gifts of grace are distributed on all things.' He is the One ' whom the Father sends in the Name of His Son,' and He co-operates with the Son and with the Father's will. The Trinity ' is a threefold Light, and a threefold Goodness, three Substances in one Essence, Father, Son, and Holy Spirit, one God '[1]—an inexactitude of expression which would not commend itself to Western experts, with whom ' Essence ' and ' Substance ' were synonymous or interchangeable terms. The same inexactitude occurs in a later chapter : ' " Holy, holy, holy, Lord God of hosts," in which hymn the Supreme Good in three Substances is praised. For there is one Essence in three Substances.'[2] In his *Expositions of the Mystic Theology* there is an orthodox appearance attaching to his mention of the ' Person of the Father, from which Person proceeds the Person of the Son by generation and the Person of the Holy Spirit by procession.'[3] But when such a statement as this is read in conjunction with the whole context of Erigena's system there appears to be a definite absence of real mutual relationship between the Divine Persons as commonly understood by orthodox theologians. Evidently he regards any similitude of human and Divine persons as impossible, and thus he rejects any serious consideration of interrelationships among the Persons in the Deity.[4]

Scotus Erigena may justly be named the first prophet of Scholasticism, though it would be more correct to state that tendencies toward Scholasticism are found in him than to point to him as actually the first of the Schoolmen. The Scholastic writers were primarily theologians ; Scotus was primarily a philosopher. The former bowed to absolute ecclesiastical authority ; the latter recognized no such authority —as witness his disagreement with the *Filioque* which had been sanctioned by the greater part of the Western Church. Moreover, his love for theological speculation induced him to assume a negative attitude in his definitions of God which quickly

---

[1] *Expositiones super Ierarchiam Coelestem S. Dionysii*, I I
[2] *Ibid*, xii 4   Further evidence of Erigena's belief in the unity of the Trinity is found in his *Comment in Evang sec. Joan Fragmentum*, I.
[3] *Expositiones in Mysticam Theologicam S Dionysii*, iii.
[4] Cf Inge, *Christian Mysticism*, pp 133 ff.

stamped him as a rationalist in the eyes of mediaeval churchmen. A second result of theological speculation is mysticism, and Dean Inge has asserted that Scotus is the father of Western Mysticism as well as of rationalism. The former trend of thought can clearly be traced through scholastic mysticism to the pre-Reformation mysticism of Eckhart. The latter trend becomes visible as Scholasticism develops a rationalistic course which was destined to find its full expression in Nominalism.

VIII

FORERUNNERS OF SCHOLASTICISM

THE tenth century yielded no writer of importance in connexion with the Doctrine of the Holy Spirit. It was too dark a period morally to encourage intense spiritual leadership, and what controversy there was had more reference to the subject of the Divinity of Christ than to the formulation of trinitarian theology. Meanwhile the attentions of the Western world were largely directed along other channels. The dissolution of the Carlovingian Empire prepared the way for feudalism, a state of social relationships based on land tenure which was probably the only system of government possible at the time. New views of the principles and ethics of society were taking shape in many minds, and Lord Bryce has shown that, at the dawn of Scholasticism, the thoughts of men were being exercised by dreams of a world-monarchy and a world-religion, which were the two legacies of an ' expiring antiquity.' ' The doctrine of the unity of God now enforced the unity of man,'[1] and it is of decided interest to note how these more insistent ideas concerning a visible union of Church and State grew out of that great truth concerning God which the Carlovingian theologians had been so careful to emphasize. The eleventh century witnessed the development of this theocratic ideal, and also the first wave of Crusading enthusiasm which proved to be one of its buttresses. Yet the religious adventure of the Crusaders was also a stimulus to intellectual intercourse and to theological discussion between East and West, and, incidentally, gave an impetus to the general revival of learning in Europe.

Into this period of change the Schoolmen brought their system. The dogmas which had been educed by the Fathers and compiled by their successors now formed attractive material for new treatment, and Scotus Erigena had pointed the way. Though the scholastic writers paid more attention to the authority of the Church than Erigena had done, they

[1] Bryce, *Holy Roman Empire*, chap vii

FORERUNNERS OF SCHOLASTICISM

were attracted by his philosophic method, which they duly harnessed to the chariot of ecclesiastical tradition. The Church was to be the mistress of this union of the sciences—a wonderful ideal, but one which unfortunately was proved impracticable by a lack of the sense of proportion displayed by the idealists. Philosophy was set a hard task to blend itself with dogmas, the exponents of which believed more in the authority of the Church for their acceptance than in the authority of the truth inherent in them. Harnack's dictum that 'Scholasticism is simply nothing but scientific thought'[1] may thus be admitted on the understanding that, even though the 'thought' might have been in certain cases profound, the 'science' was essentially external. This was the inevitable outcome of a method which set out to systematize existing dogma from the standpoint that orthodoxy as such must come first, while philosophy and the sciences must come second, in subservience to it. The externality of the scholastic method gave rise to so undue an exaltation of human reason as to lead to those two divergent streams of thought whose sources have already been noted in Scotus Erigena. Moreover, though the spirituality of the Church began to deepen again in the eleventh century, she was hindered by this very externality from impressing upon the world to any appreciable extent the importance of the regenerative work of the Holy Spirit.[2] Yet the attempt to formulate a rational setting of spiritual experience and of religious tradition, side by side with the attempt to harmonize all Godward avenues of thought, traditional and untraditional, emphasized the appeal of theology to reason and also the wrong of its isolation. In these directions the Doctrine of the Holy Spirit can be said to pass through another stage of development, even though that development was fostered in the somewhat close atmosphere of the ecclesiastical academy.

Benedict VIII

Benedict VIII († 1024) is worthy of mention at this point, for, though he was no dialectician, he introduces the

---

[1] *Hist of Dogma*, vi , p 23.
[2] Nitzsch, *System of Christian Doctrine*, §§ 139, 140 (quoted by Hare, *Mission of the Comforter*, p 441) 'The Scholastic Theology of the Middle Ages could not give a correct view of the doctrine of the appropriation of salvation, because it thought more of the ecclesiastical course of the Christian's life as it was to develop itself through the instrumentality of the sacraments than of the order of salvation'

Forerunners of Scholasticism to doctrinal study if only because of the valuable assistance which his ecclesiastical statesmanship afforded them. The Schoolmen appropriated the *Filioque* not only because it was Western, but also because it suited their philosophical exposition of the Trinity, and Benedict was the first Pope officially to recognize this addition to the Creed.[1] The belief in the procession of the Holy Spirit from the Son as well as from the Father had been steadily consolidating itself in Rome in spite of some official discouragement, and now the complete rupture between East and West removed that little sense of restraint which had previously been imposed by their union. It is the responsibility of Benedict for the definite Roman leadership of the West in this typically Occidental belief that justifies the important place assigned to him in the development of the Doctrine of the Holy Spirit. As a theologian pure and simple, Benedict is negligible. He is notable as a reformer of monasteries, and as such he received the support of the Emperor. Accordingly most of his writings are decrees connected with confirmations of certain monasteries in their privileges, and with other kindred affairs, but very occasionally a remark is found here and there which indicates the main tendency of his belief. ' May the Holy Trinity keep your love unimpaired,' he prays,[2]—where the oneness of operation of the three Persons in the human soul is clearly an article of his faith. In another decree he speaks of the Holy Spirit as proceeding from Both (*ex utroque*),[3] which is in line with his public profession. The little theology that can be extracted from his pontifical decrees on such untheological subjects reveal him to be a firm believer in the Unity of God, and in the *Filioque* as one of its main supports. Accordingly, while Erigena, a century before, had handed on to the Schoolmen suggestions for the philosophical treatment of the main Carlovingian doctrines, Benedict now passed on to them these doctrines with the valuable hall-mark of papal sanction.

LANFRANC

Another forerunner of Scholasticism is found in the person of Lanfranc (1005–1089). A noble and lawyer of Pavia, he

---

[1] Herzog, &c , *Religious Encyclopaedia* (ed Schaff) : ' The first time a Pope actually used the addition to the Creed was in 1014, by Benedict VIII, at the crowning of Henry II But from that moment the Pope himself appears as the defender of the practice of the Western Church ' (art *Filioque*).
[2] *Decretum* 4   [3] *Decretum* 39.

became a monk at the Benedictine abbey of Bec, in Normandy, which during his term as prior was an acknowledged centre of learning. The part played by him in religious controversy brought him to the notice of William of Normandy, who found him useful in his designs on England, and raised him to the Archbishopric of Canterbury in 1070, after those designs had borne fruit. In ecclesiastical history he stands out as a clever statesman with a sincere regard for Church tradition and a loyalty to Church authority. In his statesmanship he was in full sympathy with the theocratic tendencies of Gregory VII, though the English Channel had a similar effect upon him as upon many succeeding English churchmen in cooling his ardour for the authority of Rome. But, whatever might have been his powers of diplomacy, his pre-eminence in scholarship was still more pronounced, and the continuance of the revival of learning was immensely furthered by his example. While at Bec he had been engrossed in the study of theology and the sciences, and among his pupils had been Anselm, the man destined to introduce the Scholastic period. To this link between him and the Schoolmen may be added another, to be found in the debate on transubstantiation, now renewed by the activity of Berengarius. While Lanfranc was still in Normandy, he was rebuked in a letter from Berengarius for upholding the strong belief in this dogma previously expressed by Paschasius Radbertus, and for even surpassing it in asserting that unworthy communicants could partake of the reality, while not of the merits, of the changed elements. With Berengarius the Sacrament of the Lord's Supper was altogether of a more subjective nature than with Lanfranc, both as touching the change in the elements and in the benefits obtained from their reception, and in presenting his views to Lanfranc he supported his arguments by logical positions which reveal the rational tendencies of his mind. Lanfranc, however, with his sheer weight of learning, was able to bear down the immature speculations of his former friend; but the interchanges of dialectic which marked their debate definitely paved the way for the inductive methods of the Schoolmen.

The greater part of Lanfranc's teaching on the Doctrines of the Holy Spirit and the Trinity are found in a work which has long been ascribed to him, namely, certain *Commentaries on the Pauline Epistles*, including the Epistle to the Hebrews.

If these writings may be regarded as of his authorship, Lanfranc sounds as his dominant note the Unity of God, which, indeed, was the doctrine, or the aspect of it, most frequently emphasized by his immediate predecessors in trinitarian theology. 'The favour of God,' he declares, 'is not distributed through the Persons of the Father, the Son, and the Holy Spirit; but an undivided Nature of Unity, together with one action (*opus*) of the Three, is understood.'[1] 'For God is one— Father, Son, and Holy Spirit.'[2] The oneness of the Divine Nature implies a oneness of Divine energy at work in the world, and the orthodox writers did well to assert these truths in face of internal heresy and the continued menace of Mohammedanism. Lanfranc proceeds to lay stress upon the manifoldness of agency by which the Holy Spirit presents His will to men. 'The Spirit speaks in many ways (*pluraliter*) by reason of the great number of prophets, although the Spirit who fills them is one.'[3] Unity of Divine will is not incompatible with diversity in its human expression. The Divine inspiration which is the cause of this prophetic concord is manifestly regarded as soul-directing rather than verbal. Added to this is a declaration as to the part assumed by the Holy Spirit in forgiveness, He being the One 'through whom sins are remitted to the person who confesses.'[4] The Spirit is still the Origin of such remission, even though the confession be made to a priest in accordance with the practice which, for at least two centuries already, had been insisted upon by the early Mediaeval Church.

BERENGARIUS

As for that able but somewhat vacillating character, Berengarius of Tours (999–1088), there is little in his writings which bears upon the present subject. His controversy with Lanfranc, in which his position affords points of striking similarity to that of Abelard in his contention with Bernard, consumed practically the whole of his intellectual energy, so that, in the midst of the turbulence which encircled him for many years, he had no opportunity for contributing to the development of trinitarian theology.

At the time when Radbertus definitely propounded the dogma of transubstantiation he had met with some opposition,

[1] On 1 Cor. xii 5   [2] On Gal. iii 33   [3] On 1 Cor xiv 21   [4] On Heb. x. 5.

especially at the hands of Ratramnus, his contemporary, who published a work against him about the middle of the ninth century. But since then there had elapsed a century of barrenness in theological productivity during which this dogma had been allowed to pass unchallenged. When, therefore, Berengarius began to question its truth he quickly aroused the antagonism of many churchmen who were under the impression that the intervening silence meant consent. In consequence, Lanfranc turned upon him as a heretic, and as such he became the victim of constant persecution on account of his 'freethought.' It would appear that what was here upheld as orthodoxy was more a matter of the *force majeure* of an ecclesiastical majority than an appeal to ancient tradition, though certain suggestions in this direction had indeed been handed on by the Fathers. The responsibility of Berengarius for the introduction of logic into theological debate warrants his being called a Scholastic theologian; at the same time he was more rational and speculative than Anselm ever cared to be. In three of his letters he attaches importance to the work of the Holy Spirit as Truth (*veritas*) in directing the hearts of men, but he hardly touches the subject of the Being of the Spirit.

GUITMUND OF AVERSA

Beside Lanfranc, another upholder of transubstantiation against the criticisms of Berengarius, though giving to the dogma a slightly different content, was Guitmund (†c. 1095), Archbishop of Aversa. Like the Norman prelate, he is not noted for the use of speculation, but he contributed to the preparation for Scholasticism by carefully setting forth the doctrine of the Divine Unity, and by supplementing it with that analogical treatment of the mystery of the Trinity which characterized to such a degree the expositions of the Schoolmen. This is clear from his *Confession*, in which his views are seen to follow the main orthodox lines. 'I believe,' he writes, 'in the Eternal Unity of the Holy Godhead; I believe in a co-eternal Trinity in this same Unity. For the Creator of all is one God and yet threefold, since there is Father, Son, and Holy Spirit. I do not say that the Father, Son, and Holy Spirit are the selfsame Person (*ipse*); but I do say that the Father, Son, and Holy Spirit are the selfsame Thing (*ipsum*).

When I say *ipse* I refer to the Person who is Father, Son, or Holy Spirit; when, however, I say *ipsum* I refer to the Substance which is God.' This discrimination in the use of the determinative pronoun was helpful as showing the eternal distinctions in the inner Life of the Deity side by side with that essential oneness which alone makes such distinctions possible.[1]

When Guitmund proceeds to deal with the relations between the Persons of the Godhead he manifests a reverence for Augustine which expositors of the next two centuries continued to feel. The practice of pointing to indications of a trinity in the human mind had led to another practice—of contemplating the Being of God from the analogical angle, and from this viewpoint certain conclusions could be drawn in support of the theology of the Trinity and particularly of that part of it which was specifically Western. Thus he brings in an analogy of the Trinity, the second and third similitudes of which are both Augustinian and Scholastic: ' The Father is Life, the Son is Wisdom, the Holy Spirit is Love, . . . and these Three are only one Substance, because God is one.' Therefore, regarding the Spirit as Love, he draws the following inferences concerning the Divine Triunity: 'Hence it is evident that, since Love proceeds from the Father to the Son, It also proceeds from the Son to His Father. That Love is the Holy Spirit, who thus proceeds from Both. . . . The Holy Spirit is co-eternal with the Father and the Son, because He Himself, as inseparable Love, which is the same Substance, has always united the one Substance of Them Both. . . . Therefore the Son is equal to the Father, and so is the Holy Spirit.' Here, then, an analogy is used not only to exemplify doctrine but also to prove it, and it would not have appeared incongruous to Guitmund to argue from the presence of the shadow to the presence of the substance. But in the tendency of this analogical method to pare down the fine distinctions between attribute and personality, there was danger lest the shadow of one thing might be assumed to portray the substance of another, and thus the habit of certain Schoolmen of ' establishing ' from such reasoning the *Filioque* and other theological statements was based on no very secure foundation. Perhaps this writer realized the necessity of some saving clause, adding,

---

[1] ' Creditur itaque per singulos alia persona, sed non creditur in tribus nisi una substantia '

FORERUNNERS OF SCHOLASTICISM 75

as he does, 'Nevertheless, we must see to it that we do not confound the Persons.'

In his *Letter to Erfastus* he remarks upon the *Filioque* without, however, developing any reasoned defence of the 'interpolation.' Like Alcuin, he speaks of the procession of the Holy Spirit as being from the Father and the Son together as from one Divine Source,[1] and adds that the Spirit proceeds from Them Both at one and the same time (*simul*), which emphasizes the previous assertion concerning the 'one first principle.' Guitmund thus passed on to the Scholastic Age a balanced setting of trinitarian doctrine, together with suggestions as to the manner of its exposition which, in point of fact, were acted upon to the full by Anselm and his followers.

So the pre-Scholastic Age prepared the way for the more detailed system of its successor, having upheld in particular the Unity of the Godhead as shown by revelation and the economy of grace, together with the truth of the *Filioque* as confirmed by revelation, tradition, and analogy. Finally, the existence of the three Persons of the Trinity had received due consideration and confirmation, as also had the absolute Deity of the Holy Spirit, whose operations, such as inspiration and forgiveness, could be attributed to none but God Himself.

[1] ' Ita cum et Pater essentia et principium sit, et Filius aeque essentia et principium sit '

PART II

FROM THE CLOSE OF THE ELEVENTH CENTURY TO THE CLOSE OF THE THIRTEENTH CENTURY

The Flourishing Period of Scholasticism

I. Foreword
II. The Father of Scholasticism
III. The Scholastic 'Rationalists'
IV. Hildebert and the Summists
V. The Fourth Lateran Council
VI. The Scholastic Mystics
VII. The Eastern Church
VIII Alexander of Hales and Albertus Magnus
IX Thomas Aquinas

Ἄρα οὖν θεὸς τὸ Πνεῦμα, ὡς προεῖπον· δικ ναὸς θεοῦ κληθήσονται καὶ οἱ ἅγιοι ἄνθρωποι κατοικήσαντες ἑαυτοῖς τὸ ἅγιον τοῦ θεοῦ Πνεῦμα . . . Τὸ δὲ ἅγιον Πνεῦμα παρὰ ἀμφοτέρων, Πνεῦμα ἐκ Πατρός, Πνεῦμα γὰρ ὁ θεός. καὶ Πνεῦμα ἅγιον Πνεῦμα ἀληθείας ἐστί, φῶς τρίτον παρὰ Πατρὸς καὶ Υἱοῦ.—EPIPHANIUS.

I

FOREWORD

THE second main period of about two hundred years, from the close of the eleventh century to the close of the thirteenth century, reveals Scholasticism at its height. Scholasticism was a product of the most active part of Mediaeval Catholicism. It flourished at the time when the hierarchy of Rome seemed actually to be turning Europe into a mighty theocracy, and when one of its methods of success was the subjection to its own ends of the attainments of scholarship. During this period the power of the papacy rose until, in the thirteenth century, it reached its high tide under Innocent III, the greatest of all mediaeval popes, whose authority and influence outclassed even those of Gregory VII. Innocent came to be regarded as the arbiter of international disputes, and he supported his authority by the energetic promotion of ecclesiastical Orders, which, being pro-papal, were, in the mediaeval age, necessarily anti-national, and also by his encouragement of the Crusades against the Mohammedan power, of which he expected a speedy end.[1] With regard to the future of Islam, Innocent's dreams of theocratic despotism made the wish the father to the thought, for the thirteenth century witnessed the growth of Turkish power during its course and the triumphs of Islam in the Holy Land at its close, to say nothing of the crowning victory of 1453.

Foreshadowed particularly by Erigena and Berengarius, Scholasticism proper dates from Anselm and extends as far as the beginnings of the Reformation. The Scholastic method, taken as a whole, may have been more subtle than deep, and it contains much that fails to stir any warmth of enthusiasm.

---

[1] Mansi, *Sacrorum Conciliorum Nova Collectio* (Venice), xxii 957 Under the head of 'Epistolae Innocenti Papae III, ad hoc Concilium spectantes,' Innocent, who was President of the Fourth Lateran Council, remarks 'Et quidem omnes pene Saracenorum provincias, usque post tempora Sancti Gregorii, Christiani populi possederunt sed extunc quidam perditionis filius Machomettus pseudopropheta surrexit, qui per saeculares illecebras et vuluptates carnales multos a veritate seduxit. Cuius perfidia, etsi usque ad haec tempora invaluerit, confidimus tamen in Domino, qui iam fecit nobiscum signum in bonum, quod finis huius bestiae appropinquat'

Yet there is undoubted profundity in many of the writers of this period, while the mystic movement which sprang up under the aegis of Scholasticism reveals true reverence of heart together with a remarkable clarity of spiritual insight. Moreover, the painstaking devotion of the Schoolmen gave decided impetus to the definite formation of systematic theology, which, by the time of the later Scholastics, was actually in being, and was brought into a real relationship to other spheres of learning. A bold attempt was made to unify the sciences, and to treat theology as the first of them all. If indeed, Anselm pointed out the limitations of reason, he certainly pointed out its definite place and emphasized its functions, so that the 'scientific' atmosphere in which the Schoolmen worked at their systematization of dogma incidentally assigned a religious importance to the universities, in particular to the University of Paris. But the philosophy of the academy was largely controlled by ecclesiastical tradition, by the authority not so much of essential truth as of the pronouncements of the Church Fathers *ex cathedra*; hence more formality than originality characterized the majority of the works produced by this period.

Naturally, however, different attitudes arose within the circle of the Schoolmen, some being more authoritative and adhering to Realism, others being more rational and adhering to Nominalism. Herein lay a divergence of view which became intensified into the mysticism of Bernard on the one hand, and into the 'scepticism' of Abelard on the other.[1] Realism, which held the 'universals' to be themselves real, and ideas to be actually present in their subjects, kept closely to tradition, following Anselm in promoting the above union with philosophy and science; and this school of thought was predominant during the palmy days of Scholasticism. Nominalism, which laid the emphasis on the abstract in dealing with the 'universals,' asserting that ideas are from the mind and not in the subjects concerned, was in its essence rationalistic, though it was the rationalism of churchmen and not of non-churchmen; and this view was supreme in the declining days of Scholasticism. The work of Nominalism in elevating the rational above the traditional ultimately divided the two, and, after reason had turned and rent tradition, the whole attempt at union between religion and philosophy was

[1] Cf. Erdmann, *ibid*, pp. 312 ff.

abandoned. So far as Scholasticism was an embodiment of Christian philosophy hewn out of the marble of tradition, it would stand until Nominalism should undermine its pedestal. Again, if Nominalism was the rational outbreak from Scholastic rigidity, and destined to be the ultimate cause of its decay, Scholastic Mysticism was an outbreak of an opposite nature, which arose while Scholasticism was reaching to its height, and drew from its genius while revolting against its externalism. Thus Mysticism, or ' theological piety ' (Harnack's equivalent), was as yet no separate movement.[1] If the non-mystical theology of this period could be termed the scholastic of the head, Mysticism was ' the scholastic of the heart,'[2] and it straightway endeavoured to afford a common ground for both Realists and Nominalists. An effort in the same direction was made by Petrus Lombardus, who brought in the powers of reason to supplement any obscurities there might have been in the traditional statements of faith. His insistence upon Church authority first and foremost secured him an influential position among the standard teachers of Christendom, and this is evidenced by the number of ' Sententiaries,' or theologians who commented upon his great work, the *Four Books of Sentences.*

The first period of Scholasticism proper covers its rise from Anselm down to, but not including, Alexander of Hales, while the second period, which shows Scholastic thought at its full tide, begins with Alexander of Hales and is, for the most part, embraced by the thirteenth century. This century was marked by an increased study of Aristotle, now made possible by a closer intercourse between East and West, Alexander himself being the first all-round expositor of this system. Neo-Platonism as a philosophic basis became neglected, Plato stepping into the background to make way for his successor ; and, in spite of the official discouragement of the study of Aristotle, the champions of later Scholasticism pursued this new course with avidity, openly employing the Aristotelian dialectic to set forth the mysteries of revealed truth. The realm of the sciences became widened, along with their sphere of ministration to theology, and tradition tended to be more the colleague of the sciences than their mistress,

---

[1] Fisher, *ibid*, p 230   ' Mysticism and Scholasticism were not antagonists '
[2] Inge thus quotes Goethe (*Christian Mysticism*, p 6)

although the Church took care to remain the mistress of them all. This developed phase of Scholasticism found its culmination in Albertus Magnus and in his great pupil Aquinas.

In dealing with the Doctrine of the Trinity, Realism worked from the basis of Augustine,[1] and this doctrine will be seen to receive varied exposition as it is treated by one or the other of the two main schools of thought. Dr. W. B. Pope notes in Realism and in Nominalism distinct tendencies toward Sabellianism and tritheism respectively,[2] and these tendencies can be understood when the tenets of the different groups are remembered. Abelard, though belonging strictly to neither of these philosophical divisions, upheld a Trinity which laid him open to the charge of modalism. Throughout the thirteenth century, however, the atmosphere encircling the subject of the Divine Persons was not so controversial as in the twelfth. The sting of the earlier philosophical discussions was not yet drawn, but it was, for the time being, rendered innocuous.

The employment of the analogy, so common on the part of the writers of this period, might on occasion suggest that their general impression of the Doctrine of the Trinity was that of the Essence of God in conjunction with certain of His attributes. Here again, in the course of orthodox teaching, there might have been tendencies, and tendencies were difficult to avoid. But the great Scholastic theologians argued directly from attributes to persons, and constantly affirmed the existence of personal distinctions in the Godhead. In doing so, they never pursued the course of Erigena and Abelard, neither was their insistence on the oneness of the Persons secured by emptying the Persons of Their Personality, even though the difficulties of comparing human and Divine personality were frankly recognized.[3]

Twenty-one writers will be considered in the survey of this part of the history, in addition to the Fourth Lateran Council. The Eastern Church will be represented by two, while, of those belonging to the Western Church, fourteen will be drawn from the twelfth century, and five from the thirteenth.

---

[1] Harnack (*ibid*, iv 130) detects the germ of Scholasticism in his *De Trinitate*.

[2] Pope, *Compendium of Christian Theology*, 1. 278.

[3] Cf Paterson, *Rule of Faith*, 218, where the author remarks that if person be synonymous with attribute, Jesus Christ should therefore have been described as an Incarnation of the three Persons of the Trinity

II

THE FATHER OF SCHOLASTICISM

ANSELM (1033–1109), the brilliant pupil of Lanfranc, and his successor as Archbishop of Canterbury, was the real founder of the new method of expounding the dogmatic truths of the Church by working out a philosophy upon the basis of faith. In thus combining faith and reason in setting forth Christian theology, Anselm criticized the 'unreasoned' faith of the Compilers as well as the rationalism of his own age; though it is well to remember that certain of his followers admitted a wide region which human logic and intellectualism were not sufficient to explore. Nevertheless, Anselm lays great stress upon the guidance of intuition as reinforced by spiritual experience, a factor in his writings which accounts for much of their religious beauty, but which also induced the later Scholastics to regard them as insufficiently systematic. Be that as it may, the later Scholastics owed much to his system as representing an earnest effort to provide a meeting-place for faith and reason upon the common ground of the Unity of God. This purpose is exemplified to the full in his *De Divinitatis Essentia Monologium*, which he produced while at the monastery of Bec. In it he sets out to reach God through the avenue of reason, employing on the way all the *a priori* arguments for the existence of God which his Realism affords, and extending the study to the consideration of the doctrine of the Trinity.

In the preface to the *Monologium* one sentence is reminiscent of the terminology of Erigena. 'For in that I have said that the most high Trinity can be called three Substances, I have followed the Greeks, who confess three Substances in one Essence by the same faith by which we confess three Persons in one Substance.'[1] There could be no true reasoning if these terms were misunderstood. But, once they are understood,

---

[1] Also in *cap* 78, Anselm holds that the immutable *summa essentia* cannot accurately be called *substantia*, unless *substantia* is definitely put for *essentia*. He adds that the *una Trinitas* or *trina Unitas* can thus be called, quite legitimately, one Essence, and three Persons or three Substances—which is evidently what he prefers

they reveal a providential self-expression of the Being of God. The Spirit is co-eternal with the Word[1] and consubstantial with the Word.[2] 'It is true,' he continues, 'as the previous reasonings clearly teach, that the most high Spirit has made all things through His Word . . . yet They are not two, but one Creator.'[3] Their essential unity implies Their perfect unity of operation. 'For though, indeed, the Father by Himself is absolutely the all-highest Spirit (*perfecte summus Spiritus*), and the Son by Himself is absolutely the all-highest Spirit; even so, however, the Spirit the Father and the Spirit the Son are one and the same (*unum idemque*), so that the Father and the Son are not two Spirits but one Spirit.'[4] Here, then, is a real oneness of Essence which is utterly devoid of any suggestion that may concern the relation of a whole to its parts. 'So from the Father alone proceeds the whole love of the most high Spirit, and the whole proceeds from the Son alone; also there are not two Wholes (*toti*) at once from the Father and the Son, but one and the same Whole.'[5]

This argument is developed when Anselm proceeds to speak more closely of the Trinity. The Spirit possesses in every respect the attributes of the Father and of the Son.[6] It is this very truth that reveals the unity of the Trinity to be Essential. 'For all the Father (*totus Pater*) is present in the Son and in the common Spirit; and the Son in the Father and in the same Spirit; and the same Spirit in the Father and in the Son.'[7] That such reasoning appeals to the intelligence is exemplified by an analogy which is typically Augustinian. The Trinity is likened to *memoria, intelligentia,* and *amor* in man; but more—any one Person of the Trinity, taken singly, is essentially *memoria, intelligentia,* and *amor,* the other two Persons existing in the analogical counterpart of any particular One.[8] Anselm works upon this as a basis when he argues the procession question from the expressly Western point of view that the position of the Son within the Trinity is more than medial. But this in turn requires a safeguard. Such a view of the trinitarian analogy does not overlook the *proprietas* or distinctive character of each Person. 'In the highest Essence there is only one Father, one Son, and one Spirit; and there are not three Fathers, or Sons, or Spirits.'[9] The

[1] *Monol*, cap 32   [2] *Ibid*, cc 33, 37, 38   [3] *Ibid*, 37   [4] *Ibid*, 43
[5] *Ibid*, 54   [6] *Ibid*, 58   [7] *Ibid*, 59   [8] *Ibid*, 60   [9] *Ibid*, 61 and 76, &c

THE FATHER OF SCHOLASTICISM

very fact that there are three Persons in the Godhead means 'that never is the Father the Son, or the Spirit who proceeds; nor at any time is the Son the Father, or the Spirit who proceeds; nor ever is the Spirit of the Father and the Son the Father or the Son; and so any One of Them singly is perfect.'[1]

The *Monologium* in its later chapters forms an introduction to the closer exposition of the Trinity contained in the *De Fide Trinitatis*, which was written to refute the tritheism of Roscellin. Accordingly the stress of the book is laid upon the essential unity of the Trinity as against the nominal unity put forward by the opposing teaching. In upholding this unity of Essence from the standpoint of the Third Person, Anselm endeavours to eradicate any notion other than that of inexpressible intimacy between this Person and the Others. 'For,' he remarks, ' the Name of the Holy Spirit is not out of place (*alienum*) in respect of the Father and the Son, since Each is both Spirit and holy '[2]; which, again, is a reminder of his views concerning the close relationship of *memoria, intelligentia,* and *amor*. On account of the one Deity thus being three Persons, it is nevertheless not necessary that, after the Son has become incarnate, the other Persons should become incarnate too; on the contrary, it is impossible.[3] ' Indeed,' argues Anselm, ' if the Holy Spirit were incarnate, just as the Son was incarnate, the Holy Spirit would be the Son of Man. Therefore there would be two Sons in the Trinity of God.... Even if the Father had taken a man up into the unity of His own Person, the plurality of sons would create the same dissimilarities.... No Person of the Godhead other than the Son should be incarnated.'[4] Thus there are more difficulties for the unorthodox than for the orthodox! So, writes Anselm to Roscellin, 'They are called three Persons, not because They may be three distinct realities' (*res separatae*).[5] The idea of personality does not spring from the idea of separation so uppermost in Roscellin's mind, for personality in God is positive, not negative. Finally, an assertion of the procession of the Holy Spirit from the Father and the Son is brought in to strengthen the anti-tritheistic reasoning,[6] for the suggestion that the *Filioque* emphasizes the essential unity of the Trinity

---

[1] *Ibid*, 63   [2] *De Fid Trin*, cap 3   [3] *Ibid*, 4   [4] *Ibid*, 5
[5] *Ibid*, 7   [6] *Ibid*, 9

had already been made by Benedict of Aniane, Hincmar, and others.

Though Anselm preferred some of the Greek terminology, he was a vigorous defender of the Occidental doctrine of the Procession, as is clear from the distinguished manner in which he took to task the Greek opinions at the Council of Bari (1098), and also by his book *On the Procession*. This work, as might be expected, concerns the question of the *Filioque* exclusively. The two sides are at once stated in the Prologue : ' It is denied by the Greeks that the Holy Spirit proceeds from the Son, as we Latins confess.' Having thus put the case in brief, he devotes chapter i. to a general survey of the common beliefs of East and West as touching the Trinity, while refraining at this stage from any argument over their differences. Chapter ii. contains an assertion of the Personality of each of the hypostases in the Divine Essence, along with the perfect Deity and Eternity of Each. Then he reasons : ' When we confess that the Holy Spirit is from God the Father, if the Father and the Son are one and the same God, then it follows, according to the same unity of the Godhead, that He is also from the Son. . . . Because if those things are true, of which I have said above that we believe equally with the Greeks, either the Son is from the Holy Spirit, or the Holy Spirit is from the Son. That, however, the Son is not from the Holy Spirit is well known from the Catholic Faith.'[1] The conclusion reached is that the *Filioque* is the only possible position, and it is of interest to note how Anselm blends his regard for Church authority with his regard for reason. There is no doubt, he continues, but that the Holy Spirit proceeds from the Father, for this naturally follows from the assertion that He proceeds from God, because the Father is God. Can there be any doubt, then, that we are right when we declare the Holy Spirit to proceed from the Son ? For if He proceeds from God, as He does, He must proceed from the Son, because the Son is God. 'Moreover, the Father is God no " more" than the Son ; on the contrary, there is one only true God, the Father and the Son. Wherefore if the Holy Spirit is from the Father because He is from God, who is the Father, it cannot be denied that He is also from the Son, as He is from God, who is the Son.' Also, the Spirit proceeds *equally* (*pariter*) from the Father and the

[1] *De Processione Spiritus sancti contra Graecos, cap* 4

Son[1]—a statement which is again emphasized in chapter xxiv., while the main argument of chapter vii. concerning the *Filioque* is largely repeated in chapter viii. When the Mission of the Holy Spirit is considered, it is found that 'the same Holy Spirit Himself whom the Father sends, the Son also sends.'[2] Hence, an examination of the Spirit's procession and mission, and of the former in particular, seeing that it touches the essential Life of God, will reveal an *eternal* mediation of the Second Person within the Trinity which justifies the view that the Father and the Son are equally one Source of the Spirit. Only be it remembered that an agreement with the twofold procession does not warrant any inequality being attached to the Third Person. 'We who say that the Holy Spirit exists or proceeds from the Son confess Him to be neither less than nor inferior to the Son.'[3] However, on the general question of the procession, Anselm once again refers to the *Filioque* as the only logical conclusion[4] to the whole discussion, on the ground that 'the selfsame Deity is common to both the Father and the Son.'

His devotion of spirit in the midst of philosophical speculation, coupled with his endeavour to give a reasoned demonstration to faith, thus make Anselm the father of the mediaeval system. Although his maxim was that belief had to precede knowledge, his thought itself was essentially 'systematic,' and was made no less so by his attachment to ecclesiastical authority. The Forerunners of Scholasticism had prepared the way for him to a certain extent, Lanfranc's insistence upon the Divine Unity as a philosophic basis and the attraction of the analogical method passed on by Guitmund both lending useful aids, not to speak of the assistance of the universities. Yet Anselm was too great to leave even suggestions as he found them, as witness the somewhat daring way in which he treated the Augustinian analogy with a view to emphasizing the Unity of God. Anselm writes almost entirely on the subject of the Divine Being, and touches very little the work of the Spirit. With the points at issue between Realism and Nominalism this was to be expected, but the scope of his subject, though somewhat limited, was covered in that masterly manner which laid

---

[1] *Ibid*, 7 [2] *Ibid*, 9 [3] *Ibid*, 13
[4] 'Utique nihil aliud intelligi potest,' &c *Ibid*, 15; also 16, 19, and 23

the foundation of Tridentine Catholicism. Yet the Catholicism of Trent was not to be the sole beneficiary of such devotion and learning, for the whole world of religious thought will always be in debt to this saintly patron of systematic theology.

III

THE SCHOLASTIC 'RATIONALISTS'

THE term 'Rationalists' as applied to three Schoolmen of the twelfth century must in no wise be understood in its modern sense. To these men reason was not so much the substitute for faith as the great demonstrator of faith, and, as such, it took upon itself a larger content in their systems of theology. More room was given by them to the scope of the intellect as over against the traditionalism of Lanfranc and of Anselm, though they differed in their methods of combining philosophy with religion. Thus it is only with this interpretation that the term 'Rationalists' can here be applied; it was a Rationalism propounded from a distinctly ecclesiastical standpoint. Nevertheless, the 'free' tendency of their thought can be appreciated by the opposition thereto of such staunch churchmen as Anselm and Bernard of Clairvaux, the former proceeding against Roscellin, the latter against Abelard and Gilbert.

ROSCELLIN

Of these three writers, one of the two most deserving of the name of 'Rationalist' is Roscellin (c. 1050–1130),[1] canon of Compiègne, and master of Abelard. His Nominalism led him to take a tritheistic view of the Trinity, and, though he defended his position with undoubted ability, his beliefs were condemned at the Council of Soissons in 1092.[2] Anselm, whose accusation of Roscellin had secured his recantation at the Council, followed up this public blow to the Nominalist cause by his *De Fide Trinitatis* against Roscellin, which has already been noticed, together with his *De Incarnatione Verbi*. With regard to Roscellin's writings, it is probable that only a letter of his to

---

[1] Johannes Theodorus Kunneth (*Vita et Haeresi Roscelini*, 1, § 3) states that Roscellin flourished about 1137, but this is almost certainly too late a date
[2] Kunneth remarks. 'De scriptis Roscelini nil certi constat'

Abelard exists,[1] so that other sources must be resorted to for the securing of his opinions. Johannes Theodorus Künneth, in his *Vita et Haeresi Roscelini* (1756, Erlangen), contributes to the sum of knowledge concerning Roscellin's theology. ' On the subject of the Holy Trinity . . . he says that the three Persons in the Godhead are either mutually separate and distinct " things," as three angels or three spiritual beings ; or the Father and the Holy Spirit became incarnate along with the Son.' He is thus liable, comments Künneth, to the charge now of Sabellianism, now of Arianism.[2] ' In short,' his biographer continues, ' it is evidently clear that he laid down : *" Either* the Father and the Holy Spirit became incarnate along with the Son, *or* these three Persons in God are three ' things,' mutually separate from one another, just as three angels," &c. . . . So Roscellin wishes to exempt the Father and the Holy Spirit from incarnation, and to defend the Christian faith concerning the Incarnation by announcing three different and distinct beings (*res*) in God, who may differ among themselves just as three angels, yet who may be absolutely the same in will and in power. . . . This is the Roscellin heresy.'[3]

Künneth's account seems to be quite fair. However strongly Roscellin might have protested his innocence of tritheism, this protest did not hold good in the eyes of the Church, which saw the logical outcome of his Nominalism, and which was in consequence on its guard against any philosophy of religion which attached more reality to things (*res*), the concrete imitations, than to ideas, their absolute patterns. It was because Roscellin was obsessed by the notion of the

---

[1] François Picavet, in *Roscelin, Philosophe et Théologien* (1911, Paris), pp 68–74, quotes this letter in translation Roscellin denies that the Fathers (Ambrose, Augustine, Isidore) upheld such a unity of the Divine Substance as does Abelard ; he asserts the Divine unity and equality without Sabellianism ; and he denies at the same time that on account of Their possession of personal characteristics he regards the Persons of the Trinity as ' Gods.'

[2] *Ibid*, 1, § 6

[3] *Ibid*, ii, § 15. ' Itaque . . verum esse autumat : quod tres in Deo personae, non una res sint, sed tres res, unaquaeque per se separatim ' Picavet (*Roscelin*, pp 68 and 75) remarks . ' Ce qui lui appartient à coup sûr, dans tout ce qui est rapporté à ce sujet, c'est ce qui suit, sous forme de dilemme : on l'on peut dire que les trois personnes de la Trinité sont trois choses en soi, identiques par la puissance et la volonté ; on l'on doit dire qu'elles sont seulement une chose. En ce dernier cas, on sera obligé d'amettre que le Père et le Saint Esprit ont été incarnés avec le Fils . . Ainsi, pour la Trinité, Roscelin s'attache à l'unité de ressemblance et d'égalité, mais il tient surtout à éviter le sabellianisme que le rendrait hérétique à propos de l'Incarnation et l'arianisme que le conduirait à mettre la pluralité en Dieu ' Another useful work on Roscellin is by Frédéric Saulnier, *Roscelin, sa vie et ses doctrines* (1855).

reality of the concrete, or of the individual, that he was forced into the belief that there are separate Individuals in God. In process of debate he was evidently capable of malicious feelings, such as are revealed in his relationships with Anselm and his former pupil Abelard ; but as a theologian he never exerted wide influence, and the end of his life is lost in a maze of controversy.

ABELARD

Another churchman who may be termed a Scholastic 'Rationalist,' though certainly in a less degree than Roscellin, is Peter Abelard (1079-1142), the most thought-provoking writer and teacher of his time. As a theologian he was constructive as well as critical, and there is every reason for believing that the direct contribution of this brilliant and popular Schoolman to religious thought would have been more considerable had it not been for those pathetic misfortunes of his personal life which hung around the name of Heloise.

A student first of Roscellin, then of the Realist William of Champeaux, Abelard declined to adhere to either, and his own 'Conceptualism' reveals an independent turn of mind which was really responsible for the ultimate relegation to the background of the old duel of conflicting philosophies. He was essentially a 'rationalist' in outlook, and a reveller in flights of intellect. But while revolting against tradition, he submitted to the authority of the Church; for, though he took the opposite view of the mutual relations of faith and reason to that held by Anselm, faith meant decidedly more to him than it ever did to Roscellin.

The free rein which Abelard gave to his dialectical powers is exemplified by his writings on the Trinity, his central subject. The creed of the Church in regard to this must be tested by reason ; hence the rational atmosphere encircling all his treatment of the Trinity. He had thought his way through the matter far enough to revolt against the tritheism of his first master, against whom he wrote his little work *De Fide Sacrosanctae Trinitatis*, but his revolt was construed as having carried him to the other extreme, and he soon found himself confronted with the charge of Modalism. Whether he deserved the accusation of making the Persons of the Trinity mere modes of the Divine Being is extremely doubtful. What is by no means doubtful is that the period in which he lived made it difficult for nearly every expounder of the Trinity to escape some kind of accusation. At any rate, Abelard did, in fact, strongly emphasize the unity of the Trinity in his *Introduction to Theology* (or *de Trinitate*).[1] 'The religion of the Christian faith,' he writes, ' confesses the three Persons to be contained in Themselves, in all things co-equal and co-eternal, not in number of individuals (*rerum*) but in plurality of distinctive characters (*proprietatum*), truly different, God, namely the Father, and God His Son, and God His Spirit proceeding from Both.'[2] It will be noticed throughout his works how strongly Abelard stresses the procession of the Holy Spirit from the Son as well as from the Father.[3] Moreover, he asserts that 'the distinctive character (*proprium*) of the Holy Spirit proceeds from Both, and is neither created nor made. For in that it eternally subsists and is without beginning, it is proper that it should be called neither created nor made. . . . In fact, the Holy Spirit Himself also is not begotten, and since He is not begotten this means that He is not the Son ; nor, on the other hand, is He therefore unbegotten, since He is from Another, proceeding from the Father as much, of course, as from the Son.' The distinction between the Persons of the Trinity undoubtedly made here is emphasized as we read farther · ' The Holy Spirit is a Person; yet the Father, the Son, and the Holy Spirit are not one Person, but several Persons (*plures*). But, indeed, just as the Substance of these Persons is absolutely the same, so is Their glory indistinctive (*indeterminans*), and undivided Their operation and will.'[4] Abelard is at any rate free from Modalism thus far. His emphasis of the Unity of God is natural and necessary, but his insistence upon the *proprium* of each Person, the fullness of the personality of Each, and the distinctions made between Them (*diversas veraciter*), is equally firm. ' Wisdom is especially attributed to the Son, Love to the Holy Spirit, . . . yet we declare that neither the Son nor the Holy Spirit is any less omnipotent than the Father.'[5] The very name ' Holy Spirit ' suggests the Love of the Divine Goodness proceeding equally (*pariter*) from the Father and

---

[1] The books chosen to exemplify Abelard's teaching will suffice without any consideration of his *Sic et Non* (*Yes and No*), which purports to clear the ground for reasoning by attempting to resolve many contrary beliefs expressed by the Fathers into one intelligible system

[2] *Intro ad Theol*, 1 5   [3] See also 11 11, 13, 14, 15, &c   [4] i 6   [5] *Ibid*, 10

the Son[1]; while the equality of this procession must also be eternal, seeing that 'the eternity of the Holy Spirit is openly shown' (as in Gen. i. 2).[2] Again, the Deity of the Holy Spirit is unmistakably implied in our Lord's words concerning His relation to sin, when He said that sin against the Holy Spirit cannot be forgiven, although sin against the Father or against the Son can be forgiven. 'by which does He not clearly indicate that the Spirit Himself is not less than the Father or the Son, and on this account also that He is fully God, just as the Father Himself or the Son?'[3] The Holy Spirit is thus a 'self-contained' and uniform Substance which, from the very nature of Deity, is unchangeable.[4] 'Unless I am mistaken,' he adds, 'philosophers have understood the Holy Spirit as equivalent to energizing life (*vitam spiritalem*)'; but the Holy Spirit is more to him, namely, 'the Life of souls whom He causes to progress by quickening them to an increase of good works.'[5] The second book of the *Introduction* continues the same line of exposition of the Trinity, and develops into a vigorous defence of the *Filioque* against the Oriental theologians. Abelard states that 'the same Substance, absolutely uniform (*simplex*) and inseparable, which the Father is, so is the Son, just as is the Holy Spirit; for the whole Trinity is one and the same.'[6] But that this refers to the identity of relation between the Substance and each of the three Persons, and not to any identity of the Persons Themselves —which would have justified the charge of Modalism—is proved again as this second book proceeds. 'And so in God, although the Father, Son, and Holy Spirit are one and the same Essence, yet one thing (*alia*) is the individual character (*proprietas*) of the Father . . . another (*alia*) that of the Son . . . and another (*alia*) that of the Holy Spirit.'[7] Having emphasized the personal distinctions in the oneness of the Godhead, Abelard dwells upon the procession of the Holy Spirit as affecting these distinctions from the Western point of view. Hitherto he has upheld the *Filioque*, having spoken also of the equality and the eternity of the procession from the Father and the Son; now he adds that it is in the Spirit's Nature to proceed from the Father and the Son together

[1] *Ibid*, 12 [2] *Ibid*, 13 [3] *Ibid*, 14
[4] *Ibid*, 17. These sentiments are quoted again in *Theol Christ*, 1 5
[5] *Ibid*, 20 [6] ii. 10. [7] *Ibid*, 12.

(*simul*), in effect upholding the *unum principium* as expressed by earlier writers (§§ 14, 15). Nor can he rest content until he has made pointed quotations from Athanasius, Cyril of Alexandria, Chrysostom, Augustine, Hieronymus, and others, against the general position of antagonism assumed by the Eastern Church to the *Filioque*.

Though Abelard probably never intended his *Christian Theology* to be a companion volume to his *Introduction*, it might fittingly be regarded as such, as it reproduces a large portion of the latter almost word for word. In it he brings his faculty of reason to bear upon the dogma of the Trinity in its defence against many objections. He would have his readers still remember the simple (*simplex*) nature of the Divine Substance. The Unity of the Deity must on no account be allowed to fade into the background. At the same time, there are distinctions within God which the use of the analogy may express. The Christian creed includes belief in three Persons in the Godhead, namely the Father, Son, and Holy Spirit, and These may be regarded as Divine Might begetting, Divine Wisdom begotten, and Divine Favour proceeding.[1] In Abelard's analogical treatment the Spirit is always represented by the idea of love or favour, and this attitude was general among the Schoolmen. If this be true, then the Holy Spirit is obviously eternal, and an appeal is again made to the statement in Gen. i. 2.[2] Moreover, if the Holy Spirit is eternal, His procession from the Father and the Son must also be eternal (*perpetua processio*); and as He proceeds eternally from Both, He must be equally the Spirit of the Son as of the Father.[3] The third book contains a statement of faith which is a repetition of the foregoing assertions, while in more confessional form.[4] Together with belief in the oneness of God there is belief in the interrelation of the Divine Persons, so much so that, though Abelard's theology closely follows Anselm's in its 'unexclusive' treatment of the analogical

---

[1] *Theol. Christ*, 1 2. 'Potentia, sapientia, benignitas'
[2] *Ibid*, 3   [3] *Ibid*, 5 (also Book IV).
[4] 'Tenet itaque Christianae fidei religio . . unum Deum tres personas esse, Patrem, et Filium, et Spiritum sanctum , unum Deum, ac nullo modo plures deos ; unum Creatorem omnium . . Tres quippe personas dicimus ab invicem suis proprietatibus diversas, Patrem, et Filium, et Spiritum sanctum . . Nec ideo tres dii sunt aut plures, sed unus solummodo Deus in tribus personis aeternaliter atque incommutabiliter consistit . . . Sp s proprium est procedentem esse a Patre et Filio, non creatum, non factum, non genitum, sed procedentem tantum . Neque enim Pater est Trinitas   sic nec Filius nec Sp s Trinitas dici potest, sed una tantum in Trinitate persona'

representations of the Persons (viz. that the other Two are present in Each), it distinctly states that one Person cannot stand for the Three. This emphasis of the *proprium* Abelard constantly sets forth, however nearly he may incline to Modalism or Sabellianism when dealing with the nature and attributes of God. And it is no weakening of this emphasis to remark, as he does in the fourth book, that the operations of the Three are as the operation of One, that whatever One does the Others do also.[1] Such belief is essential to any notion of Divine unity as well as to any assertion of inner eternal distinctions. Nevertheless it is true that the Son alone became incarnate, and not the Father, nor the Spirit. The fourth part of the *Theologia*, in which the unity of the Divine Essence has been particularly stressed, proceeds to its close with an attack upon the Greek view of the procession, where Abelard's line of reasoning follows much the same course as that taken by Anselm, with special importance attached to our Lord's breathing of the Spirit upon the disciples. As in his previous defence of the *Filioque* in the *Introductio*, he quotes extensively from Athanasius and others of the Ancient Church in support of the Western position.

No doubt it was the wide scope which Abelard allowed to reason that, more than anything else, embroiled him with his fellow churchmen, and particularly with Bernard of Clairvaux. Any one who appreciates how much the Cross meant to Bernard will not be surprised at his opposition to Abelard on that ground alone, for the latter did not place the Cross exactly in the centre of his theory of the atonement. This might have caused Abelard somewhat to underestimate the redemptive work of the Holy Spirit, even though he wrote comparatively nothing on the subject. At any rate, his trinitarian teaching was condemned at Soissons twenty-nine years after Roscellin's had been condemned in the same place, and, though he withdrew some of the words which had given offence, he was again found guilty of heresy at the Council of Sens, 1141, and put to silence.[2] Theological accusations often have more than theology

---

[1] ' Hoc idem operari unamquamque trium personarum quod una earum operatur, ut videlicet omne id quod facit Pater faciat Filius sive Spiritus, et e converso '

[2] Cf Mansi, xxi , col 566 (following Dr Fisher's reference) In the letter of Innocent III, upholding the findings of the Council of Sens, the Pope mentions a few of Abelard's heresies (*sic*), of which the following refer to the Holy Spirit : ' Quod Pater sit plena potentia, Filius quaedam potentia, Sp s nulla potentia ' ; ' Quod Sp s non sit de substantia Patris ' , ' Quod Sp s sit anima mundi '

underlying them, and, even if Abelard were immoderate in the expression of his mind as he confronted his accusers, there is scant justification in his great works for this constant persecution, which heaped misery upon an already unhappy life. Anselm might well have been charged with Modalism since Abelard was. At all events Peter Abelard remains for all time one of the most notable pioneers not only of mediaeval[1] but also of modern theology.

GILBERT OF POITIERS

The other who can more correctly be styled a Scholastic 'Rationalist' is Gilbert, Bishop of Poitiers, or Gilbertus Porretanus (1070–1154). In him the balance swayed heavily on the side of dialectics, hence his 'Rationalism' stands out clearly against the background of a growing mysticism. The subject of the Trinity was his main theological theme, as it was Abelard's, and his faculties of reason carried him along much the same course as that which Abelard pursued. If Abelard tended to a modalistic conception of God in which the Divine oneness overshadows the personal distinctions, Gilbert went farther, namely, in distinguishing *Deus* from *Deitas*, the 'Deity' or the Divine Essence being predicated substantially, and the Persons in that Essence being regarded as 'nominals' or *proprietates*. This extreme of Realism he developed in his *Commentary on the 'De Trinitate,'* ascribed by an old, though a wrong, tradition to Boethius, and it was particularly that part of his work which deals with the second book of the *De Trinitate* that induced Bernard of Clairvaux to accuse him of heresy at the Council of Rheims, 1148.[2] These commentaries of Gilbert are found in the Basel edition of Boethius' works, dated 1570.

At the very outset Gilbert faces the question as to 'how the Trinity is one God and not three Gods.' God, he proceeds,

---

[1] Harnack (*ibid*, vi 39): Abelard 'really laid the foundation for the classical structure of mediaeval conservative theology'

[2] There appears, at first sight, to be some discrepancy between Fisher (p 226) and Erdmann (p 328), the former asserting that Gilbert distinguished *Deus* from *Deitas*, the latter denying any such distinction Gilbert himself appears to deny this distinction in his commentary on Book I of Boëthius, then he proceeds to assert it in that on Book II At least, in the *Acta Concilii* (of Rheims), Mansi xxi, being an account of the Council collected from various authors by Severinus Binius, it is stated ·
'quod Episcopus Pictavensis scripsit et dixit quod Divina essentia non est Deus,' and that he (Gilbert) was helped by 'his friends from the cardinals' 'quos habuit non paucos' . . . 'Quare et aiebat se, Divinitatem esse Deum, in illo tantum sensu concedere, quo Deus ponitur pro natura'; and by *Deus*, so Binius holds, Gilbert signified any one of the Persons.

is *solus unus*. Arius reached this conclusion by wrongly denying all *essentia* of the Godhead to either the Son or the Holy Spirit. There are other heretics in reference to the Son and the Holy Spirit, but these, like Sabellius, think out their theories in other ways. At any rate, he asserts, the oneness of God is laid down as an unalterable thesis. Proceeding from this, we find that there are those who rightly understand the Father, Son, and Holy Spirit to be distinct Persons in number, with distinct characteristics, and who believe the Son and the Holy Spirit to be God just as the Father. It is wrong, however, to say that, because the individual characteristics are distinct, the subsistences are distinct too ; for such a statement of faith would make the Father, Son, and Holy Spirit not of the same Essence but of a like Essence (*similis essentiae*). ' Again, Macedonius was perceiving aright when he stated that the Father and the Son are of one and the same Substance or Essence, and that Both are one God ; the Holy Spirit, however, they (his followers) deny to be God ; but, since the Holy Spirit is the Spirit of Both jointly, he believes that the Holy Spirit is equivalent to the Deity of Them Both, and that He has no substance.' Moreover, there are those also who regard the Father, Son, and Holy Spirit as manifestations of different aspects of the one God. Boethius, however, with the desire to destroy the ' detestable errors ' of these heretics, and to assist the infirmity of the weak, wrote on the subject of the three Persons in the one Essence. We see, then, that the Essence of the Three is *singularis* and *simplex*. ' The Father, Son, and Holy Spirit are one God in singleness of Essence, not three Gods.' This, indeed, is not in accordance with ' natural ' reasoning, which speaks of three men as three, and not as one man. But, in ' Divine ' reasoning, the Father is spoken of as God, the Son as God, and the Spirit of Them Both as God ; so that the Father, Son, and the Spirit of Both are one God alone (*singulariter*). ' The faithful say in each case : The Father is God ; again, the Son is God ; again, the Holy Spirit is God. And from this they conclude in the case of all : therefore the Father, Son, and Holy Spirit are one God.' And certainly not without reason, because they solemnly assert the underlying cause of this Divine oneness to be the complete absence of differences in the one Essence. The Arians, on the other hand, are of the opinion that there must be three different Gods in ' grades ' if each One is called God, saying that plurality must arise from ' otherness ' (*alteritas*). Not so. ' The reason of this union is absence of diversity ' (*indifferentia*). This is the Catholic faith.

From this point Gilbert proceeds to deal more closely with the exposition of the Divine Triunity, and he does not here make that distinction between *Deus* and *Divinitas* which he makes later. Rather does he state the opposite. Reference is made to ' the Substance of God, that is God or Deity.' God is a simple Substance; but ' God would not be simple if His Essence were composed of many Essences, or if forms (*formae*, original ideas in the universe) were present in Him.' The simple Essence of God is, in fact, that by which alone each One of the Persons of the Godhead is that which He is. The Persons are thus each One God, and together God; and the Catholics, in affirming these things, may be understood to draw right conclusions in accordance with due regard for Those concerning whom they are speaking. The Essence of God, then, is absolutely self-contained, and is that from which being is derived.[1] God is *ipsa divinitas sua*, so that when we speak of God from God, that is, the Son and the Holy Spirit from the Father, or the Holy Spirit from the Son, we cannot conceive of any differentiation between Them. On the contrary, the three Persons are inseparable, for They are one, one equally, and one together; for truly the Essence or οὐσία of God is single and simple. Three men together can but remain three men. It is not the same, however, in respect of the Father, Son, and Holy Spirit, although they are indeed three; and, in accordance with the number of these Persons, *actu dicendi*, the Name of God may be threefold. But, ' since the Father is God, and the Son is God, and the Holy Spirit is God, this threefold Name, I say, cannot, on this pretext, be adapted to any number, as if it were possible to assert correctly that the Father, Son, and Holy Spirit are three Gods.' The three men of the argument are still three men because of the diversity between them, which follows inevitably upon their not possessing a common substance. In God, on the contrary, there are three ' unities ' without any plurality of number ensuing, ' for They are not actually

---

[1] ' Essentia est illa res quae est ipsum esse, id est, quae non ab alio hanc mutuat dictionem, et ex qua est esse.'

(*vere*) Three.' Essential diversity alone could cause numerability, or the possibility of addition. It is diversity of character in things which causes the manifold diversity of things. Hence God does not become three Gods by any repetition of the name ' God,' for this would not be an enumeration of many, but rather the repetition of one only, in the same sense as the repetition of the word ' sun ' thrice does not thereby point to three suns. In like manner, therefore, if, with respect to the Father, and to His Son, and to the Holy Spirit of Both, God is predicated thrice, there is, after all, only one God. ' And so these Persons of the Trinity, that is, these Three differing from each other in certain characteristics, are singly and plainly one God '—a statement to which Gilbert strongly adheres, while he constantly emphasizes the fact that each Person is fully *Deus*.

Gilbert utters a warning to those who are attracted to the analogical method for the exposition of the Trinity. Certain of these analogies the Sabellians use for their own purpose, and one must beware of their error. This error will be avoided if it is recognized that the Father, Son, and Holy Spirit are distinct Persons in the one undivided Substance, so much so that the above-mentioned repetition of Their Names in the one Godhead is a repetition only *ex comparationibus*, while the use of the plural in reference to Them is a convenient form of speech which in no way detracts from Their identity of Essence.

As affording a complement to this demonstration of the Divine Unity, Gilbert is convinced of the personal character (*personalis proprietas*) of each Member of the Trinity, though, he adds, whether we speak of the Father, the Son, or the Spirit of Both, we say ' God.' The Persons of the Godhead differ only in Their mutual relation, and this *relatio* does not mean *alteritas*. Yet this relation is real. ' Indeed it is certain that the Father is other than (*alius a*) the Son, and the Holy Spirit ; and the Son other than the Father, and the Holy Spirit ; and the Holy Spirit other than the Father, and the Son ; and that each One of these Three is in that single, simple, undivided, and sole οὐσία, that is, Essence, namely, in that by which He is *alius*—one, simple, and undivided—God without any participation of unlike essence.' The word ' person ' is thus seen to possess different meanings in nature (*naturalibus*) and in theology. It has already been made clear that this otherness (*alteritas*), by which the Father, Son, and Holy Spirit are predicated as being mutually other than Themselves, is not the otherness of things.' There is no question of *aliquid* in the inner distinctions of the Godhead, but only of relation[1]; for 'the Father, Son, and Holy Spirit differ only in relation.' That this is necessarily true will be conceded when it is remembered that each Person is God; so that, even if the order in the Trinity were reversed, no differences could be detected.[2] Add to the Godhead of Each the fact that the Three together (*simul*) are one God, and any differences could still less be imagined.

Throughout this commentary on the first book of pseudo-Boethius there is a considerable amount of repetition on the subjects of the Unity and the Trinity of the Divine Life. Between these two Gilbert strives to hold the orthodox balance of trinitarian theology while giving the preponderance to the oneness of God as evidently the goal of his exposition.[3] In answer to the question as to how God can really be one and *solus* in face of the revelation of a Trinity, his first commentary shows a careful statement of the whole case which is very reminiscent of the viewpoint of Abelard. The work of the Spirit finds small place in it, and the procession none, save in such a side-remark as that *Deus* alone can proceed from *Deus*.

The Commentary on the second book of pseudo-Boethius on the Trinity is but a quarter of the size of that on the first book. In it Gilbert faces the question as to 'whether the Father, Son, and Holy Spirit may be predicated substantially of the Deity,' or be named as embracing the whole Essence of the Deity? Whether, as he reviews the question, in accordance with the analogy of the subsistences of natural reasoning, They may be predicated of the Deity—not simply *Deus* but *Divinitas*; or They may not be predicated substantially of the Deity, but in another way? 'Not a simple question,' is the remark of the author, as he reminds his readers of a conclusion of Boethius which supports the second alternative (*nullum igitur horum substantialiter praedicatur*).

[1] '[alteritas] non sit secundum res illas quibus aliquid sint ea de quibus ipsae dicuntur, sed potius secundum relationes sit.'
[2] Cf 'Ubi autem abest (haec) pluralitas, adest essentiae unitas'
[3] Cf also 'Quoniam nulla relatio potest ad se ipsam referri . sed semper ad aliud   facta quidem est illa quae dicitur Trinitatis, secundum id quod est indifferentia, scilicet vel substantiae unius . . vel operationis unius   Idcirco Pater, Filius, et Spiritus sanctus omnium non tres autores, sed unus solus autor sunt, nec tria principia, sed unum solum principium'

Each Person in the Trinity is *substantia*, and All together are one and the same *substantia*, and only one Substance or Essence. Warnings are then given against the errors of various heretics who controvert this statement of faith. The truth is that this Substance cannot be divided or separated in any way, nor is that one Essence of the Three as though it were joined together into one from so many parts; but rather is it one Essence simply, of which these Three are one (*unum*), and simple, and wholly what They are. ' Therefore that which is of the Divine Substance, that is to say, that which is predicated of God substantially, that should be common to the Three, that is, to the Father, Son, and Holy Spirit.' Again, the Father, Son, and Holy Spirit are Each the centre of origin and of operation (*principium*, and *factor*), and also together They are one centre of origin and of operation. But the state of being the centre of origin and of operation (*principalitas* and *actio*) is not Theirs in the same sense as Essence is Theirs; so that ' certain things which in the realm of time are attributed to the three Persons in common are not, however, predicated of Them substantially.' Yet, as each Person is God, and All together are one God, this much is clear, that the Deity, which is predicated of Each of Them separately, is predicated of Them at once when taken together. On this account there is one Godhead of the Three. It is clear, then, that the Name of God, that is, the Godhead in this Name which is God, is presumably predicated substantially of the Deity, that is, of God,[1] namely of the Father, Son, and Holy Spirit. We know that each Person is the Truth, but the Father, Son, and Holy Spirit are not three Truths but are one Truth, singly and simply, that is, one true Being. The unity of Essence means that those things attributed to the three Persons in unity apply *substantialiter* to Each of the Three.

Having argued thus far, Gilbert notes the proposition laid down by pseudo-Boethius that there is not one of the things by which those three are names—namely, Father, Son, and Holy Spirit—but what is not affirmed of Them all, separately or collectively. ' Clearly,' he remarks, ' it is as if Boethius said that Deity, truth, goodness, &c., are predicated substantially of the Three, and are affirmed of Them all whether regarded

[1] Cp. the foregoing footnote by Binius on the sense in which Gilbert allows the interchange of *Divinitas* and *Deus*.

separately or together. Whence it is clear that those things in general, whatsoever they may be, which can with one consent be affirmed of Each of Them separately, and yet cannot be affirmed of Them all under any single Name, are not predicated substantially, but rather in another way.' The 'other way' is referred to more pointedly at a later stage in the commentary; meanwhile, Gilbert proceeds to enlarge upon and to develop the above thesis. 'In fact,' he continues, 'whatsoever things are affirmed of any One whatever of these Three, taken separately, are not affirmed of Them all under the same single Name, and are not predicated substantially of Them. For those words, namely, Father, Son, Holy Spirit, are predicated of Them Each, whereas they are by no means predicated substantially of Them All—which is clear without a doubt.' The designation (*vocabulum*), by which each Person is what He is, is not transmissible to any other Person in the Godhead: 'by which it follows that this name " Father " is not given substantially to Him who alone is called Father; that is, the thing (*res*) which is predicated by this name is not His of whom the substance is predicated, truly.' The conclusion is thus reached that 'whereas whatever is predicated substantially of God, as of the Father, and of the Son, and of the Holy Spirit, is particularly affirmed of Them as regarded separately and together; neither indeed is the Father, nor the Son, nor the Holy Spirit spoken of as of Them all, either separately or together; so we rightly understand that the Father, Son, and Holy Spirit are not spoken of as of the Deity Itself, that is, of Those who, since They are, in the sole Deity, not only God, but are also called Deity.' Here appears the point of Dr. Fisher's criticism of Gilbert's theology. *Deus* was evidently not a wide enough term. The three Divine Persons are thus not named with regard to the whole Substance of the Godhead, whether They are spoken of singly or in union. As Each is God, God and the Divine Essence are not coincident terms; and those things which can be affirmed of each Person but not of Them all under a single Name, are predicated in another way, namely 'according to those things which are predicated by these names.' 'This means,' he adds, 'that the Trinity indeed may not be predicated substantially of God.' It is the diversity of characteristics which causes the Trinity; these characteristics are not substances; therefore

THE SCHOLASTIC 'RATIONALISTS'

the Trinity is not *substantialis*, namely, three unities by which these characteristics, and those Persons whose they are, are enumerated. This all goes to show, according to Gilbert, that the Trinity is not 'substantially predicated' of God. *Deus* and *Divinitas* are the words which can be used 'substantially,' but not *Trinitas*. No wonder Erdmann remarks on the metaphysics of these treatises!

Gilbert is thus an example of the emphasis of reason from the standpoint of Realism, as is Roscellin from the standpoint of Nominalism. His intellectualism led him to an unbalanced view of the oneness of the Godhead along lines of argument whose stages are not altogether clear. His conclusions that there is a difference between Deity and God, and that the Father, Son, and Holy Spirit are not spoken of as of the Deity Itself, or, in other words, that the Trinity and the Deity are not coincident terms, were definite grounds for Bernard's accusation of heresy; and in the account of the COUNCIL OF RHEIMS[1] there are tabulated the alleged assertions of Gilbert and also the answers given thereto by the Council. The first assertion put down to him is that the Deity is not God but the 'form' by which God is. The second of his reported assertions distinguishes 'Deity' from 'God,' who is Father, Son, and Holy Spirit. The third states that the three Persons in three unities are three, and distinct in three individual characters, which are not Themselves 'Persons,' but are three 'Eternals' (*aeternae*), differing mutually and numerically from the Divine Substance. The fourth is to the effect that the Divine Nature did not become incarnate. It may have been that the presence in the Council of his many influential friends emboldened Gilbert to advance another stage in his 'rationalism,' for the third assertion of his, if correctly reported, certainly gives the impression of such an advance upon his written work. Howbeit the Council condemned these assertions as heretical, promulgating at the same time a refutation of them *seriatim* which was issued in the form of the following Creed:

(i.) (Against the first assertion.) 'We believe and confess the simple Nature of the Deity to be God, and not in any Catholic sense can it be denied that the Deity is God, and God the Deity.'

[1] Mansi xxi, Cols 711-713 (following Dr. Fisher's reference).

(ii.) (Against the second assertion.) 'When we speak of the three Persons, the Father, Son, and Holy Spirit, we confess Them to be one God, one Divine Substance. And, conversely, when we speak of one God, one Divine Substance, we confess the one God Himself, the one Divine Substance, to be three Persons.'

(iii.) (Against the third assertion.) 'We believe and confess that the one and only God, Father, Son, and Holy Spirit, is eternal, and that no 'things' nor relations, nor characteristics, nor particularities, nor unities, nor any other subjects of this kind, which may be from everlasting but may not be God, are at all present in God.'

(iv.) (Against the fourth assertion.) 'We believe and confess that the Deity Itself, or the Divine Substance, or the Divine Nature, became incarnate, but in the Son.'

The Church, in thus refuting the theories of Gilbert and upholding the truths of revelation to which for centuries the vast majority of Christians had adhered, delivered a form of belief which was decidedly more simple and straightforward than that presented by the bishop of Poitiers. The sweeping aside of any intermediary between the Deity on the one hand, and God and the Trinity on the other, was a necessity for the practical work of the Church as well as for the correctness of theological conceptions; and the same might be said concerning the denial of the participation of the *whole* Deity in the stupendous event of the Incarnation. Thus, in guarding against the tritheistic or the modalistic tendencies of a Roscellin or of a Gilbert, the Mediaeval Church upheld, more than is often realized, the more modern conception of revelation as a means rather than an end. There has been no greater work of the Holy Spirit known in the Christian dispensation than that of applying the truths of the Gospel to human hearts: how, then, could this Divine application be expected to operate, at least to its full extent, where these truths were, even unconsciously, perverted? The realization that right thought is the basis of right action was by no means lost, notwithstanding the fact that the Church of the Scholastic period was characterized by an almost inexhaustible passion for dialectic.

IV

HILDEBERT AND THE SUMMISTS

SIDE by side with ' rational ' Scholasticism existed ' orthodox ' Scholasticism, which kept more closely to the Anselmic position. The orthodox Schoolmen could not escape the dialectical tendencies of the time, nor indeed did they so desire; rather did they harness the steeds of reason to the chariot of faith, and thus employ the methods of the 'Rationalists' in their exposition of the traditional system of theology. To such writers as Hildebert and Pullus faith was supreme, and authority an aid to its supremacy; and it is probable that their more conservative standpoint was confirmed by the reaction against the rationalist extremes, a reaction which was to be expressed definitely at Rheims. Robertus Pullus, in particular, was an exponent of the witness of tradition, and in this capacity he may be regarded as the forerunner of Peter the Lombard.

HILDEBERT

Hildebert (1055–1134), Archbishop of Tours, stands in history as a great churchman who resembles Anselm in his Realism and in his reverence for the Fathers. His *Sermons*, of which many are in existence, deal with the subject of the Trinity, though not with the same exhaustiveness as his more formal efforts. The *First Sermon on the Day of Pentecost* contains the remark that ' The Holy Spirit is said to be of the Father and the Son, because He proceeds from Both, and Each sends Him.' Consubstantiality is defined in the *Only Sermon on the Feast of the Most Holy Trinity* as that relation of two Divine Persons whereby the One exists in the Other. ' The Trinity in Unity,' he continues, ' is a Trinity of Persons in a unity of Essence.' At the same time, ' the One is not the same as the Other; nay rather is there one Person of the Father, another of the Son, and another of the

Holy Spirit.' Yet again is the balance maintained, in the *Second Sermon on the Feast of All Saints*, where Hildebert states : ' These Three are One (*unum*), and co-operate with Each Other, because the operations of the Trinity are undivided.' Therefore the oneness of God in Being and in action together with the distinctions in His inner Life which reveal the twofold procession and mission of the Spirit, are fully emphasized in the Archbishop's homiletical work.

The *Tractatus Theologicus*, which has been ascribed to him in spite of its similarity to the *Summa* of Hugh of St. Victor, can almost be said to be based on Augustine, containing as it does so many quotations from that Father. A trinitarian analogy is found in wisdom in the absolute, wisdom as proceeding from the mind, and love. This familiar designation for the third Person of the Trinity is due, so Hildebert remarks, to the fact that the Holy Spirit is the One most frequently termed in Holy Scripture the love of the Father and the Son. ' These three Persons are distinct, since the Father is not the Son nor the Holy Spirit, neither is the Son the Father, nor the Holy Spirit ; and yet these three Persons are one Substance, one God.' A note on the third Person follows : ' He who proceeds from the Father and the Son is called the Holy Spirit, who is inbreathed by the Father and the Son unto sanctification, and who, nevertheless, does not descend apart from the Father and the Son, because the Trinity is undivided. . . . Accordingly the three Persons are one God, one Substance, one Nature.' The Archbishop then turns toward the Greeks and meets them upon their own ground in their objection to the Western view of the Procession. ' The Greeks assert, on their side, that the Holy Spirit proceeds only from the Father, and not from the Son. They make this statement on the ground that no mention is made of it in the Apostles' Creed—that is in the minor Creed—nor in the Creed which was promulgated in the Synod of Nicaea, at the end of which is the observation, ' Anathema sit, quod nos ita exponimus, quasi aliter, id est contrarium.' But, as that matter is neither affirmed nor denied there, we, on our side, assert that it is not contrary to that Creed.'[1] As if any belief could be anathematized where it is not mentioned ! As if, too, there were no possibility of development ! It is interesting to see how Hildebert sincerely

[1] *Tractatus Theologicus, c* 4.

attempts to meet a definite criticism from the Oriental Church, though the argument from silence is one which both sides could turn to their own use.

The gift of the Holy Spirit, then, is one which proceeds from the Son as well as from the Father. But the writer reminds his readers that ' as both the Son and the Holy Spirit are from the Father, the Son is from the Father in one way, and the Holy Spirit in another. . . . The Son is from the Father by procession and by generation (*procedendo et nascendo*), the Holy Spirit is from the Father not by generation but by procession (*non nascendo, sed procedendo*) ; for Each One proceeds from the Father, but in an ineffable and dissimilar manner.' This terminology is noticeable as compared with that of the majority of earlier writers who had touched upon this aspect of the subject, and who are seen to distinguish between generation and procession in the sense that these functions are the peculiarities of the Son and of the Spirit respectively. Hildebert at any rate believes the ' processions ' of these two Persons to be distinct, while he regards the distinctions between them as inexplicable.[1] We know that the Holy Spirit is co-eternal, co-omnipotent, consubstantial, and co-equal with both the Father and the Son. Indeed, any reference to One of the three Persons as one part of this Holy Trinity ought never to be made ; for truly the whole Trinity is one simple and undivided Substance.[2]

Chapter vi also contains an exposition of the term ' person ' with reference to trinitarian dogma which is worthy of careful notice. Hildebert is anxious lest any one should be misled theologically by too close a comparison of human and Divine *personae* ; whereas the personal significances of God and of man are by no means the same. This may be observed in the following definition of ' person ' : A ' person ' is an undivided nature of rational substance. In the light of this, how can the Son be understood to be a Person other than the Father ? For while it can be affirmed with reason that the Father is a Person, that is, a rational substance, when, however, it is declared that He is ' another Person,' we dare not affirm that He is 'another rational substance.' Again, when we say 'The Father, Son, and Holy Spirit are three Persons,' we cannot say ' three rational substances.' Accordingly, when the

[1] *Ibid*, 5.   [2] *Ibid*, 6.

statement is made: 'The Father is a Person, the Son is a Person,' that is a rational substance, the commonly accepted meaning of the term ' Person ' is restricted by means of the very repetition of this same word. The argument here employed bears striking similarity to that contained in the first Commentary of Gilbert on pseudo-Boethius, where the principle was laid down that reiteration of the same thing does not result in its multiplication. Hildebert's principle that the reiteration of the term ' Person ' as applied to God *ipso facto* restricts the idea of separation seemingly inherent in the term as ordinarily understood, so that the Trinity in unity becomes conceivable, is a principle closely allied to the former. God is therefore one, because within the Divine Life there exist mutual relation and personal characteristics, not numerability and personal unities. In any case there is, in Hildebert's opinion, a necessity for a recast of thought when applying human terms (for want of anything more adequate) to the Divine Nature. In the use of human analogies of the Trinity there might at least be tendencies towards anthropomorphism, and such tendencies create their own difficulties. Before the book is closed, the personal distinctions within the Godhead receive further emphasis,[1] together with the individual characteristics attaching to Each, though the three Persons operate with one will as one Being.[2] There is not much in this treatise that can be called real development, though it is decidedly useful as affording a discussion on the meaning of *persona*, and as revealing another method of procedure against the Greeks.

The orthodox among the Schoolmen are further represented by the Summists, a name supplied by Erdmann to distinguish three authors of the *Summae*, or theological compilations which set forth the traditional beliefs by means of dialectical treatment of the patristic writings. These works might be styled the common denominators of faith to which the various teachings voiced by the doctors of the Ancient Church are by reason resolved. The Summists, then, together with the Sententiaries who followed with their many commentaries upon the Lombard, set forth the Rule of Faith from the ' moderate ' standpoint of the Church, never by any chance venturing to criticize ecclesiastical authority.

[1] *Ibid.*, 7.   [2] *Ibid.*, 8.

ROBERTUS PULLUS

Robertus Pullus (Robert Pulleyn—the name has many forms: *c.* 1080 – *c.* 1147), English theologian, philosopher, and cardinal, published his *Summa Sententiarum* in eight books which might have drawn their inspiration from the *Sic et Non* of Abelard, and which possibly passed on some of their own inspiration to Petrus Lombardus. The first book argues the existence of God and of the Trinity within God. The holy and glorious Trinity, inasmuch as God is one, effects, with one and the same will and power, operations which are undivided.[1] The unity of the Trinity is thus asserted at the outset, followed by a statement as to the mutual relations of the Persons. ' There are three Persons,' he remarks. ' The Father is God, and not in any sense is the Father greater (*plus*) than the Son ; nor are They Both greater than the Holy Spirit. So the Creator God is in Substance one, in Persons threefold.' When, however, Pullus considers the question of the procession of the Spirit he is cognisant of the fact of its mystery. ' In what manner the procession of the Spirit is from Both, no one will be able to explain. . . . Faith, however, is the ' evidence of things not seen.' We are constrained to believe that which will not be permitted to be clear to any of us on earth.'[2] Later on in the work the inexplicable nature of the *Filioque* is again referred to, but always in the sense that this dogma, however mysterious, must remain an article of belief seeing that the Church has so pronounced upon it. The unity of God is reached by the indwelling of Each Person in Each, as already stated by Anselm and expanded by the later expounders of the term *persona*. ' The Son is also in the Father and the Father in the Son ; the Holy Spirit is in Them Both, and Both are in Him.'[3] The function of mission belongs to the Father and to the Son ; ' but the Father sends the Son and the Holy Spirit ; the Son, however, sends only the Holy Spirit. . . . The Holy Spirit is sent by Both.'[4] The twofold Mission and the twofold Procession are here emphasized even as they were by Hildebert, and Pullus returns to this subject in the fifth book.[5] Also, whatever is said concerning the Divine Unity and the inter-relations within that Unity,

[1] *Sent*, 1. 2.   [2] *Ibid*, i. 3.   [3] *Ibid*, 1. 5   [4] *Ibid*, i 7
[5] v 4 'Tota Trinitas, aut melius Pater et Filius, tertiam personam misit, sola tertia mittebatur'

it must be remembered that each Person of the Trinity possesses and retains His own proper and peculiar character and personality.[1]

PETRUS LOMBARDUS

The contribution to theological development which Robertus Pullus made by his effort to give system to the existing cumulus of dogma was followed and overshadowed by his more celebrated colleague Petrus Lombardus († 1164), who became Bishop of Paris in 1159. He studied under Abelard at Paris, as did Pullus, but he gained over the latter by his contact with another great mind, namely Hugh of St. Victor. The very fact of Bernard's fondness for him implies that he was by no means a close follower of Abelard!

Petrus makes his public appearance with the rapid growth of papal sovereignty which was destined to reach its climax in the time of Innocent III. Indeed, the pretensions of the pontifical throne were the primary cause of that appearance. To further the ends of Rome the monk Gratian had been given the task of embodying the past decrees of the popes in a codified form to be employed in the spiritual courts. The study of this new code of canon law, known as the Decretal, was encouraged at the University of Paris, where, as an adjunct to this legal collection, a theological collection was being prepared by Petrus which was to become the great text-book for students of dogma throughout Europe. It is fittingly termed a text-book, for it is a compilation of facts of information rather than of profound thoughts, though its author had been influenced by the mystic school of the Victorines. Yet it served a useful purpose for centuries, being a *Summa* largely after the pattern of Pullus' work, and attempting, though not with complete success, to present as an ordered whole the patristic teachings together with the more recent reasonings of the early mediaeval period. Like the *Summa*

---

[1] 1 8 One of the most noted of the pupils of Pullus and also of the critics of Scholasticism, namely John of Salisbury (c 1115–1180), Bishop of Chartres, was too 'practical' a churchman to excel in theology, but in his poem *Entheticus de dogmate philosophorum* (§ 705) he asserts the unity of God in Being and operation, and, in addition, the 'propriety' or individual character of each Person

' Nam Pater et Natus cum Flumine sunt Deus unus,
  Sed retinet proprium prosopa quaeque suum . . .
  Sint licet unius naturae, numinis, actus '

'Flumen' was an unusual designation for the Holy Spirit; presumably with reference to Him as being poured out upon mankind

of Pullus, it is both dialectical and authoritative, containing objections and answers thereto which are supported by quotations from the Fathers in general and from Augustine in particular. It is indeed difficult in certain parts to discover the views of Petrus among masses of Augustinian extracts, so definitely does he prefer the use of authority to that of reason. It is to this fact that Erdmann[1] attributes its wide use as a basis of study to the comparative neglect of the *Summa* of the more original Pullus. The official atmosphere in which it was composed might also have conduced to its celebrity. At least the *Summa* of Petrus stands in history as the great example of a new stage in the methods of the Schoolmen, its author accordingly being styled *Magister Sententiarum*; and commentaries continued to be written on his work after the Reformation had become an accomplished fact.

The *Summa* of Petrus Lombardus is composed of four books, of which the first considers the subjects of God and the Trinity in the course of forty-eight chapters or *distinctiones*. The statement is made at the outset that the Trinity is said to be one God,[2] and of one and the same Substance or Essence.[3] Moreover the Trinity is one God ' in inseparable equality,' so that 'there is unity in Essence and plurality in Persons, and therefore They are not three Gods, but one God—mutually co-equal.' 'For,' he adds, ' of the Father, Son, and Holy Spirit there is one Essence, which the Greeks call ὁμουσία.'[4]

The assertion of the Divine oneness as the necessary foundation of all thought concerning God is followed by a closer consideration of the mutual relations within that oneness, illustrated by that recourse to the analogical of which the Summists and the Sententiaries were so fond. An analogy (*assignatio*) of the Persons of the Trinity as found in the human mind is presented as *mens, notitia*, and *amor*, love naturally proceeding from the pure intellect and its conception or idea. The force of such a similitude is that ' in that Holy Trinity there is one God the Father, who alone begets one Son essentially from Himself; and there is one Son, who alone is begotten essentially from one Father; and there is one Holy Spirit who alone proceeds essentially from the Father and the Son.'[5] A glance at the Catholic Faith substantiates

---

[1] *Hist of Phil*, 1, p 341   [2] *Sent*, lib 1, De Mysterio Trinitatis, Dist. i 2.
[3] *Ibid*, ii 1   [4] *Ibid*, 2   [5] *Ibid*, iii 25

this position, argues the Lombard, for the Church holds that the three Persons are one God and one Substance or Essence or Divine Nature; also conversely, that the one God, or the Divine Essence, consists of three Persons[1]—an instance of the appeal to authority which characterizes the Summist theology.

Having laid down these premises, Petrus proceeds to discuss the subject of the Third Person. His pneumatology is comprehensive and typically Western. The teaching of the Church and the revelations of trinitarian analogies both support the Occidental view of the procession; consequently it is known that the Holy Spirit is from the Substance of the Father and the Son, since He proceeds from Them Both. This means that the Spirit did not 'come from nothing,' but from the 'common Substance' as indicated.[2] Again, as the Substance or the Essence of the one God is correctly spoken of as unchangeable (for It is not changed, nor can It be changed),[3] and as the Holy Spirit proceeds from that Essence, or from God, the Holy Spirit Himself must be God.[4] If, then, the Holy Spirit is God, the next step is to examine the question of His procession from God, the question at issue between the Latins and Greeks. Petrus at once makes the assertion, 'which many heretics have denied,' that the Holy Spirit is from the Father and the Son, and proceeds from the Father and the Son.[5] 'The Greeks, on the other hand, assert that the Holy Spirit proceeds only from the Father, and not from the Son.'[6] The Oriental Church is therefore quite heretical on the point! But, at any rate, it is common knowledge that the Greeks confess the Holy Spirit to be the Spirit of the Son, as also the Spirit of the Father.[7] Further, according to the authorities and the teachers even of the Greek Church, the procession of the Spirit from the Son is all but openly asserted. 'Therefore,' he exhorts, 'let every tongue confess that the Holy Spirit proceeds from the Father and the Son!'[8]

If, again, the Holy Spirit proceeds from Them Both, certain other questions arise. Does the Spirit proceed to any greater degree from the Father than from the Son? Did He proceed from the Father before He began to proceed from the Son? These two queries are answered in the negative. The procession

---

[1] *Ibid*, iv. 3 [2] *Ibid*, v 10 [3] *Ibid*, viii 3 [4] *Ibid*, x. 5.
[5] *Ibid*, xi 1. [6] *Ibid*, xi. 2. [7] *Ibid*, xi 4. [8] *Ibid.*, xi. 5.

is equal and simultaneous ; while, as touching the Mission of the Spirit, both Augustine and Hilary testify that He is sent by the Father through the Son, the twofold Source of the Mission thus not being so apparent.[1] Reference, however, must be made to the terms 'generation' and 'procession,' which refer in particular to the second and third Persons. A quotation is made from Augustine to show that these are different functions affecting the Son and the Spirit respectively,[2] but indeed we are unable, according to Petrus, to distinguish between the generation of the Son and the procession of the Holy Spirit ' while we live here.' One fact at least remains · the Holy Spirit is the Spirit of Both by virtue of proceeding from Both.[3] Should any one, however, desire to study more closely the significance of these two terms, let him be careful to avoid confusion between them. It is with this in mind that we do not speak of the Holy Spirit as begotten, for if we ventured to speak thus we should be blamed for belief in the existence of two Sons in the Trinity[4] ; while, on the other hand, any designation of Him as unbegotten would involve us in a confession of two Fathers.[5] The above distinction must be kept, even though it passes human understanding.

Taking, then, the one function of the procession of the Spirit, Petrus passes on to show that it is twofold, apart from any allusion to the *Filioque*. It is, for instance, eternal and ineffable, whereby the Spirit has proceeded, eternally and timelessly, from the Father and the Son : it is also temporal, whereby He proceeds from the Father and the Son for the sanctification of the race.[6] Again, the procession, mission, or gift of the Holy Spirit from the Father and the Son and from Himself is regarded as twofold in another sense, namely visible and invisible. For He was given in the representation of a visible creation as on the day of Pentecost, and in other ways ; and He is given every day invisibly as He flows into the minds of those who are faithful.[7]

The nineteenth 'distinction' resumes the topic of the inter-relations of the Persons, and with it the safeguard of appeal

---

[1] *Ibid.*, xii.
[2] *Ibid*, xiii 2   Augustine, *de Trin*, lib 5. 'Spiritus Sanctus procedit a Patre non quomodo natus, sed quomodo datus vel donum. Filius autem procedit nascendo, exiit ut genitus'   [3] *Ibid*, xiii 3
[4] Petrus quotes this caution from Aug *ad Orosium*
[5] *Ibid*, xiii. 5.   [6] *Ibid*, xiv 1   [7] *Ibid*, xvi 1.

to the pronouncements of the Church. The Catholic Faith claims co-eternity and co-equality for the three Persons. 'The Son is equal in all things to the Father, and the Holy Spirit to the Father and the Son'; while an earlier paragraph [xv. 14] asserts the Son and the Spirit to be no less than the Father on account of Their being sent by Him. 'For no One of These precedes Another in eternity, or exceeds Another in greatness, or surpasses Another in power; for the Father is not prior to nor greater than the Son or the Holy Spirit, nor the Son prior to nor greater than the Holy Spirit.'[1] The equality of the Persons receives further emphasis in the course of the work, but Petrus follows, though more conclusively, the line already taken by Pullus in declaring that in no respect can Two of the Persons be regarded as being together greater than One, nor the Three greater than Two; 'nor is the Essence greater in the Three than in Two, nor in Two than in One; because the whole is in Each.'[2] This opens up the question of the meaning of *persona* in reference to the inner Life of God. Let it then be said at once that none of the three Persons is a 'part' of God or of the Divine Essence, 'for each One of Them is true and full God, and the whole and full Divine Essence.' Such a statement could never be made concerning God if any idea of partition or numeral complement were at all admissible in reference to the Trinity.[3] Take, for instance, reasons Petrus, the animal *genus*, or stock, of which the horse is a *species*, or distinct kind. We can speak of three horses as three animals; but we cannot in this case refer at once to the *species* in the plural and to the *genus* in the singular as in the statement that 'Three horses are one animal,' for 'just as three horses are spoken of with a particular name, so are three animals with a general name. Therefore, since we confess three Persons to be one Essence, not three Essences; since three horses are called three animals, not one animal; it is evident that *genus* is not indicated by the name of *essentia*, nor *species* by the name of *persona*.'[4] The same uniqueness of significance attaching to these terms explanatory of the Trinity is further illustrated by recourse to the human contrast much in the same manner as it had already been employed by Hildebert and Gilbert. The three Persons of the Trinity are one Essence, but not in

[1] *Ibid*, xix. 1   [2] *Ibid*, 4.   [3] *Ibid*, 7.   [4] *Ibid*, 8.

the same sense even as three men are of one nature. 'For the Father and the Son together are not greater in Essence than the Father alone or the Son alone, but these three Persons together are equal to each One singly. . . .[1] The Father is perfect, also the Son, also the Holy Spirit, and each single One of Them is pronounced to be perfect. For that very reason It should be called a Trinity (*Trinitas*) rather than a triplicity (*triplex*).'[2]

Distinctio xxiii. is devoted almost entirely to a careful distinction between and harmony of the senses of Greek and Latin terminology with regard to the Trinity. Where the Latins speak of three Persons, the Greeks speak of three hypostases or substances (§ 4). At least it must be borne in mind that the Father, Son, and Holy Spirit are three Persons and not three Gods, and support is given to this admonition by the testimony of Scripture and of Augustine (§ 6). Even so, the Persons are distinguishable by Their several characteristics of being Father, of being Son, and of proceeding from Both; so that this mutual relation negatives both tritheism and Sabellianism.[3] This procession from Both incidentally sanctions the 'Spirit of God' and the 'Spirit of Christ' as interchangeable terms for the Holy Spirit, and He dwells within us as such.[4] But, though the Holy Spirit has from eternity been existent, He has not always exercised the functions of a Source (*principium*). 'The Father from eternity is the Source of the Son, and the Father and the Son the Source of the Holy Spirit, because the Son is from the Father and the Holy Spirit from Both. The Holy Spirit, however, is not a Source from eternity, but He began to be, for He is only called a Source with regard to the creatures. When, therefore, the creatures began to exist, the Holy Spirit also began to be their Source.'[5] *Distinctio* xxxvii. deals with the inquiry as to how God can be generally in the universe. The Spirit of God is not locally confined: He is everywhere, and always everywhere. The Divine omnipresence is thus an attribute which distinguishes God from the angels who, though spirits, are locally confined, being circumscribed or 'bounded-in'

[1] *Ibid*, 12.　　[2] *Ibid*, 19
[3] *Ibid*, xxv 10　'Paternali enim proprietate distinguitur hypostasis Patris ab hypostasi Filii, et hypostasis Filii filiali proprietate discernitur a Patre, et Spiritus sanctus ab utroque processibili proprietate distinguitur.'
[4] *Ibid*, xxxiv. 2.　　[5] *Ibid.*, xxix 2

personalities (*circumscriptibiles*). The Holy Spirit, on the other hand, knows no such limitation.

Petrus Lombardus came to be regarded in due course as the great authority for theological students of the West, but a charge of heresy was eventually brought against him by the Mystic Joachim of Floris, who deposed that he had taught a Quaternity in God. Indeed, the very task of a Summist was dangerous as it was laborious, for in reducing the opinions of the past into a text-book for the future Petrus needed only to have joined together the one Essence of Realism and the three Persons of Nominalism to have produced the alleged Quaternity. But, fifty-one years after his death, he was acquitted of the charge by the Fourth Lateran Council, which ruled that the *divina essentia* as interpreted by him did not involve a fourth *persona*. That this acquittal was but simple justice is manifest from his own distinct statements in the *Sentences*.[1]

ALANUS MAGNUS

The reputation of being the most brilliant, while not the most prominent, of the Summists belongs to Alanus Magnus († 1203), Bishop of Auxerre, surnamed 'de Insulis' from his birthplace of Lille, and known as 'Doctor Universalis' on account of his theological activity. Of the products of this activity one alone is here considered, namely, the *De Arte, seu de articulis Catholicae Fidei*; for, though other writings of his bear on the Trinity, they are essentially more argumentative and apologetic than systematic. The *De Arte*, too, is described by Erdmann as 'the shortest but most important of Alanus' works,' the prologue containing the information that it is directed against heretics and Mohammedans. It is a *Summa* in reduced compass, composed of five

---

[1] e g *ibid*, x 7 'Tria ergo sunt, et non amplius' Petrus Lombardus found another critic in Gerhohus of Reichersberg (1093–1169), ecclesiastical reformer and anti-scholastic His statement concerning Christ as 'one Lord together with His Father and the Holy Spirit' (*Epist* 15) is indicative of the emphasis which, throughout his writings, he lays upon the unity of the Trinity This unity of the Deity embraces the Trinity and the incarnate Son in a striking passage 'Cum ergo Patris ingeniti, et Filii eius unigeniti, et amborum doni simulque hominis hoc dono concepti et sanctificati, atque in unam personam Trinitatis assumpti sit una Divinitas, qua et Pater Deus, et Filius Deus, et Spiritus sanctus Deus, et Spiritu sancto conceptus homo Deus nominatur, recte de his omnibus una aequalitas praedicatur, quorum una divinitatis essentia, vel natura cognoscitur et virtus eadem' (*Epist* 23) Gerhohus is, indeed, concerned primarily with the Doctrine of the Son, that of the Spirit only being brought in incidentally This is still more apparent in the more formal treatise, *Liber de Gloria et Honore Filii Hominis*, where the Spirit is constantly represented as the 'Cause' of Christ's Birth, and almost exclusively as such

books, of which the first is entitled : *De una omnium causa . de uno eodemque trino Deo*, and which, accordingly, is the book to be discussed in reference to the Doctrine of the Spirit.

Substance, in the abstract, consists of Matter and Form, which are the cause of substantial co-inherence.[1] The substance of anything possesses a threefold cause, namely, matter, and form, and their unity (*compago*), which three in turn are derived from one and the same cause.[2] For nothing is *per se*, or is *sui causa*,[3] therefore everything must have a cause outside of itself, and every cause is greater than its effect.[4] The first cause (*causa suprema*), however, does not possess *proprietas* or *forma*,[5] qualities or form, and it is indeed necessary that there should be a first and most simple cause. ' It is clear, then, that there is one only first cause of all things, which, for the sake of reasoning, we call God.'[6] God, the First Cause, thus holds the same place in the theology of Alanus as does the Divine Essence in that of Petrus. He is that which is conceived by process of ratiocination as the highest and the unchangeable Origin of all. That being so, God is eternal,[7] boundless, incomprehensible, ineffable, unnameable. ' Therefore God cannot be comprehended by the human intellect.'[8] It is for this reason that ' we discern God by no knowledge, but by faith alone. For nothing can be known which cannot be understood. But we do not apprehend God by the intellect . . . therefore we do not by knowledge. So we take for granted as led by reason that God Himself exists ; we do not know (by human perception), but we believe Him to exist. For faith, for definite reasons which are not sufficient for knowledge, is essentially anticipation. Consequently faith is in every way above opinion, but below knowledge.'[9] The intellect, at least, is unable to fathom the mysteries of the Deity, for Alanus in the Prologue has already defined *intellectus* as that ' power of the mind which comprehends a thing by the assistance of form.' As, however, God is formless, He cannot be so comprehended.

Faith and reason, then, together indicate that ' all is in God, and God is in all.'[10] God is essentially everywhere, being confined to no locality (*nusquam localiter*).[11] But that there

---

[1] Edition found in the *Thesaurus Anecdotorum Novissimus*, published by Bernardus Pezius in 1721, tom 1, pars 11, *lib* 1, sent 5
[2] *Ibid*, 6   [3] *Ibid*, 8   [4] *Ibid*, 10   [5] *Ibid*, 11   [6] *Ibid*, 12
[7] *Ibid*, 15   [8] *Ibid*, 16   [9] *Ibid*, 17   [10] *Ibid*, 21   [11] *Ibid*, 22

are mutual relationships within that Divine Unity Alanus proceeds to show by recalling his previous words concerning substance. 'Matter, and Form, and their unity are truly,' he remarks, 'three different things which are originally required in the creation of any substance. From this it is manifest that the effect in the creation of one and the same substance is clear evidence of the existence of a Trinity in one and the same Creator. And three Persons are stated to be this Trinity, the first the Father, the second the Son, the third the Holy Spirit. Their descriptions and natures prove that the Form and the Matter are quite different things. Moreover, it is obvious that neither of these is its own unity,' seeing that something else (*aliud*) is brought into being by their union.[1] This unconventional analogy of the Trinity receives further treatment in the course of the twenty-fifth *Sentence*, where the Trinity is perceivable in the operation of creation. ' Though in any creation of substance a proper order can allot Matter to the Father, Form to the Son, Unification to the Holy Spirit, yet the whole Trinity must operate in any one of the three.' Matter as touching the very basis of substance corresponds to the first Person of the Trinity; Form, which has its origin in Matter, we fittingly assign to the Son; as for their Unification (*compositio*), to whom could we apply this unless to the third Person of the Trinity, who is called the Holy Spirit? There is thus in created things a reflection of the inner light of God's Nature which serves to emphasize the fact of the Trinity as already imparted by revelation. We know, too, that all the Persons work in and through Each in the unity of the Godhead. Moreover, seeing that any One of these Persons is God, and that God is the one Author (*artifex*) of all things, it remains that the whole Trinity operates invisibly in accordance with the three similitudes already mentioned.

The Holy Spirit, then, being equivalent to the unity (*compago* or *compositio*) of Matter and Form, is thus the bond (*nexus*) and, in consequence, the love of the Father and the Son, and can correctly be said to proceed from Both.[2] Reason has accordingly tested and upheld faith in its declaration that the Father, Son, and Holy Spirit are equal in power and nature, because Each is God and the Three are one God.[3] It is clear,

---

[1] *Ibid*, 24   [2] *Ibid*, 26   [3] *Ibid*, 27, 29

therefore, concludes Alanus, that the Doctrine of the Trinity is based upon the essential oneness of the three Persons in the Unity of the Godhead, this Godhead being nothing else (*nihil aliud*) than a Unity.[1]

A summary of orthodox or Summist theology emphasizes the real attempt here made to produce a balanced exposition of the Trinity from the Western standpoint. Analogies drawn from the human mind and from the nature of created substance point to corresponding mutual relationships within the Creator; while certain objections arising from the human conception of the term ' person ' as affecting the Triunity of God are carefully examined and answered by the aid of contrasts from human and animal life. The denial of any numerical superiority among the Divine Persons, enforced by the statement that the whole Essence is in Each, explains the Unity of the Deity which faith and reason alike demand; for God is certainly *unum*, seeing that each Person is *alius, non aliud*. This Unity forms the background of all the above teachings of the Summists. The absolute oneness and indivisibility of God, to which the Holy Spirit is regarded as especially contributing as the common Bond of Love, constitute the necessary basis of trinitarian theology, a basis which is seen to be in no wise impaired by the incarnate life of One of the Persons. Firm belief is expressed in the twofold procession of the Spirit, which is also equal and simultaneous; and the *Filioque* is argued from tradition, from reason, and from analogical induction. The Eastern Church, indeed, is regarded as having no case, the Greek Fathers having substantially admitted the procession from the Son, which admission cannot now be covered by any Greek inexactitudes concerning the Creeds!

Though the full Deity of the Holy Spirit receives constant assertion and proof, the work of the Holy Spirit receives little more than bare assertion. Mention is frequently made of His part in the conception of Jesus, and of His function as Origin of creation. His Mission to the race takes place with a view to the sanctification of the human heart, and the same purpose is attached to this Divine operation under the name of the temporal procession of the Spirit, more particularly in its present invisible manner. As the Inspirer of the soul, the Holy Spirit brings into it the presence of the whole Trinity.

[1] *Ibid*, 28, 30.

In spite of their desire to set forth the dogmatic teachings of the Church in reasoned form, Hildebert and the Summists frankly recognize the inadequacy of reason in face of such Divine mysteries. Full knowledge of these mysteries is impossible, while reason can only lead in the direction of full knowledge by the formation of opinion. Between the two, so the Summists conclude, is the rightful place of faith, which, as affording conception, if not comprehension, is thus sufficient to enable the mind to grasp those truths of revelation which experience proves and reason approves.

V

THE FOURTH LATERAN COUNCIL

THIS, the most prominent of the Lateran Councils, was convened in 1215, and presided over by Innocent III, then at the height of papal power as the virtual ruler of East and West. Seventy decrees were promulgated by the Council, among them being the first, which set forth the Catholic faith 'against the various errors of heretics,' and the second, which condemned the book of Abbot Joachim against Petrus Lombardus on the subject of the unity of the most blessed Trinity.[1]

The first Decree, *De fide catholica*—containing, incidentally, the first formal sanction of the dogma of transubstantiation—states the full trinitarian teaching of the West. ' We firmly believe and simply confess that there is one only true God, eternal, boundless, omnipotent, unchangeable, incomprehensible, and ineffable, Father, Son, and Holy Spirit, in truth three Persons, but one Essence, Substance, or entirely simple Nature. The Father is from nothing, the Son is from the Father alone, and the Holy Spirit is equally from Both, always without beginning and end. The Father begetting, the Son being begotten, and the Holy Spirit proceeding ; consubstantial and co-equal, co-omnipotent and co-eternal, one Origin of the universe, the Creator of all things invisible and visible, spiritual and corporeal. . . . For the devil and the other demons were certainly by nature created good by God, but they themselves on their own account have become evil. . . . This Holy Trinity is indivisible in accordance with a common Essence, and in accordance with personal characteristics.' To the above statement concerning the Trinity and the operation of the three Persons as of the one Origin of all good is added a reference to Jesus Christ as ' made incarnate by the joint action of the whole Trinity.'[2] There is thus no

---

[1] Mansi xxii , *Concilium Lateranense* iv , *Generale*, from the history of the Council, appearing as the prologue [2] *Ibid* , cols. 981, 982.

new development in the actual expressions embodied in this Decree, but there is undoubted interest in the adherence to the *Filioque* on the part of a Council which purported to be Ecumenical! Seeing, however, that the Pope had forced his ecclesiastical supremacy upon the East, and also that, in consequence, the Greek Church was represented at the Council by Latin patriarchs, it is hardly to be wondered at that, in the Oriental view, this Assembly was not warranted in speaking for the whole of Christendom. In short, no conversion of the Greeks to an acceptance of the *Filioque* ever took place. Yet it is noticeable that the Councils of the West never indulged in charges of heresy on this subject against the Greek opinion, even though such charges were by no means wanting in the works of individual Latin writers.

The second Decree, *De errore abbatis Joachim*, deals with the charge which had been brought by Joachim of Floris against Petrus Lombardus, accusing the famous Master of teaching a quaternity in the Godhead by establishing the Divine Essence with such distinction from the three Persons as to necessitate a fourth Person. This charge was decisively dismissed by the Council, whose ruling was drawn up as follows:

> ' We condemn and reject the pamphlet or criticism which the Abbot Joachim published against the Master Petrus Lombardus on the unity or Essence of the Trinity, calling him a heretic and a madman with reference to what he said in his *Sentences*, seeing that a certain supreme Object (*summa res*) is Father, Son, and Holy Spirit, which Object is neither begetting, nor begotten, nor proceeding. From this he claims that he was setting up not so much a Trinity as a quaternity in God, namely the three Persons, and that common Essence as the fourth, evidently protesting that what the Father, the Son, and the Holy Spirit is, is no Object (*nulla res*), nor Essence, nor Substance, nor Nature; although he admits that the Father, Son, and Holy Spirit are one Essence, one Substance, and one Nature.
>
> ' We, however, with the approval of the Sacred General Council, believe and confess with Petrus that there is one certain Supreme Object, indeed incomprehensible

and ineffable, which is truly Father, Son, and Holy Spirit, at the same time three Persons, and any One of the same singly. And therefore in God there is a Trinity only, not a quaternity; because any One of the three Persons is that Existence (*res*), to wit, Substance, Essence, or Divine Nature, which alone is the Origin of all things, beside which any other cannot be found. And that Existence is not begetting, nor begotten, nor proceeding, but is the Father who begets, the Son who is begotten, and the Holy Spirit who proceeds; so that the distinctions are in the Persons, and the unity is in the Nature. Therefore, though the Father is *alius*, and the Son *alius*, and the Holy Spirit *alius*, yet Each is not *aliud*; but That which is the Father is the Son, and the Holy Spirit, in every way the same; that They may be believed to be consubstantial in accordance with the orthodox and Catholic Faith. . . . The Father and the Son possess the same Substance, and thus the Father and the Son are the same *res*; and so too the Holy Spirit who proceeds from Both.'[1]

In the opinion of the Council, Joachim's argument meant, ultimately, that the Trinity is no Substance or Essence, though he himself confessed the opposite. The Church hereby upheld the essential reality of the Divine Oneness, guarding against a quaternity by declaring any One of the Persons to be equivalent to the whole and the sole Essence of God. Indeed, the Catholic teaching up to this point is quite against any numerical conjunction of the Essence with the Persons; ' but,' comments Durandus,[2] ' the decree only denies a quaternity or fourth *res* being reckoned numerically along with the three Persons, which is obviously clear from the context; for—in replying to the reasoning of Joachim, who wished to conclude against the Master from his own saying that he states that the Essence neither begets, nor is begotten, nor proceeds, therefore It is not the Father, nor the Son, nor the Holy Spirit, but a fourth Object (*res*)—the Pope rejoins that it does not follow, since that supreme Object (*summa res*), even if It does not beget as Father, nor is begotten as Son, nor is breathed as Holy Spirit,

[1] Cols 981-6. [2] Durandus († 1334), *Sent.*, lib 1. dist 26, q 1.

is nevertheless Father, Son, and Holy Spirit.' This is an indication at once of the final authority of Innocent III in the Council,[1] and of the continued influence of Augustine in the Western Church.

[1] Trevor, *Rome*, p 233 · ' The canons are said to have been all written by himself, no one venturing to oppose or criticize his draft '

VI

THE SCHOLASTIC MYSTICS

THE Mysticism which originated from Scholastic minds during the twelfth century was a revolt of an essentially orthodox nature against the rigidity of the dialectic-systematic method of the age. The need was felt of a warmer individualization of that theology which was already receiving such exhaustive treatment, and this very reaction from within has given rise to two opposing views of itself. One explains Mysticism at this stage as simply Scholasticism from another standpoint. But it is doubtful whether Harnack is altogether justified in blending the subjective Schoolman with the objective Mystic, and in asserting that ' Mystic theology and Scholastic theology are one and the same phenomenon, which only present themselves in manifold gradations as the subjective or objective interest prevails.'[1] Indeed, his definition of Mysticism has been criticized by Dean Inge as portraying a Ritschlian love of austere moralism whose view of Christianity appears to be one of excessive objectivism far away from the Christian Mysticism of much of the thought of St. John and St. Paul.[2] The ' Ritschlian position ' would certainly have much to learn from the doctrine of a Holy Spirit, and the question accordingly seems larger than the mere variation of one outlook. Again, the fact that Bonaventura and, in later years, Gerson attempted a reconciliation between Scholasticism and Mysticism hardly warrants any theory of their identical character. Hence the statement which upholds a real oneness of these two appears to be too extreme for fact. The other view explains Mysticism as an entirely different movement, with a decidedly hostile attitude toward Scholasticism, taking for an example Bernard's attack upon Abelard. But, though Mysticism was in its essence antagonistic to Scholastic ' Rationalism,' it does not follow that it was so to Scholasticism as a whole. Scholastic ' Rationalism ' and Scholastic orthodoxy were by no means one and the same thing. In this case, as

[1] *Hist. of Dogma*, vi , p. 27   [2] *Christian Mysticism*, p. 346.

in many others, the correct version appears to be the mean between two extremes. The Mysticism of the twelfth century was a reaction against Scholasticism on the part of Scholastics. It was definitely Scholastic in its literary method; in fact, it was as yet no separate movement. True, certain of these Mystics might well have been regarded by the greater part of the Mediaeval Church as theological adventurers, but they were not, on the whole, hampered by charges of heterodoxy. Bernard, for example, possessed, or rather was possessed by, a strong passion for the orthodox faith as handed down by the Fathers and interpreted with the authority of the Church. The writers here considered did in no wise belittle the Word of God or the value of revelation, nor was the place given by them to personal experience to any degree independent of the general experience of Christian believers. With the exception of Joachim, who, nevertheless, was also zealous for orthodoxy (!), they were singularly free from theological eccentricity, and did not go to the extreme of confusing faith with feeling. The Scholastic Mystics, as their name implies, thus looked in the direction more of an alliance than of enmity between Scholasticism and Mysticism; but, while not deserving the name of opponents, these were not affinities enough to be lastingly united. Scholastic Mysticism was, indeed, an unpromising marriage!

The Doctrine of the Holy Spirit is primarily that of God in human life, and the genius of Mysticism was the working out of this truth supremely from the standpoint of the individual. Scholastic or Gallo-Romanic Mysticism, as a movement, did not travel so far toward this end as did the later Germanic, but it made considerable progress. Its stress upon the illuminative side of the Divine relationship with man brought into prominence the Doctrine of the Holy Spirit with far more reference to the Spirit's work than is found in the Summists[1]; while their love of the contemplative produced a passion for the suffering Jesus in such men as Bernard, Francis of Assisi († 1226), and Anthony of Padua († 1231), which led to a self-denying piety of a most practical order.

That there were, indeed, extravagant offshoots of Scholastic Mysticism is not surprising. Amalric of Bena († 1207) taught

---

[1] The outlook of the Summists was to that of the Mystics much as the Pauline to the Johannine

that the incarnation of the Holy Spirit in himself and his followers superseded that of the Son of God, and that therefore this latest revelation of the Spirit dispensed with the sacraments ; but the sect which bore his name died out after its condemnation at the Fourth Lateran Council. The Fratricelli, a century later, declared themselves filled with the Spirit and accordingly sinless, also as having no need of the sacraments ; but their immoderations were responsible for their ultimate disappearance during the latter part of the fourteenth century.

BERNARD OF CLAIRVAUX

' The religious genius of the twelfth century, and therefore also the leading spirit of the age '[1] is Bernard (1091-1153), Abbot of Clairvaux in Champagne, the ascetic statesman of the Church, the secret of whose power lay in that passionate piety which characterized his life even from childhood. He was a Scholastic traditionalist in the sense that he aimed at making the content of tradition his own by means of mystical contemplation, and he found a ready sympathizer in William of Champeaux († 1122), who strove with success against Roscellin and with failure against Abelard, the famous pupil of them both. The differences between Bernard and Abelard revealed clearly the antagonism of the method of faith to that of mental inquisition and conclusion. To the former the *love* of the Lord was the beginning of wisdom, and the mystical idea of union with God in Christ was realizable by way of affectionate adoration of the suffering Jesus. It was this adoration that somewhat kept in the background of his thought the doctrines of the Holy Spirit and the Atonement, though he relates these two in a way hardly encouraging to a distorted view of his traditionalism which sees in him no love for doctrinal development.[2] The Spirit of God is treated

[1] Harnack, *ibid*, vi. p 10
[2] W B Pope (*Compendium of Christian Theology* ii , p 428) asserts that, in the doctrine of salvation as taught by the mediaeval mystics, love was simply faith itself ' in its self-renouncing and Christ-embracing character ' The stress, however, was undoubtedly laid by Bernard on imitation of Christ rather than on redemption by Christ And yet Bernard was a soul-winner, proclaiming the truly evangelical message that no human merit can of itself suffice for salvation In remarkable contrast to this are Bernard's eloquent support of the second Crusade of 1146 as a means of expiation of sin, and his belief that the monastic life was essential to his own acceptance with God It may be granted that the subjectivism of his contemplation of the sufferings of Divine Love was taken up by the whole spirit of monasticism more than was ever his intention But in reviving the influence of the monasteries, and, as the ' uncrowned pope ' and the ' oracle of Europe,' in re-establishing the power of the Papacy, Bernard delayed the Reformation for a considerable time On the other hand, to style him ' one of those who obtained the prize in the race of superstition ' is an extremism characteristic of Gibbon.

9

by him more in reference to His operations than to His Being, while as regards the latter his attitude is definitely Western.

His *Sermons on the Feast of Pentecost* are noteworthy if only from the fact that his early fame was due to his preaching. 'The Holy Spirit is God Himself. . . . And therefore, with regard to the Holy Spirit, if I allow that it is not procession by which He proceeds from the Father and the Son, nevertheless I know that it is something, namely inspiration. For there are Two from whom and by whom He may proceed. The procession from the Father and the Son has made darkness its hiding place; but the procession toward men is beginning to be known to-day, and is already manifest to the faithful.'[1] The eternal procession is regarded as always partly shrouded in mystery, but the temporal procession as a fact proved by human experience. Concerning the eternal procession, however, an exhortation is found in the third sermon of the same series which guards against a misconception of an 'order of precedence' in the Trinity: 'Understand that the Father is the principal Spirit, not because He is greater, but because He alone is from nothing, while the Son is from Him, and the Holy Spirit from Both.' The priority is solely one of source.

The twofold procession of the Spirit is again stated along with a recurrence of the unusual emphasis found in Bernard on His work in the hearts of men. 'Concerning the Holy Spirit Scripture bears witness in that He proceeds, breathes forth, indwells, fills, glorifies. He is said to proceed in two ways; whence and whither? Whence? From the Father and the Son. Whither? To the creatures. By proceeding He predestines; by breathing forth He calls whom He has predestined; by indwelling He justifies whom He has called.'[2] This suggests the existence of the controversy on predestination which was then in its initial stages. It is more significant still in the declaration of the close connexion of the work of the Holy Spirit with justification. This is emphasized by an important statement in one of his letters touching the Spirit's part in the Atonement. 'Wherefore,' he writes, 'since we hold fast a twofold sign of our salvation, the twofold outpouring of blood and of the Spirit, neither is of benefit without the other.'[3] This is striking testimony to the necessity

[1] *In Festo Pentecostes, Sermo* 1.   [2] *Sententiae,* § 2
[3] *Epistola* 107 (*Ad Thomam Praepositum de Beverla*).

of the complementary work of the third Person of the Trinity on the part of one for whom the second Person was preeminently the subject of contemplation.

In his little book *On Love* Bernard dwells on that aspect of the Nature of God which for centuries had been ascribed particularly to the Holy Spirit. ' God is Love. The Holy Spirit is denoted especially by the name of Love. He Himself is the Love of the Father and the Son, . . . also whatever can be common to Them Both. . . . For the Spirit is He who imparts life to the spirit of man, and teaches and trains him to love God.'[1]

Throughout the works of Bernard of Clairvaux there is little reference to the Being of the Spirit save in connexion with passages which refer to His operations or His gifts. The attention given to this other side of the Doctrine of the Holy Spirit was long overdue, and accounted for much of the power of Bernard's teaching, contrasted as it was with the background of Scholastic disquisition.

Hugh of St. Victor

A bridge across the gulf which separated the mysticism of Bernard from the outlook of the 'rational' school was constructed in the monastery of St. Victor, the famous foundation of William of Champeaux in Paris, by the Victorines Hugh and Richard. Hugh of St. Victor (1096-1141) may indeed be regarded as the pioneer of French Mysticism, for Bernard owed much to his system of thought, as also did Petrus Lombardus; and his influence as writer and theologian was immense. To Hugh, faith comes first, speculation second; and, while faith has no relationship to the absurd or the incredible, reason cannot seek to probe into the supernatural. Moreover, faith, as the gateway to knowledge, is affected by personal experience which, in turn, is encouraged by both Hugh and Richard by means of introspection. In this standpoint of his the mysticism of Hugh is seen more clearly than in his writings which bear upon the Trinity.

A survey of his theological work reveals the considerable place given by him to scriptural exegesis, in which, as in that of Bernard, his Western orthodoxy touching the Doctrine of the Spirit is clearly set forth. In the *Quaestiones in Epistolas Pauli*,

[1] *Tractatus de Charitate*, cap 10

which have been ascribed to him, the Latin view of the Procession is set forth in the course of his treatment of the Epistle to the Romans. 'Unity,' he writes, 'is said to be in the Father, equality in the Son, . . . truly, therefore, is the Holy Spirit called the union (*concordia*) of unity and equality; so that the Holy Spirit may thus be regarded as being from Both, for He is equal to Both. I assert this with sound Catholic faith.'[1] The fact that the Holy Spirit is the Bond of the Trinity is believed to presuppose the truth of the *Filioque*, which, again, is made still more credible by the mutual equality of the Persons.

The latter period of Hugh's literary activity yielded the *Summa Sententiarum*, a reasoned statement of belief which in all probability dominated the mind of Hildebert when at work upon his *Tractatus Theologicus*. The first Tract of the *Summa* deals with the Being of God and the Trinity, and the Unity of God is at once carefully guarded. 'God is one and not three, one omnipotent, one eternal, one immeasurable, and so forth.' On the basis of this he declares that 'the distinct character (*proprium*) of the Holy Spirit proceeds from the Father and the Son. But in regard to that by which the Father is God, omnipotent, wise, and so forth, He is not distinguished from the Son and the Holy Spirit, because the Son also is God, omnipotent, and the like, and the Holy Spirit in like manner.' It is thus desirable to emphasize those attributes which are common to all the Persons of the Trinity as well as the *proprium* which conveys the sense of distinction in the case of Each. The question of the Procession brings in the consideration of distinction, and in his assertion of a procession of the Son and his mode of distinguishing it from the procession of the Spirit he was followed closely by Hildebert. 'The Son, too,' writes Hugh, 'proceeds from the Father, as He Himself shows in John, saying, "I came forth (*processi*) from God and have come into the world" (ch. viii.). And so the Son is from the Father by procession and generation; the Holy Spirit, however, is from the Father not by generation but by procession. For Each proceeds from the Father, but in an ineffable and dissimilar manner. Hence the Holy Spirit is not begotten, because, seeing that He is from the Father

---

[1] Q 283 The *Filioque* and the Godhead of the Spirit are upheld also in Q 37, while the *Filioque* is again argued in Q 285.

and the Son, if He were begotten He would at once have two Fathers; and so in the Trinity there would be confusion in which there would be both two Fathers and two Sons.'¹ But it is of first importance to notice that, in this Trinity which is inseparable though the Persons are distinct,² 'the Holy Spirit is co-eternal, co-omnipotent, consubstantial, co-equal . . . with the Father and the Son.'³ That there is thus no possibility of the Divine Spirit being a creature is emphasized in the *Miscellanea* in the following statement ' There are three spirits, the Spirit of God, the spirit of man, the spirit of the devil. The Spirit of God and the spirit of the devil are immovable, the one in good, the other in evil. The spirit of man is turned now hither, now thither.'⁴ It is a statement which also reveals the need of man for the guidance of the Holy Spirit.

Reference may be made to another of Hugh's later works, the *De sacramentis Christianae Fidei*, for an analogical exposition of the Trinity in which the essential attributes of God, namely power, wisdom, and love, receive special consideration.

RICHARD OF ST. VICTOR

Of the life of Richard of St. Victor († 1173) little is known, but his writings on the Doctrines of the Trinity and the Holy Spirit are of greater interest than those of his master. Richard's outlook was more subjective, and his method more contemplative, than Hugh's, and, while much of what he said concerning the Holy Spirit had already been said by others, he imparted an intimacy of touch to a subject which was evidently of little use to him if it only formed part of a reasoned statement of an intellectual position.

His theology under this head is found principally in the *De Trinitate*, a rather bold work after the Augustinian pattern. He is anxious at the outset to lay stress upon the fact of the Divine Unity. 'I have said of my God that He is one and threefold, one substantially but threefold personally. . . . I have said that in the true Godhead there is only one Substance, that in the unity of the Substance there is a plurality of Persons, Each, again, being distinct from every Other in characteristic. Daily I hear concerning the Three that They are not three

¹ *Cap* 7   ² *Cap.* 11.   ³ *Cap* 8   ⁴ *Lib* 1 § 130

eternals (*aeterni*) but one Eternal, that They are not three uncreated nor three immeasurable beings, but one uncreated and one immeasurable Being. I hear concerning the Three that They are not three omnipotents but one Omnipotent; no less do I hear that They are not three Gods, but that there is one God; nor three Lords, but that there is one Lord. I find that the Father is not made, nor begotten; that the Son is not made, but begotten; that the Holy Spirit is not made, nor begotten, but proceeding.'[1] The very revelation of mutual distinctions within the Godhead would appear, in Richard's view, to minister to the idea of Divine unity, which, in turn, receives emphasis from a consideration of the Nature of the Persons concerned. ' It is impossible that the Divine Persons should not be wholly co-eternal.'[2] Again, ' it must be well observed that, just as true love requires a plurality of persons, so the highest love requires an equality of persons.'[3] Thus there is one and only one Divine Substance which is possessed by each Person of the Trinity, and this truth is constantly brought into prominence in the course of the book. Godhead and Divine Substance are one and the same thing, which proves that each Person, being God, possesses the one and the same common Substance.[4] ' The Trinity of Persons is one identical Substance. But,' comments Richard, ' if that is incomprehensible which nevertheless the human mind knows by experience, how much more incomprehensible is that which no human experience reaches!'[5] A warning is hereby given against a despairing scepticism toward which the finite intellect may on occasion be attracted when discussing verities pertaining to the Infinite. These verities, however, remain. The oneness of the Substance of Father, Son, and Holy Spirit underlies the considerations (1) that Each of Them is God, eternal and omnipotent,[6] and (2) that They have varied relationships to Each Other.[7] ' We deny,' he pronounces, ' that in this Trinity there are three Substances.'

Richard then takes up the subject of the inner distinctions in the Life of God. The term ' Trinity ' implies that here is no question of mutual dissimilarity or inequality.[8] It also utterly repudiates any possibility of a quaternity: ' For the

---

[1] *Lib* i *cap* 5   [2] iii. 6   [3] *Ibid*, 7.
[4] *Ibid*, 8; cf *ibid*, 23, ' Summa autem Trinitas constat in unitate substantiae.'
[5] iv 2   [6] vi 20.   [7] *Ibid*, 25.   [8] iii 24

THE SCHOLASTIC MYSTICS 133

distinguishing character (*proprietas*) of one Person, as is evident from the premises, consists alone in giving, of Another alone in receiving. Between These, again, is another Person who mediates (*media*) in giving as in receiving. . . . Hence a fourth distinguishing character is understood to have no place in the Godhead, from whom the idea of a quaternity is altogether excluded. Therefore it is assured that in the Divine Nature there certainly cannot be a fourth Person.'[1] As to the third Person, however, it has been proved that He is not united to the First by a relation of generation (*germanitate innascibili*), and that He cannot rightly be called His Son; but we do know that He, who is the Third in the Trinity, proceeds from the Two Others,[2] that He proceeds at once (*simul*) from the Begotten and the Unbegotten,[3] and that He proceeds in an equal manner (*pari modo*) as much from the Father as from the Son.[4] This procession, too, is timeless: ' For indeed it is certain that the spirit which proceeds from a man is not consubstantial with the man himself. The Spirit of God, on the other hand, is decidedly consubstantial with Him, and is altogether equal to Him in all respects. . . . Therefore, seeing that the Holy Spirit is called the Spirit of God, the procession which concerns Him who is eternal is itself designated eternal.'[5] One other truth, moreover, must not be overlooked: ' No one receives the fullness of the Godhead wholly from the Holy Spirit, and, for that reason, He does not portray the image of the Father in Himself. Behold the reason why the Son only, and not the Holy Spirit also, is called the Image of the Father.'[6]

' There is,' remarks Richard, ' one will in the Trinity in everything, one love, one goodness without trace of difference.'[7] Indeed, the mystic sense of this deep thinker was responsible for his attachment to Augustine's view, which regarded the Trinity Itself as the necessary conclusion from Divine Love. The highest form of love can only be fully expressed towards the highest form of object, and therefore the position of the second Person in the Godhead can be appreciated. Less obviously, perhaps, the argument is extended to the third Person, who is the embodiment of the mutual love (*condilectio*) of the Others. This conception of the third Person is more

---

[1] v. 15; also 20. [2] vi. 8, 10 [3] v 13 [4] vi 13
[5] *Ibid*, 9 [6] *Ibid*, 11 [7] v 23.

passive than active, yet it is one full of interest for the modern mind.¹

His sermon *On the Mission of the Holy Spirit* enforces the function of the Spirit as the creative principle of the universe. He speaks of the Spirit as the One from whom are all things, through whom are all things, who in the beginning created the heaven and the earth, through whom all things were made, and without whom nothing was made. 'Therefore this Spirit will be the same as the Father, the same as the Son, because the Father, Son, and Holy Spirit are one God, one Substance, one Nature, one Godhead, one Majesty.' The personal distinctions are obscured here, just as, indeed, they are somewhat obscured by the love argument for the Trinity; but the whole Trinity is regarded as operating through the Holy Spirit for the creation and preservation of the existing order, while the Godhead of the third Person is manifest. The Spirit, however, is related to mankind in a sense in which He could not be to the rest of creation. 'The same Spirit is present only to rational creatures, yet to all whether good or bad, to the happy and to the miserable likewise. . . . For no one can say " Lord Jesus " save in the Holy Spirit.' There must first be the exercise of spiritual discernment.

In a letter written to Bernard of Clairvaux with special relation to the distinguishing characters of the Persons of the Trinity, Richard discusses the question of the equality of the Holy Spirit as affecting Substance and precedence. 'According to the thought of Augustine,' he writes, 'the Son is co-equal with the Father, not the Father with His Image. Rightly, therefore, is equality attributed not to the Father but to the Son. But why, you ask, not also to the Holy Spirit? But if you concede that the Son alone in the Trinity is called the Image of the Other, consequently you will allow that equality may be attributed to the Son alone, not however at the same time to the Holy Spirit also. Certainly in these things, which are spoken of with reference to Substance, equality is attributed not only to the Son but also to the Holy Spirit, but with reference to precedence (*principalitatem*) the Son alone possesses this, and not the Holy Spirit.' For all that, a uniform

---

¹ Cf W P Paterson, *Rule of Faith*, pp 221-2 ' The highest level is reached in the reciprocal love of two persons when there is a third personal life which is the object of their common love and devotion ' But, as Dr Paterson suggests, this is somewhat of a development of the Augustinian *condilectio* as upheld by Richard

relationship exists between the Persons of the Trinity from whatever viewpoint.¹ And Bernard would doubtless value Richard's opinions on a side of pneumatology which was no forte of his own, for there was much in common between these churchmen of Clairvaux and St. Victor.

JOACHIM OF FLORIS

Joachim (1145–1202), Abbot of Floris (Fiori) in Italy, was a very different type of theologian from Bernard or the Victorines. From the obscurity of his life's history two facts can be gleaned which reveal a gulf between him on the one hand, and the authorities of the Church on the other. The first is reminiscent of the Fourth Lateran Council, which dismissed his charge of a Divine Quaternity against Petrus Lombardus, and condemned his own tendency to tritheism which had been responsible for it. The second is his remarkable theory of dispensations, whereby the reign of the Holy Spirit would presently² supersede that of the Son, which had already followed that of the Father, and thus, in Montanist fashion, would take the place of both law and Gospel.³ His theology of the Spirit is set forth in his *Liber concordiae novi ac veteris Testamenti*, a striking production which attempts to harmonize various occurrences in both Testaments, and from which doctrinal allusions to the Spirit need to be carefully extricated.

According to Joachim, ' the Father, Son, and Holy Spirit are not three first principles but one first principle (*principium*)'; and yet there are three Persons in the One Godhead, for, ' if God were one Person, three distinct operations should not be sought for.' One of these distinct operations belongs to the Holy Spirit, who works in the hearts of spiritual men,⁴ and who proceeds from the Father and the Son.⁵ The Holy Spirit is described as ' the love of God ' in more places than one, and, as such, He represents the final expression, or the *tertius status*, of Divine sovereignty. ' The first dispensation (*status*) must be attributed to the Father, the second to the Son, the third to the Holy Spirit.' This is an allusion to his

---

¹ ' Uniformiter autem habent tam Pater quam Filius ad Spiritum amborum, et e converso uniformiter se habet idem Spiritus tam ad Patrem quam Filium '
² A D 1260 (Herzog, *Ency*)
³ Cf Milman, *Latin Christianity*, vol 1 p 47
⁴ *Lib* ii *tracta* 1 § 6, also *lib* v § 2 (1612 edition)
⁵ *Ibid* , § 7, for *Filioque* see also §§ 8, 9, 13, 14, 26, 29, 30 ; *lib* ii *tr* ii, § 5 ; *lib*. iv., §§ 1, 3, 5, 36, 39.

belief in the successive reigns of the Persons of the Trinity, adding as he does that, whereas 'Christ came into the world, the Holy Spirit still comes.'[1] Nevertheless 'the Holy Spirit was given by the Father just as by the Son,' and although He was given twice, He Himself is but One.[2]

This author constantly emphasizes the fact that the Persons of the Trinity are distinct,[3] though his emphasis of this distinctness was too unbalanced for the Fourth Lateran Council. He is careful to add, however, that the Persons are inseparable, which can be seen by the way in which the Holy Spirit co-operates with the Father and the Son[4]; also, 'it is unreasonable . . . that the Holy Spirit, who is of the same Nature together with the Father, could proceed from the Father Himself if He were not one (*unum*) with the Father, or from the Son if He were not one with the Son.'[5]

The second book of the *Concord* contains assertions that the Holy Spirit spoke through the prophets,[6] and that the gift of tongues is imparted by the Holy Spirit by means of the imposition of hands.[7] The third book, again, yields more references to the third Person of the Trinity. Speaking of the Son and the Spirit Joachim remarks: 'One should not be considered greater or less, before or after, the Other,' for there is between Them the highest equality, the same glory, and co-eternal majesty. Indeed, the three Persons of the Trinity abide in the very height of majesty (*culmen majestatis*).[8] It should be remembered, however, that, even though the Holy Spirit was specially operative in the incarnation of Christ,[9] Christ did not thereby become the Son of the Holy Spirit; but rather He is One from whom the Spirit proceeds.[10] 'Nothing,' he writes 'may the Son do without the Holy Spirit; nothing may the Holy Spirit do without the Son.'[11] The Holy Spirit, then, works particularly in the human and the moral sphere, increasing the sum of good in man,[12] and this operation of His in the heart is an essential to salvation.[13] Moreover, the fertilizing power of the Spirit can banish barrenness of soul in the Body of Christ as in its members. 'The

---

[1] *Ibid*, § 8 [2] *Ibid*, § 9
[3] *Ibid*, §§ 9, 11; see also *lib.* 11, *tr* ii, § 7; *lib* iv, § 1.
[4] *Ibid*, § 14. [5] *Ibid*, § 26 [6] *Tr* 11 § 1; see also *lib* iii *part* i §8 [7] *Ibid*, § 5.
[8] *Part* i § 3 The complete equality of the Persons is asserted again in §§ 13 and 16.
[9] *Ibid*, § 14 [10] *Ibid*, § 9 [11] *Ibid*, § 18. [12] *Ibid*, §§ 5, 7.
[13] *Ibid*, § 6: 'opus sine quo non est salus'

THE SCHOLASTIC MYSTICS

Church,' he adds, ' has been made fruitful (*fecundata*) by the Holy Spirit.'[1]

The fourth book states that the operations of the three Persons of the Trinity are the same. Certain definite actions are assigned to the Spirit, who, nevertheless, works in complete accord with the Father and the Son.[2] Thus all through the *Concord*, Joachim is true to the ' mystical ' mind in laying the stress upon the work of the Spirit rather than upon His Being, and in avoiding many of the subtleties associated with the dialectics of most of the Schoolmen, even while, on the other hand, he certainly introduces subtleties and fantastic aberrations of his own! His treatment of the whole subject from a moral point of view, by which the personal Life of God was regarded as entering into the life of the Church and of human hearts, energizing the former and imparting salvation to the latter, served a useful purpose in the closing years of the twelfth century.

BONAVENTURA

The last theologian to be considered under the head of Scholastic Mysticism is Bonaventura, or Giovanni di Fidanza (1221–1274), a pupil of Alexander of Hales at Paris, and a great teacher and prolific writer, who rose to be Cardinal-Bishop of Albano. His piety gained for him the title of ' Doctor Seraphicus,' and was of such a rigorous nature that his death is said to have been due wholly to ascetic exhaustion. An extreme Romanist, he was also in heart a Victorine. The fact that he became General of the Order founded by Francis of Assisi points to the mystical tendency of his mind, though he presented this mysticism in the systematized form expected of a Sententiary building on Summist foundations. His devotion to Petrus Lombardus never induced him to discount the prime necessity for spiritual illumination as a means of arriving at Divine truth. If philosophy must do obeisance to theology, theology itself must make the mind do obeisance to the heart ; for, in the quest for union with God, heights which are unreachable by the intellect are attainable by the soul. As may thus be expected, the Commentary written by Bonaventura on the First Book (*De Dei Unitate et Trinitate*)

[1] *Ibid.*, § 10   [2] § 36.

of the Sentences of Lombardus is of a more practical character than most of the similar work of the Sententiaries.

Bonaventura states that, according to the Catholic Faith, there are only three Persons in the Deity, not more nor less, ' and, in support of this, there is brought forward the reason of necessity and fitness.' This reason he proceeds to expound in a strain reminiscent of Richard of St. Victor. ' There cannot be fewer than Three,' he writes, ' for supreme happiness requires love (*dilectio*) and mutual love (*condilectio*). . . . Whence, the first Person, since He cannot be begotten (*innascibilis*) and breathed forth (*inspirabilis*), begets and breathes forth; the second, since He cannot be breathed forth, but is begotten, does not beget, but breathes forth; the third Person, however, since He is breathed forth and proceeds from One who begets, neither begets nor breathes forth. And therefore it is impossible that there are more than Three. . . . There will be only three Persons,' he continues, ' One, who only gives, in whom is Love by Nature (*amor gratuitus*); Another, who only receives, in whom is Love by indebtedness (*amor debitus*); and One mediating, who gives and receives, in whom is Love mingled (*amor permixtus*) from Both.'[1] The whole Trinity is, in fact, implied at the beginning of Genesis by the words ' In the beginning God created,' &c., (I. 1, 2).[2] ' It must be remarked, however, that plurality of persons, together with unity of essence, is characteristic of the Divine Nature alone, the like of which neither is found in the creature nor *can* be found nor rationally conceived. Therefore in no way is the Trinity of Persons understandable through the creature, by rationally ascending from the creature into God.'[3] Yet analogies of the Trinity are plentiful, and carry considerable weight. A trinity of personal attributes such as *unitas, veritas,* and *bonitas* is certainly indicative of the triune Life of God[4]; while the human similitudes of (1) *memoria, intelligentia,* and *voluntas,* and (2) *mens, notitia,* and *amor,* both of which he borrows from Augustine,[5] demand attention as being full of suggestion in the same direction. It is possible to grasp a Trinity in God by means of these analogies by attributing the factors in a human trinity to the highest

---

[1] *Dist* ii (of Lombardus, *Sent* 1), *quaest* iv, *conclusio*
[2] *Ibid*, *Dubium* viii, Reply   [3] *Dist* iii part 1 *q* iv, *concl*
[4] *Ibid*   [5] (1) *Ibid*, p ii., *q* 1; (2) *Ibid*, p ii, art ii, *q* ii.

THE SCHOLASTIC MYSTICS 139

Trinity of all. Taking the last of the analogies above-mentioned, Bonaventura asserts that these three eternal effects can be ascribed to God as touching the Divine Substance, so that a Trinity in the Deity can be perceived through the corresponding faculties in man.[1] He adds that recognition of the Trinity in respect of personal attributes was arrived at by the philosophers, whose views commanded his respectful attention. ' The Father, Son, and Holy Spirit are united in one Deity or Essence, but possess distinction by reason of the plurality of the Persons.'[2] There is, however, one will (*voluntas*) in the Trinity.[3]

The subject of the Holy Spirit receives careful treatment from the tenth *Distinction* onwards. He is regarded as the Love with which the Father loves the Son.[4] ' The Father and the Son are united in breathing forth the Holy Spirit, which union is love.'[5] The Holy Spirit is thus the Love and the Unity of the Father and the Son, as stated in the conclusion to the following question ; so that ' although the Son and the Holy Spirit have Their source from the Father in a different manner, on the contrary the Father and the Son breathe forth the Holy Spirit in the same manner.' These and other considerations leave no doubt as to the Spirit's Godhead [6]

The way is thus prepared for a discussion in the next *Distinction* of the question of the Procession, concerning which Bonaventura is uncompromisingly Western. Quotations are made from Scripture and early Christian writers, from which, *auctoritatibus et rationibus*, the truth of the faith is asserted—that the Holy Spirit proceeds from the Father and the Son. ' The Greeks and the Latins agree upon the authority of Scripture, which says that the Holy Spirit is of the Son and

---

[1] *Ibid*, art ii, q iii, *concl* ' Ista tria possunt Deo attribui secundum substantiam, ut per mentem intelligamus mentem in Deo, et per notitiam in anima notitiam in Deo, et sic de tertio '

[2] *Dist* iv, art *unicus*, q ii *concl* Another analogy of Bonaventura's given by Erdmann (*ibid*, p 397) is *pondus, numerus, mensura*, in things. Another point of view of Bonaventura is described by Inge, *Christian Mysticism*, p 146 ' His proof of the Trinity is original and profound It is the nature of the Good to impart itself, and so the highest Good must be *summe diffusivum sui*, which can only be in hypostatic union '

[3] *Dist*. xi, art. *unicus*, q 1   [4] *Dist* x., art i q ii., *concl*.

[5] *Ibid*, art ii, q 1 *concl* Cf *ibid*, q iii, *concl* ' Persona illa, quae est amor, non tantum dicitur Spiritus, sed Spiritus sanctus Non sic Filius dicitur sanctus, quia generatio est motus naturalis, circa quem non attenditur sanctitas vel puritas, sicut attenditur circa amorem voluntatis '   [6] *Ibid*, q iii *concl*.

is sent by the Son ; but they differ over reason and revelation. . . . The Greeks have compared the Spirit to the breathing forth of an outer breath, but the Latins to the breathing forth of an inner love.' Indeed, the most vigorous of the defenders of the *Filioque* were those who usually spoke of the place of the Holy Spirit within the Trinity in terms of love and intimacy. Moreover, he adds a note to the effect that while the early Greeks did not confess the *Filioque* they did not flatly deny it ; ' but,' he continues, ' their scurrilous progeny have added to the paternal madness and say that He proceeds from the Son only temporally. And therefore the Roman Church condemns them as so many heretics and schismatics.'[1] And yet the very acceptance of the *Filioque* provides more problems for solution. 'If, then, it is asked whether the Holy Spirit proceeds from the Father before He proceeds from the Son ; if " before " in duration, is meant, it is untrue ; similarly if " before " in causation is meant ; similarly if " before " in source is meant. If, however, " before " in authority is meant, so that " before " (*prius*) is the same as "more prominently" (*principalius*), it is true.'[2] Yet 'the Father and the Son are one Source (*principium*) of the Holy Spirit.'[3] The Holy Spirit, again, proceeds from the Father through the mediation of the Son, and also immediately *per se*.[4] While, too, precedence in authority alone is allowable in the case of the procession of the Holy Spirit from the Father being ' before ' that from the Son, reason allows us to assert that the generation of the Son is before the breathing-forth of the Holy Spirit.[5] The distinction between these two functions must be carefully guarded. ' Just as the Holy Spirit is not the Son, so neither is the procession of the Holy Spirit generation.'[6] Further, ' generation and breathing-forth, or procession, differ not only according to mode of speech, but also according to a difference of source and condition.'[7] A confusion of the Persons follows upon a confusion of functions peculiar to Them.

The commentary on *Distinctions* xix. to xxix. brings

---

[1] *Dist* xi , art *unicus*, q i , *concl*

[2] *Dist* xii , art *unicus*, q 1 *concl* Cf *ibid* , q ii , *concl* ' Dicendum quod Sp s dicitur procedere a Patre principaliter, et per se . principaliter, quia auctoritas est in Patre ; per se, quia non tantum mediante Filio, sed etiam immediate. Non tamen plenius procedit a Patre, nec perfectius '

[3] *Dist* xxix , art ii , q 1, *concl*   [4] *Dist* xii , see also q. iii , *concl*

[5] *Ibid* , q. iv , *concl*.   [6] *Dist* xiii , art *unicus*, q ii , *concl*.   [7] *Ibid* , q iii *concl*.

THE SCHOLASTIC MYSTICS   141

back the thought to the interrelations of the Divine Persons. Their unity of Essence is fundamental,[1] and Their mutual equality perfect.[2] The term *persona* is used with reference to the Divine *substantia*,[3] so that the Trinity *can* be substantially predicated of God, as against the opposite view upheld by Gilbert of Poitiers in his commentary on pseudo-Boethius. The pseudo-Boethian definition of a Divine *persona*, with its differentiation from that of a human *persona* already revealed in Gilbert's commentary, is sanctioned as being in accord with revealed truth.[4]

Bonaventura is the chronological link between the ' systematized ' Mysticism of Scholasticism's flourishing period and the ' unsystematized ' Mysticism of its period of decay. Directed against the rigidity of dialectical Scholasticism, the former remained a movement from within, the latter became a movement from without. Theological rigidity was constantly confronted by Mysticism, so that when even the theology of the Reformation also became rigid there was a Protestant Mysticism to oppose it. The genius of Mysticism brought the Doctrine of the Holy Spirit into prominence along practical lines, and the same is perceivable to no small degree in the Mysticism of the Scholastics, which, indeed, partly paved the way for the school of Eckhart and Tauler.

[1] *Dist* xxiii., xxiv.
[2] *Dist* xix , p 1, art *unicus* q i , *concl*
[3] *Dist.* xxv , q 1 (Cf his comment on *Dist* iii , p ii , art ii , q iii , *concl*)
[4] *Ibid* , q ii (Rupert of Cologne († 1135), another Scholastic Mystic, was also an expositor of the Trinity)

VII

THE EASTERN CHURCH

SINCE the schism between the Churches of the East and of the West had become open in the eleventh century, the gulf then revealed had gradually become wider and in consequence more difficult to be bridged. The *Filioque*, which had been receiving the official sanction of Rome, had also been receiving the official anathema of Constantinople. The religious bitterness, in which the East appears to have been the more proficient, was largely due to a political bitterness which was, again, closely related to the very existence of two Empires. The Crusades, which might have achieved a *rapprochement* between the Greeks and the Latins as a means to their adventurous end, succeeded in drawing together sections of the world of intellect, but they actually thrust wider apart the great ecclesiastical sections of Christendom. The fourth Crusade, diverted by the Venetians against the Eastern Empire, led, in 1204, to the foundation of the Latin Empire at Constantinople, and, accordingly, to the representation of the Eastern Church at the Fourth Lateran Council by Western bishops. Hence, though Constantinople was lost to the Latins in 1261, the religious hatred directed against them on the part of the Greeks was implacable, and the situation was aggravated by the falsity of Michael Palaeologus, who presented himself at the Council of Lyons (1274) with the pretence of negotiating a union with the Latin Church on the strength of his forged letters of Greek bishops.[1]

Whatever its motives may have been, the papacy had constantly expressed desire for reunion with the Eastern Church, but that desire had never received encouragement of any duration from the latter. Theologically the Greeks stood aloof from the West. They were essentially Oriental in outlook, still adhering to the content of faith as presented by John of Damascus, but allowing that content to remain

---

[1] Cf Gibbon, *Rome*, vii 65-69.

THE EASTERN CHURCH

practically unsystematized and merely reiterated by what unprogressive literary activity they exhibited. During the twelfth century Nicholas, bishop of Menthone, wrote on the dogma of the Procession, while during the thirteenth century Blemmydes, a Greek monk, is seen to be actually defending, in a debate at Nicaea, the Latin view of the Procession. The adoption, however, of the Western opinion by a Greek was as exceptional as that of the Eastern opinion by a Latin, and any such exception did in no way alter the course of Greek theology. This is clear from the works of but two of its representatives, both of whom being of some repute and of differing qualifications.

THEOPHYLACT

The first is Theophylact († c. 1110), the famous scholar who became Archbishop of Achrida, in Bulgaria, in 1078, and whose *Commentaries*, while yielding little that had not already been said by the Fathers, were masterpieces of exegetical labour, particularly so for the period in which he lived To him the Holy Spirit is 'the fountain of wisdom,'[1] an appellation reminiscent of Latin references to the Son; He is the One who is the Origin, the Setter-in-motion, of the life of mankind.[2] But it is when the Archbishop arrives at iii. 31–34 of St. John's Gospel that he turns aside to attack the Latins for their belief in the *Filioque*. ' It is not out of place,' he writes, ' to speak here, as the thought has come to me, of how the Son possesses the Spirit, and how He is called the Spirit of the Son. For the Apostle also says, " He sent forth the Spirit of His Son into your hearts, crying ' Abba, Father'" (Gal. iv. 6). And again, " But if any one hath not the Spirit of Christ he is not His " (Rom. viii. 9). For the Latins, wrongly taking up these things and thinking of them amiss, say that the Spirit proceeds from the Son. We, however, say this to them first of all, that it is one thing to be *from* any one, and another thing to be *of* any one. For instance, it is without doubt that the Spirit is, on the one hand, the Spirit of the Son, and this has been settled in accordance with all Scripture ; but, on the other hand, that He is from the Son, not once does the Scripture testify, in order that we

[1] Com on St Mark ix, 3–7 : ἡ πηγὴ τῆς σοφίας.
[2] On St John's Gospel, 1. 1 : τὸ κινοῦν τὰς τῶν ἁπάντων ψυχάς.

might not introduce two sources of the Spirit, both the Father and the Son. . . . Believe thou that the Spirit indeed proceeds from the Father, but that He is supplied to the world through the Son, and this shall be for thee the canon of orthodoxy.'[1] Theophylact pays no attention to the claim of Western theology that the Father and the Son together are one Source (*principium*) of the Spirit. So, in reference to xv. 26, 27 of the same Gospel, he remarks that the Son sends the Spirit—who is given to men by the Father through the Son—returning to the subject of the Procession with a useful distinction embodied in a definition of the term: ' And whenever thou shouldst hear that " He proceeds," do not consider the procession to be a mission such as that on which the ministering spirits are sent, but the procession of the Spirit is a natural subsistence (φυσικὴ ὕπαρξις).' Again, the Spirit is not less than the Son on account of His later appearance,[2] for He is fully God.[3] Many other statements are made in these Commentaries concerning the Holy Spirit, but they are unworthy of special notice, as having been emphasized previously by Latins as well as by Greeks.

Theodorus Lascaris

The second representative of the Greek theology of this period is Theodorus Lascaris II, who became Emperor of the East in 1255, and died in 1259. To him theology was more a matter of intellectual nicety than of spiritual application, for, while he undertook to write upon one aspect of the Doctrine of the Holy Spirit, in personal character he was warlike, passionate, and cruel. Gibbon's description of him leaves little indeed from which any development of the present doctrine may be expected! Nevertheless his defence of the Greek view of the Procession is interesting as being imperial, and also as imparting a touch of verdure to a considerable stretch of literary sterility in Eastern theology.

Lascaris begins his pamphlet[4] by asserting the Greek

---

[1] . . . Ἡμεῖς δὲ πρῶτον μὲν τοῦτό φαμεν πρὸς αὐτούς, ὅτι ἄλλο ἐστὶ τὸ εἶναι ἐκ τινος, καὶ ἄλλο τὸ εἶναί τινος· οἷον, τὸ Πνεῦμα εἶναι μὲν τοῦ Υἱοῦ Πνεῦμα, ἀναμφίβολον, καὶ παρὰ τῆς Γραφῆς πάσης βεβαιούμενον, εἶναι δὲ ἐκ τοῦ Υἱοῦ, οὐδεμία Γραφὴ μαρτυρεῖ, ἵνα μὴ δύο τοὺς αἰτίους τοῦ Πνεύματος εἰσάξωμεν τόν τε Πατέρα καὶ τὸν Υἱόν . . . Πίστευε σὺ τὸ Πνεῦμα, ἐκ τοῦ Πατρὸς μὲν προιέναι, δι' Υἱοῦ δὲ χορηγεῖσθαι τῇ κτίσει, καὶ οὗτος ἔσται σοι κανὼν ὀρθοδοξίας

[2] *Ibid*, xvi 12–14   [3] On 1 Cor xii 6, 7

[4] Latin title *De Processione Spiritus Sancti*; Greek text edited by H B Swete (Williams & Norgate, 1875).

position, namely that the Holy Spirit proceeds from the Father, and from the Father only. 'On the one hand,' he writes, 'we say that He does not proceed from (ἐκ) the Son, but, on the other hand, we believe and hold that He is supplied to us through the Son for cleansing and sanctifying.' St. John xv. 26 shows that the Spirit proceeds from the Father alone. Yet the Westerns insist that He proceeds from the Son also, seeing that St. Paul calls Him 'the Spirit of Christ.' To this the Emperor makes reply by using the identical words of Theophylact, ' that it is one thing to be *from* any one, and another thing to be *of* any one.' The Scriptural witness is to the effect that the Holy Spirit is τοῦ Υἱοῦ, but not ἐκ τοῦ Υἱοῦ, 'in order that we may not bring forward two sources of the Spirit, the Father and the Son.' A possible difficulty in his argument he finds in St. John xx. 22, which describes the breathing by Christ of the Holy Spirit upon the disciples; but he doubts the truth of any wide interpretation of this statement on the ground that there would therefore be no urgency for the Gift at Pentecost, when the Spirit was given by the Father. In his opinion, what really happened on this occasion was that Christ bestowed upon His disciples 'one grace (χάρισμα) of the Spirit,' namely, the power to forgive sins. Numerous quotations follow from the Greek Fathers in support of the belief in the single Procession.

As anticipated, there is nothing of note in the contribution of this Eastern Emperor save a striking similarity between his thought and expression and those of Theophylact. That Lascaris should have been so close an imitator of a writer who flourished a century and a half before him is testimony enough to his own lack of theological initiative, and, again, to the scantiness of pertinent literature in the Oriental Church. His opinions from the Greek standpoint were, however, manifestly decided, and no less so because he once desired to establish the pro-*Filioque* Blemmydes in the Patriarchate of Constantinople.[1] At that time, it must be remembered, the Latin Empire was already established there.

---

[1] See Herzog, *Encyclopaed*, art 'Blemmydes.'

VIII

ALEXANDER OF HALES AND ALBERTUS MAGNUS

THE thirteenth century brought Scholasticism to its height in the great theologians from the Mendicant Orders who introduced their fuller knowledge of Aristotelian philosophy. Aristotle helped to make the thought of the Schoolmen deeper as well as wider, so that the climax of Scholastic effort reveals an exhaustive treatment of dogma such as was unknown to the age of Anselm and his immediate successors. Faith, or 'dogmatic conviction' (Lord Acton's preference in referring to certain mediaeval churchmen), now received a closer examination in the light of, and in conjunction with, a vast range of knowledge; and from this knowledge no detail was omitted which might serve to present the system of the Christian religion as a proved and ordered unity, with a meaning and purpose beyond question. True it is that the aim of thirteenth-century Scholasticism was largely one of 'reducing to the service of the Church all the forces of the understanding and the whole product of science';[1] hence the Church looked on approvingly. This hope was indeed strengthened by the fact that the same century saw the Papacy also at its height, when the Popes certainly did not deserve the pontifical title of *servus servorum Dei* which had been in use since Gregory the Great. Yet the later Scholastics loved theology for its own sake, and their personal piety was undoubted; the saintliness of Bonaventura, the friend of Aquinas, is a ready instance. Again, as toward the close of the century the universal grip of the Church slackened with the wane of its power, there followed an emphasis upon individual character and the claims of conscience[2] which turned to good account the highest spiritual truth which the learned divines could impart.

[1] Harnack, *Hist of Dogma*, vi. 154
[2] Lord Acton, *Lectures on Modern History*, 31, 32   Cf Harnack, *ibid*, vi 23: 'The Realism that was represented by Albert and Thomas, acting upon impulses received from Augustine, made excellent use of experience'

This new departure in Scholastic thought is presented particularly in still more elaborate commentaries on the *Sentences* of Lombardus, and in independent *Summae* which are themselves characteristic of a new outlook. Such a departure, which came to be most perfectly represented by Thomas Aquinas, the greatest of all Schoolmen, had for its pioneer ALEXANDER OF HALES († 1245), an Englishman who was destined before his death to win fame at Paris as a noted teacher of theology. The great work of the 'Irrefragable Doctor,' and the only work of which his authorship is authentic, is the *Summa Universae Theologiae*, a massive production in four parts, the first part of which bears upon the Doctrine of the Spirit. It is not a commentary on Lombardus but an example of the above-mentioned independence of thought, in which pros and cons are adjudicated by conclusions which, in turn, are supported by philosophical as well as by Biblical and theological authorities.

Like many of the Schoolmen, Alexander manifests anxiety to uphold the Unity of the Deity, and to preserve it unimpaired, whatsoever is revealed concerning interior relationships. There are personal distinctions in God with regard to source, but the Essence of God is one nevertheless.[1] 'Truly and really do we confess a plurality of Persons in the Godhead, because there we believe in a plurality of Existences; and not on that account do we intend to disagree with the unity, as, for instance, *vice versa*, while we believe firmly in the unity of the Essence, we do not preclude the plurality of Persons' The sole distinction between the Persons as to Their Being lies, he repeats, in Their source.[2]

His reasoning is seen at its closest in his treatment of the question of the Procession, from which he emerges as a Latin enthusiast, altogether impatient with the shortsightedness of the Greeks! What, then, is meant by the term 'procession'? The answer is: 'When the Spirit Himself proceeds or is brought forth (*producatur*) from the Father who has the power, not from any other, of bringing forth; and is brought forth by the Son, or proceeds from Him as from One who has the power from Another; and is brought forth from the Substance of the Father and the Son alike to Them in Nature; He is therefore generated (*generatur*) from the Father and the Son.' He

---

[1] (1622 edition) *quaestio* 14.   [2] *q* 44

adds, however, that, in the stricter sense, the Spirit must be spoken of as proceeding rather than as being generated.[1] *Quaestio* 43 follows with a defence of this twofold procession, which he bases on the fact that the Son is Spirit, even as is the Father, while the Greeks, on the other hand, have been regarding the Son too much as a *Verbum corporale,* and as therefore not to be associated with the Father as one Spirit-Source. ' The Latins speak more truly and correctly than the Greeks,' he observes (also in *q.* 46). ' Away with the Greeks, who confess that the Divine Spirit proceeds from the Father only ! Prosperity to the Latins, who confess that He proceeds at once from the Father and the Son ! ' ' The Holy Spirit,' he continues, ' is from the Father and the Son, just as love (*amor*) is from mind (*mens*) and understanding (*intelligentia*) '—which is one Augustinian triad with *intelligentia* substituted for *notitia.* To this analogy he adds in the following *membrum* a second, which is evidence of the influence upon him of Richard of St. Victor. ' By reason of the highest love which is understood in the Person of the Father, exists the reason of the generation ; the highest mutual love (*condilectio*), however, which is understood in the Person of the Father and in that of the Son, is the reason of the procession of the Holy Spirit from Them.' Again, the consideration of the relation of these functions emphasizes the distinctness between the Persons due to Their source, for ' while the generation of the Son is *per modum naturae,* the procession of the Holy Spirit is *per modum voluntatis.* Just as, in the order of nature, nature is before will, even so the generation of the former is before the procession of the latter.'[2] The invisible mission of the Spirit brings with it also the revelation of the Father and the Son, whose *condilectio* is the source of His procession.[4] ' The Holy Spirit,' he concludes, ' subsisting in the same Trinity, will be neither less than, nor inferior to, but equal in all respects to, both the Father and the Son.'[5] The *Summa* of Alexander is undeniably a system of careful thought, but of a Sententiary form of it which makes too much of the system, and therefore too little of the practical side of the Doctrine of the Spirit which had appealed so strongly to the Victorines.

[1] *q* 42, *articulus* 2   [2] *q* 43, *membrum* 4   [3] *q* 46
[4] Erdmann, *Hist of Phil* 1 p 390, mentions Alexander's discussion in the third part of the participation of all three Persons of the Trinity in the Incarnation
[5] *q* 47

ALBERTUS MAGNUS

The same in a more philosophical sense may be said of Albertus Magnus (1193–1280), General of the German Dominicans and, for a brief two years, Bishop of Ratisbon. Though partially eclipsed by his brilliant pupil, Thomas Aquinas, his breadth of learning won for him the title of ' Doctor Universalis,' which, together with his piety and useful service to the Church, led to his receiving the title of ' Magnus.' The deeper Aristotelianism of Alexander is developed under his treatment as he brings together the sciences around theology as their mistress. This he does while regarding dogmatics as something more than a system of mere intellectual knowledge, and also without losing sight of tradition or of personal experience. Albertus is responsible for a *Summa Theologiae* as also for a *Commentary on the Sentences* of Lombardus, but after the glimpse at this later Scholasticism through Alexander's *Summa*, it may now be to fuller advantage to take the second glimpse at it through the other form of the *Commentary*.

'It must be held faithfully,' he writes, 'that the one and only true God is a Trinity—Father, Son, and Holy Spirit—and this Trinity is God, of one Substance or Essence. . . . The Father, Son, and Holy Spirit are of one Substance and are one God in inseparable equality; so that there is unity in the Essence and plurality in the Persons. They are not three Gods, but one God.' The absolute Unity of God is thus never to be forgotten even in face of a warning which Albertus gives against confounding the Persons. He holds the Father, Son, and Holy Spirit to be one God by Nature (*naturaliter*); ' for of the Father, Son, and Holy Spirit there is but one *essentia*, which the Greeks call *homousion*, in which the Father is not one thing (*aliud*), the Son another, the Holy Spirit another; rather, in personal terms, is the Father one Person (*alius*), the Son another, the Holy Spirit another.'[1] ' Therefore these Three are not three lives, but one Life; not three minds, but one Mind, one Essence,' so that the highest unity marks the Trinity. To Albertus, the Augustinian triad of *memoria*, *intelligentia*, and *voluntas* represents three that are one, in the sense that they are all functions of the same mind while each possesses its own *proprietas*. This human analogy of

[1] *Distinctio* 2

the triune God is correspondingly significant, *dilectio* being another analogical simile of the Holy Spirit. So he remarks: ' In this highest simplicity of Nature . . . there are three Persons . . . and not one Person.' A second triad in human life is that of *mens, notitia,* and *amor,* which is once more suggestive of the Trinity, especially as ' *notitia* is not less than *mens,* nor *amor* than both.' These terms, however, are not to be regarded as representing exclusive possession of the properties named, but rather particular possession in each case of what is the general possession of the Three.

The same *distinction* (3) contains a trinitarian confession which is worthy of note : ' I believe that the Father, Son, and Holy Spirit are one God, the Maker and Ruler of the whole creation ; that neither is the Father the Son, nor the Holy Spirit either the Father or the Son ; but that They are a Trinity of Persons resembling One Another. . . . The faith of patriarchs, prophets, and apostles declares that the one God is a Trinity. Therefore in that Holy Trinity there is one God, the Father who alone has begotten one Son essentially from Himself, and there is one Son who alone is begotten essentially from one Father, and one Holy Spirit who alone proceeds essentially from the Father and the Son. Moreover this Whole (*totum*) cannot be one Person; that means to beget oneself and to be begotten from oneself and to proceed from oneself; for, as says Augustine in the first book *de Trin.,* " Nothing exists which begets itself in order to exist." '[1] *Distinction* 4 follows with a continued insistence on the Divine Unity, asserting that, together with revelations of mutual relations within the Divine Life, that Life Itself is one and the same God, one Substance or Essence or Nature, and that this is the Catholic faith as demonstrated by Augustine.

When Albertus comes to deal with the subject of the Holy Spirit more particularly, he does so as a decided Western, having evidently taken his cue from Alexander on the question of the Procession as regards both the spirit of approach to it and the space allotted to it. The Holy Spirit, who is the *amor* or *charitas* of the Father and the Son, is thought of in reference to a temporal procession as well as an eternal, the temporal procession corresponding to the invisible mission of Alexander's *Summa.* As to the eternal procession, ' the Holy Spirit proceeds

---

[1] Nulla res est quae seipsam gignat ut sit '

from the Father and the Son as the love wherewith They love One Another,' the Father and the Son being one Source of the Holy Spirit. Not that the property, or even the simile, of love is thereby exclusively applicable to the Spirit. The Substance of the Three is one, and on that account each Person is called Love, certainly no less so by reason of the first Two being the *principium* of the Third.[1] 'This must be said,' he continues, 'that the Holy Spirit is from the Father and the Son, and proceeds from the Father and the Son, a fact which many heretics have denied. Indeed, that He proceeds from Both is established by many testimonies of Divine utterances.' Albertus adds his conviction that the Holy Spirit proceeds as a distinct Person from the Father and the Son as from one Source. 'The Greeks, on the other hand, say that the Holy Spirit proceeds from the Father and not from the Son. . . . Another thing has been added by the Latins—*Filioque*'— which addition can be argued from silence as well as from statement, for, though St. John's Gospel (xv. 26) declares that the Holy Spirit proceeds from the Father, it does not add ' only.' Then, after quoting Athanasius, Didymus, and Cyril in support of the twofold procession, he turns to the Eastern writers themselves. ' See ! ' he exclaims, ' we have open testimonies by doctors of the *Greeks* by which it is shown that the Holy Spirit proceeds from the Father and the Son. Therefore let every tongue confess that the Holy Spirit proceeds from the Father and the Son ! '[2] There is reason, too, for the supposition that Albertus had ground for this reference to the Latin view of the procession as adopted by certain Greek theologians. One case of this has arisen in the preceding chapter, while one of the Eastern Fathers, Cyril of Alexandria, might almost be termed another.[3]

In accordance with the usual outline of such a work, the Commentary considers next the relationship of the procession of the Spirit to its twofold Source. In this connexion Albertus asserts that the Spirit does not proceed more or less from the Father than from the Son, nor does He proceed from the

---
[1] *Dist* 10   [2] *Dist* 11
[3] Swete, *H Sp in the Ancient Church*, 269 On the other hand, Hilary is an instance of a Western Father who leaned to the Eastern view (*ibid* , 304) Yet Albertus, in upholding the *Filioque*, makes the following comment on a quotation from Hilary (!) · ' Ecce aperte dicit Spiritum sanctum a Patre per Filium et mitti et esse ; quod non est intelligendum quasi a Patre per Filium minorem mittatur vel sit , sed qui ex Patre et Filio est, et mittitur ab utroque ' (*dist* 12)

Father before or after He proceeds from the Son. Rather does He proceed immediately from Both as from one *principium*, and is also sent by Them Both as by one Source of His mission. This, however, does not belittle the truth that 'the Father is the Source (*auctor*) of the procession whereby the Spirit proceeds from the Son,'[1] even though the procession from the Father and the Son is equal and simultaneous. Again, distinction must be made in thought between procession and generation, the former having relation to two 'sources,' the latter to one. But, as to any vital distinction between these Divine functions as we know them, Albertus states that 'no distinction can be made by us between the generation of the Son and the procession of the Holy Spirit' Such a question does not affect the human race practically; it does not touch the spiritual experience. At the same time, for the purpose of clear thinking, 'we say that the Holy Spirit should not be spoken of as begotten or unbegotten,' and we must continue to affirm this if we would avoid the difficulty of either two Sons or two Fathers in the Trinity.[2] Albeit, the order in the Trinity is not mechanical. 'It is not surprising if the Holy Spirit may be said to be sent by or to proceed from Himself, since the Son also may be said to be sent by Himself.' Indeed, 'that the Son has been sent by the Holy Spirit is established by authorities,' namely Isa. ix. 6, 7, xlviii. 16, and lxi. 1, 2, which is quoted by Christ in Luke iv. 18, 19.[3]

Toward the close of the Commentary Albertus discusses the term *persona* in its reference to the Deity. We say, 'The Father is a Person, the Son is a Person, the Holy Spirit is a Person'; but we may not say 'The Father, Son, and Holy Spirit are one Person' when They are three Persons. The three Persons, on the other hand, are one Substance and one God. Once more the difference between the Greek and Latin terminology receives attention in a quotation from Augustine, who wrote that, while the Greeks spoke of 'one Essence, three Substances, three Hypostases,' the Latins spoke of 'one Essence or Substance, three Persons'; and, in spite of misunderstandings arising from the word 'person' as applied to the Divine Life, he follows Alexander in expressing his preference for the Western expressions. The word 'person' is used to denote each Member of the Trinity because 'what

[1] *Dist.* 12.   [2] *Dist.* 13.   [3] *Dist.* 15.

a person is, is common to the Three.'[1] All he has said, so he concludes, is the proper Catholic teaching on the subject of the Persons of the Deity, a subject which reveals the personal ' propriety ' of Each and, at the same time, Their unity in the one Godhead as evidenced by the Scriptures.[2]

[1] *Dist* 23 . 'Tribus commune est id quod persona est '
[2] *Dist* 25, in which reference is again made to the unsatisfactory nature of the Greek equivalents

IX

THOMAS AQUINAS

OF all the Schoolmen the outstanding figure is Thomas Aquinas (1227-1274), the first truly great theologian of the mediaeval period. Born near Aquino, a town between Rome and Naples, and reared amid noble surroundings, he entered the Dominican Order against the desires of his family, becoming a pupil of Albertus Magnus at Cologne. Here in course of time he began his lectures on the *Sentences* of Lombardus, and after transferring to Paris he gained marked distinction as a philosophic theologian, securing also immense reputation throughout Europe. By the command of the Pope the ' Angelic Doctor ' lectured in various seats of learning, always regarding with veneration the tradition and authority of the Church while declining all offers of ecclesiastical preferment. As a theologian he developed many of the ideas of his master, though, in his own work, philosophy and theology are balanced and combined more than they had ever been by Albertus. Again, while making full use of Aristotle as an exponent of the prevailing Realism, he went beyond Albertus in the stress which he placed on Scriptural revelation as a means of enabling man to know facts essentially out of the reach of human reason. In the contemplation of God the soul is aided more by revelation than by reason, and such contemplation meant so much to Aquinas that, influenced as he probably was by his friend Bonaventura, he is said to have given an impulse to Mystic thought. To him theology is essentially speculative, and, being such, it requires spiritual appropriation, with the result that ' ultimately no conflict can arise between reason and revelation.'[1] The existence of the Trinity, for example, is necessarily a matter of revelation, but reason can justify it now that it has been revealed ; and the same can be taken as the attitude of Aquinas in reference to the Doctrine of the Holy Spirit, His Nature and His operations.

[1] Harnack, *ibid*, vi, 155.

His *Commentary on the Sentences* of Lombardus (a good folio edition of which is that published at Venice in 1586) varies but little from that of Albertus, being the embodiment of his earliest labours. The method of his reasoning in the Commentary takes the same form as that afterwards adopted in the *Summa Theologica*, the conclusion being reached after discussion of both sides, then the conclusion itself explained and expanded. The views expressed in the Commentary are found also in the *Summa*, there being no need, therefore, to give them separate consideration.

A later publication belonging to the Paris era of his life is the *Summa contra Gentiles*, a work of an apologetic order which treats of natural religion in the first three books and of revealed religion in the fourth. Accordingly it is the fourth book which applies to the Doctrines of the Trinity and the Holy Spirit. The earlier reasoning is gathered up in the statement that a certain way is opened up to man whereby he can ascend in the knowledge (*cognitio*) of God, the First Cause, in whom the most perfect unity exists. The natural light of reason needs to be supplemented by revelation, and even then our knowledge of God is imperfect. Revelation, however, affords matters for our discussion which must be believed concerning God while they are beyond human reasoning (*supra rationem*), and such matters pertain to the doctrine of the Trinity [1] God thinks and knows in relation to Himself as the Word, and loves Himself as Holy Spirit, so that in the generation of the Son and the procession of the Spirit there are seen to be eternal *distinctiones* in God by which the Divine oneness is preserved without diversity or separation. This is upheld by the authority of Scripture, as in Matt. xxviii. 19, 1 John v. 7 [A.V.], John xv. 26, &c.[2] Aquinas then refers to certain reasons put forward in support of the view that the Holy Spirit is a creature, and proceeds to controvert these in the 17th chapter, entitled ' Quod Spiritus sanctus sit verus Deus.' 1 Cor. vi. 19 shows that our bodies are a temple of the Holy Spirit, and as our bodies are ' members of Christ ' (*ibid.*, vi. 15), these statements together point to the Godhead of the Spirit. For, ' since Christ is true God, it would be inappropriate that the members of Christ should be a temple of the Holy Spirit, unless the Holy Spirit were God.' Again, ' to sanctify men is a work

[1] (Edition published in 1664 by Petrus Maffre) Book iv , chap. i.   [2] Chap. xv.

characteristic of God (Lev. xxii. 9); but it is the Holy Spirit Who sanctifies (1 Cor. vi. 11; 2 Thess. ii. 13); therefore the Holy Spirit must be God.' A perusal of Rom. viii. will reveal that the Holy Spirit shares the Divine Nature, and that His operations for and in the soul are essentially Divine. The operations of the Spirit in creation (Job xxxiii. 4) emphasize His Godhead, for creation can only be the work of God. Again, the Spirit searches even the deep things of God (1 Cor. ii. 10, 11), which is not within human possibility (cf. Matt. xi. 27); 'therefore the Holy Spirit is not a creature.' 'According to the above-mentioned comparison the Holy Spirit is to God just as the spirit of man is to man.[1] But the spirit of man is essential (*intrinsecus*) to man and not of a nature strange to him, but it is actually part of him. Therefore the Holy Spirit is not of a nature strange to God.' This is another form of the argument from human to Divine personality. A further indication of the Deity of the Spirit is found in various passages of Scripture which relate how God, by His Spirit, spoke through the prophets (Acts i. 16; 2 Pet. i. 21, &c.); 'clearly, therefore, in the Scriptures it is understood that the Holy Spirit is God.' Moreover, the Holy Spirit is the Revealer of mysteries, and the Instructor of the soul; so He must be Divine. It is fair reasoning, then, that Divine operations mean Divine Nature. The Father and the Son have the same operation, hence They must have the same Nature. Likewise there is a unity of operation attached to the Son and the Holy Spirit (Matt. x. 20); 'therefore the Nature of the Son and of the Holy Spirit is the same; and, consequently, the Nature of the Father, since it has been shown that the Father and the Son possess one Nature.' Further, what has already been said concerning the 'temple of the Holy Spirit' may be emphasized by additional Scripture passages (1 Cor. iii. 16; 2 Cor. vi. 16), while the Godhead of the Holy Spirit is definitely stated in connexion with the sin of Ananias (Acts v. 3, 4). The passage which speaks of the diversities of gifts but the same Spirit (1 Cor. xii. 4-11) refers not only to the operations of the Spirit as Divine but also to the Being of the Spirit as such, the Spirit, too, dispensing His gifts entirely in accordance

---

[1] Cf Beet, *Manual of Theology*, pp 108, 109, on 1 Cor 11 10, 11. Aquinas' parallel, in exposition of this passage, is—Holy Spirit · God · spirit of man · man Dr Beet's parallel is—Holy Spirit · spirit of man · God · man The former is really the Pauline setting and it also serves more obviously the purpose of the argument

with His own judgement. Finally, ' To adopt as sons of God cannot be the work of any other than God. . . . The Holy Spirit is the Cause of adoption, so says the Apostle in Rom. viii. . . . Therefore the Holy Spirit is not a creature, but God.'

Having demonstrated the Deity of the Holy Spirit, Aquinas proceeds in the 18th chapter to show, as its title signifies, ' That the Holy Spirit is a subsistent Person.' ' Since,' he writes, ' certain people hold that the Holy Spirit is not a subsistent Person, but is either the Godhead Itself of the Father and the Son (as some Macedonians are said to have declared), or even some accidental perfection of the mind bestowed upon us by God, as, for example, wisdom or love, or other such created accidents ; against this it must be shown that the Holy Spirit is not anything of the kind :

1. ' Accidental forms, to be sure, do not properly work, but rather do people make use of them conformably to the decision of their own will. . . . But the Holy Spirit works conformably to the decision of His own will, as it has been shown. Therefore the Holy Spirit must not be regarded as some accidental perfection of the mind.

2. ' The Holy Spirit, as we are taught from the Scriptures, is the Cause of all the perfections of the human mind (Rom. v. 5 ; 1 Cor. xii. 8). Therefore the Holy Spirit must not be regarded as some accidental perfection of the human mind, seeing that He Himself is the Cause of all such perfections.

3. 'Scripture makes it clear that the Holy Spirit is not the Essence of the Father and the Son, in which case He could not be distinguished personally from Them. For the Holy Spirit proceeds from the Father (John xv. 26), and receives from the Son (John xvi. 14), which are functions not of the Divine Essence but of a subsistent Person.

4. ' Holy Scripture manifestly speaks of the Holy Spirit as of a Divine subsistent Person (Acts xiii. 2, 4 ; xv. 28), which would not be spoken of the Holy Spirit unless He were a subsistent Person.

5. ' Since the Father and the Son are subsistent Persons, and of the Divine Nature, the Holy Spirit would not be numbered with Them unless He were a Person subsisting in the Divine Nature ; but He is numbered with Them (Matt. xxviii, 19 ; 2 Cor. xiii, 14 ; 1 John v, 7 [A.V.]).

From which it is clearly shown that not only is He a subsistent Person just as the Father and the Son, but also that He possesses a unity of Essence along with Them.[1]

'Therefore,' he resumes, 'we, instructed by the testimonies of the Holy Scriptures, hold this firmly concerning the Holy Spirit that He is true God, subsistent and personally distinct from the Father and the Son.' Not that distinction involves separation; *intellectus* and *voluntas* in God are essentially one, and every act of the will is 'rooted in love.' But in God the act of the will proceeding by love is an eternal distinction, and therefore Essential; so that Love, as being in God and as eternally directed toward Himself, is named Holy Spirit.[2]

The Holy Spirit, again, is the Creator, the *principium vitae*, the Originator of *res* by His own will and out of the inward compulsion of Divine Love. 'Therefore the Love by which He loves His own Goodness is the cause of the creation of the universe (*rerum*). . . . The Holy Spirit proceeds by way of the love whereby God loves Himself; therefore the Holy Spirit is the first principle of creation' (Ps. civ 30). He is also the Cause of the varied developments of matter (Gen. i, 2). 'If, therefore, impulse and motion belong by reason of love to the Holy Spirit, the government and creation (*propagatio*) of matter are fitly assigned to the Holy Spirit.' This implies that the Spirit is Lord as well as Creator (2 Cor. iii. 17).[3]

At the same time, unity of Divine Essence means unity of operation. 'All that God works in us must be as by an effective Cause, by the Father, Son, and Holy Spirit together. Yet the Word of wisdom, by means of Which we get to know God, and Which has been sent to us by God, is peculiarly representative of the Son. And similarly the love with which we love God is peculiarly representative of the Holy Spirit.'[4] The love by which God is in us and we in God is especially through the mediation of the Holy Spirit. So, too, our gifts from God, our adoption as His sons and consequently the revelation to us of Divine mysteries, our forgiveness of

---

[1] § 5 figures as § 4 in the Latin edition used here
[2] Chap xix 'Esse igitur Dei in voluntate sua per modum amoris non est esse accidentale sicut in nobis, sed essentiale . Quia vero omnis intellectualis motus a termino denominatur, amor autem praedictus est quo Deus ipse amatur; convenienter Deus per modum amoris procedens dicitur Spiritus sanctus'
[3] Chap. xx
[4] Aquinas naturally applies the same to *charitas* as to *amor*.

sins by Him together with our being inwardly renewed and cleansed—all these functions are particularly functions of God through the Holy Spirit. Hence the Divine operation maintains its unity while it is being effectuated through one of the Persons,[1] and it is a truth which Aquinas further exemplifies. ' The Holy Spirit makes us lovers of God. . . . He gives to us the status of God's friends ; and, since He makes Him to dwell in us and we in Him, as it has been shown, it follows that through the Holy Spirit we have joy in God and encouragement in face of all the adversities and assaults of the world.' It is this Love of God, exercised through His Spirit, that makes us sons of God, prompting us to do God's will from the motive of love, a motive which can appeal to those who are spiritually free, thereby creating within us an attitude to God which mortifies the fleshly side of our nature.[2]

With Chapter xxiii. Aquinas begins his formulation of the dogma of the Trinity as such. In the 16th chapter he reminded his readers of the position of the Holy Spirit as a creature in the teachings of Arius and Macedonius. He now speaks of the relation of the Holy Spirit to the Father and the Son in proof that He is not a creature. The first evidence under this head is His derivation from the Others. Seeing that the knowledge (*scientia*), power (*virtus*), and operation of God compose His Essence, these qualities as possessed by the Son and the Holy Spirit are from the Father, these as possessed by the Son being from the Father alone, while these as possessed by the Holy Spirit are from the Father and the Son. The second evidence is His mission, by which He is sent visibly and invisibly. He descended upon Christ at His baptism in the form of a dove, and in fiery tongues upon the Apostles ; so that from the outpouring at Pentecost there have been visible manifestations of His mission from the Father and the Son, a mission, too, which implies no inferiority to Them. Again, ' it is clear,' writes Aquinas, ' from what has been said, that the Son proceeds from the Father by way of the knowledge with which God knows Himself, and the Holy Spirit proceeds from the Father and the Son by way of the love with which God loves Himself.' It is thus the particular

---

[1] Chap xxi Cf also chap xxiii., ' Manifestum est quod ad Spiritum sanctum pertinet amor quo Deus nos amat '   [2] Chap. xxii.

function of the Holy Spirit to cause men to be lovers of God, and, as the Possessor of this function, He indwells in them, being sent to them—in this case invisibly—by the Father and the Son. Thirdly, 'the Holy Spirit is not excluded from the Godhead because the Father and the Son are occasionally considered together without mention being made of the Holy Spirit. For neither can God the Father be comprehended without the Word and Love, nor conversely; and for this reason all Three are understood to be Three in One.' For instance, Matt. xi. 27 receives this comment: '" Neither does any one know the Father except the Son "; although both the Father and the Holy Spirit know the Father.' Indeed, several passages (John xvii. 3; Rom. i. 7; 1 Cor. viii. 6, &c.) imply that any Divine attribute which pertains to one of the Persons must be understood also to pertain to Them All, as required by the oneness of God.[1] But, adds Aquinas, though the Holy Spirit is true God, the fact that He has a true Divine Nature from the Father and the Son does not make Him Their Son!

Chapter xxiv. is devoted to the consideration of the procession of the Holy Spirit, and to the defence of the Western view that He proceeds from the Son as well as from the Father. 'It is manifest from Holy Scripture,' he writes, 'that the Holy Spirit is the Spirit of the Son (Rom. viii. 9). It is shown from the words of the same Apostle that the same Spirit is of the Father and of the Son, for the text just quoted (from the Epistle to the Romans) is added after he had said "If the Spirit of God dwell in us." Yet it cannot be said that the Holy Spirit is the Spirit of Christ in this sense alone that He as Man possessed Him (Luke iv. 1, 3), for from the statement in Gal. iv. 6, the Holy Spirit makes us sons of God inasmuch as He is the Spirit of the Son of God.[2] . . . But the Holy Spirit cannot in any sense be called the Spirit of the Son of God except in respect of source, because this distinction alone is met with in the Godhead.' Hence the Spirit has His source in the Son and thus proceeds from Him. Again, 'the Holy Spirit is sent by the Son (John xv. 26),' and His mission by the Son implies an authority of the Son in relation to the Holy

---

[1] '   per hoc enim tacite scriptura insinuat, quod quicquid ad divinitatem pertinens de uno trium dicitur, de omnibus est intelligendum, eo quod sunt unus Deus'

[2] Adding that adoption takes place ' per assimilationem ad filium Dei naturalem '

Spirit, yet an authority 'not of lordship or of superiority, but according to source only; so, therefore, the Holy Spirit is from the Son. And if any one may say that the Son likewise is sent by the Holy Spirit, since it is stated in Luke iv. 18 that the Lord said that the words of Isaiah were fulfilled in Himself ['The Spirit of the Lord is upon me,' &c.], it must, however, be borne in mind carefully that the Son is sent by the Holy Spirit in respect of the nature which He assumed. It remains, therefore, that in respect of the eternal Person the Son has authority over the Holy Spirit.' Again, John xvi. 14 means that the Spirit receives the Divine Essence of the Son. The following verse is then taken in conjunction, with the remark: 'If all things which belong to the Father belong also to the Son, the authority of the Father, in accordance with which is the source of the Holy Spirit, must also belong to the Son. Therefore, just as the Holy Spirit receives from the Father of what is the Father's, so He receives from the Son of what is the Son's;' and this conclusion is supported by citations from the Fathers, including certain Greek Fathers who are represented as agreeing with the Latin view.

The *Filioque* is next reasoned from the fact that the Father is the Source of two functions, *paternitas* and *spiratio*. 'The Son is from the Father, so also is the Holy Spirit. Therefore the Father must be related both to the Son and to the Holy Spirit as the source (*principium*) to that which is from the source. Now He is related to the Son by reason of paternity, but He is not so to the Holy Spirit; because then the Holy Spirit would be a Son. For paternity is spoken of only in respect of the Son. Hence there must be another relation in the Father by which He may be related to the Holy Spirit, and which may be called a "breathing-forth" (*spiratio*). Similarly, as there is in the Son a certain relation by which He is related to the Father, which is called "filiation" (*filatio*), there must be in the Holy Spirit also another relation by which He may be related to the Father, and which may be called "procession." And so as touching the "origin" of the Son from the Father there are two relations, one in the Person "originating," the other in the Person "originated," namely paternity and filiation; and two others as touching the "origin" of the Holy Spirit from the Father, namely breathing forth and procession. But paternity and breathing forth do not set up two Persons, but relate to the one Person of the Father, seeing that they are not mutually in opposition. Neither therefore would filiation and procession set up two Persons, but would relate to one Person, except that they are mutually in opposition. It is impossible, however, to concede any other opposition than that which relates to source. Therefore there must be an opposition as touching source between the Son and the Holy Spirit, so that One is from the Other.' The *Filioque* is thus a necessity in thought to account for the allowed distinction between the second and third Persons of the Trinity, for, adds Aquinas, 'if the Father alone be the Source of the procession of the Holy Spirit, the Holy Spirit would thus not be distinct from the Son. . . . Hence,' he continues, 'for the purpose of conserving the distinction between the Holy Spirit and the Son, it does not suffice to say that the Son proceeds by way of understanding (*per modum intellectus*) and the Holy Spirit by way of will (*per modum voluntatis*), unless, along with this, it is also stated that the Holy Spirit is from the Son.' Further, 'the Father and the Son are so one in Essence that They differ only in this, that This is the Father, and This the Son; so that whatever else there is is common to the Father and the Son. But being the Source of the Holy Spirit has nothing to do with (*est praeter*) the relation of paternity and filiation; for the relation by which the Father is Father is different from that by which the Father is the Source of the Holy Spirit. Therefore, being the Source of the Holy Spirit is common to the Father and the Son.' The chapter concludes with the assertion: 'Hence the Son is the Source of the Holy Spirit.'

In the following chapter Aquinas considers objections to the *Filioque* on the ground that in certain passages it is not expressly mentioned, but he meets them with the assertion that the *Filioque* is herein implied on account of the oneness of Essence of the Father and the Son. Then in Chapter xxvi. he argues that there can only be three Persons in the Godhead. 'For the Divine Persons, since They agree in Essence, can be distinguished only by relation of source. Now it is clearly not within reason that these relations of source should hold in respect of any procession extending to things without (for what proceeds in this manner would not be co-essential with its own source); but the procession must remain within (*interius*). A procession of this kind, remaining within its own source, is found only in the action of understanding and will. . . . Therefore there can be in God only two Persons proceeding, One by way of understanding, as the Word, or Son; and the Other by way of love, or as Holy Spirit; there is also one Person not proceeding, namely the Father. Hence there can be only three Persons in the Trinity.' The same conclusion can be reached by considering the implications of the term 'procession,' according to the manner of which the Persons are distinguishable. 'The mode of a Person (*modus personae*) as regards procession can only be threefold; for instance, it may be one of not proceeding at all, which belongs to the Father; or one of proceeding from One who does not proceed, which belongs to the Son; or one of proceeding from One who does proceed, which belongs to the Holy Spirit. Therefore it is impossible to maintain more than three Persons.' Aquinas adds that the distinction between the Persons of the Godhead rests solely upon Their mutual relations.[1] Finally, Chapter xxxix. contains the assertion that the Incarnation of the Son does not involve the Incarnation of the Father or the Holy Spirit, 'seeing that the Incarnation did not happen in respect of the oneness of Nature in which the three Divine Persons agree, but in respect of hypostasis and individual character (*suppositum*) according to which the three Persons are distinguished.' Only one Person of the Trinity is herein affected.

More famous even than the *Summa contra Gentiles* is the *Summa Theologica*, the work of his last years. It is a compendium of theology pure and simple, being known as the first attempt at a complete theological system. As such it still remains the great standard of Roman Catholic teaching.

To Aquinas 'sacred doctrine is knowledge, derived from the higher principles which are peculiar to God and the saints,'[2] so that spiritual things must be spiritually discerned. Beginning with the subject of God, we find that He is simple (*q.* 3), perfect (*q.* 4), good (*q.* 6), infinite (*q.* 7), omnipresent (*q.* 8), immutable (*q.* 9), and eternal (*q.* 10). Thus God in His absolute oneness and infinite perfection is the One by whom exists the

---

[1] Chap xxvi also contains this trinitarian analogy. 'Mens ipsa, mens concepta in intellectu, et mens amata in voluntate'

[2] *Summa Theol*, Paris edition, 1853, by Drioux, *quaest* 1, art 2.

order of the whole universe. The unity of the Divine Nature excludes the thought of a plurality of Gods, as also does the 'infinitude of His perfection.' Indeed, a one only First Cause is a necessity to all thought, as the philosophers have shown. Moreover, the very oneness of the universe reflects the oneness of its Creator, for it is God who reduces all things to one order,[1] displaying in that order His attributes of love, justice, mercy, providence, and power.[2] Within the Godhead any procession must follow the course of the operation of the Divine Mind, and a procession *ad intra* remains within its own source. So the Word is begotten by the Father by reason of 'similitude in Nature.' But there is another procession *ad intra*, namely that of the Holy Spirit. 'Beside the procession of the Divine Word which follows the action of God's understanding, there is another procession of love which follows the action of His will. . . . For there is a procession of love only in order in respect of the procession of the Word. For nothing can be loved by the will unless it has been conceived in the understanding.' The procession of the Son is thus by reason of likeness (*secundum rationem similitudinis*), while the procession of the Spirit is by reason of will (*secundum rationem voluntatis*); 'and therefore, because He [the Spirit] proceeds in the Godhead by way of love, He does not proceed as begotten, or as Son, but rather does He proceed as Spirit; which name denotes some vital motion and impulse.' There is no third procession in the Godhead beside these.[3]

There are real relations revealed within the Deity, but the distinctions between them are respective rather than absolute. 'In God,' remarks Aquinas, 'there are only four real relations —paternity, filiation, spiration, and procession—which alone exist really and inwardly in God.'[4] Spiration, or 'breathing forth,' is the term used in respect of the Source of the Spirit's procession, while 'procession' is that used in respect of the One who proceeds. Attention is drawn to the fact that 'equality and likeness in God are not real relations, but only relations of reason.'[5]

Connected with the term 'relation' is the term 'person,' defined by Aquinas as 'an indivisible substance of rational

---

[1] *Ibid*, q 11 [2] *Ibid*, qq 20–25 [3] *Ibid*, q 27
[4] *Ibid*, q 32, contains these four, together with *innascibilitas*, as the five only *notiones* in the Deity [5] *Ibid*, q 28

nature,' and applied in a far higher sense to God as expressing the perfection of His Nature.[1] Since there are real relations within the Godhead, and the word ' person ' distinctly implies relation, there are Persons in the Godhead—three Persons or Substances in one Essence, or, in Greek terminology, three hypostases. The act of procession belongs 'actively' to the Father and the Son, ' passively ' to the Holy Spirit ; and, seeing that in the Deity love is co-essential because it is Divine, the procession of love is not spoken of as generation.[2]

' In the Godhead, the name of Trinity must be used to signify determinately the very same that plurality signifies indeterminately.' The ' Trinity ' means a unity of order and of Essence, and, in this connexion, triplicity (*triplicitas*) ought not to be used of God because it implies that three persons might be more than one.[3] ' It is impossible,' he continues, ' to arrive at a conception of a Trinity of Divine Persons by means of natural reasoning. . . Certainly those things which pertain to the unity of the Essence can be learned of God by means of natural reasoning, but not those things which pertain to the distinction of the Persons. On the contrary, he who endeavours to demonstrate the Trinity of Persons by natural reasoning doubly detracts from faith.'[4]

The Father is the One from whom are the Son and the Holy Spirit ; accordingly He may be regarded as Their Source (*principium*)—a statement which implies no other authority than the fact that He is Their Source.[5] Regarding the Holy Spirit, various objections are cited by Aquinas to the effect that the name ' Holy Spirit ' is not a distinguishing characteristic (*proprium*) of any Divine Person ; but he quotes 1 John v. 7 (A.V.) in opposition to these, with the conclusion that ' the name of " Holy Spirit " is the distinguishing characteristic of the Divine Person who proceeds as Love.' However, the *procession* within the Deity which is by way of love does not possess a particular name ; wherefore also the relations which govern this procession are unnamed. It would seem, then, that the name of the Person who proceeds in this manner does not possess a particular name, for the same reason. But custom has named the conceptions of ' procession ' and ' spiration '

---

[1] *Ibid*, q 29 Cf q 39, where *persona* is described as ' relatio subsistens in divina natura,' the Persons of the Godhead being distinguished really by reason of an ' opposite real relation '
[2] *Ibid*, q 30 [3] *Ibid*, q 31 [4] *Ibid*, q 32 [5] *Ibid*, q 33

as such, so that it is convenient to take from Scriptural usage the name of 'Holy Spirit,' 'in order to signify the Divine Person who proceeds by way of love.' Augustine is called in to support the arguments (i.) that the Holy Spirit is common to the Father and the Son, being both 'Spirit' and 'Holy'; (ii.) that, as the word 'Spirit' implies impulse and motion, 'it is the distinguishing characteristic of love, in that it moves and impels the will of the person loving toward the person loved.' The relation of these facts in and to God warrants the attribution of 'holiness' to the Spirit.

On the subject of the *Filioque*, Athanasius is asserted to be able to hold his own against the false and unnecessary attitude of the East, as set forth in the Creed of Constantinople and in such writers as John of Damascus. The conclusion of Aquinas is that 'the Holy Spirit necessarily proceeds from the Son, because, if He did not so proceed, He would not be distinguished from Him personally.' Care is required in distinguishing between the Divine Persons so as not to overlook the oneness of Their Essence. They are distinguished by 'opposite relations.' The Father has two relations with the Son and the Holy Spirit which are not opposite; hence they constitute the one Person of the Father. On the other hand, this reasoning would make the Son and the Holy Spirit one Person, since Their relations to the Father are not mutually opposite, and this would be heretical. 'Therefore the Son and the Holy Spirit must be related to Each Other by opposite relations. Now there cannot be in the Godhead any opposite relations other than relations of source. But opposite relations of source are understood in respect of the principle, and in respect of what is from the principle. Therefore it remains that we must say, either that the Son is from the Holy Spirit, which no one says, or that the Holy Spirit is from the Son, which we confess. And with this, indeed, the mode of the procession of Each One is in perfect accord.' A second 'proof' of the *Filioque* is then recalled, to the effect that Love must proceed from the Word because 'we do not love anything unless we have apprehended it by a conception of the mind.' It is of course impossible, adds Aquinas, to conceive of any material distinction between the Persons of the Trinity. The Greeks themselves understand that the procession of the Holy Spirit bears some relation of order to the Son: 'for they concede the Holy Spirit to be the Spirit of the Son, and to be from the Father through the Son ; and certain of them are said to concede that He is from the Son, or that He is breathed forth by Him, yet not that He proceeds from Him ; which seems to be either ignorance or impudence.' At least, Scripture clearly indicates that whatever is spoken of concerning the Father must also be understood of the Son, with the one exception of those things in which They are distinguished in respect of opposite relations. ' So then, when it is stated that the Holy Spirit proceeds from the Father, even if it should be added that He proceeds from the Father only, the Son would not thereupon be excluded.' Moreover, the procession of the Holy Spirit is co-eternal with its own Source, thus being eternal, and therefore not following in order of time the generation of the Son. Also the Father and the Son together are one Source of the Holy Spirit, who proceeds from Them as the united love (*amor unitivus* or *mutuus=nexus*) of the Two. And ' just as the Father is not more like Himself than He is like the Son, so neither is the Son more like the Father than is the Holy Spirit.'[1]

The three Persons of the Deity are of one Essence (John x. 30, 38),[2] and are thus unlike persons that are human. For in the Deity the relations and individual natures that are in the Persons are also the Persons Themselves. Paternity is the Father, filiation the Son, and procession the Holy Spirit. ' The individual natures determine and distinguish the Persons, but not the Essence ' ; and ' the Divine Persons or Hypostases are distinguished by Their relations rather than by Their Source.'[3] ' There is only one Father, one Son, and one Holy Spirit in the Godhead ; for forms of one kind (such as paternity, filiation, &c.) are multiplied only in respect of matter, which does not exist in God.'[4] Moreover, these Three are necessarily equal to One Another, on account of the oneness of the Divine Essence. For ' quantity in the Godhead is nothing else than Its Essence. Whence it remains that, if there were any inequality among the Divine Persons, there would not be among Them one Essence. And so the three Persons would not be one God ; which is impossible. Therefore equality *must* be maintained among the Divine Persons.'[5]

[1] *Ibid*, q 36   [2] *Ibid*, 39   [3] *Ibid*, 40   [4] *Ibid*, q 41
[5] *Ibid*, q 42   He adds that the order of Nature of the Divine Persons is without priority

Finally, in Question 43 (in eight articles), Aquinas touches upon the Mission of the Holy Spirit. He declares that 'it is fitting for a Divine Person to be sent, inasmuch as He has His source in another Person.' A mission which is a distinct act, otherwise than generation and breathing forth, is of a temporal nature; 'wherefore a "sending" or a "giving" are spoken of only temporally, generation and breathing forth only eternally.' This mission of the Spirit refers only to the bestowal of Divine grace. So the Son and the Holy Spirit can manifestly be 'sent,' seeing that They are Both from the Father[1]; for 'since it becomes the Son and the Holy Spirit to dwell by grace within the mind of a rational nature, and also to be from Another, it must also become Them to be invisibly sent.'[2] Further, the missions of the Son and of the Holy Spirit are not separate from each other, for these Persons Themselves are not separate, and also both Their missions are of Divine grace. For though all gifts are attributed to the Holy Spirit, since it is He who bestows the greatest gift of love, certain gifts are nevertheless attributed to the Son, such as those which belong to the intellect. In addition, however, to the invisible mission of the Son and of the Holy Spirit, 'it became the Son and the Holy Spirit to be sent visibly; the Son as the Author of sanctification, the Holy Spirit as the Evidence (*indicium*) of sanctification. And so the Son is said to be less than the Father by reason of an assumed nature. But the Holy Spirit did not assume into the unity of a person the visible creature in which He appeared, that what was adopted by Him might be predicated of Him. Wherefore it cannot be said that He is less than the Father on account of a visible creature [of the dove, or of fire].' The creaturely forms in which the Spirit of God was manifested were not assumed to enable Him to *do* anything, but were simply signs or evidences;[3] while it must be remembered that 'in the case of mission, as of procession, a Person is sent only by that Person from whom He eternally proceeds; that is, the Son is sent by the Father, the Holy Spirit by the Father and the Son.'

Mention of the work of the Spirit is not so frequent in the

[1] 'Missio importat processionem'

[2] The Father cannot be 'sent,' but He can 'indwell' (John xiv 23)

[3] 'Spiritus sanctus visibiliter dicitur esse missus, inquantum fuit monstratus in quibusdam creaturis, sicut in signis ad hoc specialiter factis Neque oportuit quod creatura visibilis ad hoc formata esset assumpta a Spiritu sancto in unitatem personae; cum non assumeretur ad aliquid agendum, sed ad indicandum tantum'

Summa Theologica as in the *Contra Gentiles,* and its lack of the experimental element is disappointing. At the same time, Thomas Aquinas was a Schoolman with the aim of a Schoolman, and the way in which he marshals scripture and philosophy in the cause of orthodoxy is brilliant indeed. The charge that he makes the Trinity practically three aspects of the one God cannot be substantiated ; on the other hand, he leaves Albertus far behind in consideration of the more ' practical ' side of the Doctrine of the Spirit. Schoolman though he was, he felt what he taught ; and Scholasticism reached its climax in one who, for depth of piety and of learning, is unsurpassed in the history of the Mediaeval Church.[1]

---

[1] Thomas Aquinas had an ardent disciple in Aegidius Colonna (1247–1316), Archbishop of Bourges, and a writer on the *Sentences* Raimundus Lullus (1235–1315) also figures in this period, but his complicated reasonings afford nothing particularly worthy of note in this connexion.

PART III

FROM THE CLOSE OF THE THIRTEENTH CENTURY TO THE BEGINNING OF THE SIXTEENTH CENTURY

THE PRE-REFORMATION PERIOD

    I. FOREWORD
   II. DECADENT SCHOLASTICISM
  III. THE SCHOLASTIC REVIVAL
  IV. THE ANTI-SCHOLASTIC MYSTICS
    V. THE EASTERN CHURCH
  VI. THE PRE-REFORMATION REFORMERS
 VII. THE HUMANISTS

'The Dove lights on no carrion'—LANCELOT ANDREWES.

'Some think that the love of the Father and blood of the Son will do, without the holiness of the Spirit of God, but they are deceived . . There is a sort that think the holiness of the Spirit is sufficient of itself; but they (if they had it) are deceived also; for it must be the grace of the Father, the grace of the Son, and the grace of the Spirit, jointly, that must save them.'
—JOHN BUNYAN.

I

FOREWORD

THE two centuries here under survey contain the history of a long preparation for the Reformation, a preparation to which differing schools of thought made their contributions. After Thomas Aquinas it soon became clear that the 'rationalistic' outlook introduced by Duns Scotus meant ultimately the suicide of Scholasticism, and that the demolition of one structure would also mean the erection of another. Speculative Thomism, which stood in the main for Catholic orthodoxy, and the more critical Scotism which followed Duns, made the Doctrine of the Trinity one of their points of collision, the former not desiring to probe so deeply into the personal distinctions of the Godhead as the latter.[1] The separation of philosophy from theology which Duns Scotus had begun was carried to greater lengths by Occam and Durandus, whose Nominalism completed the disintegration of the Scholastic system. Occamism, which was decidedly sceptical as compared with Thomism, thus succeeded in driving a wedge between authority and science, the same revealed truth in which Occam himself sincerely believed being actually disparaged by him on account of its alleged illogical nature!

Scholasticism remained influential until the death of Gabriel Biel (1495), but during the fourteenth century the German School of Mysticism arose and endeavoured to explain the Deity and His relations with the race from an entirely different standpoint, much of its thought possessing a pantheistic tendency. The need for a new ground of appeal can be seen by the fact that the movement at the commencement of the fifteenth century for the regeneration of Scholasticism took a mystical turn, though Scholasticism and Mysticism, being ecclesiastical and subjective respectively, were two points of

[1] This attitude of the Scotists is reminiscent of that of the Nominalists of the twelfth century Free thought with reference to the Trinity will be seen in its extreme in Socinianism, which had no regard for the authority of the Church

view which could never quite coincide.[1] Fourteenth-century Mysticism was not an exclusively clerical movement. It embodied and expressed a passion for personal piety which emphasized the necessity for the indwelling of the Spirit,[2] and, as such, it represented the very opposite of the Nominalism of the Occamists, while in its idea of salvation as being attainable largely through self-abnegation it resembled the Scholastic Mysticism of the earlier period. It is true that Mysticism, in its desire for union of the soul with God, laid stress upon the Divine Unity rather than upon the Trinity, but this simply signified the importance of the former without implying any denial of the latter. Though these Mystics were introspective and not dialectical, they were no less Catholic than the Schoolmen. At the same time the majority of them insisted on the practical and experimental side of religion, and thereby helped to prepare the way for the Reformation. So also, as may be expected, did the pre-Reformation Reformers, and this in spite of the fact that, with the exception of Wyclif and Huss, they remained within the fold of Catholicism. These heralds of the Reformation indeed failed in their attempts at reform even as the Paris doctors failed in theirs, but they did succeed in preserving the continuity of the essential features of Catholic theology.

Inseparable from the great drift towards the Reformation was the Renaissance. Like Mysticism, Humanism was not exclusively clerical; it also had a practical character. It was a liberalizing movement directed not against the Church (though critical of it) but against ignorance, and therefore against the exclusive rigidity and subtlety of Scholastic reasoning held responsible for it. If the system created by the Schoolmen had already received its defeat at the hands of the Nominalists, the Humanists gave it the *coup de grâce*. The study of the New Testament in Greek, which had become possible before as well as after the fall of Constantinople, helped forward the desire for truth as over against the desire for the abstruse. Hence the work of the Humanists was preparatory to the work of the Reformers in that it revealed the narrowing effect of much of the prevailing theology of the

---

[1] It has been said that Scholasticism ended in Roman Curialism, Mysticism in the Reformation. The Mystics also laid a new emphasis upon Bible study

[2] The Mystics worked from within to without in their discovery of God (Inge, *Christian Mysticism*, pp. 27 f.)

age. In addition, that experimental view of religion which the Reformers preached, when they emphasized the work of the Holy Spirit in the human heart, was clearly foreshadowed in the writings of Colet.

The Doctrine of the Holy Spirit in this period will be illustrated by twenty-eight writers apportioned approximately to their several centuries thus : one to the thirteenth, ten to the fourteenth, ten to the fifteenth, and six to the sixteenth. There is also one writer taken from the Eastern Church, between which and the Church of the West a wider gulf than ever can be seen. In this case, however, the chronological grouping of sources has but little significance as showing any varied interest in the subject under review. During the thirteenth century the great Scholastics had already written extensively on the Doctrines of the Holy Spirit and the Trinity, while the mass of the sixteenth-century contributors still remain to be considered in connexion with the Reformation itself. Nevertheless it is possible that even more might have been written on these doctrines in the thirteenth and fourteenth centuries had not the Doctrine of the Atonement consumed much argumentative energy during the former, and a sacramentarian development of Scholasticism during the latter.

II

DECADENT SCHOLASTICISM

THE edifice of the Schoolmen, which had received no real strength from its Aristotelian buttresses, was shaken to its foundations during the early part of this period by certain of its professed upholders. First among these is the Englishman ROGER BACON (1214–1294), whose aim cannot in point of fact be defined as pro-ecclesiastical or pro-Scholastic in actual practice. Philosopher, mathematician, and natural scientist, he displayed a knowledge so extensive as in those days to be regarded as magical, and he applied his great learning in part to the exposition of dogma. His physico-theology is seen in the *Opus Majus*, his principal work, written during his first imprisonment at the request of Pope Clement IV. In the fourth part, under the head of mathematical science, he observes that the Trinity is symbolized by the form of a triangle, each of its angles being distinct and yet embracing the whole space. ' It is impossible,' he urges, ' for the blessed Trinity and the Unity of Essence to be more adequately represented by the example of a rational creature than by means of geometry.' For again in a single triangle there is a unity of essence together with a distinction between the three angles which contain this essence or the whole space within the triangle. These are nevertheless distinct angles even while embracing the whole, and such geometrical truths point to similar truths not in human life but only in God. Euclid speaks of erecting an equilateral triangle upon a given line ; in the same figure, then, given the Person of the Father, the fact of a Trinity of equal Persons in the Deity can also be appreciated.[1]

Part vii. treats the subject of moral philosophy from various standpoints, and of these the theological is of interest as reviewing the Doctrine of the Trinity. Moral philosophy sets forth this doctrine as a truth arrived at through

[1] Chap. v , on *Mathematicae in Divinis Utilitas* (ed J H Bridges, Oxford, 1897).

revelation rather than through reason. ' The metaphysician,' continues Bacon, ' has been able to teach sufficiently that God is, that He is naturally (*naturaliter*) comprehended, that He is of infinite power, that He is One, and that He is Threefold (*trinus*). But how in that case there may exist a Trinity he has not been able fully to explain ; and for that reason this must be verified here.' Accordingly the statement is made that ' there exists a Blessed Trinity—Father, Son, and Holy Spirit.' Anticipations of a Divine Trinity there have been before Christ in the teachings of Plato, Porphyry, and Aristotle, though naturally they are merely anticipations. These pre-Christian philosophers had conceptions of a second Person in the Deity, but, adds Bacon, the existence of a Holy Spirit was not so easily understood by them, ' for it is more difficult to understand the procession of the Holy Spirit from two distinct Persons than the generation of One of Them from Another.' The Christian Doctrine of the Trinity, however, is presented in a short statement to the effect that there are three Persons in the one Godhead, equal in love and in power ; that the Son and the Holy Spirit derive from the Father ; that the Personality of Each is distinct and real ; and that no fourth Person is at all possible. The very Nature of God, which is Love, demands a plurality of Persons within It for the purpose of Its own self-expression ; and this is a truth which mathematics can illustrate, though not prove.

Duns Scotus.

The beginnings of division between theology and philosophy, between the Church and Scholasticism, as illustrated by Bacon's treatment at the hands of Bonaventura, the General of his Order, are intensified by Duns Scotus (1266–1308), one of the most brilliant of the Schoolmen. Joining the Franciscan Order, he studied at Oxford, then lectured there and, from 1304, at Paris on theology and philosophy. Attracted as he was by Nominalism, he brought to bear upon the labours of his predecessors that rational tendency which promoted the Thomist and Scotist controversy and prepared the way for the Nominalism of Occam. His practical mind criticized the speculative outlook of Aquinas, holding the basis of theology to be essentially practical He was unorthodox in reference to the method of demonstrating theological truth, but not so in reference to the truth itself[1]; and, while he emphasized the personal distinctions within the Deity more than Aquinas had done, the strict Catholicism of his teaching was never called in question.

His views on the Doctrines of the Trinity and the Holy Spirit are concisely set forth in his commentary on the first book of the *Sentences* of Lombardus, written at Oxford (*opus Oxoniense*).[2] In the simple and undivided Essence of the Godhead there is the Father, together with two distinct and opposite emanations, the Son, by way of Nature, and the Holy Spirit, by way of Will. The Father and the Son are one Source of the Holy Spirit. The fact, however, that the Son proceeds *per modum naturae* and the Holy Spirit *per modum voluntatis* at once suggests that Their processions could not be simultaneous, the first necessarily being before the second.[3] The Holy Spirit is referred to as Love, and as 'personally distinct.' He who is brought forth as Love is not begotten; and 'this Person I speak of as Holy Spirit, because the Son is not brought forth in such a manner.'[4] Indeed, the Son, having been previously brought forth by the power of the One who begets, possesses the productive principle of the Holy Spirit *before* the Holy Spirit is brought forth.[5] But this implies no conflict of productive principles, the Father and the Son breathing forth the Holy Spirit in every sense uniformly and simultaneously. In exterior activity, however, such as in the work of creation, simultaneous action is extended to the Three, who here operate as One.[6] Yet the consideration of the interior harmony of thought and action characteristic of the Godhead never weakens the emphasis of Duns Scotus on the subject of the personal distinctions, and he continues to insist upon the distinction between generation and procession.[7] This distinction is illustrated by the respective modes of manifestation adopted by the Son and the Spirit, thus:

[1] Cf Erdmann, *ibid*, 1, pp 485, 501. For points of difference between Aquinas and Duns see *ibid*, pp 489 ff
[2] Ed 1639, with expositions of the *Scholia* of Duns by Franciscus Lychetus
[3] *Dist* 8, q 4 'Sic haec conclusio Filius prius producitur a Patre quam Spiritus sanctus' (Lychetus); also *dist* 11, q 1 (Lychetus) Duns upholds the *Filioque* again in Vol iii of this edition, *Theorema* 14, § 19 He further notes the eternal distinctions of the Deity in the *scholium* to *dist* 25
[4] *Dist* 10 The expositor Lychetus at this point attacks Occam on several grounds, asserting that the *voluntas Dei* is *not* the *principium* of the Holy Spirit.
[5] *Dist* 11, q 1
[6] *Dist* 12, q 3
[7] *Dist* 13 Lychetus comments 'Non proprie ignis dicitur generari. Modo Sp s non dicitur generari, quia talis productio non est per modum naturae'

' Since the Holy Spirit did not unite to Himself the nature of a perceptible form (*signum*) by which His procession used to be manifested; therefore it is unreasonable that those things which are applicable to the nature of such a form should be applicable to the Holy Spirit. But the Son united to Himself human nature in the oneness of a Person; therefore those things which are spoken of the nature are truly spoken of the hypostasis (*suppositum*) subsisting in that nature; and therefore the Son can be called less than the Father by reason of the united nature. This is not so, however, with the Holy Spirit, because He does not have being in a special manner in such a nature, except, as it were, in form.'[1] Similar opinions had already been expressed by Aquinas.

The *scholium* of Duns in reference to the eighteenth *distinction* of Lombardus is principally concerned with definitions of terms. The *proprietas* of the third Person of the Trinity is, he remarks, generally characterized by the name ' Holy Spirit.' Not that by the word ' Spirit ' is understood merely a spiritual or an intellectual nature, for, by that interpretation, this term is common to all three Persons. But it is recognized that ' Holy Spirit ' is the designation of the one Holy Will of the Father and the Son, as breathed forth by Them[2]; and as such He is present to Himself as the Source of infinite love, and is therefore self-contained as Holy Spirit. Again, the Holy Spirit may be discerned by the term ' Gift,' relating to Him as ' the united Love of the Father and the Son, whereby the Father lavishes love upon the Son, and He [the Son] returns the same love.' The name ' Holy Spirit ' signifies eternal procession, or an eternal distinction within the Godhead. It also points to a direction of operation in respect of God's creatures which is not suggested by the generation of the Son, for the Son proceeds by way of Nature and not of Gift.

Consistent with the importance which his system of philosophy attaches to the individual, Duns insists that the Persons of the Trinity are Themselves positively distinguished from One Another. The Father, for instance, is personally distinguished from the Son and the Holy Spirit by that by which He is constituted in personal Being. As to the mutual

---
[1] *Dist* 14   [2] ' Accipiendo " Spiritus sanctus " pro spirato voluntate unica et sancta Patris et Filii, quia talis voluntas habens objectum infinitum, infinite diligibile sibi praesens est principium sufficiens producendi amorem infinitum, et per consequens per se stantem, qui " Spiritus " dicitur '

relations of source, even if they are real, these neither distinguish nor do they constitute the Persons.[1]

NICOLAS OF LYRA.

Among the Scotists may be reckoned Nicolas of Lyra (c. 1270–1340), a French Biblical commentator of whose personal life comparatively little is known. His opinions with regard to the procession of the Spirit receive frequent expression in his works, and are consistently Western. On the text 'When the Comforter is come, whom I will send unto you from the Father' (John xv. 26, R.V.), he comments: 'In this He [Jesus] makes known the Holy Spirit as proceeding from Himself inasmuch as He asserts that He sends Him': and the addition—'even the Spirit of truth, which proceedeth from the Father'—is one 'in which He shows that the Holy Spirit proceeds from the Father because He proceeds from Both.'[2] Mission thus implies source, which is by no means an unusual argument. What *is* unusual, is to find the procession from the Father asserted on the ground of the truth of the *Filioque*!

Nicolas makes some interesting observations on St. John xvi. The Holy Spirit is essentially the Truth and the effective Teacher of the same. He is not from Himself but from the Father and the Son, which is the reason of His not speaking from Himself. 'What things soever He shall hear, these shall He speak' (v. 13. R.V.)—'that is, to you. But this must not be understood generally of everything which the Holy Spirit hears from the Father and the Son, because He receives from Them infinite knowledge; but it must be understood of everything pertaining to salvation and to the guidance of the Church.' The statement 'He shall glorify Me; for He shall take of Mine' &c. (v. 14), is explained 'by proceeding from Me. And it must not be understood by this that He receives part of the Essence of the Son; because He is indivisible, and therefore if He takes anything He takes all. But every word proceeding from any one naturally reveals him; so also the Holy Spirit, proceeding from the Son and receiving all His Essence, reveals Him wholly (*totum ipsum*). And that the Holy Spirit proceeds from Him He shows in His next remark.' This next remark of Jesus contained in v. 15 draws the

---
[1] *Dist* 26, various *scholia*   Duns observes that perfection in the absolute is infinite, but not *proprietas hypostatica*.
[2] Ed 1634

following observation from Nicolas: 'All things which are the Father's are imparted to the Son with the exception of the paternal character in which He is distinguished from the Son ; and in consequence the power of spiration (*virtus spirativa*) is imparted to the Son.' This must be so seeing that the power of spiration and the paternal character, as such, are not related exclusively. ' And this is the reason why the Holy Spirit proceeds from the Son just as from the Father, because They are one (*unum*) in power of spiration.' Finally, the noted interpolation 1 John v. 7 (A.V). is brought in as an authority for the Doctrine of the Trinity thus : ' The Blessed Trinity reveals Itself to the saints in a distinction of Persons, an emanation of the Word from the Father, and of the Holy Spirit from Both.' The Father is unbegotten, the Word is begotten by Him, and the Holy Spirit proceeds from the Father and the Word. ' And these Three are One,' that is ' in Essence, and so are one God, above all, full of glory.'

WILLIAM OF OCCAM AND DURANDUS

With William of Occam (Ockham or Ockam) (†.c. 1349) there flowed in the full tide of nominalistic thought which was to sweep away the foundations of mediaeval Scholasticism already weakened by the work of the Scotists, and clear the way for the later scepticism. Occam is said to have been a pupil of Duns Scotus at Paris, where also he afterwards lectured. As critic, logician, ecclesiastical politician, and pioneer of the later Nominalism, he employed his versatile mind with varying fortunes, meeting with decided opposition in the promotion of his philosophy[1] ; but, in spite of the opposition, his followers became numerous, and include such celebrities

[1] Among those who strove in vain to stem the tide of Nominalism were Thomas Bradwardine († 1349), Archbishop of Canterbury, and Antoninus († 1459) In Bradwardine's philosophical work *De Causa Dei* there is little by way of contribution to the Doctrine of the Spirit in a treatise which lays stress upon God in His unity. But for that very reason he would ascribe the Divine attributes to the Holy Spirit, whose Godhead he distinctly affirms (1 42, &c) He is ardent in his defence of orthodoxy against heresy, declaiming against the Arians who say that ' the Holy Spirit is a temporal creation of the Son,' against the Donatists who assert that ' the Son is less than the Father, and the Holy Spirit less than Both,' and against the Sabellians ' who assume among the Father, Son, and Holy Spirit a unity and identity of Essence and of Person ' Neither is Each Person of the Trinity God *successively* (1 22 ff) The Holy Spirit is stated to have been instrumental in the Birth of Christ, being also sent into the world by Christ after His resurrection (*ibid* , 32) : He is thus by no means ' an incorporeal nothing,' as the Epicureans and Sadducees suggest (*ibid* , 36) Whereas the name of love may be given to Each Person of the Trinity, it is peculiarly the possession of the Holy Spirit (*ibid* , 42), who, as the Divine Goodness and Will (11 13), proceeds equally from the Father and the Son (*ibid* , 30) Bradwardine's outlook was Augustinian

as Durandus, Buridanus, Marsilius of Inghen, and Biel. He completed the divorce of theology from philosophy by abandoning Realism—the only force which could maintain their union. As long as a thing and its idea possessed equal reality, so long was there a common ground for faith and science; but when the Occamists began to declare that universal ideas are merely names, they abandoned theology to the realm of revelation and to the guardianship of Church authority. Thus what Erdmann calls the 'dualism' of Occam arises when he criticizes certain doctrines (including the Trinity) as illogical, and then confesses his Catholic adherence to them as being true in one sense if not in another! In this dualism lay the forces of disruption. It was not that Occam was less orthodox than Duns, or that he was intentionally insincere. His disparagement of theological 'contradictions,' followed by his pious adhesion to them, was evidently designed to show that reason and authority *both* have place in the world of thought, though the result of his teaching was that they could no longer live together. The very importance which he attached to philosophy left his theology somewhat anaemic, and in his *Questions on the four books of Sentences* (Lyons, 1495) he does not justify all the dogmatism of his predecessors.[1] Yet his impatience at the hair-splitting subtleties which characterized so much of the theology of the Schoolmen was his unconscious contribution to the gathering forces which culminated in the Reformation.

The views to which Occam gave expression may, to curtail repetition, be found substantially in the *Commentary on the Sentences* written by DURANDUS of Sancto Porciano (St. Pourçain) (†1334), Bishop of Meaux, styled by Wagenmann 'the most prominent representative of Scholasticism in the fourteenth century.'[2] Answering in the Prologue the preliminary question as to whether theology is a science, he replies that it is not properly and strictly such, for, while it is invaluable as a practical guide to the Christian life, it cannot displace the authority of reason, which is no longer to be regarded as

---

[1] Erdmann (*ibid*) i p 513. 'He will have nothing to do with the statement that the Son has His cause in the understanding, the Holy Spirit in the will of the Father Both proceed from the nature of God, and understanding and will are the same'

[2] Herzog, *Encycl* His *Commentarii in Sententias Theologicas Petri Lombardi* was, according to Wagenmann (*ibid*), recommended by Gerson to his pupils as the best work on the subject The edition Venice, 1595, contains many misprints

the handmaid of faith but as its own mistress. This outlook clearly shows the author's break with Thomism, and also the standpoint from which he conducts his examination of the content of the *Sentences*. A threefold Personality, he resumes, is inherent in God, and therefore it is impossible for God to be other than threefold (*trinus*) ; but neither this fact nor its possibility can be demonstrated. ' In the Godhead nature cannot be distinguished,' so that our knowledge that God is one and also threefold is by Divine goodness (*virtute divina et miraculose*). ' For,' proceeds Durandus, ' we say that the distinction of the Divine Persons is effected through Their relations, and not through Their self-existence (*per absoluta*). . . . For if it might be effected through Their self-existence it would necessarily follow that it might be effected either through the Divine Essence Itself being pluralized, which is impossible, or through something self-existent being added to the Essence, and thereby causing a true and real *compositio* in God, which again is impossible.' The article of the Trinity, however, is in his opinion ' very obscure to the human reason ' (*q.* 1). Its truth certainly cannot be demonstrated by reference to facts contained in the world of creation (*q.* 2.). Indeed, since the Infinite cannot be the subject of a finite science, God is not the subject of theology : rather is salvation the subject (*q.* 5). The Unity of God, however, is the only basic principle of philosophic thought.[1]

The syllogistic method employed by Durandus tends occasionally to obscure his own views; these are, nevertheless, usually embedded in modifications of earlier statements. Like Occam, he is critical of the use of fine distinctions. In the Godhead, Essence and relation are the same, and therefore it is impossible that those things which are one in the Godhead through the Essence are really distinct through the relations. ' All the faithful hold that there is one God in respect of Essence, and that there are three Persons, distinct in relations of source ' ; and they demonstrate this by referring to the two most perfect operations in God of understanding and will, asserting the Word to be the product of the former, and Love of the latter. ' It has been shown,' however, ' that an article of faith, especially that of the Trinity, cannot be demonstrated. . . . The impossible does not follow from the possible.' It thus remains

[1] *Lib* 1, *dist* 2, *q* 1.

to deal with the reasons by which previous writers, in particular the Thomists, have endeavoured to demonstrate this article. With regard, then, to the above argument for the Trinity, 'it is absolutely false,' he declares, 'because, among the blessed, the functions of understanding and will by which they see and love God are most perfect operations; and yet through the function of understanding no Word is formed or brought forth, neither through the function of will is any Love brought forth; therefore that argument[1] is absolutely false.' There are reasons for this conclusion. 'Firstly, it cannot be asserted, because emanations (*productiones*) in the Godhead are really distinct; but to will and to understand do not really differ; therefore they are not emanations. Again, to bring forth and to be brought forth cannot coincide in all persons, because one person does not bring forth (as the Holy Spirit), while another is not brought forth (as the Father). But to understand and to will coincide in all persons, therefore they are neither bringing forth nor brought forth, and so they are not emanations, neither actively nor passively. . . . Wherefore in no way through the functions of understanding and will can a plurality of emanative persons be demonstrated.' Hence, adds the author, the existence of the Trinity cannot be proved by human reasoning.[2]

In passing to the consideration of *Distinction* 3, Durandus notes that Lombardus, having established the unity of Essence and the Trinity of Persons by means of authorities (*per auctoritates*), proceeds to establish them by means of natural reasoning (*per rationes naturales*), and then illustrates the Doctrine of the Trinity by means of analogies from the creatures (*per similitudines creaturarum*). He concedes that 'there is in every creature some representation of the Trinity leading us to some kind of idea of the Trinity, although confused. . . . For in every creature is found unity of essence, also three things which equally correspond to the three Persons, although confusedly. For every creature proceeds from God by power according to an order of wisdom, and by reason of Divine goodness; and these three are assigned to the three Persons.'[3] Illustration or suggestion, however, is not demonstration, and the smallness of the writer's concession only serves to

---

[1] 1 e 'Omnis perfecta operatio terminatur ad aliquod operatum,' &c
[2] *Ibid*, q 4
[3] *Dist* 3, q 4

DECADENT SCHOLASTICISM 185

emphasize his principle that reason cannot establish matters of faith. Accordingly he is sceptical of there being in the mind of man any true likeness (*imago*) of the Trinity, for Divine Infinity has no likeness in any creature; neither therefore has the Trinity.[1]

There are, however, distinctions in the Godhead which are acknowledged by the Church even while they cannot be wholly embraced by human reason. We speak of the Holy Spirit as proceeding by way of will, not by way of nature. He is brought forth by the impulse of love (*per actum diligendi*), from which also Love (*amor*) is derived. 'The Father and the Son of necessity breathe forth the Holy Spirit.' The Son proceeds from One, but the Holy Spirit from Two; and since the Spirit proceeds from Both with equal perfection, and not more perfectly from Both together than from One of Them alone, He is said to be brought forth by way of will, and not by way of Nature, as the Son.[2] The question then arises as to whether 'Holy Spirit' is the proper name of any one Divine Person; and at first it would appear not to be, 'because everything which exists and is not tangible substance (*corpus*) is Spirit; but the Father, and any one Divine Person, exists and is not tangible substance; therefore He is Spirit. Also it is certain any One of Them is "Holy"; therefore "Holy Spirit" is not a proper name characteristic of any Divine Person, but is common to any One without distinction. Moreover, what is applicable to the whole Trinity is not applicable to one Person alone; but the name "Holy Spirit" is applicable to the Trinity, in accordance with John iv. 24, "God is a Spirit."' For all that, there is another view which may be taken as correct. 'In another way, however, the name is used in relation to spiration, and thus is applicable alone to the third Person in the Godhead. . . . Since, therefore, the Father is Spirit and the Son Spirit, and Each is Holy, the third Person proceeding jointly from the Father and the Son is appropriately called "Holy Spirit"'; and that name is all the more appropriate to the Spirit seeing that He proceeds as Love *per modum voluntatis*.[3] It must be remembered that there are only three Persons in God as

---
[1] *Ibid*, part 2, *q* 1.
[2] *Dist* 6, *q* 2   The Son is certainly not the Son of the Holy Spirit, since He does not proceed from the Holy Spirit *per generationem*, but from the Father alone *modo naturae—Lib* iii *dist.* 4, *q* 1   [3] *Dist* 10, *q* 1.

represented by the three relations of paternity, filiation, and spiration,[1] and that these Persons are equal.[2]

In introducing the matter of the *Filioque*, Durandus mentions in this connexion the difference ' from us ' of the Eastern divines, who agree that the Holy Spirit is ' the Spirit of the Son, consubstantial with the Son,' but deny that He proceeds from the Son. ' Every opinion,' he writes, 'states that the Holy Spirit proceeds from the Father. Either, then, the Spirit proceeds immediately from the One who begets, and in that case is Himself begotten ; or mediately through the Other, who is begotten. Therefore the Spirit must be from the One who is begotten, which is our proposition.' The Son and the Holy Spirit, then, are brought forth from the Father in this ' order of source,' but there is no question of precedence in Nature or in time ; it simply remains that here is the order by which one thing is from another. ' It is certain, however, that the Son is not from the Holy Spirit ; therefore the Holy Spirit is from the Son.' Again, ' wherever there is plurality without order, there exists confusion. In the Godhead, however, there is plurality without confusion ; therefore in this connexion there exists plurality along with order. But it is known that in the Godhead there is no order by which one thing is after another, as has been shown ; therefore there is here an order by which one thing is from another, which is the same conclusion as the above.'[3] Moreover, 'if the Holy Spirit were immediately from the Father only, as is the Son, His procession would be generation, just as the procession of the Son, because He would proceed by way of nature as the Son, as is clear from what has been said above on *Distinction* 6. This, however, is impossible, for in that case there would be two Persons begotten, that is, two Sons in the Godhead.' The statement embodied in the *Filioque* is thus the only possible inference. Certain it is that the function of breathing forth the Spirit is not a *distinguishing* characteristic of the Father as Father.[4]

[1] *Ibid*, q. 2.
[2] *Dist.* 19, q 1.
[3] *Cp dist* 20, q 2, where an order of Nature is argued from the very existence of a *principium*, but this order does not affect the Divine Essence, for 'realis ordo requirit distinctionem realem, sed in divinis non est distinctio naturae, accipiendo naturam pro essentia vel pro parte essentiae'
[4] *Dist* 11, q 1 ' Pater producens communicat producto filio omne illud in quo ei non opponitur, nec repugnat distinctioni personarum, sed pater non opponitur filio quoad spirare, nec repugnat distinctioni patris et filii communicatio spirationis, ergo spirare potest filio communicari '

The next question arising from this discussion is ' whether, if the Holy Spirit did not proceed from the Son, He would be distinguished from Him.' Durandus considers the suggestion that the personal characteristics (*proprietates*) of the Son and the Holy Spirit would be sufficient for distinction between Them, but he is not of the same mind ; for ' as the Father is one Person having two characteristics according to which He is called " begetting " and " breathing forth," so there would be only one Person emanating from the Father, having two characteristics according to which He would be called " breathed forth " and " begotten." ' Neither are the differing relations between the Persons sufficient for such distinction. ' There is a plurality of differing relations in the Father who brings forth, and they do not distinguish Him among a plurality of Persons. Therefore differing relations are not sufficient cause of a distinction of Persons ; but if the Holy Spirit should not proceed from the Son, nor conversely, there would not be any differing relations between Them ; therefore They could not be personally distinct, but only as one person differs from himself in respect of different characteristics.'[1] The importance of the twofold procession leads to the assertion that the Father and the Son are one Source (*principium*) of the Holy Spirit, since They Themselves are One, differing only in the mutual relations of Fatherhood and Sonship which do not affect the act of spiration.[2] ' Further, the Holy Spirit is brought forth perfectly by the Father, and perfectly by the Son ; therefore the Father and the Son are at one in respect of the measure in which They bring forth the Holy Spirit.' The Holy Spirit may thus be regarded as the bond (*nexus*) of the Father and the Son,[3] and, following from this, the generation of the Son must not be prior to the spiration of the Holy Spirit. These two functions in the Life of God are simultaneous ; and, should trinitarian analogies be brought from the realm of creation purporting to demonstrate the contrary in the uncreated Trinity, our attitude, observes Durandus, would be that ' the one does not perfectly represent the other.'[4] It may be added that while ' the Holy Spirit proceeds no more

[1] *Ibid*, q 2
[2] See *Dist* 29, q 2 · ' vis spirativa quae est ratio producendi Spiritum sanctum est una in patre et filio, ideo,' &c
[3] *Ibid*, q 3   For the Spirit as *nexus*, cf Swete, *Holy Spirit in the N T*, p 152, and *Holy Spirit in the Ancient Church*, p 213 (the interpretation of Athanasius)
[4] *Dist* 12, q 1

completely nor perfectly from the Father than from the Son,' yet 'the Father breathes forth more prominently (*principalius*) than the Son; indeed, He breathes forth from Himself, while the Son breathes forth from Another.'[1] As to the term itself, 'procession' is more fittingly applied to the Holy Spirit because (1) of the scarcity of terms in these matters which pertain to the Holy Spirit; (2) of the suitability of the term 'procession,' itself being by way of will; (3) the Holy Spirit proceeds from more Persons than does the Son, who proceeds from the Father only.[2] The general use of the term, with special application to the Holy Spirit, also serves to maintain the necessary distinction between procession and generation.[3]

The temporal, as well as the eternal, procession of the Holy Spirit claims the attention of Durandus at this point. He speaks of the Spirit as proceeding temporally when He works in the soul of a believer unto sanctification of life; not meaning by this the procession of a gift of the Spirit, but of the Spirit Himself as given by the Father and the Son. The Spirit, thus given, causes recognition and then love of the goodness (*meritoria*) of God.[4] In answer to the question whether the Holy Spirit may be given by holy men, it is stated that He can be given in two ways: 'in one way directly—by authority, in the other way indirectly—through the ministerial office. In the first way the Holy Spirit cannot be given by any creature whatsoever, by angel or man, neither in Himself nor in His gifts; not in Himself, because the Holy Spirit can be given by authority only by Those from whom He has His source, for in the Godhead there is no authority of Person over Person but by reason of source. . . . Hence the Holy Spirit is given by authority only by the Father and the Son, and not by any creature; nor can the Holy Spirit be bestowed as a Gift unless by Those according to whose will He exists, to be possessed by us. Those, however, are only the Father, Son, and Holy Spirit, who have one and the same will.' Similarly, the gifts of the Spirit cannot be granted by any creature by authority. But 'in the other way, the Holy Spirit can be given indirectly through the ministerial office, and in this manner the Spirit can be given by (*ab*) men who

---

[1] *Ibid*, q 2.   [2] *Dist* 13, q 1.   [3] *Ibid*, q 2.
[4] *Dist* 14, qq 1, 3. Durandus adds that this procession is distinguishable from eternal procession in that it is effected *novo modo* for a special purpose which involves a *terminus*.

are not only good but also bad, as long as they are administering the Sacraments of the Church. . . . Again, He can be given here and there by all such through their preaching (*praedicatio*) as they commend the way of salvation. And, beside these ways, the Holy Spirit can be given by good men by gaining Him equally through prayer (*oratio*). These things, then, having been made known, man returns from sin to grace through repentance ; and therefore the Holy Spirit can be given in these ways by the good and the bad, not only by men but by angels.'[1] The difficulty concerning the efficacy of a Sacrament when administered by evil-living priests had already been met in the Early Church with the assertion that it is the Holy Spirit who dispenses grace, and not the ordained person, whose part is only ministerial.[2] Durandus could have expressed this view more consistently had he maintained the term of mediation (*per*) rather than of agency (*ab*). At least, the Mediaeval Church would hardly have asserted that the Spirit of God can be given by evil angels, if indeed that is what Durandus ventures to suggest.

The Mission of the Holy Spirit is next considered. The writer here states that His visible mission to the Apostles in fire at Pentecost was with a view to His graces being diffused by them to others. On the other hand, His invisible mission is at present directed alone to the sanctification of humanity.[3] But, as to the visible mission of the Spirit, were the forms in which He appeared real objects? The answer is in the negative, ' for it is clear that the Voice which was heard at Christ's Baptism was not the real voice of a creature possessed of animal life. Neither does the fire which appeared upon the Apostles seem to have been real fire ; for real fire burns, but that particular fire burned nothing.' As to the reality or otherwise of the body of the dove which figured in the Baptismal scene, Durandus preserves an open mind. Once more, ' the Breath in which the Holy Spirit was given to the Apostles after the resurrection (John xx. 22) could have been real breath, such as was evident at the time ; possibly, however, it was not then a Mission in the proper sense of the word, but the bestowal of some virtue through the mediation of a visible sign, as at present in the Sacraments ; though in the Sacraments we do

---
[1] *Ibid*, q 4
[2] See Swete, *Holy Spirit in the Ancient Church*, p 395 (Cyril of Jerusalem).
[3] *Dist* 16, q 1.

not affirm that a visible mission takes place.' Concerning, then, these visible manifestations of the Spirit, the conclusion reached is that they were forms (*species*) only, and not real objects (*res verae*).[1]

Finally, Durandus notes a now familiar definition of ' person ' as ' an indivisible substance of rational nature,' but he prefers that of *res intentioni subiecta*, expressive of the possibilities of the powers of Mind, so that ' the name of " person " indicates neither substance nor relation, but derives from both ; so that in the Godhead that of which " person " is predicated is not relation only, nor Essence only, but is constituted of both Essence and relation.'[2] In answer, then, to the question of the 25th *distinction*, ' whether " person " is spoken of at once of God and the creature,' Durandus says ' yes,' if the term is conceived as *nomen intentionis*; but ' no,' if it is conceived as *nomen rei* (*q.* 1). The three Divine Persons must not be called three divisible objects (*res*), for They may be understood to be three Substances, which is incorrect. In our present reasoning, however, *res* represents relation, not substance, and therefore the three Persons are three Objects of relation (*res relativae*) (*q.* 2). They are eternal relations within the Infinite Mind, and are Themselves real.[3] A real relation, by the way, is ' a name given to a single Divine fact which in no sense is really pluralized, but only in thought, and therefore a real relation in the Godhead is not the same as in the creatures.' Accordingly, equality is not a real relation within God, but is a relation of reason, or of source ; and, as to the ' reality ' of relation in this connexion, it is important in the mind of Durandus to maintain a clear distinction between the Divine nature and the human.[4] ' All Essential attributes,' he continues, ' are common to all the Persons.' Certain specific attributes are, nevertheless, conveniently ascribed to different Persons ; thus ' power, which characterizes Source, is ascribed to the Father, who is the principal (*primum*) Source ; wisdom, however, which belongs to the understanding, is ascribed to the Son,

---

[1] *Ibid*, q 2

[2] *Dist* 23, q 1 Otherwise—' quicquid distinguitur et est incommunicabile hoc habet per proprietatem relativam, ergo illud de quo persona dicitur in divinis includit essentiam et proprietatem relativam ' In *dist* 33, q 2, the author distinguishes between *proprietates personales* (e g *paternitas, filatio, processio*) and *proprietates relativae* (e g *spiratio, communio, innascibilitas*)

[3] *Dist* 26, q 2

[4] *Dist* 31, q 1 The thought of God as in everything and in every place should help to maintain this distinction *Cf dist* 37, qq 1, 2

who proceeds by way of understanding ; goodness, again, is ascribed to the Holy Spirit, who proceeds by way of will. . . . The distinction of the Persons is real, but the distinction of the attributes exists in thought (*secundum rationem*).'[1] Thus the Father loves the Son and us ' with the Holy Spirit,' that is, with Essential love, which is ascribed to the Holy Spirit ; for ' no one loves except with a love which proceeds from himself, even as action is understood to proceed from the one who acts.' But this Essential love proceeds not as *aliquid productum*, as affecting any real distinction in God, but only in thought by reason of its being ascribed to the Holy Spirit. On account of this ascription, therefore, the Father is said to love ' with the Holy Spirit.'[2]

GABRIEL BIEL

The teaching of Occam and Durandus was continued and developed by Gabriel Biel (c. 1425-1495), Nominalist philosopher and professor of theology at Tubingen. Biel is commonly known as the last of the Schoolmen, but though this is incorrect he may reasonably be styled the last of the noted Schoolmen.[3] As such he is briefly considered here. His *Sacri Canonis Expositio* connects the Spirit of God with the gift of grace, which is regarded as necessary for the soul and as being bestowed along with the Spirit. ' He is given,' he writes, ' for the personal sanctification of the recipient ; . . . not always, however, for personal sanctification, but always for the benefit of the Church.' The gifts of the Spirit, too, are granted rather to the Church than to the individual.[4]

But it is in his *Commentary on the Sentences* that his theological system is most clearly seen. This work reveals much repetition of the views of the earlier Nominalists as touching the Doctrine of the Holy Spirit. Thus, at the outset, goodness is mentioned as a distinctive attribute of the Spirit of God.[5] ' In the Godhead,' he continues, ' the Father possesses fertility (*fecunditas*) for the purpose of bringing forth the Son as also

---

[1] *Ibid*, q 3   [2] *Dist* 32, q 1
[3] It is of interest to note that the spirit of Scholasticism remained in the history of dogma long after Biel, as witness two post-Reformation Sententiaries, Dominicus Soto († 1560) and Estius († 1613) Others there were, truly, who continued the method of Scholasticism, but not its spirit Cf Herzog, *Encycl*, art. ' Wendelin ' († 1652)
[4] *Lectio* 2   [5] *Lib* 1, *dist* 3, q 9 (ed 1574).

the Holy Spirit, and communicates to the Son fertility for bringing forth the Holy Spirit.¹ These three Members of the Trinity are, however, not three Gods, but three Persons in one God ;² and, being such They are co-eternal.³ So ' of the three Divine hypostases, one only is bringing forth, the second is both bringing forth and brought forth, the third alone is brought forth ' ; that is, the Son is brought forth by way of understanding, while the Holy Spirit, as Love breathed forth, has as His Source the fertile will (*voluntas fecunda*) of God. All these three hypostases are co-equal, as well as co-eternal.⁴ The Holy Spirit is of necessity God just as the Son, so that equal importance is attached to Their processions from the Father, the former being brought forth by spiration, the latter by generation. These processions, however, must be kept distinct in the mind, for a function by nature (*naturaliter*) is not the same as that by will, as a gift (*per voluntatem libere*) ; and the Son is surely not brought forth by way of will. The distinction can again be seen in that the Son is called the Image of the Father (2 Cor. iv. 4 ; Col. i. 15), whereas the Holy Spirit is not spoken of as such, but as the Gift of Them Both ⁵ From this follows the next argument, that the Holy Spirit proceeds from Them Both, and both Athanasius and Duns Scotus are quoted in support of the *Filioque*. ' The Father,' he concludes, ' is from nothing, the Son is from the Father only, and the Holy Spirit is equally from Both. . . . The Holy Spirit proceeds eternally from the Father and the Son, not as from two Sources, but as from one Source ; not by two spirations, but by one single spiration.' According to Biel the Greeks themselves recognize that they have had the worst of this long debate. By none of their lines of argument is it found that the Holy Spirit does not proceed from the Son ; ' nay rather Holy Scripture appears to intimate this and to assert that He certainly proceeds from the Son. Wherefore the Greeks, even while they think the opposite, have to affirm that the Holy Spirit proceeds from the Son ! '⁶ The writer might have had in mind, among other

¹ *Ibid*, q 10   ³ *Dist* 4, qq 1, 2, *dist* 8, q 1
² *Dist* 9, intro and q 1.   ⁴ *Dist* 10, q 1
⁵ *Ibid*, q 2   See *dist* 13   the Son being *natus*, and from One, the Spirit being *datus*, and from Two
⁶ *Dist* 11, q 1   Cf *dist* 12, q 1 (on the one spiration), and q 3 (on the uniformity of the one spiration)

cases previously reported by Westerns, the recent waverings of the Patriarch Gennadius II. The truth of the twofold procession of the Spirit receives constant emphasis in the course of the Commentary, and is brought in to support the other truth of the Essential Unity of the three Divine Persons; while, in his declaration that no distinction between the Son and the Spirit would be possible apart from the *Filioque*,[1] Biel follows Durandus, Duns Scotus, and Thomas Aquinas. Nearly a century after Durandus, Pierre d' Ailly had also expressed the same opinion, though he was not of Biel's school.

This period, in which appeared the gulf between theology and philosophy, yielded comparatively little in respect of the work of the Holy Spirit, and even in this the ecclesiastical medium loomed large. The Being of God claimed more attention in that it attracted minds with a tendency to the abstruse. The eternal Distinctions within the Godhead received particular emphasis, in which the more picturesque forms of analogical treatment gave way before what may be termed Divine psychology. The word 'person' as applied to the Deity continued to be carefully scrutinized, while the *Filioque* was declared to be a rational necessity, not only for the distinction between the Persons but also for that complete absence of confusion in plurality which means perfect Unity. But the Scholasticism of the Nominalists, now sceptical, now ecclesiastically rigid, contained no inspiration for needy humanity. A sincere attempt to supply this came from the German Mystics.

As a postscript to this chapter mention may be made of the Italian theologian Petrus Galatinus (†1539). Of his life comparatively little is known. References to the Holy Spirit are found in the first book of his work *On the Talmud* (ed 1561), and show him to be typically Western. He declares that the procession of the Holy Spirit from the Father and the Son are here intimated openly enough, the Spirit of Elohim, or of God, being regarded as the Spirit of the Messiah Picturesquely mediaeval, he speaks of the Father and the Son as the two nostrils of one nose, and therefore as the one and only Source breathing forth the Holy Spirit This procession 'from the Divine nostrils' proves that the Holy Spirit is true and perfect God. The inspired Jewish writers asserted that the 'third Person in the Godhead is brought forth from eternity by the Father and the Son by way of

[1] *Dist* 11, *q*. 2.

will in one single spiration, really distinct from Them indeed, but essentially the same along with Them' (chap. vi). He is the mutual Love of the Father and the Son. As *intelligentia* has its source in *memoria*, and *voluntas* in both, so the Son is begotten by the Father, and the Holy Spirit proceeds from Both. Also, as the former three are not three minds, but only one mind, so the latter Three are not three Gods, but one God (chap. viii.).

III

THE SCHOLASTIC REVIVAL

FEAR lest theology and philosophy had been finally separated stirred a group of Schoolmen to attempt to reunite them by working from the standpoint of piety rather than that of reason, and thus rejuvenating Scholasticism with mystical ideas. In thought the new Scholastic 'Mysticism' comes midway between the Scholasticism of Durandus and anti-Scholastic Mysticism; and, though the teachings of Eckhart and his colleagues actually preceded the Scholastic 'Revival' and accounted somewhat for it,[1] this 'Revival' will be dealt with at once in order to preserve the continuity of the study of Scholasticism in its variations. It is well to remember also that, while the influential period of Scholasticism was rapidly drawing to a close, the influence of Mysticism remained, and continued after the Reformation. Both these movements, however, made their own contributions to Reformation theology.

PIERRE D'AILLY

Two holders of the Chancellorship of the University of Paris figure in this chapter, namely Pierre d'Ailly (Petrus de Alliaco) and Jean Charlier de Gerson. D'Ailly (1350–c. 1420), as Cardinal-bishop of Cambrai, was as much a statesman as a theologian, but, though he held firmly to ecclesiasticism, he did so with that liberal spirit which is characteristic also of his work as a divine. Nominalist as he was, he emphasized the spiritual origin of the knowledge of spiritual things, and he calls to mind Aquinas in the importance which he attached to faith as against the subtleties of Occamism. His *Quaestiones super Primum Sententiarum*, as Erdmann shows, do not make his distinction from the Occamist writers so clear as do others of his works, yet they embody his opinions concerning the Doctrine now under review. 'The Father, Son, and

---

[1] Nicolas of Cusa had been a pupil of Eckhart

Holy Spirit,' he writes, 'are three equal Persons and one Essence. The Holy Spirit proceeds from the Father and the Son as from one Source,' and is breathed forth by Them uniformly and equally. It is necessary that the Holy Spirit should proceed from the Son, otherwise He would not be distinguished from Him.[1] 'The Father and the Son do not breathe forth the Holy Spirit by virtue of Their being One, nor by virtue of Their being distinct.' They are, nevertheless, one Source of the third Person.[2] Of these three Persons the Holy Spirit has been regarded particularly as Love; yet, in point of fact, He is not so to any greater degree than They are. It has simply been a matter of custom in theological language, for, after all, He is brought forth by the mutual love of the Others, and therefore is Their Bond (*nexus*).[3] Even so, the Mission of the Holy Spirit has for its particular object the cultivation of love for God in the human soul (*ut faciat nos diligere Deum*). 'The Holy Spirit sanctifies or accepts no one unto life eternal save him in whom is love'; which is a development of a statement as to the twofold manner of the Spirit's immanence in creation, He being in one way in all creatures generally, but in another way, specially, only in rational creatures who are just and holy.[4] The notice which is given by d' Ailly to the work of the Spirit is an indication of the new method of approach adopted by this group of Schoolmen.

John Gerson

John Gerson (1363–1429), the pupil and successor of d'Ailly, was, however, more of a Mystic than his master. Without adopting any of the extravagances associated with German Mysticism, he would have nothing to do with the extreme subtleties of the prevailing Scholasticism, and in all his reasoning he was naturally subjective. In accord with this outlook, the exposition of his theology takes a sermonic rather than a sententiary form, his sermons on the Holy Spirit and the Trinity affording a clear insight into his mind with reference to those doctrines. In the first Sermon *De Sancto Spiritu*, written in 1403, is found an assertion of the instrumentality

---
[1] *q* 8, art 1 (cf *q* 10, art 1)   [2] *Ibid*, art. 2
[3] *Ibid*, art 3   'Pater et Filius mutuo se diligendo producunt Spiritum sanctum'
[4] *q* 9, art 2

of the Spirit in the conception of Jesus, followed by the request :
'Come again, O sweet and kindly Spirit, and recreate in us
the spiritual world, even as in seven days Thou didst construct
the material world.' Such a prayer is fitting, because the
Holy Spirit is peculiarly 'the Spirit of love and unity.' But
there are also two other Divine characters, namely 'the Spirit
of justice and truth,' and 'the Spirit of grace and beauty,'
the former representing the Son, the latter the Father. 'Why
then is the Holy Spirit said to quicken and unify the soul more
than the Father and the Son ? The reply is that He Himself
is the Bond (*nexus*) of the Father and the Son, and proceeds
by way of will. Other questions there are,' he adds, ' concerning the procession of the Holy Spirit from the Father and the
Son, and the error and schism of the Greeks ' ; which remark
of itself implies Gerson's adherence to the Western opinion.[1]
Another sermon on the Holy Spirit contains the statement
that the Father and the Son are said to be joined together
into one (*in unum*) by the Holy Spirit ; yet ' however much
the operations of the Trinity are undivided, they are not so
inwardly, but outwardly.' The Spirit, too, is present in all
creation, His immanence being due entirely to His own will.[2]
Further assertions are made in other homilies. 'The Holy
Spirit gives gracious comfort in abundance by bestowing the
shield of firm belief in God,' while the difference which the
gift of Himself makes to men was strikingly illustrated by the
Apostles, 'who, before they received the Holy Spirit, were
simple men, without education and learning, but who surpassed
and vanquished with their wisdom all the most subtle of the
world's teachers.' So does the Spirit inhabit the spiritual
mind.[3] Then let Him be admitted into the soul as a welcome
guest (*hospes*).[4]

Two sermons *On the Holy Trinity* allude to the place of the
third Person in the inner Life of God. It may be asked, 'If
the Father is God, and the Son God, and the Holy Spirit God,
is it not allowable to conclude that there are three Gods ?
Indeed, my soul, no ! No conclusion can be reached in that
manner, and this thou canst perceive on account of what I
have said ; since the Father, Son, and Holy Spirit can possess
only one power, the same perfection, one and the same goodness,

---

[1] Vol 2, serm 1 (ed 1706) [2] *Ibid*, serm 3
[3] Vol 3, serm. 2 [4] *Ibid*, serm 4.

one life, one knowledge, there is absolutely one Being (*res*) in respect of these Three. Among the creatures, of course, this would not obtain.' For all that, human analogies of the one Essence in the three Persons are suggestive while not exactly parallel. 'No less dost thou possess three capacities, which are memory, understanding, and will. From memory there is begotten knowledge, and from memory and knowledge there proceeds will, and love. . . . From which it follows that the Holy Spirit proceeds from the Son as from the Father, contrary to the error of the Greeks.'[1] The particular attributes of the Persons receive attention in the second sermon on the Trinity, might being ascribed to the Father, wisdom to the Son, liberality and goodness to the Holy Spirit.[2]

In these writings as well as in his dissertations on mystical theology can be seen Gerson's preference for the theological as compared with the philosophical. Though far more conservative in his ecclesiastical views than d'Ailly, he displayed a reverence for the experimental side of religion which brought the operations of the Holy Spirit definitely to the fore. No better course could have been taken for the discouragement of unedifying controversy.

NICOLAS OF CLÉMANGES

A pupil of d'Ailly and Gerson who assimilated ideas from them both was Nicolas of Clémanges (*c.* 1360–*c.* 1437), Rector of the University of Paris and afterwards Archdeacon of Bayeux. In the history of dogma he is not outstanding, being the author of no great theological treatise; yet even as an understudy of his more celebrated teachers he has an interest of his own. In the *De Corrupto Ecclesiae Statu*, whose authorship by Nicolas has been challenged, a statement occurs to the effect that the Holy Spirit reveals the meaning of Scripture-prophecies (chap. xxii.). His advanced views on ecclesiastical matters, expressed in a book on the subject of the General Council, contain interesting references to the Doctrine of the Spirit. He agrees with Ambrose that every truth which is spoken by any one is from the Holy Spirit, the Spirit of Truth; so that the holy men whose words are recorded in the

---

[1] *Sermo primus de Sancta Trinitate*   [2] *Sermo alius de Sancta Trinitate*

Scriptures were filled with the grace of the Spirit. Next to the authority of the Scriptures, in his opinion, comes the authority of a General Council, with whose members the Spirit is present, directing them and leading them to a beneficial end. For the Spirit is called the Spirit of discipline, not of doctrine, because He makes a man teachable rather than a teacher, and then Himself teaches him concerning everything. But with regard to the dictum that 'a Council cannot make a mistake,' what guarantee is there that the Spirit is allowed to guide the majority of those who attend? Certainly the Spirit has no control over a carnal and contentious assembly, met to discuss only carnal questions. The obvious conclusion (*cf. Epistola* 102) is that no carnally-minded men should be sent to a General Council, but only the spiritually-minded, who are under the direction of the Holy Spirit. Nicolas, however, does not lose sight of the spiritual possibilities even of the carnal mind, seeing that it is fashioned in the image of the Trinity.[1]

Allied to d'Ailly and Gerson in the attempt to bridge the gulf between theology and philosophy from the other side was RAYMOND OF SABUNDE, Regius Professor of theology at Toulouse, who produced a celebrated work on Natural Theology about the year 1435.[2] His aim was to reunite revelation and reason, authority and 'free thought,' by showing the essential necessity of the one to the other; but his method of working from natural to revealed religion left little scope for an expression of his mind on the Doctrine of the Holy Spirit. His outlook, however, together with that of Gerson on the other hand, were combined in a theologian of unusual insight and versatility, who commenced to bridge the gulf from both sides at once. NICOLAS OF CUSA (1401–1464) rose by sheer merit to the position of cardinal, in spite of his being notably in agreement with d'Ailly on such questions as the papacy and its relationship to General Councils and secular government[3]; and before receiving this final ecclesiastical preferment he had already acted as Envoy Extraordinary to Pope Eugenius

---

[1] See his treatise *On the Prodigal Son* (chap ii) : ' O humana creatura ad nobilissimam aeternae Trinitatis imaginem condita !'

[2] Erdmann (*ibid*, p 525) remarks that, while d'Ailly and Gerson did not wish to break with philosophy, Raymond did not wish to break with theology

[3] The growing belief in the ultimate authority of a General Council found particular expression in the proceedings of the anti-papal Council of Basel, 1431–1449

IV.[1] The extracts from his many works here considered are taken from the folio edition published at Basel by Henri Petri in 1565, and illustrate the truth of Erdmann's assertion that 'the rays which emanated from Erigena, that epoch-making sun of Scholasticism, are gathered as in a focus in Nicolas, who brings Scholasticism to a close.'[2]

His first publication, *De Docta Ignorantia*, together with the *De Conjecturis*, which immediately succeeded it, contain the fundamentals of his philosophy. The former begins with certain observations concerning the Absolute, in which exists the highest unity. 'This unity, seeing that it is the highest, is not capable of multiplication because it is itself all that it can be,' neither more nor less. 'The Deity is therefore Infinite Unity.'[3] Unity, then, must necessarily be eternal, and equality also eternal seeing that it precedes both inequality and otherness (*alteritas*). That their bond of union (*connexio*) is also eternal, is shown from the following argument : Two causes, the effects of the first of which are prior to those of the second, cannot possess unity, for unity is by nature prior to dual causality. Dual causality produces division. Therefore the bond of union which joins unity to equality is by nature prior to division. But division and otherness are together by nature. Therefore the bond of union is prior to otherness, and is accordingly associated by nature with unity and equality. But both unity and equality are eternal. Similarly, then, their bond of union must also be eternal. 'Hence unity, equality, and their bond of union are one (*unum*) ; and this is the much-discussed threefold unity.'[4] The threefold nature of God does not, however, interfere with His absolute unity as the substance or sum of all being. Generation, for instance, as applied to the Deity, is the generation of unity from unity, and is thus one repetition of unity ; the procession from Both is accordingly the uniting of unity and its repetition or equality. The

---

[1] Gabriel Condulmieri (1383–1447), who was elevated to the papacy in 1431 as Eugenius IV is known not so much as a theologian as a strife-making pontiff who deserved many of his misfortunes Even so, his *De Septem Ecclesiae Sacramentis* is worthy of notice The form of Baptism is ' Ego te baptizo in nomine Patris, et Filii, et Spiritus sancti quoniam cum principalis causa, ex qua baptismus virtutem habet, sit sancta Trinitas ' The form of Confirmation is ' Signo te signo crucis, et confirmo te chrismate salutis in nomine Patris, et Filii, et Spiritus sancti ' The gift of the Spirit, who supplies strength to confess Christ before the world, accompanies the imposition of hands, so that this sacrament has an effect similar to that of Pentecost The form of Ordination (for a priest) is ' Accipe potestatem offerendi sacrificium in ecclesia pro vivis et mortuis In nomine Patris, et Filii, et Spiritus sancti '

[2] Erdmann, *ibid*, p 532   [3] *De Doct Ign.* 1, chap v   [4] *Ibid*, chap. vii

THE SCHOLASTIC REVIVAL

Filioque is seen to rest upon a philosophical basis as well as the Divine Unity, the former arising from and contributing to the latter. ' Procession,' reasons Nicolas, ' is spoken of as a certain " extension " from the one to the other. . . . Hence it is said to proceed as a bond of union from unity and the equality of unity. There is, indeed, no uniting bond of one thing only ; on the contrary, unity proceeds from unity to equality, and from the equality of unity to their union. Quite correctly, therefore, is it said to proceed from both ; . . . and though the equality of unity is begotten from unity, and their uniting bond proceeds from both, yet unity, and the equality of unity, and their bond of union proceeding from both, are one and the same thing.' So in the Trinity there are conceived *id*, and *idem*, and communion between them ; or *iditas*, *identitas*, and *communitas*. In that our most holy Doctors have called unity the Father, equality the Son, and the bond of union the Holy Spirit, they have done this on account of a certain parallelism in respect of those conceptions.' The Holy Spirit, then, joins together the Father and the Son by virtue of the similitude of Their self-same Nature, and in doing so He exercises the natural function of love.[1] The conclusion of Nicolas at this point is that, while the *unicum simplicissimum maximum* of the Trinity cannot be adequately set forth by mathematics, this *maxima unitas* cannot rightly be understood at all if it is not understood as threefold. ' For, if Unity is the greatest and most perfect Intellect which, without those three correlations—*intelligens*, *intelligibile*, *intelligere* (perceiving, perceivable, and to perceive)—can be neither intellect nor the most perfect intellect, he, who does not arrive at the Trinity of Unity Itself, does not rightly conceive Unity.' Moreover, the greatest Unity can only be a Trinity from the standpoint of Its possessing undividedness (*indivisio*), internal distinction (*discretio*), and their union (*connexio*), while the very meaning of *connexio* necessitates its procession from both.[2]

---

[1] *Ibid*, IX ' Amor enim naturalis (seu Spiritus sanctus) alterum cum altero connectit, et hoc propter similitudinem eiusdem naturae, quae in eis est, quae a patre in filium descendit '

[2] *Ibid*, x ' Unitas enim, non nisi trinitas est, nam dicit indivisionem, discretionem, et connexionem ' . . . et quoniam indivisio est, tunc est aeternitas sive absque principio, sicut aeternum a nullo divisum , quoniam discretio est, ab aeternitate immutabili est ; et quoniam connexio sive unio est, ab utroque procedit, adhuc cum dico unitas est maxima trinitatem dico ' For an interesting parallel see Illingworth, *Personality Human and Divine* (1894), pp. 73 f.

As Nicolas continues his discussion of the Doctrine of the Trinity in the 19th chapter he presents geometrical analogies, arising from his own study of mathematics, in a manner which savours of the *Opus Majus* of Roger Bacon. In an equilateral triangle the three equal sides represent the Trinity, while the one line, divided into three, represents the Essence. It is the changing emphasis of the human mind that accounts for variation in the presentation of the Doctrine. Augustine supports the statement that ' where distinction is indistinction, the trinity is a unity; conversely, where indistinction is distinction, the unity is a trinity. So also concerning the plurality of Persons and the unity of Essence. For where the plurality is a unity, the Trinity of Persons is one and the same thing, along with the unity of Essence. Conversely, where the unity is a plurality, the unity of Essence is a Trinity in Persons; and these things clearly appear in our example, where a most simple line is a triangle, and, conversely, a simple triangle a lineal unity.' The true view, however, concludes the author, is obtained not by considering one Object and then three Objects, or conversely, but by considering one and the same Object as either One in Three (*unitrinum*) or Three in One (*triunum*).[1] Accordingly ' the Father is the first Person, although the Son is not the second as coming afterwards; but since the Father is the first, without priority, consequently the Son is the second, without posteriority, and the Holy Spirit the third as equal to Them in Nature.' In the Trinity the *ipsum maximum* is threefold, and not fourfold, or fivefold, &c., just as the triangle is the simplest form of polygon, and upholds the highest perfection of unity in itself.[2] And is not the circle also descriptive of the Divine Triunity, consisting as it does of centre, diameter, and circumference?[3] The name of God, or of the *Primum Maximum*, should thus be interpreted as One and All, or—better—All in One (*omnia uniter*), which is a more correct term than Unity, since God is over all and in all. The Divine Unity, too, being infinite, is not opposed by otherness, or plurality, or number.[4]

The subject of the Unity of God receives further treatment in the second book of this same work. ' Absolute Unity,' resumes Nicolas, ' is necessarily threefold, not indeed con-

---

[1] *De Doc. Ign.*, xix   [2] *Ibid*, xx   [3] *Ibid*, xxi   [4] *Ibid*, xxii

THE SCHOLASTIC REVIVAL

cretely (Erdmann's equivalent for *contracte*), but absolutely.
... In the Godhead, Unity does not exist concretely in the Trinity as a whole in its parts or a universal in its particulars, but the Unity *Itself* is the Trinity. Therefore any One of the Persons is the Unity Itself; and since the Unity is a Trinity, one Person is not Another. In the universe, however, it cannot be so, because those three correlations, which in the Godhead are called Persons, have Their being in action only as together in unity. This must carefully be noted, for, in the Godhead, so great is the perfection of the Unity, which is the Trinity, that the Father is God in action, the Son is God in action, the Holy Spirit is God in action; the Son and the Holy Spirit are in action in the Father, the Son and the Father are in action in the Holy Spirit, the Father and the Holy Spirit are in action in the Son, thus the Divine Unity clearly cannot exist in the concrete, for the correlations are not subsistences by Themselves save in a state of union (*copulate*).'¹ God, then, who is Spirit, is the One from whom all motion descends. From Him, too, descends the created spirit of the universe, without which nothing is one, or is able to subsist. ' And this is the motion of a loving linking-together of all things into a unity, that there may be one universe of all things. Therefore, just as all possibility remains in the Absolute, which is the Eternal God, and all form and action in absolute Form, which is the Word of the Father, and the Son in the Godhead; so all motion of joining together, also the proportion and the harmony which unify, exist in the absolute Bond of union of the Divine Spirit, so that He, as God, is the one principle of all things, in whom are all things, and through whom are all things, in the unity of the Trinity.'² It is in the Incarnation of the Son that the work of the Holy Spirit as Creator and absolute Love is most perfectly made manifest,³ He being also the cause of the absolute union of the two natures in Christ. The unity of the Church triumphant

---

¹ ii 7 Nicolas continues · ' Non potest enim contractio esse sine contrahibili, contrahente, et nexu, qui per communem actum utriusque, perficitur ' The Holy Spirit is called *nexus infinitus*
² *Ibid*, 10 Erdmann's digest (*Hist of Phil* E tr , i , p 538) reads ' The universe exhibits a limited image of the Trinity, in the fact that in it the idea contained in the Divine Word joins itself, as form, with matter, the possibility of being, to produce a unity which appears in motion, this really animating principle of the world '
³ iii 5 The *Dialogus de Annunciatione* also speaks of the Holy Spirit's operation in the conception of the Son of God, He, as *nexus* and *amor*, imparting virtue to Mary See *Excitationum, libb* iv v

is, moreover, due to the Holy Spirit.[1] Human cognition, however, is not sufficient to grasp the things of God, concerning which it is, by itself, in the darkness of ignorance.[2] The *De Conjecturis* points to the same conclusion. In our reasoning concerning principles we shall be led astray unless we keep to the standpoint of unity being itself trinity, and not the unity of a plurality of principles.[3] Even so, the psychological analogy, as a method of comprehending God, serves but to illustrate the Infinite Mind from the finite, and therefore can never be exact.[4]

In the *De Concordantia Catholica*, another of his earlier works, there is little concerning the Doctrine of the Holy Spirit save a reference to the famous Nicene Council, when the Spirit manifestly sat with the Fathers and presided over them in their deliberations.[5] This point might not have been entirely lost upon the members of the Council of Basel, for this book, which was published after two years of its sessions, attained considerable publicity. In the *Idiota*, however, there are recurrences of a line of thought in demonstration of the Trinity already adopted in the *De Docta Ignorantia*. The Holy Spirit is the Bond which binds all things together (*connectens*, *uniens*, *nectens*) into an ordered whole, in us and in the universe, which clearly points to His Deity. ' Equality proceeds from unity— so does the Son from the Father ; and union proceeds from unity and its equality—so does the Holy Spirit from the Father and the Son.' Here also, the well-known triad of *unitas*, *aequalitas*, and *connexio* forms the basis of the author's conception of God.[6] Again, matter, form, and the union of both constitute one substance, namely, the human mind, and are a figure of that Triunity which is found in the Eternal Mind. Manifestly it is the unity in particular which Nicolas is anxious to emphasize in this analogy, the substance of the mind being one (*imago unitatis unientis*) and the inner equality also one, as being derived from the unity of the substance.[7] God, then, is absolute Infinity itself, inaccessible, incomprehensible,

[1] *De Doc Ign*, 12   [2] *Ibid*, 6
[3] *De Conject*, 1 10 (*de ultima unitate*)
[4] Erdmann, *ibid*, p 539 (on *De Conject*, 11. 14) : ' God's thinking produces things, man's thinking represents them '
[5] *De Concord Cath*, 11   [6] *Idiota*, i
[7] *Ibid*, 111 Cf *Philosophus* · ' Quando autem nostri dicunt theologi, unitatem pro Patre, et aequalitatem pro Filio, et nexum pro Spiritu sancto capientes ; quomodo Pater est unus, Filius est unus ; unde hoc? '—*Idiota* · ' A singularitate personae : sunt enim tres singulares personae, in una divina substantia '

unnamable, invisible, and incapable of multiplication ;[1] but in Him we see love, love loving or lovable, and the bond of love (*amabilis nexus*) ; or unity unifying, unity unifiable, and the union of both. The writer in his *Vision* thus addresses the Deity : ' Nothing is in Thee which is not Thine Essence Itself.' So God is ' the most simple and absolute Essence itself '—which at the same time is ' a threefold Essence ; and yet there are not three objects in it because it is the most simple.' There is plurality here because there is unity, and unity because there is plurality. ' The plurality of the Three is plurality without the plural number, for a plural number cannot be a simple unity for the very reason that it is a plural number. There is therefore no numerical distinction of the Three because the distinction is Essential ; for number is essentially distinguished from number. And since the unity is threefold it is not the unity of the singular number ; for unity of the singular number is not threefold. O most wonderful God, who art neither of the singular number nor of the plural, but art over all plurality and singularity, One in Three and Three in One ! ' So do *pluralitas* and *singularitas* in the Godhead coincide ; ' as if any one should say " one, one, one "—he says " one " three times ; he does not say " three," but " one," and this " one " three times.' The ' one ' is always present to the mind, whatever power of multiplication affects it ; similarly the plurality which exists in God is ' otherness without otherness, since it is an otherness which is identity.' This plurality without otherness Nicolas reaches through introspection. ' For so, Lord, Thou dost permit me to see love in Thee, because I see myself as loving. And since I see that I love, I myself, I see that I am lovable ; also I see that I am the most natural union of both—I am loving, I am lovable, I am their union. So the love is one, without which none of the three could exist. I am one, who am loving, and that self-same one who am lovable, and that self-same one who am the union arising out of the love wherewith I love myself ; I am one and not three (*tria*). Let it be, then, that my love is my essence, just as in my God ; in that case, in the unity of my essence there would be a unity of three predicates, and in the trinity of the three predicates a unity of essence, and the whole would exist in my essence concretely, even as I see it exist in Thee

[1] *De Visione Dei*, chap xiii

truly and absolutely.'[1] Again, since God is *intellectus intelligens, intellectus intelligibilis*, and their *nexus* or union, the created intellect can grasp the truth of this Divine unity with Divine guidance,[2] the Spirit in particular encouraging the conceptions of the rational mind.[3] For as the sun's power descends upon vegetable life, promoting and perfecting its growth, so that, by means of the most welcome and natural ripening virtues of heavenly warmth, good fruit is produced, even so the Spirit of God descends upon the intellectual life of good men, ripening and perfecting their capacities for goodness, so that, by means of the warmth of Divine love, fruit is produced which is most welcome to Him. Human experience bears testimony to the manifold ways in which the Spirit guides the intellect, how He is the Source of prophecy, the Interpreter of mysteries, the Teacher of knowledge, the Bestower of various gifts which are all *perfectiones intellectualis spiritus*, the Spirit of spirits, the Impulse of impulses, who fills the whole world, the medium of Divine comfort, and the Inspirer of holy desires and right choices.[4] Hence the guidance of the Holy Spirit leads to our belief in the fact that He Himself is the Divine union by which God the Father is united to God the Son : and that, on this account, He is an infinite union, for He embraces absolute and essential identity.[5]

The necessity of bearing in mind the Essential oneness of God throughout all exposition of the Trinity is repeated in the *De Ludo Globi* and the *Dialogus de Possest*. With my mind I think (*cogito*), I consider (*considero*), and I determine (*determino*), the second mental function is begotten by the first, while the third proceeds from the others ; but there is only one 'living impulse,' which is completely self-contained. Similarly, but infinitely, are there three interrelated distinctions in the most perfect Life of the Deity.[6] Thus, in the one First Cause, there is unity, equality, and their union, and this threefold character is entirely necessary to His being at all the First Cause or the Being of Beings (*entitas entium*). 'God, then, *because* He is Creator, can only exist as one and threefold ' ; the Father being unity or Existence, the Son the equality of unity, and the Holy Spirit the union or love of unity and equality.[7] Accordingly the Doctrine of the Trinity

---
[1] *De Visione Dei*, 17   [2] *Ibid*, 18.   [3] *Ibid*, 19.   [4] *Ibid*, 25
[5] *Ibid*, 20   [6] *De Ludo Globi*, 1   [7] *Ibid*, 11

portrays Divine Unity and not a plurality of Gods, so that, though the inner distinctions of this Unity remain distinct, the identity of Nature and of Essence belonging to such distinctions entirely exclude any notion of otherness (*aliud*).[1]

Nor is the work of the Spirit overlooked by Nicolas. He is the Divine Cause of all perfections, and therefore the Source of various gifts to mankind. 'As in the Word of Truth the Father begets all things, so in the Spirit, who proceeds from the Father and the Son, all things are perfected. For the Spirit fills the world, that is, He leads it on to a state of perfection, and all things which possess knowledge of language are all in the Father paternally, all in the Son filially, all in the Holy Spirit perfectly. In the Father all things have their essence, in the Son their power, in the Holy Spirit their operation.'[2] The Spirit effects perfection of life in the living, perfection of knowledge in the intelligent. 'All these things are effected by the one Spirit, who is the blessed God, so that every creature may ascend through perfection more nearly (as much as the state of his nature allows) to the Divine likeness, that is, to the consummation of peace.'[3]

Of more interest as touching the Doctrine of the Holy Spirit are the *Extracts* from the sermons of Nicolas, published in ten books. In this collection the theology of the Spirit is set forth in a less formal manner, while the work of the Spirit is treated in more adequate proportion. The writer states that the three principles in God form one eternal Essence; which is not incredible, for in temporal nature we see the principle of paternity, the principle of filiation, and the principle of both, or the bond of love proceeding from the principle of both. Moreover, in every perfect action of God three correlatives are necessarily found; since nothing acts in itself, but in something effective which is distinct from it, while the third arises from the first two correlatives, thereby completing the action.[4] These correlatives exist in the Divine Essence as three Persons, wherefore we speak of God as threefold. Though

---

[1] *Dialogus de Possest* 'Video Deum aeternaliter, et eundem Deum de Deo aeternaliter, ac eundem Deum ab utroque aeternaliter procedentem'

[2] Or 'Deus Pater est omnia in omnibus, Deus Filius potest omnia in omnibus, Deus Spiritus sanctus operatur omnia in omnibus Ab esse autem et posse procedit operari.'

[3] *De Dato Patris Luminum*, chap v

[4] 'Agens, agibile, agere'

justification is associated with the Spirit as being peculiarly His work, the operations of the Trinity are undivided in this as in the work of creation, for God is one. In spite of this, the Jews seek to evade the revelation of the Trinity by speaking of three of God's attributes—Divine wisdom, goodness, and power; but Nicolas adds that their position has already been undermined by his namesake of Lyra in his commentary on the Old Testament, while the Gospels naturally supply still fuller evidence. The three Persons, therefore, are one God. Whatever belongs to God belongs equally to Them All, since Each is *alius*, not *aliud*. For of the Father, Son, and Holy Spirit there is one Essence, a co-equal glory, a co-eternal majesty. 'And since the one God is threefold, there spring forth from God creatures of three kinds, those that are spiritual only, those that are corporeal only, and those that are united from both. The spiritual are the angels and intelligences, the corporeal are the vegetable growths, the things capable of feeling, and the elements. The united nature, as if proceeding from both, is man'[1]—a remarkable conclusion from the triune Nature of the Creator.

The Holy Spirit, who is the Spirit of Life, makes us heirs of God and joint heirs with Christ, bringing us into a filial relationship to God.[2] There is no salvation apart from the Holy Spirit, for He it is who alone diffuses the love of God in our hearts, making us holy since He is holy. 'The mission of the Holy Spirit is a going forth of love from the Father and the Son to the creature for the sanctification of the creature. Only a rational or intellectual nature is capable of sanctification. . . . And holiness is nothing else than grace making a man joyful, or love which the Holy Spirit infuses by His coming.' But this is a state requiring a preparatory process, over which the Spirit presides. The beginning is marked by meditation, judicially severe, concerning sins and their punishment, which is 'servile fear' but also 'the beginning of wisdom.' Then follow reflections upon the good gifts of the Creator and consequent shame of wrong-doing. Further reflection, should it be centred no longer upon self and punishment but now upon the things which pertain to the honour and adoration of God, will be the reflection of sonship, and is the first gift. Sanctifying love ensues, 'for without love man

---

[1] *Excitat.*, 1.   [2] *Ibid*, 11.

is nothing'; and it is the Holy Spirit, the Love-Bond, who gives this love as the bond of union of God and man. 'Since, therefore, love is the principle of life, all sin, since it is contrary to love, is subject to death.' But the Spirit of Divine Love is water, fire, perfume, in fact all those things which cause spiritual growth and cleansing. In creation, too, He is the power holding together all creatures; and since from *connexio* descends *motus* (motion), and so from infinite *connexio* infinite *motus*, He is therefore omnipotent, His goodness appearing in His creative work. The first attention of Nicolas, however, is here devoted to the work of the Holy Spirit in the human soul, He being the Cause of its new birth wherever there is belief on the Son of God. We, whom God the Father has created and whom God the Son has regenerated and adopted, are instructed by God the Paraclete, through whose guidance and goodness we attain to sonship in God, and in whom we are finally translated from this world to the kingdom of eternal peace.[1] Again in the fourth book, and also throughout the *Extracts*, there is frequent mention of the use made by the Holy Spirit of faith in Christ[2] in order to produce sonship of God in the heart, the Church being regarded as the special instrument or the medium of the Holy Spirit in this connexion.

The study of Divine relations with man affords a trinitarian analogy of an experimental nature. God is represented as a magnet, whose form is the Father, whose power is the Son, and whose operation is the Holy Spirit; and, as such, He attracts the iron, which represents the human spirit. So, 'in the Absolute Essence which attracts, I see Him who attracts, I see His power, and also the Union of Both; and the whole Essence is Spirit.' This Divine Power of attraction is effective since 'the Word of God, or the Wisdom of the Father, through the mediation of the Holy Spirit whom He sends upon the rational spirit, attracts it and sets it in motion' by the diffusion in it of Divine love. Hence the whole Trinity operates for our salvation; 'Christ teaches us how we ought to prepare ourselves so that the Spirit, the Paraclete, may come upon us,' the Spirit who is given by the Father. And when the Spirit does come upon us, He imparts grace and illumination, speaking to our intellect and arousing it to action whereby

[1] *Ibid*, iii   [2] Cf 'fides non est nisi donum Spiritus'—*Ibid*, x

fruit is produced from the good seed already within us. Possession of the Holy Spirit (who purifies and illumines) ensures victory over evil spirits (*maligni spiritus*), for it is the pledge of our Divine adoption.[1] But there could be no moving of the mind such as that of which Nicolas writes, except for the impelling activity of the Holy Spirit, which can produce even love for an enemy. The Spirit is therefore correctly termed not only ' the Spirit of salvation ' but also ' the Liberty of the mind.' He is the glory proceeding from pure and omnipotent Intellect and from omnipotent Intellect begotten by It. He is the Light of Life sent into the reasoning faculty of our mind to reveal truth and eternally to impart new life, presenting all things that the Word of God speaks. ' And since He is the Spirit of Truth, or the Intellect of the Word, He is accordingly the Spirit of Jesus, who is the Word of God, and the Truth. Hence this Gift of the Spirit of Truth proceeds from the Father and the Son, or Word, and is sent by the Father in the name of the Son.' The interrelations of the Divine Persons may again be appreciated experimentally : ' In adoption we understand that the Spirit proceeds from the Father, who adopts us ; and in admission we understand that the Spirit is sent by the Son. Admission carries with it participation of the Spirit of Love. . . . Thus He proceeds from the Father and is sent by the Son just as the spirit of teaching proceeds from a master and is sent through his language (*per verbum*) to the pupils.' That this illustration conveys no weakening of the writer's belief in the *Filioque* is shown by a succeeding analogy which likens the Trinity to water, of whose essence are the fountain, the river, and the sea proceeding from both. Nicolas adds, however, that in the Godhead, as illustrated here, no procession occurs in any sense of succession in time, for eternity is the principle of itself.[2]

' The Spirit leads our hearts upwards to God, but the flesh leads them downwards.' Guided thus by the Spirit we continue to explore with reverence God's triune Nature. Even Aristotle says truly that the First Cause is threefold, yet ' there cannot be three first causes, for unity is before all plurality.' The emphasis in the Doctrine of the Trinity varies with the point of view. They are three Persons when

---

[1] *Ibid*, v The possession of the Spirit is also the pledge of eternal life —*Ibid*, vii.
[2] *Ibid.*, vi

we consider Them in Their hypostases ; but when we consider Them in Their eternity, They are one Cause. But in the First Cause there appears a Trinity of causation—*causa efficiens, causa formalis*, and their bond, which is *possibilitas* and *actus*. So from power, form, and motion we reach the conclusion that God who is the ' Giver of Life ' is both Three (*trinus*) and One.[1] The third hypostasis of this Trinity of causation, namely motion, appears in the statement : ' The Spirit of God moved upon the face of the waters ' (Gen. i. 2) ; and again in the dispensation of grace as perfecting our ' inner man ' (cf. Eph. iii. 16 ; 2 Cor. iv. 16).[2] In the last book of the series the human intellect once more figures in illustration of the Divine Triunity, containing, as it does, intellect, the expression of conception or idea, and the spirit of desire or longing. 'Wherefore in every operation of the intellectual nature there shines forth a resemblance to God's causation. And it appears how perfection requires a trinity, namely Father, Son, and Holy Spirit.' So this desire of the mind is the Spirit, in whom are united the powers of that rational mind, which in discursive reasoning are mutually distinct. This Spirit Christ gave to mankind after His Ascension, and the presence of love in the mind is a sign that the Spirit of Love dwells within it. Hence ' in the universe there are various creatures, spiritual and corporeal, and, through one omnipotent Spirit who fills all things, these are held together.' Through this same Spirit also, human hearts are sanctified, becoming holy and pure by possessing Him. ' Should you say, " In what is this Spirit recognized ? " I answer, " In poverty in respect of the world of flesh, which means abundance in respect of the world of spirit."'[3]

Further observations concerning the Trinity are found in the second of his three volumes entitled *Cribratio Alchoran*, containing a ' sifting ' of Mohammedan teaching. In every part of the universe, according to Nicolas—in angels, in men, in the animal, vegetable, and mineral worlds—there exists the triad of fruitfulness, a bringing forth (*partus*), and love. ' And whence has the world these things, so that it is necessarily threefold even as it is one, save from the Creator ? . . . Therefore, just as a created thing is one in three, so also is the

[1] *Ibid*, vii [2] *Ibid*, ix [3] *Ibid*, x

Creator ; since a thing created by itself is nothing, and everything which exists subsists in this way, since it is the image and likeness of the Creator. So the trinity which is seen in the creature is created by the Trinity even as a copy is by the original, and a cause by a cause. God is therefore triune, and He has created a triune universe according to the image and likeness of Himself. In the Divine Nature, then, there is fruitfulness, offspring (*proles*), and love,' which are the Father, the Son, and the Bond of Them Both. Another reflection of the Trinity is found in the intellect, which is composed of fruitfulness, idea or intellectual conception, and will[1] ; another in Love, which is composed of uniting love or unity of love (*uniens amor, unitas amoris*), equality, and their union, which are not three eternals but one eternity. Finally, a comparison of Deity with humanity also serves to point to a Trinity in the Godhead. We do not speak of three humanities but of three men, for humanity and man are not identical. But Deity and God are identical on account of the most simple Divine Essence.[2] Wherefore, even as there is no plurality of Deities, so there is no plurality of Gods. Also, there are only three persons in humanity, namely, I, thou, he ; and these three persons are of the same humanity. Even so is God threefold in Persons and one in Essence and Deity—a conclusion which is supported by the baptismal formula given by our Lord (Matt. xxviii. 19).

The temporary character of the Scholastic ' Revival ' was largely the outcome of its nature of compromise. Influenced by the Mystics of the school of Eckhart and the new quest upon which they had already embarked, they were impressed with the necessity of a more intimate application of those fundamentals of the faith which had been receiving such reasoned and scientific exposition. At the same time, their foundation was ecclesiastical, their monitor the authority of the Mediaeval Church, ever suspicious of any new search for truth, and, in consequence, their thought always remained essentially scholastic. For all that, their widened vision and clearer insight into the religious needs of a developing Europe caused

---

[1] Cf *Excitat*, x —' Spiritus seu voluntas,' and a passage in *ibid*, vi , which interprets the petition in the Lord's Prayer, ' Thy will be done,' as referring to the effectual working of the Holy Spirit on earth, *voluntas* being equivalent to the Spirit !

[2] Recalling the opposition of the Church to the contrary assertions of Gilbert of Poitiers

them to present theology in a more practical manner, so that the work of the Holy Spirit, particularly in the adoption and sanctification of the human soul, received greater attention at their hands. Indeed, the attitude of Nicolas in all his consideration of the Holy Spirit's relation to mankind may be summed up in one of his epigrams, ' No one is happy unless he is a son of God.'[1]

[1] *Excitat*, vi

IV

THE ANTI-SCHOLASTIC MYSTICS

UNLIKE the earlier Mysticism of the Victorines and the later Mysticism of the Scholastic Revival, the Mysticism of the German type which flourished in the fourteenth century was definitely anti-scholastic. It was the direct negative to the question whether man can by searching find out God. It was a striking recoil from the long conventionalism in Scriptural interpretation and from the maze of Nominalist dialectic which had been outstanding features of the Scholastic system.[1] To say bluntly that the Mystics preferred the authority of the Holy Spirit to that of Aristotle would be to cast an undeserved slur upon theologians who, while they were Schoolmen, were spiritually-minded. At the same time there had been in existence too great a tendency to dislodge Divine guidance from its first position, and this tendency was now roundly countered by men whose outlook was not only anti-Scholastic but also anti-worldly.

At this point Mysticism begins to take shape as a distinct phenomenon, as a movement in itself, so that when taken in conjunction with the Renaissance it figures as one of the two main sources of a new river of free thought which was destined to overflow its banks in the Reformation. Yet Eckhart, Suso, Tauler, and Ruysbroek were all genuine Catholics, bent truly on popularizing religion, but without any separatist motive. There were, indeed, dangers of exaggeration in the subjectivism of their system which were to receive correction at the hands of the still more practical Reformers,[2] while their insistence on the possibility of union with God, to the subordination of the Atonement,[3] also on the statement that God teaches

---

[1] The deification of things (*res*), found in extreme Nominalism, is related to Pantheism, and Pantheism (as Eckhart illustrates) is akin to Mysticism. Thus there was a link between the first and the third, in cause if not in effect.

[2] Inge, *Christian Mysticism*, p 57, notes in history an extreme mysticism which was 'little more than a dramatization of the normal psychological experience' These, however, he calls 'pseudo-mystics'

[3] See Pope, *Christian Theology*, ii, p 428

THE ANTI-SCHOLASTIC MYSTICS

individuals as distinct from the Church, aroused the suspicion of the ecclesiastical authorities. For all that, their devotional works rest upon an essentially orthodox foundation, and the air of singularity which attaches to their movement was due in no little measure to the fact that the mystical spirit has always been more congenial to the Eastern temperament than to the Western.[1]

Dean Inge's definition of Mysticism as 'the attempt to realize, in thought and feeling, the immanence of the temporal in the eternal, and of the eternal in the temporal'[2] prepares us to expect in this chapter a greater emphasis on the Divine Unity than on the Divine Trinity. Throughout this section, too, the familiar designation of the Holy Spirit as Love is much in evidence.

MEISTER ECKHART

Johann Eckhart (1260–1327), generally called 'Master,' and possessing ever widening influence in the circles of the Dominican Order, was the first and the chief of these speculative Mystics. Thoroughly conversant with Aristotelian philosophy, he taught theology from pulpit and desk, his scholars at Cologne including Suso and Tauler. In his extant writings[3] there is little to indicate any definite development of doctrine save from the pantheistic standpoint. He largely identifies the Deity with *Natur*, and his work is one protest against binding God, who is essentially Spirit, within set formulae. He dwells upon the power, creatorship, and sole reality of God, and, while he admits the existence of the Trinity, he asserts that the contemplative soul is desirous only of union with God in His Unity of Love, in which character He has most clearly revealed Himself. Within this Unity of Love, which is God, there are three equal, eternal, and Personal distinctions of Father, Son, and Holy Spirit. The Holy Spirit, as the love-bond of the Father and the Son and as that eternal distinction in the Deity corresponding to the human will, is immanent in the world as Divine love, and illuminates and draws humanity upwards to its true Divine

---

[1] Cf Swete, *Holy Spirit in the Ancient Church*, p 148 n, on Dr Inge's reference to a connexion between the German Mystics and Methodius, the Eastern Father
[2] *Ibid*, p 5
[3] *Eine Theologische Studie* (Martensen, Copenhagen, 1842).

end which is God Himself. But on the exact mutual relations of the Persons Eckhart remains somewhat obscure.

HEINRICH SUSO

Of the remaining three Mystics here considered, the one who came most fully under Eckhart's influence was Heinrich Suso (1300-1365), also a Dominican. An ascetic, writer, preacher, and passionate admirer of his master, he has been styled the poetic spirit of the movement, and, like Eckhart, his mind was occupied more with the Divine Essence than with the Divine Persons. A 'dialogue' between Maiden and Minister, in the *Appendix Quarundam Sublimium Quaestionum*,[1] reveals certain of his trinitarian opinions. The very fact that from the supreme and essential Goodness there can proceed a supreme Emanation clearly reveals in the Holy Trinity a consubstantiality or communion of Substance which must itself be supreme. It also reveals that the highest equality and identity of Essence, together with undivided power, belong to the three Divine Persons. But 'that a Trinity of Divine Persons is able to subsist in a unity of Essence cannot be explained in words.' These sublime facts are for belief rather than for argument. Thus we believe that the reciprocal love (*amor reciprocus*) of the Father and the Son is named Holy Spirit, and this mutual love (*amor mutuus*), which is the Holy Spirit, 'is distinct in Person, but is one God in one Essence along with the Father and the Son.' Since this Emanation is by way of will and of love, the third Person in the Godhead, who emanates from the flowing forth of love (*ex amoris perfluvio*), proceeds both from the Father and from His own express Image; but this Person is not a Son, nor can He be called begotten. Since, again, this love exists in the will intellectually or spiritually, or exists as a certain inclination and uniting power of love in the One who loves toward Him whom He loves, the emanation of will, which is love, belongs to the third Person, and is called Holy Spirit. 'The Father and the Son simultaneously bring forth the Holy Spirit, and the Unity which is the Essence of the first origin is also the Substance of the three Persons together'; so that the three Persons do not exist apart from Each Other, but cohere at once in unity of Essence. The warning is

[1] *Appendix Q S Q* (ed 1588), chaps XIX-XXI

repeated that the mystery of the Three in One and the One in Three is altogether too deep a subject for explanation in language. Suso shrinks from debate and prefers contemplation. Even so, his mind is neither aloof nor abstruse. He holds that the Church's means of grace, in particular the Sacraments, are necessary to spiritual growth. The Cross is central to his teaching, and his view of Jesus, which closely resembles that taken by Bernard, was as real a stimulus to a practical spirit-filled life in his own case as it was in the case of the other.

JOHANN TAULER

The other noted Dominican pupil of Eckhart was the famous preacher of the movement. Johann Tauler (1290–1361) was early attracted by mediaeval devotional literature, and he proceeded to turn to good effect the impressions received from his master and later from other Mystics in Germany. His devotional mind was of a more practical type which discourages unreality. He was eager to reach the people, and in this he succeeded, becoming the human instrument of a great revival of spiritual life in the Rhine region. Accordingly his opinions on the subject under review are in the main set forth in his sermons, which have seen many editions, and which are singularly free from the extravagances so often associated with 'mystical' utterances. The Holy Spirit, for instance, teaches us by means of Holy Scripture and Church tradition.[1] Taught thus, we learn that ' our most loving Creator is present with us as Father, Son, and Holy Spirit,'[2] a most Holy Trinity truly mirrored in the three very notable powers of the human mind—memory, understanding, and will.[3] The most fundamental article of the faith declares that the Father, Son, and Holy Spirit are only one God[4]—God in a unity of Essence and in a Trinity of Persons.[5] ' As the one God the Trinity is Holy and should ever be revered. . . . Concerning this Trinity we are unable to employ suitable expressions, and yet something must be said concerning It. . . . No created intellect can at all comprehend that that super-essential

---

[1] *Sermones* (Paris, 1623), *Dominica* III, *Adventus, Sermo* 1.
[2] *Dominica Infra Octavas Epiphaniae, Sermo unicus*
[3] *In Nativitate Domini, Sermo* 1
[4] *Dominica* 1 Post Octavas Ep phaniae, Sermo 1
[5] *Dominica* IV ; Post Pascha, Sermo II

unity, so simple in Essence, is also threefold in Persons, that the Persons are distinguished from One Another, that the Father begets the Son, that the Son proceeds from the Father and yet remains within in perfect knowledge of Himself, . . . and that out of that knowledge with which They comprehend Each Other proceeds inexpressible Love, namely the Holy Spirit. . . . So, indeed, the Son and the Holy Spirit are one (*unum*) with the Father; but great is the distinction between the Persons,'[1] for in the Divine operations can be traced the Father in the work of His omnipotence, the Son in the light of His eternal wisdom, and the Holy Spirit in the work of His great, beautiful, eternal, and boundless love. To the soul that is aware of this life has a new meaning.[2] Throughout his sermons Tauler, in common with the other Mystics of his school, gives the designation of Love to the Holy Spirit, and to these thinkers such a designation would have been impossible apart from a full acceptance of the Spirit's Godhead.[3]

With regard to the presence of the Spirit in the soul—a subject dear to the heart of Tauler—he declares that it is possible to be certain of this presence when striving to follow Christ, but that such certainty completely vanishes when sway is allowed to bodily passions.[4] Yet the Holy Spirit has seven gifts in His bestowal for all who desire to tread in the upward way, namely, the fear of the Lord, holiness, knowledge, courage, prudence, understanding, and wisdom.[5] And upon the larger question his words are conclusive: 'Nothing clearly is more profitable than that we retain the true, pure, and simple faith concerning one God in a Trinity of Persons, not in various ways, but simply and plainly.'

JAN VAN RUYSBROEK

Many of the sentiments contained in the writings of Eckhart, Suso, and Tauler are found also in *The German Theology*, a booklet by an unknown Mystic, afterwards edited by Luther. But it was left to the Dutch mind to produce a Mysticism of a truly practical character which, in conjunction with the teachings concerning mystical union, embraced considerations

---
[1] *In Festo Sanctissimae Trinitatis, Sermo* ii
[2] *In Parasceve* (ἡ παρασκευή—the Preparation), *Sermo* ii
[3] Cf *In Festo Pentecostes, Sermo* v
[4] *Dominica* iv , *Post Pascha, Sermo* i
[5] *In Festo Pentecostes, Sermo* iii

THE ANTI-SCHOLASTIC MYSTICS 219

of human nature and the necessity for its regeneration.¹ The leader of the Flemish interpreters of the mystic sense was Jan van Ruysbroek (1293-1381), *Doctor ecstaticus*, who, like the other theologians of this chapter, wrote in the vernacular, the first Latin translation of his works published at Cologne in 1552 being the one here used. To Ruysbroek contemplation is invaluable as a means of uniting man to God, and in this connexion the stress is again laid on the Divine Essence rather than on the Persons. Whether the discourse be of the Trinity, of the special attributes of the Spirit, or of His special work, it is always guided by the constant recognition of the Divine Unity as the fundamental.

The Trinity, then, is exhibited in Divine nature. 'The Catholic faith instructs us that God is a Trinity in Unity and a Unity in Trinity; that His nature is to know and to love Himself, and within Himself to delight in Himself; and that these three [hypostases] in Him are unchangeable and eternal, without beginning or end,' the goodness of the Divine will being effected by the Holy Spirit.² The Trinity is exhibited also in human nature. ' Our life lives impregnate (*ingenita*) along with the Son within the Father's Substance, and is begotten from the Father along with the Son, and from both These emanates as one along with the Holy Spirit. Thus we live eternally in God, and God in us.'³ Pantheistic tendencies are in evidence here, though not so clearly as in the writings of Eckhart.

With regard to the gift of the Holy Spirit Ruysbroek has something to say when commenting upon the Feast of Pentecost. ' " And they were all filled with the Holy Spirit " (Acts ii. 4), that is, with Divine Love, which, being One, brought with It the Father and the Son, and in this way they received at once the holy and adorable Trinity. . . . It must likewise be understood that Christ gave the Holy Spirit to His disciples at three stages and for a threefold reason. He gave Him to them before He suffered, when He bestowed upon them the power of working miracles, namely, of healing the sick, of expelling demons, of raising the dead, all of which were but physical operations (*corporalia opera*) since they themselves

¹ The distinction between practical and speculative Mysticism is made very clearly by Erdmann, *History of Philosophy*, 1 , p 557
² (*Op omn*) *Speculum Aeternae Salutis*, chap xvii
³ *Ibid* , chap xviii

were following Christ at that time with a love which was in a measure only tangible, physical, or fleshly. Again, He gave Him to them after He had risen from the dead, in order that through Him they might accomplish spiritual actions and works, namely, that they might baptize, remit sins, and teach the truth; inasmuch as already their spiritual love was surpassing and overcoming their physical or fleshly love. Thirdly, at last He gave Him to them after He had ascended into heaven, in order that through Him they might effect and achieve Divine works, and be one with God. . . . In any case, they all received the Holy Spirit, that is to say, the Perfume of Christ.'[1] Herein is seen the necessity for spiritual growth for the gradual conquest of sin, and for the consistent raising of the standard of human affection, before any measure of oneness with God, or the greatest gifts of the Spirit, can possibly be attained. Eckhart would hardly have deemed such a process necessary, especially to the first disciples; but, as compared with the Dutchman, he was accustomed to think more of nature and less of grace.

In his book entitled *On the Ornament of the Spiritual Marriage* Ruysbroek mentions, as the special attributes of the Holy Spirit, ' love, holiness, liberality, pity, mercy, infinite faithfulness, illimitable kindness, riches abundantly scattered, unbounded goodness, . . . a flame of fire inwardly penetrating the Father, the Son, and all the saints in a delightful unity.' Yet the speciality of the Spirit's attributes is due to His place in the Unity of the Godhead, and therefore can never obscure such Unity. ' The Father and the Son breathe one Spirit who is the Will or the Love of Both; and He neither begets nor is begotten, but is the eternal Breath of Each. And these three Persons are at the same time one God and one Spirit; Their works and actions which proceed from Them are common to Them, inasmuch as they operate by virtue of the one most simple Nature.'[2]

Ruysbroek's *True Contemplation* touches upon the operations of the Holy Spirit as those of a distinct Person within God, and draws to a close with his accustomed emphasis on the Divine oneness. ' In very truth,' he writes, ' the Father together with the Son gave to us the Holy Spirit, who is the

---

[1] *In Tabernaculum Foederis Commentaria*, chap lxix (*de Pentecoste*).
[2] *De Ornatu Spiritalium Nuptiarum*, ii, chap xxxviii

THE ANTI-SCHOLASTIC MYSTICS

Love of Both ; and the Holy Spirit Himself gives Himself to us bountifully, also all His gifts. And the same Holy Spirit who, as we have remarked, is the Love of God, demands nothing from us but love.'[1] The Holy Spirit, as the Divine fountain of life and as eternal Love, dwells within those who love Him,[2] and this indwelling is active, being manifest in all good works.[3] ' Here, by the way, it should be realized that, though from our outlook we assign many names to God, His Nature is but one, in three distinct Persons who are Father, Son, and Holy Spirit, one abundant Nature (*Naturam foecundam*) in a Trinity of Persons.'[4] This view receives a final elaboration in a later chapter : ' The Trinity indeed abides eternally in a unity of Nature, and the unity of Nature in a Trinity of Persons ; and in this bond a vital and abundant Nature exists to all eternity. . . . And this very Essence is the Nature of the Persons, who possess three characteristics, namely, paternity, filiation, and voluntary breathing (*voluntaria spiratio*). . . . So then the Nature is one in Itself, and abundant in the Trinity of Persons ; and the Trinity lives in the Unity and the Unity in the Trinity. . . . For the Trinity *is* the Unity of the Nature ; but It contains three Persons, distinct in fact and in thought (*re et ratione*), who are Father, Son, and Holy Spirit, who, indeed, are three distinct Persons and also one undivided Godhead, in no way separable. . . . Again, any One of the Persons is God, seeing that He contains within Himself the whole Nature of the Godhead. Yet we have no right to speak of three Gods, for They are a Unity. . . . In all things the three Persons are at once co-eternal and co-equal in Essence, in life, and in action.' The Father is first according to reason and order, while the Son is second as being begotten from the Father. ' Moreover, out of this mutual regard of the Father and the Son proceeds eternal Delight (*complacentia*) which is the Holy Spirit, the third Person in the Godhead, proceeding from the Father and the Son inasmuch as He is the Will and the Love of Both, and proceeds eternally from Them Both, and flows back again into the Nature of the Godhead.'[5]

The orthodoxy of the Anti-Scholastic Mystics is thus beyond dispute. The emphasis laid upon the Divine Unity in their

---
[1] *De Vera Contemplatione, Opus Praeclarum*, chap xxv
[2] *Ibid*, xiii [3] *Ibid*, xv [4] *Ibid*, xvi. [5] *Ibid*, xxviii.

expositions of the Doctrine of the Trinity in no sense ran counter to the teaching of the Church, for it was natural to those who were constantly handling the great theme of God in His exterior relations with the soul. These Mystics adhered to the Western view of the Procession as based upon the entire *mutuality* of the bonds which exist between the Father and the Son. What distinguishes them is the warmth of their treatment of Divine truths. Their tendencies to pantheism arose largely from their desire to impress the people of their day with the dignity of human nature, with the need for spiritual development, and therefore with the wonderful fellowship possible with the Spirit of love. Their doctrine of the mystical union was never entirely 'mystical' in any narrowly subjective sense. Holy Scripture, the Sacraments, and even Church tradition were regarded as necessary aids, while the Dutch school faced the fact of sin, demanding good works as a proof of the Spirit's indwelling. The mystical revolt against dogmatic rigidity, which had at length been expressed outside Scholastic boundaries, readily lent itself to exaggeration during the following two centuries, but its spirit developed throughout the Reformation, and the movement enters upon a new phase in the modern period with the genius of Boehme.

V

THE EASTERN CHURCH

SINCE the middle of the thirteenth century the sharp division between the Churches of East and West had become more and more accentuated. For this state of affairs religion continued to share the responsibility with politics, the animosity of churchmen being encouraged by the animosity of statesmen. Occasionally, indeed, there happened to be political motives for friendliness which necessitated attempts at theological adjustment, but these attempts all proved futile, and after the downfall of the Eastern Empire the motives themselves which prompted them no longer existed. This notwithstanding, the attempts at agreement and even at reunion which took place during the mediaeval period in the West are full of interest for the student of doctrinal development. Fear of the Turk drove the Eastern Emperor John Palaeologus I to present himself to the Pope in 1369, when Urban V had the satisfaction of witnessing his assent to the *Filioque*. In 1438 a notable effort to achieve union was made at the papal council held at Ferrara, afterwards at Florence, where, in response to the pressure of the Latins, the Greeks agreed dogmatically to the Augustinian interpretation of the Procession. Further than that they refused to go, and it might have been that their strong objection to the insertion of the *Filioque* in the Creed was due as much to their disinclination to reunion as to their enthusiasm for ' orthodoxy.' It is more than possible that even their dogmatic agreement was signified from considerations of personal safety during their residence in Italy. At all events, the Greek attitude at the Council was a familiar compromise which would no more succeed then than it had done previously in the case of Leo III. To crown all, the Eastern Church vigorously refused to confirm the nominal adhesion of her delegates, while John Palaeologus II, who had himself journeyed to Ferrara with his theologians, also, in course of time, renounced this delusive union altogether. So the gulf which separated the two sections of Christendom yawned more widely than ever, particularly when, after the capture of Constantinople, the Turks offered to shield the Greek Church from papal domination.

GENNADIUS

Of this momentous section of Church history in the East the outstanding religious character is Georgios Scholarios (c. 1400–c. 1468), who became patriarch of Constantinople in 1453 as Gennadius II. From his many writings his first Confession of faith may be taken as illustrative of his position during the first period of his career. 'God,' he declares, 'is an invisible Being, intellectual and inexplicable. God is a resounding Wind, a sleepless Eye, an ever-moving Mind. . . . There is one God of gods and Lord of lords, and no Other beside Him. . . . We speak of Three and One. . . . Understand this, that because of this God is called inexplicable, since we cannot comprehend His Nature, nor is His Person like us. . . . Yet God is one, while the Persons of the same Godhead are three. . . . Just as there is one sun, though the sun possesses its ray (ἀκτίς) and its light (φῶς), so also does it imply this concerning God. There is one God, but of the one God there are three Persons, Father, Son, and Holy Spirit, ... one God and not three Gods. And as the sun's disc begets the ray, and from the sun and the rays proceeds the light, so the God and Father begets the Son and His Word, and from the Father and the Son proceeds the Holy Spirit.[1] And the Holy Spirit is everywhere . . . and lightens every man, and does not leave any place.' Further analogies of the Trinity receive mention: 'Life (ψυχή) and reason (λόγος) and breath (πνοή) are one Life and three Persons.' In fire, too, there is the fire itself (πῦρ), its property of heat (καυστικόν), and its property of light (φωτιστικόν). 'Common is Their Essence, common Their timelessness, common Their power, goodness, and justice; and the Father, the Son, and the Holy Spirit possess all things equally, with the exception of Their distinctive characteristics (πλὴν τῶν ἰδίων αὐτῶν). . . . I affirm one Source in God, and this is the Father; He begets

---

[1] καὶ ὥσπερ ὁ δίσκος ὁ ἡλιακὸς γεννᾷ τὴν ἀκτῖνα, καὶ παρὰ τοῦ ἡλίου καὶ τῶν ἀκτίνων ἐκπορεύεται τὸ φῶς· οὕτω ὁ Θεὸς καὶ Πατὴρ γεννᾷ τὸν Υἱὸν καὶ Λόγον αὐτοῦ, καὶ ἐκ τοῦ Πατρὸς καὶ Υἱοῦ ἐκπορεύεται τὸ Πνεῦμα τὸ ἅγιον.

the Son and breathes forth the Holy Spirit. . . . And behold They are co-eternal (συνάναρχοι), and no One is before and no One after in the Holy Trinity.'[1]

The belief in the *Filioque* asserted in this Confession is remarkable as coming from one who was destined to fill the highest office in the Eastern Church, and at first sight it might afford some ground for the assertion, constantly made by Latin theologians, that the Greeks themselves were realizing the truth of the twofold Procession. But this was in fact far from the truth. Policy and not conviction prompted Scholarios to trim his first creed to suit Western tastes, for, as an official of the court, he had attended John Palaeologus II to the Council of Ferrara prepared to assist his imperial master in his desire for the proposed ecclesiastical union of East and West. It was after his homecoming, when he discovered the Greek hostility to the Ferrara compromise, that he altered his attitude to the question of union, and with it his attitude to the dogma of the Procession. The second period of his career may be said to open with his exchange of court life for monastic seclusion, when, under the new name of Gennadius, he began to write against the Western view. The Confession which he presented to the Sultan after his elevation to the patriarchate, at least thirteen years after his return from Florence, could hardly have been this first Confession in view of the historical events already noted. Internal evidence points to his second Confession as the one then presented, as being more in harmony with the Greek view. Otherwise there is little addition to the phraseology of the first Creed. There occurs a further trinitarian analogy of mind (νοῦς), reason (λόγος), and breath (πνεῦμα) ; also the statement, ' We call the will of God the Spirit of God, and Love,' which serves to demonstrate the agreement of both Churches in regard at least to the distinctive attributes of the Spirit of God. In his book entitled *Of one God in a Trinity* is found a philosophical discussion which treats of the personal distinctions eternally existing in the Godhead. But of the genuineness of his antagonism to the *Filioque* no trace of doubt could remain after a perusal of two further works, *On the Procession of the Holy Spirit* and *On the Addition to the Creed*, both of which are strongly anti-Latin in sentiment.

[1] The word τριάς seems first to have been brought into general usage by Origen

In the East, indeed, there had occurred isolated cases where exception had been taken to the prevailing opinion concerning the Procession, but such cases had been rare in the extreme. During the seventeenth and eighteenth centuries also, certain Western divines ventured to assert that the Greeks really believed in the *Filioque*. This, however, was complete fiction.[1] The Greek Church has always been careful to distinguish between the temporal procession or mission of the Holy Spirit from the Son to the race, and, on the other hand, His eternal or metaphysical procession from the Son. This is clear from the *Orthodox Confession of the Eastern Church* (1643) and from later declarations from similar sources; clear also from the Conference at Bonn in 1875 when the Old Catholics (who seceded in 1870) and Anglo-Catholics agreed to surrender the 'unauthorized' addition. But no Western surrender has been effected, the practices of East and West still diverge, and there is at present little sign of any further appeal to the mediation of John of Damascus.

[1] The Greeks, on their side, would have been justified in retorting upon the case of Simon Episcopius († 1643), a Dutch theologian who held to their own view very strongly.

VI

THE PRE-REFORMATION REFORMERS

IN the long struggle against papal domination one indirect part had already been played by the great fourteenth-century Mystics. Another indirect part was being played by d'Ailly and Gerson, who ventured to criticize within narrow limits certain abuses of the Church. A more direct part, however, was now played by certain notable men, who may correctly be termed forerunners of Luther, not, indeed, as root and branch opponents of the Catholic system either in dogma or in authority, yet as holders of evangelical opinions which were in the main based upon Holy Scripture. Heralds of the Reformers were many, among them being the Lollards, the Hussites, the followers of Savonarola, and the Waldenses whose piety was openly acknowledged by Louis XII. Whatever else may be said concerning this whole preparatory movement as touching its connexion with ecclesiastical, political, or social causes, it was in itself fundamentally spiritual, arising out of the religious experiences of human hearts left cold by what Romanism had offered, and hungering for saving truth stripped of all cloakings and unrealities.

JOHN WYCLIF

Pre-eminent among the guiding spirits of this preliminary movement is John Wyclif (c. 1320–1384), often alluded to as 'the morning star of the Reformation.' Owing much as he did to Occam and to Bradwardine, Wyclif was reputed to be the first schoolman of his day, his intellectual power in debate as in knowledge being quickly recognized at Oxford, his *alma mater*, which at that time outshone even Paris.[1] The Oxford period of his life, before 'the schoolman was transformed into the pamphleteer,' was in its nature scholastic, Augustine continually furnishing the bases for his Latin productions.

---

[1] So John Richard Green, *History of the English People*, pp 228 f.

The mediaeval universities were, however, essentially democratic, and so paved the way for those more powerful days when he appeared as the noble religious patriot, to assume like the Mystics the language of the people as the literary and sermonic vehicle of his thought. Thus in the history of Church and State he appears less as a theologian than as a thunderer against the fetters of the ecclesiastical system, a champion of individual liberty of conscience, and a firm believer in the supremacy of the authority of God's Word, a fact to which was closely related his gift of the first English Bible to his fellow countrymen. But in the history of dogma he is outstanding, even though in his treatment of the doctrine of God he reverts to a scholastic method which affords no material development.

To Wyclif the Holy Spirit possesses Divine Substance and is therefore fully God.[1] He it is who inspires the Holy Scriptures,[2] and 'in the meaning of the Evangelist no one sins against the Holy Spirit but he who sins against the mercy of God by finally despairing.'[3] Further statements concerning the Holy Spirit are found in the sermon on John xv. 26, typical of the sermons in Latin which were delivered before the University of Oxford. One of the causes of Jewish accusation of the Apostles, he remarks, lay in this, that in the absence of Christ the Holy Spirit had descended upon them, illuminating their minds and bestowing upon them the authority of love and the power of working miracles. 'And note that it is sufficiently implied that the Holy Spirit proceeds equally from the Father and the Son, otherwise He who is the Truth would not assert that He sends Him.' Nor does it follow in this particular instance that the One who sends has naturally some priority of source or some dignity over and above the One who is sent. 'And it is clear that Christ in not mentioning that the Holy Spirit proceeds from Himself teaches two things : firstly, that between the Father and Himself there is a priority of source, and this by reason of the fact that the Father cannot be sent by any one ; secondly, by teaching that the Holy Spirit does not proceed from Him in respect of His manhood, He implies that He Himself is God, and that no man ought

---

[1] *Ad Argumenta Emuli Veritatis* (ed. Loserth, Wyclif Soc Pub , 1913)
[2] *De Fide Catholica* (do.)
[3] *Epistola de Peccato in Spiritum Sanctum* (do.)

THE PRE-REFORMATION REFORMERS 229

to boast of the Gift that God may have given him.'[1] Again, 'to the Father is ascribed power, to the Word wisdom, and to the Holy Spirit grace or favour.'[2] Also in one of his later sermons, delivered in English during his more influential years, he declares, 'The Holy Ghost is another Person and another Thing, but He is none other God,' and speaks constantly of the Trinity as of one God.[3]

Wyclif's last and most important work is the *Trialogus*, or *Dialogorum Libri* iv., written two years before his death. In the form of a conversation between three persons (Pseudis and Phronesis being the characters quoted here), the first book treats in a surprisingly dialectical manner the Doctrine of the Trinity. In his reasoning God the Father knows Himself in the Son, and knows actually how much He can know Himself in the Holy Spirit, the second kind of knowledge being necessary to the existence of the first. 'And these three Persons are absolutely and necessarily co-eternal, co-equal, and proceeding in order. For the Father is before the Son in source, and the Father and Son are before the Holy Spirit in source. . . . And any One of these three Beings (*res*) is essentially very God. . . . Since They are one God and not three Causes, so They are not three Gods. Or again: The Father and Son are one Source (*principium*) of the Holy Spirit seeing that conjointly They are the principle of the Holy Spirit; and the whole Trinity is the selfsame Source of every creature.'[4] 'The intellectual mind is threefold, namely, memory, reason, and will. Therefore,' he concludes, 'the God who creates it is threefold.'[5]

John Huss

While Wyclif was engaged upon his *Trialogus*, King Richard II. of England married Anne of Bohemia, who was a decided admirer of the Reformer's life and work. This event had a double effect. On the one hand, it promoted an influx of Bohemian students into Oxford, from which they took back again the reforming atmosphere of a University held in high repute at Prague. On the other hand, it was responsible for the conveyance of larger quantities of Wyclif's books by

---

[1] *Sermo* 30, vol. i (ed Loserth, 1887). [2] *Sermo* 33, vol. iii. (do., 1889).
[3] Sermon 199, vol ii (ed Arnold, Clarendon Press, 1871)
[4] *Dialogorum* 1, chap. vi. (ed. 1753). [5] *Ibid*, chap. vii.

the Queen's Bohemian followers on their return to their own country after her death (1394). In Bohemia John Huss (c. 1369–1415) had already begun to head a protest against ecclesiastical arrogance, and now, under the influence of Wyclif's teaching, his attitude became more aggressive, his movement for reform more widespread. Strange it is that, though the University of Paris was associated in liberal ideas with that of Prague, of which Huss was rector, it was due principally to the enmity of the former that Huss was martyred at Constance. This, however, only serves to show the immense difference between the lengths to which d'Ailly, the Paris Chancellor who took an active part in his condemnation, and Huss himself were prepared to go in the direction of reform. To defend the rights of individual conscience and Scriptural authority he went to the stake; and his followers lived on after the Council of Constance to prepare the way for the Reformation on the continent, while the followers of Wyclif lived on to prepare the way for it in England. For all that, it is no very far cry from Huss the popular reformer to Huss the sententiary. Doctrinally the Bohemian theologian was more conservative than Wyclif, though in places he follows the latter's teaching closely; and his scholastic propensities found free play in his Commentary on the *Sentences*. Occasionally, however, in the course of this work, he reveals some impatience at the Lombard's fine distinctions.

The Commentary declares at the outset that ' the Father, the Son, and the Holy Spirit are one and the same God,' the Holy Spirit being ' the Spirit of truth who, in proceeding from the Father, infallibly teaches all truth.'[1] To the Father power is particularly ascribed, to the Son wisdom, and to the Holy Spirit favour (*benevolentia*). ' Accordingly, " The uncreated Trinity " is put into the title of the question because It is Itself the Origin of all created things; therefore I assert at the commencement that the uncreated Trinity consists of Father, Son, and Holy Spirit, one God, simple, immeasurable, eternal, unchangeable, omnipotent, and omniscient. . . . It is also clear that in the unity of the Divine Nature there are three Persons, of whom the first is from no Person, the second by generation is from the first alone, and the third by a common spiration is from the first and the second. But this is so

[1] Super iv Sent 1, *A Inceptio* 1 f.

because the Trinity of Persons does not exclude unity from the Essence.'¹ 'The Father is not before the Son, nor the Son after the Father; nor, again, is the Holy Spirit after the Father and the Son. . . . There cannot be any priority since the same Essence exists in all the Divine Persons, and They Themselves exist together as a mutually related Nature.' Huss still follows Wyclif closely when he adds that there is indeed one, but only one, priority allowable in the Godhead, namely that of order. The procession of the Holy Spirit is an operation second in order to that of the generation of the Son in deriving from the Father as the First Cause.² Moreover, it is absolutely necessary that the Holy Spirit should be brought forth from the Father *and* the Son . . . and the Father and the Son are one Source in breathing forth the Holy Spirit; so there are not three Causes.'³ But it must be observed that, while the Father and the Son are certainly one Source, the Holy Spirit must be spoken of as proceeding from ' Them,' and not as proceeding from ' It,' merely because They are one common Source.⁴ As Love, He is the common Bond of the Father and the Son, the Bond within which the Father and the Son love One Another, for in natural affection love is shared in common.⁵ And, since this is so, can the Holy Spirit Himself be any other than God?⁶

In the opinion of Huss, the eleventh ' distinction ' reveals, in brief, two facts : ' The first is that the Holy Spirit proceeds from the Father and the Son ; the second is that the Greeks assert the opposite—in their talk, but in reality they agree with us, and certain of their doctors are expressly of our opinion.'⁷ No doubt the period of *rapprochement* between East and West, noted in the last chapter, was mainly responsible for this sweeping assertion, which was written within its limits. As for any reality of agreement, there was little or none, and allowance must be made for this commentator's wish being father to the thought. He then states the case for the *Filioque* analogically : ' Since the Holy Spirit is equivalent to personal volition, and the Word to personal knowledge, it is clear that the Holy Spirit proceeds from the Son because volition proceeds

---
¹ *Ibid.*, *Inceptio* 2
² ' Pater est prima causa et plus influit causando tertiam personam quam secundam personam '
³ *Ibid.*, *dist.* ix. 4. ⁴ *Ibid.*, *dist.* xi. 3. ⁵ *Ibid.*, *dist.* x. 1, 3
⁶ *Ibid.*, 4 ⁷ *Ibid.*, *dist.* xi. 1.

from knowledge. Also the same is evident from the likeness existing in the human similitude of the Trinity, that the third element (*res*) generally proceeds from both those which precede it, as, for instance, the will proceeds from the understanding and the memory.' Beside this, the Scriptures speak of the Holy Spirit as the Spirit of the Son.[1] The next ' distinction ' develops the argument, and, in the words of Huss, what it amounts to is this : ' The master (Lombardus) maintains three things ; firstly, that the Holy Spirit does not proceed from the Father before He proceeds from the Son ; secondly, that He does not proceed chiefly, more fully, or more actually from the Father than from the Son ; thirdly, that He is said, with greater propriety, to be from the Father, because the Son owes it to the Father that He brings forth the Holy Spirit.'[2] So is the Holy Spirit, as Love, the eternal Gift of the Father and the Son.[3]

Attention is called to the manner in which Lombardus distinguishes between procession and generation. The former affects the action of two of the Persons, is humanly rational, and is by way of will ; while the latter affects the action of One alone, is humanly ' irrational,' and is by way of nature. These, however, are distinctions which Huss himself does not labour.[4] But prominence is given to the declaration that ' the Father, Son, and Holy Spirit are equal by reason of the highest simplicity and unity of Their Essence, and not in respect of Their relation.'[5] Here is the equality not of co-ordination but of Infinity. Then in *Distinctions* xv. and xvi. the commentator shows that, as a Gift to mankind, the Holy Spirit bestows Himself ; he also discusses the visible manifestations of the Spirit and of the Son.

In the other books of this same work little concerns the Doctrine of the Spirit. Huss agrees with Wyclif in explaining that the sin against the Spirit of God is ' the sin of obstinacy and of despair,'[6] and mentions that the flesh of Jesus was preserved from moral defilement by the action of the Spirit in descending upon Mary, thereby cleansing her from all sin.[7] It is a sane treatment of the *Sentences*, revealing ripe scholarship but also a disinclination to carry dialectic to extremes. Such extremes, indeed, were impossible to such a man, whose

---

[1] *Ibid*, 5 [2] *Ibid*, *dist.* xii 1 [3] *Ibid*, *dist* xviii [4] *Ibid*, *dist* xiii. 1–5.
[5] *Ibid*, xxxi 1 [6] II., *dist.* xliii 2 [7] III., *dist* iii

outlook embraced issues too great to be contained within any narrow circle of intellectualism.

JOHANN VON WESEL

In Germany one of the precursors of the Reformation was John of Wesel (†1481), Nominalist philosopher at Erfurt, who emphasized the authority of the Scriptures as the rule of faith and boldly attacked the system of indulgences. He is of note especially as being brought as an old man in 1479 before Gerhard Elten of Cologne, the Dominican Inquisitor, on various charges which are reported at length in an elaborate account of his trial.[1] Presumably the real reason for his arrest lay in his unpopular Nominalism, but when face to face with his judges he was confronted with various accusations of heresy, one of which is of present interest. ' Seventhly, questioned as to whether he had at any time declared or published that Sacred Scripture does not say that the Holy Spirit proceeds from the Son, or from Both, and as to what he himself believes in the matter: He admits that he has written these things, but has not published them. Again, he does not believe that the Holy Spirit proceeds from the Father and the Son as from one and the same Source, because it would appear to him that this cannot be found in the text of Sacred Scripture. . . . Ninthly, questioned as to whether he believes that the Church, the Bride of Christ, is governed by the Holy Spirit: This he believes.' The record shows that at this point the trial stood adjourned, and that during the adjournment his judges took counsel concerning his reply on the subject of the Spirit's procession from the Son, deemed by them to be unsatisfactory. On the resumption of proceedings the record continues : ' With regard to the seventh question he persists in the reply given. He still considers that all Christians ought to believe in those words of John, " The Holy Spirit proceeds from the Father " (John xv. 26), more than in these, " The Holy Spirit proceeds from the Father and the Son." He believes that the article of the Nicene Council, " The Holy Spirit proceeds from the Father and the Son," is false. He is doubtful whether a council legitimately convened does directly receive a Divine infusion from the Holy Spirit, and from Christ its Head. Once more, he is convinced that

[1] ' Examen Magistrale ac Theologicale Doctoris Joannis de Wesalia . . . Haereticae . . . inquisitoribus . . . Elten et . . . Sprenger ' (ed. 1530–1540).

the belief that the Holy Spirit proceeds from the Father and the Son is not contained in the Biblical canon either expressly or virtually.'

Seeing that this account of the trial comes principally from the pen of Elten himself, there is little doubt that it is prejudiced. Proof of this is afforded by the above allusion to the *Filioque* as being an article of the Nicene Council, whereas, as Wesel must have known, neither council held at Nicaea, in 325 or in 787, so much as mentioned the matter. To all appearances, Wesel preferred simply to take the Eastern view of the Procession, and accordingly said so ; and it is improbable that this particular view figures among those which he ultimately modified in order to escape the stake. His theological opinions certainly did not influence the minds of his accusers, save possibly to a fiercer hatred of himself. The whole incident shows how deep-seated the belief in the *Filioque* had become in the West.

JOHANN WESSEL

But the chief among the pre-Reformation Reformers in Germany was John Wessel (1420–1489), between whom and Wesel there are striking parallels, alike in Nominalism and in championship of the authority of Scripture as against that of the Church. Thus it is not surprising that Luther edited and published in 1522 a collection of the works of this his principal German herald, under the title of *Farrago Rerum Theologicarum*. In discoursing of the Providence of God, Wessel declares that there is only one Holy Spirit, who proceeds from the Eternal as a Gift, and who Himself bestows gifts in many various ways. For as the Holy Spirit breathes upon us where and when He desires, we are aware of a moving in our hearts which is from Him ; and the love of this eternal Spirit of the Father and the Son transcends while it partakes of the best affections of both human sexes.[1] Yet it is as one God with undivided action that the Father, Son, and Holy Spirit keep on seeking men,[2] even while it is particularly through the Holy Spirit that love is shed abroad in the hearts of God's sons.[3],[4]. Consideration of the Incarnation brings the thought that in this great act the Father and the Holy

---

[1] ' Scio Spiritum aeternum Patris et Filii amicum et amicam, sponsum et sponsam confiteor et scio '

[2] *De Providentia Dei.*   [3] *De Potestate Ecclesiastica*   [4] *De Sacramento Poenitentiae.*

Spirit were also involved, with one result that Christians often use the name Jesus when they have actually the whole Trinity in mind. It brings also another thought, that in the days of His flesh Christ possessed the Gift of the Spirit without measure.[1] 'The Holy Spirit Himself is the Perfume (*unguentum*) which Christ won for us by His death.' Again, 'Spiritual wisdom is that which is taught and inspired by the Spirit of wisdom, and this Spirit is God.'[2] The *Farrago* is full of such epigrams.

Girolamo Savonarola

The same year in which Wessel died saw in Italy the rise of Savonarola (1452–1498), a great preacher rather than a great character, whose aim was the moral and political reform of his own country. The Renaissance, with its mediaevalism, was then holding over Florence an unholy spell which a wealthy papacy made no attempt to break; and it was left to Savonarola to create a great religious movement. This he accomplished so thoroughly that for several years the City experienced theocratic rule of a remarkable type. During this period, however, the Dominican orator began to preach political revolution, giving way to such extremism as resulted in his being strangled and burned, along with two of his Dominican disciples, by order of the Pope.

On the subject of the Holy Spirit his opinions are set forth in that most important of his works, *The Triumph of the Cross*, written at the close of his life against the semi-pagan brilliance of the Italian Renaissance. The Trinity, he asserts, cannot be divided.[3] God is one and the same and infinite although He is threefold,[4] 'a plurality of Gods being impossible.'[5] The spiritual Nature of God is an axiom, for 'no philosopher doubts that God is not matter, nor any form of matter, nor any compound (*compositum*), but absolute Impulse,'[6] and Spirit.[7] 'We believe,' he continues, 'that the crucified Christ Himself is true God and true Man, the Son of God, one in Nature with the Father and the Holy Spirit, and distinct among the Persons.'[8] 'For Christ commanded and desired that God should be believed to be Triune (*trinus*); that is to say, the Father, the Son, and the Holy Spirit are one God in three Persons who are

---

[1] *De Incarnatione et Passione* [2] *De Sacramento Poenitentiae*
[3] *Triumphus Crucis*, I. I. [4] *Ibid*, 5 [5] *Ibid.*, 9. [6] *Ibid*, 7.
[7] II. 2. [8] *Ibid*, 7.

really distinct, but who are One in Substance and Essence, and most simple in Being.'[1]

It is, however, in the third book of the *Triumphus* that Savonarola expresses himself at length on the Doctrine of the Trinity. 'We confess,' he writes, 'the three Persons who are really distinct, namely, the Father, Son, and Holy Spirit, to be one God. . . . We say again that God is One, most simple and infinite, and we do not challenge anything concerning God which is approved by true philosophy, however much we may assert that He is Father, Son, and Holy Spirit. Not as says Sabellius nor as says Arius do we say. . . . But proceeding in the royal and middle way, we affirm as against Sabellius that the Father, Son, and Holy Spirit are three really distinct Persons; yet as against Arius we affirm that They are one in Nature, and co-equal in power and glory. . . . Wherefore the distinction between Them does not exist in the same way as it does among the creatures in that one Person has something that Another has not. . . . The Holy Spirit has whatever the Father and the Son have; but He is distinguished from Them in this particular, since He has it from Them, while They certainly do not receive it from Him. . . . Again, the procession of the Holy Spirit is from the Father and the Son by way of love, for love is the bond and the union of all. But since in the natural realm nothing is found which equally proceeds immediately from two things equally perfect, as the Holy Spirit proceeds from the Father and the Son, for that reason not so particular a name was devised for the procession of the Holy Spirit as for the procession of the Son; but, in general, procession is the name used in respect of the One who proceeds from the Father; though, since we say that the Holy Spirit proceeds by way of will or of love, we call His procession from the Father the breathing forth of a First Principle. . . . So therefore the three Persons exist as One in Substance, and are distinguished by opposite relation.' Then, in view of the intellectual pride of his day, he adds: 'Though human impotence does not suffice for the understanding of this, nevertheless we ought not to be sceptical of the Holy Mysteries which are revealed to us. For it is ridiculous to suppose that nothing is true except what we can measure by the rule of our own intellect.'[2]

[1] *Ibid*, 13   [2] III 3.

This caution, however, does not in any sense alter the fact that Savonarola's theology of the Holy Spirit and of the Trinity is truly mediaeval both in spirit and in setting. His reforming zeal never aimed at influencing existing theology. Aquinas remained his foundation, and he himself lived and died within the Church of Rome. He was, in fact, a Reformer only in morals and in politics, while in both these realms his outlook was mediaeval. Indeed, it was on account of his reaching *backward* in an attempt to revive the old Dominican asceticism that he was condemned by the Pope—not on account of any step forward to new ideas. ' No man having drunk old wine desireth new ; for he saith, The old is good ' (Luke v. 39). Such may be said of Savonarola. But even the revival of the old was far too drastic for such a man as Alexander VI.

JACOBUS FABER (STAPULENSIS)

Finally, in France the chief pioneer of the Protestant movement was Jacobus Faber (Jaques Lefèvre) (1455–1536), surnamed Stapulensis from his native town of Etaples. His connexion with the revival of learning links him to the Renaissance ; but, on account of his translation of the Bible into French and his general adherence to Lutheran principles, he is linked more closely to the Reformation. In view of the fact, however, that he never broke with the Roman Church, always cherishing the hope that her reform would come quietly from within, he is associated with the pre-Reformation Reformers rather than with the Reformers themselves. His works include a commentary on *The Orthodox Faith of John of Damascus*, beside commentaries on the Gospels and the Epistles, and from these his Commentary on St. John's Gospel, written and published in 1522, may be selected as containing examples of his pneumatology.

' God is a Spirit,' he writes, ' and those who worship Him must worship Him in spirit and in truth. The Father begets, the Son is begotten, the Holy Spirit is breathed forth. . . . So these diversities—to beget, to be begotten, to be breathed forth—are those by which One is Father, Another is Son, Another is Holy Spirit. And these Three are One (*unum*), and one God.' The Paraclete, the Comforter of the apostles, came openly after the Lord's departure, but He always came secretly while He was present. 'But as long as the Lord was plainly present in the world, the Holy Spirit (although He is the Spirit of Truth, that is, of the Son) was with the Father, and absent from the world; but after the Lord was received up to the Father and was plainly absent from the world, He sent Him from the Father. . . . Certain it is that the Paraclete, that is the Holy Spirit, has proceeded from the Son even as He has proceeded from the Father.'[1] At least, now that He has been poured out upon the world, His regenerating power is manifest, for 'those whom the Holy Spirit arrests He unexpectedly makes spiritual.'[2] The sixteenth chapter, too, gives evidence that the Holy Spirit was sent by the Son even as the Son was sent by the Father. Then the incident of the breathing of the Holy Spirit upon the apostles as recorded in the twentieth chapter of the Gospel is considered, receiving the following comment. 'On that occasion the Lord gave the Holy Spirit to the apostles in one way; in another way on about the fiftieth day after. And each manner was necessary for the world.' The explanation follows that the bestowal of the Holy Spirit in St. John's account had particular application to the Lord's followers in that it conveyed authority for remitting sins. This gift Faber believes has never been withdrawn, nor will be withdrawn till the Last Day, even though there may be changing forms of its employment.[3]

Thus these heralds of the Reformation, with but one exception, received and passed on the accepted teaching of the Church with regard to the Holy Spirit and His place in the Deity, never forgetting to remind their readers of the fact that God is One. To the Doctrine of the Trinity they gave careful thought without being abstruse, substituting for the extreme subtlety so often found in Scholasticism an attitude of simple belief which recognized the inadequacy of the human intellect in face of infinite mysteries. Most striking, however, is their insistent emphasis upon the authority of the Bible as the Rule of Faith, with the consequent enforcement of its inspiration by the Holy Spirit, the infallibility of the Spirit's teaching as therein contained, and the regenerating and sanctifying power of the Spirit as therein preached. Accordingly, the pre-Reformation Reformers speak of the Holy

---

[1] *Comm. in Evang Joannis* (ed 1522), on chap xv
[2] *Ibid*, on chap. xvi.   [3] *Ibid.*, on chap. xx

Spirit's operations in the soul in conjunction with a more direct and conscious relation of the soul to Him, the ground of such relation being the Atonement wrought by Christ. They carried on this discussion in a distinctly evangelical spirit, ignoring alike the intermediaries of scholastic sacramentarianism and of mystical progression. But the doctrine of justification by faith, which was the great spiritual message of the Reformation, they left to Luther to proclaim.

VII

THE HUMANISTS

THE revival of learning associated with the Humanists of the fifteenth and sixteenth centuries was as the introduction of fresh air into a well-used atmosphere. In 1438 ecclesiastics from the East brought Greek with them into Italy, where the classical movement of Rienzi had been rescued from its political groove by Petrarch ; and during the following year certain of them proceeded to England to teach their ancient language. The stimulus given to the new intellectualism by the fall of Constantinople and by the patronage of Nicholas V made Italy the centre of light. Here the Renaissance took philosophical and artistic forms, ranking gratification of taste before doctrine and thereby revealing those sceptical tendencies so strongly denounced by Savonarola. Philosophy was now divorced from theology. The efforts of the Schoolmen to combine science and philosophy were completely discredited, and the Humanists, who employed their knowledge of Greek in the study of the New Testament as well as of Plato, widened the breach by adopting a critical attitude toward this authority. Moreover, the appearance of politics, in the more modern sense of the term, supported the progress of religious and philosophic thought in its protest against the theological rigidity which had long been one of the chief features of mediaevalism. In his day Boniface VIII had come into contact with the rising sense of nationality which the papacy itself had encouraged in order to defeat the Empire ; and now, with the exception of Italy and Germany, which still endured the antique government of the Holy Roman Empire, the great states were modernizing themselves while the Church remained mediaeval. Accordingly, along parallel lines of inward and outward movements, the domination of system was passing away and the individual was coming to his own, a fact which the work of the pre-Reformation Reformers serves only to emphasize.

In Germany and in England Humanism took upon itself a

THE HUMANISTS 241

more theological character with such spiritual minds as Reuchlin and Erasmus, Colet and More, whose views on the Doctrine of the Holy Spirit reflect in part the individualism of the time. But Humanism itself was an essentially mediaeval phenomenon,[1] anti-ecclesiastical in part while not definitely anti-dogmatic; consequently the theology of the Trinity is presented by these four writers in quite a familiar form.

JOHANN REUCHLIN

Prominent among the Humanists is Johann Reuchlin (1455–1522), a great classical scholar and Platonist, and a pioneer of the Renaissance in Germany. While in Rome in 1482 as ambassador from the Elector he applied to be a student of Argyropulos, an aged exile from Constantinople, who was teaching Greek in that city to distinguished audiences; and it was Argyropulos who, on hearing his new pupil read into excellent Latin a passage from Thucydides, exclaimed with emotion, 'With our exile Greece has passed over the Alps.' But, even more than as a classic, Reuchlin is famed as a Hebraist, and he incurred the bitter hostility of the German Dominicans for upholding the necessity of studying the mind of the Jewish people in their own writings. His *De Verbo Mirifico*, which he published in 1494, is based on the Jewish theosophy of the Cabbala. In this work may be seen his fondness for the study of the Scriptures in their original tongues, but in devoting the main portion of it to the consideration of the Old Testament and the pagan philosophers, he gives little attention to the New Testament, which accounts for the scantiness of material relative to the Holy Spirit. God is a Spirit, he declares.[2] No one, however, knows the Mind of the eternal God but he within whom is His Spirit and to whom He reveals Himself; just as no being knows the thoughts of a man save only his own spirit which is in him.[3] Within this one most simple God exists the Holy Spirit, who has been spoken of as 'Fire' by Moses, Ezekiel, Plato, and others.[4] Full knowledge of the whole Trinity has been gained by no one,[5] though the analogy of mind, reason, and feeling (*sensus*), found in the human intellect, indicates that partial knowledge

---

[1] Pius II, one of its promoters, made a vain attempt to revive the glories of the mediaeval papacy
[2] *De Verbo Mirifico*, ii 6 (ed 1561)   [3] *Ibid*, 13   [4] *Ibid*, 16   [5] iii 4

of this mystery has already been attained.¹ Then, before proceeding to consider the Eternal Generation of the Son, he delivers this judgement: 'It should be openly professed that the true eternal God is One, immeasurable, unchangeable, incomprehensible, omnipotent, and indescribable—Father, Son, and Holy Spirit—three Persons truly, but one Essence, Substance, Nature, utterly simple. . . . There are three "hypostases," which in Latin is translated "Persons." . . . And the Catholic faith is this, that we worship the one God in a Trinity, and the Trinity in a Unity; neither confounding the Persons, nor dividing the Substance.'²

John Colet

Though Reuchlin enjoyed the friendship of Wessel ever since he had studied under him at Basel, and also greatly influenced his young relative and pupil Melanchthon, he himself shrank from any tendencies toward Church reform. Not so, however, did John Colet (c. 1467–1519), Dean of St. Paul's, who, on the contrary, associated with his Humanism a passion for reform which fills his powerful sermons and writings. Colet's learning thus possessed a distinctly religious aim. An ardent student of the Bible and, in particular, of the New Testament in its original tongue, he had no sympathy with the Scholastic system, with its subtlety and championship of the supreme authority of the Church. On the other hand he was content to place Jesus Christ at the centre, and from that centre to labour straightforwardly for the bringing about of a widespread moral revival; and, indeed, the secret of his greatness as a preacher lay in his directness and simplicity. It is not surprising, then, to observe that during his sojourn in Italy in 1493 he was influenced not by the enthusiasts for art but by Savonarola. Yet, persecuted as he was on account of his open dislike of certain Romish practices and his plain speaking concerning abuses, he, like Faber, desired reform to come quietly from within; accordingly he worked for the spiritual uplift of the English Church without seeing any necessity for her separation from Rome.

Colet was a firm believer in the power of the Holy Spirit to regenerate and sanctify the human heart, but to the development of the Doctrine he contributes little. In his treatise *On*

¹ *Ibid*, 7. ² *Ibid*, 8.

the Church he sets forth the Divine Spirit as the great permeating Force of Good, as God Himself indwelling and guiding man ; and in his *Lectures on the Epistle to the Romans*, delivered at Oxford, which reveal his dislike of Scholasticism, he emphasizes the Holy Spirit's work of regeneration in the soul, cleansing it from sin and imparting to it the new life. In his book *On the Sacraments of the Church* he states that ' By God the Father, through the Son, with the Holy Spirit, all things exist, are formed, and are perfected ' ;[1] and that ' Confirmation truly testifies to the sure giving of the Holy Spirit . . . for it is the sacrament of the giving of the Spirit.'[2] There is no doubt whatever that Colet helped to prepare the way for the Reformation in England not only by the enlightenment caused by his learning, but also by his constant insistence on the efficacy of God's work in the individual heart, the Church being rightly regarded as a channel of such efficacy, but in no sense as the inevitable intermediary between God and the individual.

SIR THOMAS MORE

A ready sympathy with Colet in his desire for reform was forthcoming from one of his close associates, Sir Thomas More (1478-1535), Lord Chancellor of England and author of the *Utopia*, who, together with the Dean, was attracted more by the reforming party in Italy than by the artistic. Nevertheless he remained a consistent and staunch Romanist, in direct opposition to the more popular expression of reform then in full swing on the continent, and from his assumption of the Chancellorship he shared with Fisher the recognized leadership of the Catholic party in England. Most of his theological writings are concerned with the particular heresies of the period, some of them being directed against Tyndale and Luther ;[3] hence the paucity of his remarks which bear upon the Doctrine of the Holy Spirit. His *Dialogue Concerning Heresies* contains the statements that God is a spiritual Substance and is omnipresent, and that the Holy Spirit is ' the Giver of life ' ; but no noteworthy declaration on this subject ever flowed from his pen.

---

[1] *De Sacramentis Ecclesiae*, 1
[2] *Ibid*, 9
[3] Cf J R Green, *English History*, p 315, where More anticipates that the dogmatism of Luther will check the quiet reforming work of the Renaissance

DESIDERIUS ERASMUS

Fortunately this need not be said of the brilliant friend of More and Colet, Desiderius Erasmus (1466-1536), styled by Lord Acton 'the King of the Renaissance.' Of Dutch birth and yet, in another of Acton's phrases, 'an international character,' he led the Humanist protest against the superstitions of the Church, even though the results of his scholarship tended to uphold her dogmatic beliefs. At the same time it was evident to him that the Renaissance had weakened the sense of sin and narrowed the scope of theology by its new attention to Homer and Plato, and while he could not agree with Luther's doctrine of the depravity of human nature he shaped his learning to the distinctly religious end of presenting to the world the Person of Christ and the message of His gospel in all its simplicity.[1] Accordingly he follows Colet in his dislike of the current systematic theology and of the Schoolmen who had been mainly responsible for it; though in his *Exposition of the Common Creed*, written in English in the form of a dialogue between Disciple and Master, his own views of God are by no means without system.

'I know,' he writes, 'that there is but one God, which Name for all that comprehendeth three Persons · that is to say, the Father, which only is of none other; the Son, which was begotten of the Father before all time; the Holy Ghost, which proceedeth from Them Both. . . . Let not man's wit imagine here any transitory or bodily thing. All things here are eternal, unspeakable, and incomprehensible, to the understanding of which man's reason is obscure and blind; and they are perceived only by faith. They are three, distinct in properties, but They are all Three of one and the same Substance or Nature, or of one Essence . . . of one almightiness, of one majesty, of one wisdom, and of one goodness. There is indeed an order in this Trinity, but inequality there is utterly in it none at all. For None of Them is posterior to the Other in time, neither is One of them inferior to Another in dignity. The Deity of Them all three is one, and They three are one

---

[1] A striking evidence of this lies in his popular editions of the Greek Testament, in the third of which he restored the famous interpolation concerning the Trinity, 1 John v 7 (A V) (Cf Herzog, *Encycl*) Yet Erasmus, with peace-loving conservatism, pursued an uncomfortable middle way between the Catholic and the Lutheran positions, being in sympathy with many of Luther's ideas but steadfastly opposed to any personal break with the Church In a letter of his to Melanchthon in 1524 he states that he had separated the cause of literature from the cause of Luther

God. . . . The Father hath the first place, the Son hath the second, the Holy Ghost hath the third, which is charity or love and a certain unspeakable bond or knot of Them Both. . . . Even so doth the same Spirit glue the Church unto Christ.' At this point Erasmus mentions certain analogies of the Trinity : (1) the sun, the sun's beams, and the heat proceeding from both ; (2) mind, reason, and will emanating from both ; (3) a fountain, a river flowing therefrom, and fertility arising from both. These internal distinctions typified here are, however, contained within the one Divine Substance, and ' substance' is defined as ' a thing substantially being of itself.' The oneness of the external actions of the Three appears, for instance, in the creation of the world, ' for the Father hath made all creatures by the Son, the Holy Ghost working together with Them Both.' But when he turns to consider these internal distinctions, Erasmus, bearing in mind his definition of ' substance,' continues : ' Certain men have said that the Holy Ghost is not a Substance, but that He is nought else but the emotion (*concitation*) or stirring of a godly mind. But this motion or stirring of our mind is indeed caused and cometh of the Holy Spirit, but it is not the very Holy Ghost's Self.' This Self truly exists behind these emotions, and, as the Spirit of God, He is called ' Holy ' in order to distinguish Him from spirits that are evil. The matter of the *Filioque*, with the divergent opinions thereon of East and West, receives in conclusion a brief notice which shows Latin sympathies : ' For as the Son is argued and proved to be of the same Substance with the Father because He is begotten of the Father, even so is it concluded and gathered that the Holy Ghost also hath the same Nature with Them Both, forasmuch as He proceedeth and cometh forth of Them Both.'[1] Procession from Both thus indicates Deity in common with Both.

In their emphasis of faith before reason as the right attitude of mind with reference to the Trinity, their declarations as to the new life brought about by the regenerating and sanctifying power of the Holy Spirit, and their eagerness to place popular versions of the Scriptures in the hands of the masses, the Humanists closely resemble the pre-Reformation Reformers. The need of a more practical theology undoubtedly existed, and if, in their attempt to meet that need, the Humanists

[1] *Expo/ycyon of the commune Crede*, § 2 (ed. 1533)

succeeded only in bringing about an intellectual reformation, their success was none the less a definite step forward.[1] Spiritually, however, the Renaissance was incomplete, for it raised hopes which could alone be fulfilled by a renaissance in human hearts ; and when Luther burned the Pope's Bull in the market-place at Wittenberg he knew that he was standing for deeper things than those for which the Humanists had ever stood.

[1] See Bryce in reference to the Renaissance, *Holy Roman Empire*, p 241 ' The agitation was not merely speculative There was beginning to be a direct and rational interest in life, a power of applying thought to practical ends, which had not been seen before ' Bellarmine calls Laurentius Valla, the great Italian Humanist, a forerunner of Luther.

PART IV

FROM THE BEGINNING OF THE SIXTEENTH CENTURY TO THE BEGINNING OF THE SEVENTEENTH CENTURY.

The Reformation and its Immediate Results.

I. Foreword
II. The Theology of Luther and Melanchthon
III. The Reformed Theology of Zwingli
IV. The Reformed Theology of Calvin
V. The Theology of English Protestantism
VI. Later Lutherans and the Philippists
VII. Early Socinianism
VIII. The Counter-Reformation

Spiritum sanctum mundum superavit.—MALDONATUS.

Regnum Spiritus est carnis abolitio.—CALVIN.

I

FOREWORD

THE theological thought of the Middle Ages resulted in three outstanding forms of belief: Reformation theology, Socinianism, and Tridentine Catholicism. The Reformation maintained the continuity of dogmatic development by reason of the fact that in its inception it was directed not against the Church but against the corruptions of the Church. It was ' a restoration of Pauline Christianity in the spirit of a new age.'[1] So while the Turks were being expelled from Western Europe, there advanced on the continent a great movement, impelled by the Spirit of God, which, in the words of Lord Bryce, ' was in its essence the assertion of the principle of individuality, that is to say, of true spiritual freedom.' Humanism, with its individualism and love of intellectual liberty, had migrated from Italy to Germany during the sixteenth century, thereby laying the foundations of a love of spiritual liberty. Hence the Reformation which came upon Europe when it was beginning to take its modern shape proved to be more than the reformation of the religion of Europe. It meant the reformation of Europe itself.

The interpretation of this new spiritual individualism soon became varied. Luther's ' mysticism ' and Zwingli's ' rationalism ' were incompatibles. The former disliked the Renaissance; the latter embraced it. The former emphasized justification by faith; the latter the sovereignty of God. The former upheld the real Presence of Christ in the Sacrament; the latter regarded all such allusions as metaphorical. The former allowed a place for the direct guidance of the Holy Spirit side by side with the guidance of Scripture; the latter adhered to the authority of Scripture alone. Thus the genius of the Reformation, as interpreted by Luther and Melanchthon, laid stress upon the inward working of the Holy Spirit in the soul and the reality of direct personal relationship with Him,

[1] Harnack, *Hist. of Dogma*, vii p 169

Holy Scripture being attestable as the Rule of Faith by this same Divine witness. One of the marked features of the Reformation was its championship of Scriptural authority against Church authority upheld as this had been by the subtleties of men who thought more of Aristotle than of Scripture. The Protestant Confessions of this period embody this attitude, for they are all based on Scriptural authority. But even this position had its dangers. Zwingli and Calvin gave to it a rigidity which Luther and Melanchthon disavowed, and set up an infallible Bible in place of an infallible Church.¹ The possibility of the adoption by Protestantism of tyrannical methods was feared by Erasmus, who, when writing to Melanchthon, had little that was good to say of Zwingli and his followers, whose conduct, in his view, showed clearly that they were not led by the Spirit.

In revolt against this later rigidity arose certain mystical sects of comparatively short duration. The revolutionary Anabaptists of the sixteenth century declared that, as they possessed the direct guidance of the Holy Spirit in matters of faith and knowledge, they could therefore do without the Bible altogether. This was an obvious exaggeration of mysticism, and naturally it treated the Doctrine of the Trinity with scant respect. Less extreme was that form of mysticism established by Caspar Schwenkfeld (1490–1561), a man of unimpeachable character, who in 1544 wrote an *Epistle on the Holy Trinity* which is found in his *Christlichen orthodoxischen Bücher und Schriften*. In addition to these types of Protestant mysticism, a type of Catholic mysticism arose in Spain with the Alombrados or Illuminati, who laid claim to being directly guided by the Holy Spirit, asserting that such guidance was the only needful authority. It was, as Dean Inge remarks, ' a familiar type of degenerate mysticism,'² resembling the Anabaptists in a multitude of excesses. Socinianism, however, was non-mystical though anti-trinitarian.

In order to uphold the mediaeval system against which the Reformers protested, the Roman Catholic Church in the

---

¹ Cf Auguste Sabatier, *The Religions of Authority and the Religion of the Spirit*, p 175. ' To the early Reformers the proposition, " the Bible is the Word of God," was the shout of the soul saved from sin and death, and set free from all outward servitude, bound solely by the inward monitions of the Spirit of God With their successors the same proposition became an abstract theorem, a truth of logic from which one had only to deduce the consequences '

² *Christian Mysticism*, p 217n

Counter-Reformation took strong measures, which, in part, were directed to the removal of certain of her own irregularities. While her theology as set forth at Trent had the effect of ascribing justification to good works rather than to faith, it remained, as would be expected, definitely trinitarian. The same can be said of the theology of her opponents. Divines, both Lutheran and Reformed, faithfully adhered to the ecumenical creeds, asserting God to be One in Three and the whole Godhead to be contained in Each of the Three. Sanctification is particularly the work of the Holy Spirit, yet it is one in which all Three co-operate. But it was along their line of spiritual individualism that the Reformers made here their distinct contribution, namely an *experimental* aspect of the Trinity, in which Father, Son, and Holy Spirit stand revealed in the salvation of *one* soul. While, then, the universal priesthood of believers did not come to be expressed as an article of faith until somewhat later, dogmatic truths were even now beginning to be tested by the facts of personal experience.[1]

The Formula of Concord, which closed the synergistic and other controversies and which remains one of the chief standards of Lutheran belief, together with the Canons of Dort, which embodied the opinions of the Reformed Churches, will not receive consideration in this study for the reason already given in the Introduction; neither will the discussion of the theology of English Protestantism be extended to the controversy between Anglo-Catholicism and Puritanism, as represented respectively by Hooker and Cartwright. Among the authorities on the Doctrine of the Holy Spirit discussed in the following chapters are twenty-four writers and nine formal Confessions of faith. These all occur in the course of a single century.

---

[1] It is of interest to note that both the seventeenth and eighteenth centuries began with the emphasis being laid on the Being of the Holy Spirit, and end with its being laid on His work in the individual life

II

THE THEOLOGY OF LUTHER AND MELANCHTHON

Martin Luther

WHILE resident at the University of Erfurt, Martin Luther (1483–1546) had become thoroughly acquainted with Nominalism, particularly the Nominalism of Occam. But it was not long before he came under the influence of the German Mystics, with the result that he completely broke with Aristotle and the scholastic system identified with him, and came to believe intensely in *direct* contact between the soul and God. Yet his regard for the ethical, which prompted his revolt against the cheap goodness offered by papal Indulgences, was a deciding factor in preventing him from becoming a Mystic in the then accepted sense of the term. Another deciding factor was his spiritual conservatism, which permitted him to exchange, but never to abandon, authority. To his mind, therefore, the 'enthusiasm' of Carlstadt and his followers, who claimed the Spirit's guidance without need of Bible or Sacraments, was intolerable, and their wild subjectivism is strongly confronted by him in the Schmalcald Articles. That the Holy Spirit indeed uses the Sacraments and the Scriptures as recognized channels of Divine efficacy always remained his firm conviction, though in regard to the latter he would make due allowance, as the Holy Spirit Himself might direct, for the human limitations of the writers.

The word conservatism as applied to Luther is, however, of merely comparative import and by no means belittles the mighty fact that this great reformer brought the urgent question of individual salvation right to the forefront. The Reformation itself is accounted for by the single religious experience of this one man, for the development of which experience he went back by way of Augustine to St. Paul. It was natural, then, that the doctrine of justification by faith should receive the first attention at his hands. To him justification was *per*

THEOLOGY OF LUTHER AND MELANCHTHON 253

solam fidem, and faith a mystical gift rather than an intellectual possession. Both faith and love had been regarded by the Schoolmen as necessary to salvation, and in speaking of salvation by faith alone Luther meant by faith what most of the Schoolmen, at any rate, meant by love. Now to the Schoolmen love was a primary effect of the Holy Spirit, and Luther in his Commentaries and Biblical lectures speaks frequently of the work of the Spirit in the soul, influencing the soul towards a reliance by faith upon the merits of Christ on the ground of which alone justification can be obtained. Salvation is thus the gift of God, bestowed by the Spirit of God.

Hence the work of Luther was in its essence the elevation of personal experience, and his very insistence on the Scriptures as an aid to experience rested upon the simple truth that the Bible was, to all intents and purposes, but a newly opened Book. The statements of Scripture he was disposed to accept without attempting scientific explanations. His conservatism already noticed induced him to assume quietly the great doctrines as handed down through the centuries. Concerning the dogma of the Trinity he declined to speculate, preferring to leave such a pursuit to the more metaphysical divines of his own country and of Southern Europe. But he held to the dogma as outlined in the Foreword, regarding Each of the three Persons as fully God, and All Three together as One in that unique manner in which three men could never be one. He saw the Father revealed in the Son who again is revealed by His Spirit, and this revelation of the Divine Triunity he found secondarily in nature as well as primarily in grace. So, in the writings of Luther, there *is* pneumatological and trinitarian development, but it is experimental, not philosophic or speculative, which justifies Harnack in saying that he ' was only great in the rediscovered knowledge of God which he derived from the gospel, i.e., from Christ.'[1] But this was just the greatness that the world needed.

PHILIPPUS MELANCHTHON

The theologian, however, of the early days of the Reformation was Philippus Melanchthon (1497–1560), grand-nephew of Reuchlin, professor of Greek at Wittenberg, and composer of the first Protestant Confession. In temperament more peaceful

[1] Harnack, *Hist of Dogma*, vii., pp 171, 172.

than Luther, he stands out especially in his later life as a strongly convinced Protestant, though certain of his purely theological opinions received slight modification. He demonstrates the continuity in trinitarian thought maintained by the theology of the Reformers,[1] and the rare combination of Humanist and Reformer which existed in him is responsible for careful exposition of the Doctrine of the Trinity such as Luther never stayed to undertake. This exposition is found principally in his *Loci Theologici*, published by him in 1521, which is the first great Protestant work of systematic theology. In this he describes God as ' a spiritual Essence, intelligent, eternal, true, good, . . . the Father, who has begotten the Son, His Image, from eternity ; the Son, the co-eternal Image of the Father ; and the Holy Spirit, proceeding from the Father and the Son.' These internal Divine relations nevertheless co-exist in one external Divine relation : ' I have said that the creatures have been fashioned by the Father, the Son, and the Holy Spirit. . . . The eternal Divine Essence is One.' With the indivisible unity of God in the background, Melanchthon proceeds to examine the term ' person,' which he defines as ' an indivisible, intelligent, and incommunicable substance.' ' It is common knowledge,' he continues, ' that the ancient acknowledged writers of the Church distinguish between these two words οὐσία (essence) and ὑπόστασις (hypostasis), and assert that there is one οὐσία, namely the Essence of the eternal Father, Son, and Holy Spirit, but three ὑποστάσεις, namely Three really subsisting . . . and distinct.' Thus at the Baptism of Christ the three Divine Persons are plainly seen. ' There are therefore three Persons of the Godhead, immeasurable, co-eternal, ὁμοούσιοι (consubstantial). . . . And not only is the Son begotten from reason (*cogitatio*), but also the Holy Spirit proceeds from the will of the Father and the Son.'

Concerning the Holy Spirit Melanchthon shows that, in the opinion of many, He is merely ' an impulse (*agitatio*) created in men,' or at least that He is ' the Father Himself as possessing or exercising power—apart from another Person.' But this position is controverted by the evidence revealed by Christ's Baptism already noted, by the incidents connected with Pentecost, and by the baptismal formula as given by Christ. Accordingly the

[1] Cf W P Paterson, *The Rule of Faith*, p. 265.

THEOLOGY OF LUTHER AND MELANCHTHON 255

Holy Spirit is not the impulse but 'the One causing the impulse (*agitator*), who proceeds from the Father and the Son and is sent for the sanctification of hearts.' Other considerations lead to the same conclusion. The fact that prayer is directed to the Holy Spirit 'teaches not only that the Holy Spirit is a Person, but also that He is omnipotent, all attentive, and saving.' Moreover, Christ promised '*another* Paraclete' (John xiv. 16) as personal as Himself; and 'if "the Spirit" meant a created impulse He would be a teaching, not another Teacher from the Father and the Son, hearing and receiving,' who is given in response to human faith. At this point a number of Biblical quotations follow in proof of the Godhead and Personality of the Holy Spirit.[1] In a later edition of the *Loci* he adds to the first an elaboration of his synergistic view which upholds in the work of conversion the freedom of the human will and its co-operation with the Holy Spirit, as against the strictly Lutheran or monergistic view which asserts the impotence of the human will and the consequent unaided work of the Holy Spirit.

In his *Examination of those who are heard before the Rite of Public Ordination* the above definitions of the Godhead and of the term *persona* are repeated. The Son is said to be begotten because He is 'the Image of the Father,' and the Spirit to proceed from the Divine Will, seeing that He is Himself the Divine Love. The analogy of the Trinity as here set forth, namely mind (*mens*), reason (*cogitatio*), and impulse (*agitatio*), is interesting as assigning to the Son the same similitude as Nicolas of Cusa assigned to the Father.

The synergism of Melanchthon indeed brought about some divergence of opinion between himself and Luther as touching the part taken by the Holy Spirit in justification; but, while he made room for a certain moral or ethical response on the side of man, he insisted upon the primary importance and the essential nature of the work of the Spirit.[2] The Spirit, he felt, would guide the Church to the true knowledge of Christ, and in this assurance he was engaged in prayer to the Holy Trinity on the very day of his death.

---

[1] *Loci Theologici*, ed 1565
[2] This was recognized by Contarini in his conversation with Melanchthon at the Colloquy of Ratisbon, 1541, though not in so forensic a sense Melanchthon deemed it unnecessary to make room for any such moral response in the sanctification of baptized infants

Kaspar Cruciger

Luther employed as his secretary one who had studied under himself and Melanchthon. Kaspar Cruciger (1504-1548), who assisted the great Reformer in this way while carrying out his own professional duties at Wittenberg, necessarily figures more as an understudy than as a theologian of independent thought. That he was, however, no mere mouthpiece is evident from his *Exposition of the Nicene Creed*. ' Concerning the Essence of God,' he writes, ' all the Gentiles stray from the truth. . . . The Mohammedans deny that there is any Son of God begotten from the Essence of the Father. They deny that a Holy Spirit proceeds from the Father and the Son. . . . So let this definition of God remain untouched even as it has been taught by God and continued through the prophets, Christ, and the Apostles : God is a spiritual Essence, intelligent, eternal, true, good, just, merciful, pure, utterly free, of boundless power and wisdom—the Eternal Father, who has begotten the Son, His Image, from eternity, and the Son, the co-eternal Image of the Father, and the Holy Spirit, proceeding from the Father and the Son—as indeed it has been disclosed by the sure word of God, in that the Eternal Father, together with the Son and the Holy Spirit, has founded and ordered heaven and earth and all creatures.' There follows the other part of the article on the Godhead, that ' there are three consubstantial Persons (*personae homousiae*), the eternal Father, the Son the Word (λόγος), who is the Image (εἰκών) of the Eternal Father, and the Holy Spirit ; . . . and we strongly affirm that there are neither more nor less.' A statement here follows that there is one Holy Spirit, having His Substance from (*ex*) God, who, on the ground of the redeeming work of the Son, appeared as the Sanctifier, by whom God is perceived as being over all and in all.

The Holy Spirit, the Person who proceeds from the Father and the Son, indwells in the human soul, encouraging the virtues of godly fear, faith, love, courage in confession, tolerance, chastity, and fostering the life eternal. Upon the personality of the Holy Spirit Cruciger insists. Paul of Samosata, Photinus, Macedonius, and the Mohammedans denied the personality of the Spirit, interpreting the name ' Holy Spirit ' to represent ' simply emotions that are created in men's hearts.' On the other hand the New Testament abounds in evidence concerning the Spirit's personality, as witness the Baptism of Christ, the Gift at Pentecost, the formula of baptism into the threefold Name, Christ's promise of *another* Paraclete (John xiv. 16), and 1 Cor. xii. 4 ff., where St. Paul refers to the Spirit as the Giver of all good gifts. In support of this, passages are quoted from the Old Testament and from Epiphanius, Basil, and other Fathers.

The distinction between generation and procession is another matter which commands the attention of Cruciger. The source of the former function is intelligent power, the source of the latter function, will ; ' for the Holy Spirit is the impelling Force (*agitator*), or essential Love, as it were the Fire of love in which the Father embraces the Son and the Son the Father. . . . Again, the distinctions attaching to the Persons are twofold. Some are interior, as to beget, to be begotten, and to proceed ; others have been assumed in favours toward the Church, inasmuch as the Son was made a Sacrifice on our behalf, and the Holy Spirit is sent into our hearts.' Creation, however, is the common work of the three Persons, which is clear from Genesis i.[1] In these extracts appears the influence of Melanchthon.

JOHANN BUGENHAGEN

Lutheran theology was carried a stage farther by Johann Bugenhagen (1485-1558), an unostentatious statesman of the Reformation. In his *Exposition of the Third Chapter of Matthew* he points to the whole Trinity (truly a mystery uncomprehended by any one) as present and as revealed at the Baptism of Jesus (iii. 16, 17). ' The Father appeared in the voice, the Son in our flesh, the Holy Spirit not in the substance but in the form of a dove, who in the day of Pentecost appeared in fire.' Similarly ' the Father pronounces us to be sons of God through Christ, in whom we are baptized, and the Holy Spirit begets us again unto a living hope, . . . if indeed we are baptized in accordance with the instruction and command of Christ in the Name of the Father, the Son, and the Holy Spirit.'[2] He follows Luther in emphasizing the Sacraments as channels whereby spiritual efficacy may be

[1] *Enarrationis Symboli Niceni Articuli Duo* (ed 1548)
[2] *Enarratio in III cap Matth* (ed 1543)

received by faith. In his *Notes on Ten Pauline Epistles* he states that the Holy Spirit, who is the Spirit of Christ, is personal, since it is possible to sin against Him (Acts v. 3, 9). But here again, as throughout his writings, the mass of references to the Holy Spirit concern His regenerating operations in the soul. Bugenhagen is among those Reformers who consistently unite the work of the Spirit to the work of justification, regarding each as indispensable to the other. To him justification implies not only the imputation of righteousness through faith in Christ but also the living, purifying presence of the Spirit in the believer. This setting of the doctrine was all the more effective for not being exclusively forensic.

THE AUGSBURG CONFESSION

The theology of the Lutheran Church is completely and systematically set forth in its first great creed presented by the German Protestants to Charles V at the Diet of Augsburg, 1530, and known as the *Augsburg Confession* (*Confessio Augustana*). This document of twenty-one articles was composed by Melanchthon on the basis of an earlier confession of seventeen articles drawn up by Luther, which was considered insufficiently comprehensive for the occasion. While the Protestant principles herein embodied did not fail to impress the Catholics at the Diet, the efforts of the peace-loving Melanchthon to disarm their hostility by what he himself called 'mild language' succeeded in introducing into the Confession that very spirit of compromise which Luther, in his enforced absence at Coburg, feared would be introduced.[1]

The trinitarian part of the Confession is based on the ecumenical creeds. 'With us the Churches, with full consent, teach that the decree of the Nicene Synod concerning the unity of the Divine Essence, and the three Persons, must truly and without any hesitation be believed: namely, that there is one Divine Essence which is both called, and is, God, eternal, incorporeal, indivisible, of unlimited power, wisdom, goodness, the Creator and Preserver of all things visible and invisible; and yet there are three Persons of the same Essence and power,

---

[1] Though Luther gave his general approval to the contents of the Confession, he deeply regretted the absence of certain statements from the contents, in particular his conviction that the Pope was anti-Christ (cf Acton, *Lectures on Modern History*, p 102) Melanchthon, however, would never have given his consent to such an insertion

THEOLOGY OF LUTHER AND MELANCHTHON 259

co-eternal, Father, Son, and Holy Spirit.'[1] Further references to the Holy Spirit concern His work in the human heart. ' Christ . . . sanctifies those who believe on Him by the Holy Spirit sent into their hearts, who is to rule, comfort, and quicken them, as well as defend them against the devil and the strength of sin.'[2] Justification is not by merit, but by grace through faith, ' since they believe that they are received into grace '[3]—an inward assurance which no Catholic could tolerate. The statement follows that the Holy Spirit is given through the instrumentality of the Word and the Sacraments.[4] Faith, however, is necessary to the reception of the Holy Spirit even in the sacraments, for there is no spiritual efficacy or power of justification in the sacraments *ex opere operato*.[5] It is nevertheless conceded that baptism 'is necessary to salvation,' for the original sin in the soul will end in eternal death to those ' who are not born again through baptism and the Holy Spirit.' The Word of God and the guidance of the Spirit through it and through the sacraments together form the true basis of faith. But faith itself is a result of Divine influence. The human will is impotent apart from a definite receiving of the Holy Spirit through the Word, for ' the natural man receiveth not the things of the Spirit of God ' (1 Cor. ii. 4.)[6] Similarly, good works are impossible apart from the indwelling of the Spirit of God, who alone can create new affections. If, however, such new affections are not developed, and justification is not followed by a desire for sanctification, the indwelling of the Holy Spirit becomes no longer possible.[7] Theologically these clauses represented, in the main, Luther's own position. They provided the boundaries within which the Lutherans were granted toleration twenty-five years later by the Treaty of Augsburg, from which the followers of Zwingli and Calvin, who did not exactly fit inside those boundaries, were significantly excluded.

The *Apology* or *Defence of the Augsburg Confession* (*Apologia Confessionis Augustanae*), written by Melanchthon in answer to the Catholic Confutation of the Confession, was not accepted by the Diet, and was accordingly published by its author

[1] (ed 1535) Art 1   [2] Art III   [3] Art IV   [4] Art V   [5] Art XIII
[6] ' humana voluntas non habeat vim sine Spiritu sancto efficiendae justitiae Dei seu justitiae spiritualis   sed haec fit in cordibus cum per verbum Spiritus sanctus concipitur ' (cf Art XVIII)
[7] ' Damnant Anabaptistas qui negant semel justificatos posse amittere Spiritum sanctum '

early in the following year. Many times larger than the document on which it comments, it follows closely the main ideas therein contained. ' Our adversaries,' it states, ' approve of the first article of our Confession, in which we set forth that we believe and teach that there is one Divine Essence, indivisible, &c. ; and yet there are three distinct Persons of the same Divine Essence, co-eternal, Father, Son, and Holy Spirit. This article we have always taught and defended.' But the divisions of opinion between the Lutherans and the Catholics concerned matters other than the Trinity. Melanchthon reasserts in this *Apology* that the doctrine of justification by faith alone is the necessary gate of entrance to the higher life of love,[1] which, together with the ' new works ' arising out of it, is dependent entirely upon a personal reception of the Holy Spirit and His regenerating power.[2] With regard to the sacraments, ' we call them rites which have the injunction of God, and to which is attached the promise of grace.' But here, again, the bestowal of grace is dependent entirely upon the personal attitude, and the Scholastics are condemned in that they held justification to be effected *per ceremoniam*, without faith. Melanchthon, however, considers that the Sacraments are essential to the new life, and therefore that baptism must be administered even to little children, in order that the promise of salvation may be applied to them.[3] Ordination is allowed to be a sacrament if it concerns the ministry *of the word*.[4] The stress of the *Apology*, which ranks high as a second Lutheran symbol, is clearly laid upon the inward rather than upon the outward in treating of the conditions which govern the reception of spiritual efficacy, and one necessity which it lays down for the existence of a true Church is that the Holy Spirit should dwell in the hearts of its members.

Luther and Melanchthon received from their predecessors the doctrine of the Holy Trinity and passed it on to their successors enriched by the attention given by them to the economical Trinity as manifested in the experience of salvation.

---

[1] ' Nos quoque dicimus quod dilectio fidem sequi debeat '

[2] ' Regeneramur et Spiritum sanctum accipimus ut nova vita habeat nova opera, timorem, dilectionem Dei '

[3] ' Necesse est baptizare parvulos, ut applicetur iis promissio salutis . . quia salus cum baptismo offertur '

[4] An extension of Luther's personal opinion, which had no place for a sacrament of orders essentially distinguishing priests from laymen.

The work of the Holy Spirit through the Word and the Sacraments was emphasized by them as never before, the Word of God being interpreted by the inward authority of the Spirit rather than by the outward authority of the Church, and the Sacraments, while necessary to salvation, being judged efficacious not 'of themselves' but according as the grace of the Spirit is received through them by faith. The doctrine that will ever be supremely associated with the theology of Luther and his great colleague is that of justification by faith alone. Whether the human will be impotent or potent as an aid to the saving work of the Spirit, both divines held that the Spirit is necessarily the origin of the faith by which justification becomes a personal fact, also the origin of the assurance by which the believer knows that justification has become a personal fact. The doctrine of justification in course of time tended, in their system, to lose that wholly forensic aspect which it possessed when first expounded by Luther, and to be proclaimed side by side with the doctrine of union with God; thereby linking, in thought, to the imputation of righteousness the purifying indwelling of the Holy Spirit, by whom sanctification is then carried forward on the ground of the redeeming work of Christ. Throughout all their consideration of the work of the Holy Spirit in the soul, these early theologians of the Reformation were careful to assert His true personality, and, at the same time, most strongly to deny the idea of His being merely a created impulse or emotion.

III

THE REFORMED THEOLOGY OF ZWINGLI

DURING Luther's lifetime Protestantism of a non-Lutheran type began to spread rapidly over Europe and continued so to do afterwards. For this Luther's own conservatism and lack of organizing ability were mainly responsible, so that, on his death, the government of the Lutheran communion passed completely into the hands of the civil power. The chief pioneer of this new type of Protestantism was ULRICH (or HULDREICH) ZWINGLI (1484-1531), whose headquarters were at Zurich. Certain differences between the great Reformer and himself have already been noted. Though Zwingli had been decidedly influenced by Luther and had also founded his theology upon the Pauline Epistles, his religious outlook was coloured by his Humanism, his 'rationalism,' and his zeal for political and social reform. It cost him little agony of soul to be a more extreme Protestant than Luther, and the same practical setting of his mind directed all his treatment of Divine truth. Accordingly he declined to enter into any speculative or metaphysical discussions concerning the Trinity, being content to give the doctrine a bare adhesion. Thus in his *Fidei Ratio*, presented by him to the Emperor at the Diet of Augsburg, he states: 'I both believe and know that there is only one God, that in Nature He is good, true, powerful, . . . that God is Father, Son, and Holy Spirit, three Persons indeed, but Their Essence one and simple.' Similarly, in his *Fidei Expositio*, also written in 1530, he declares that the Father, Son, and Holy Spirit are neither creatures nor separate Gods, seeing that the Scriptures refer to Them together as 'God.' 'And since these Three are One, one Essence, one οὐσία—that is, Existence—one perfection, one power, . . . the Names or Persons are three, but All and Each are one and the same God.'[1] In doctrines pertaining to salvation, however, Zwingli took a deep interest, discussing them freely in both the above documents, in his commentaries

---

[1] Ed Niemeyer, 1840.

on the Gospels and Romans, and in his *Articuli Fidei*, which in 1523 he put forward in a debate at Zurich. It is thus the work, not the Being, of the Holy Spirit that consumed his energies as a theologian. He believed that the Holy Spirit influences man to the exercise of faith by which alone he may be justified in the sight of God, and, after justification, dwells within him in order to unite him to God. This he felt was true Scriptural doctrine, which also the Lutherans presently came to feel, though to him justification by faith was much more a matter of the intellect than of the experience. It was the intellectualism of Zwingli that led him to advocate predestination as the logical conclusion of Luther's Augustinian doctrine of the impotence of the will. Baptism he considered to be non-essential to salvation, and the Holy Communion to be primarily commemorative; hence his break with Luther. Yet through the symbolism of the Holy Communion he believed that grace could be received by faith from Christ as present in His Spirit, and this he did not hesitate to assert.

JOHANNES OECOLAMPADIUS

Side by side with Zwingli stood Johannes Oecolampadius (1482–1531), who, after a period of constant intercourse with some of the great Christian exponents of Humanist culture, threw the weight of his influence on the side of the Reformation, becoming at Basel one of the outstanding leaders of the movement in Switzerland. With Zwingli he formed a close friendship, which was cemented by his adoption of Zwingli's position with regard to the Holy Communion. That he disliked scholastic speculation as much as his friend is revealed in his pneumatology, throughout which the stress is laid not upon the Person of the Holy Spirit but upon His operations within the soul. His *Sermons on the Epistle to the Colossians* are an illustration in point. The Holy Spirit is to be adored along with the Father and the Son,[1] with whom He eternally reigns.[2] As God, He inspired the patriarchs, prophets, and Apostles,[3] and now continues to implant in men true love and true religion.[4] Justification is by faith alone, by faith prompted by the Spirit, and succeeded by the Spirit's indwelling —a belief which figures prominently in the course both of these sermons and of his *Commentary on the First Epistle of*

[1] In *Ep ad Col* (ed 1546), *Sermo* 1   [2] *Sermo* 5   [3] *Sermo* 20   [4] *Sermo* 2

St. John. The omnipresence of the Holy Spirit and His work in and through the universal Church are twin subjects which receive more attention in his writings than in those of Luther. On the other hand, he inclined to Luther's view, disfavoured by Zwingli, which joined to the authority of Scripture that of the guidance of the Holy Spirit, vouchsafed directly to all followers of Christ.

WOLFGANG FABRICIUS CAPITO

During these years the Reformed theology of the Zwinglian school was enriched by the adhesion of Wolfgang Fabricius Capito (1478–1541), a scholar of depth and of versatility, who had been theological professor at Basel. After embracing the new movement he took up his residence in Strassburg, where he soon became renowned for his able and moderate advocacy of the Reformation. In his treatment of the creative and saving work of the Holy Spirit he does not neglect His Person; on the contrary, in his *Hexemeron Dei Opus* he leads through the former to the latter. The terms 'Holy Spirit' and 'Spirit of God' are to him synonymous. No description of the Divine Spirit will suffice which likens Him simply to air or vapour; rather does He resemble 'a most violent wind.' 'The reality of this circumstance [Acts ii. 2] seems to exist in order that the sword of truth may repel what people generally imagine, namely that this very Spirit of the Lord is a creature, and created, forsooth, before He became a Principle of creation! . . . For from the Scriptures they have assurance that the Spirit of God subsisted before the beginning of things. . . . Therefore the Spirit of the Lord is neither an instrument (*organum*) nor a servant of God as external things are, and as we men are.' He is Himself the eternal God. 'Seeing, then, that the Spirit is God, this means that He possesses the spiritual Nature common to the three Persons.' At the same time, the Spirit of God is indeed a Person distinct from the Father and the Son, for in the beginning He moved upon the waters (Gen. i. 2), a fact which also demonstrates His Deity. As in nature[1] both the Unity and the Trinity of God stand revealed,

---

[1] 'In eadem divinitate utraque persona erat, et alia apud aliam, et non in alia. Ideo Spiritus Dei erat apud Deum in principio, qui cum Patre et Filio erat in eadem Divinitate' In creation the Holy Spirit is regarded as completing the work of the Son 'Ergo nunc duas habemus personas in uno Deo, Verbum quo creantur, et Spiritum Dei quo ornantur creaturae'

so also in grace. 'The Father has adopted us through the Son, and through the Holy Spirit dwelling within us.' Hence, 'among the Persons of the Deity this is the natural order: God the Father, the Word, and the Spirit,'[1] the Third of whom spake by the prophets. Accordingly the Spirit has been a Subsistence *per se*, since distinct action has been attributed to Him. 'God, the Creator, and the Word breathe forth the Holy Spirit, and He is breathed forth from Them, for He proceeds from Both.' Capito is careful to state clearly that the Father, the Word, and the Holy Spirit are one God and not three Gods, and are one God simultaneously; yet his own particular emphasis appears to be laid upon the Trinity of Divine Persons, and, in consequence, upon the distinctiveness of the operations of Each of the Three.[2] Of these, he adds, the Third Person is the One who permeates all things in general, and the Church in particular.[3]

MARTIN BUCER

Chief among the collaborators of Capito in Strassburg was Martin Bucer (1491-1551). While he took Zwingli's view of the Sacrament of the Lord's Supper as against Luther's, his moderation fitted him for fulfilling the rôle of mediator between these two leaders, as also for discharging, later on, the duties of theological professor at Cambridge. Cranmer, at whose invitation Bucer crossed over to England, found in him an invaluable assistant in consolidating the new Protestantism, so much so that during the reign of Queen Mary his body was exhumed and burnt. No extremism could thus be expected to mar the writings of such a theologian, who, in gentility and restraint of spirit, so closely resembled the peace-loving Melanchthon.

Unlike his friend Capito, Bucer devoted little attention to the doctrine of the Trinity and to the place therein of the Holy Spirit; but, in common with the majority of the earlier Reformers, he concentrated his mind on the work of the Spirit in salvation and sanctification. In his *Constans Defensio* it is asserted that the Scriptures are inspired by the Holy

---

[1] Like his contemporary Galatinus and others, Capito sees in the word *Elohim* a signification of the Holy Trinity
[2] 'Non est earum actionum communio, nisi in comparando, sed potius divisio personarum hinc elucet in uno et simplici Deo'
[3] Ed. 1539.

Spirit, that the Spirit fills the justified soul, and that He is given by the imposition of hands at Confirmation and at Ordination ;[1] this reference to the rite of confirmation being made in an evangelical, rather than in a sacramental, sense. In the *Commentary on St. Matthew* the Holy Spirit is spoken of as the Fire which purifies the hearts of men in response to their faith, and as the Water which fertilizes barren minds into pious fruitfulness. As such He is called ' the Spirit of Christ,' ' the Spirit of God,' and Divine ' Unction.' ' Moreover, the Saviour has named this Holy Spirit the Paraclete, which means not so much the Comforter as the Advocate (*patronus*), Exhorter, and Encourager.' The Holy Spirit is the ' Finger of God ' which operates in all persons who are Christ's, ' for He Himself is God, even as the Word,'[2] being sent by the Son from the Father, and by the Father in the Name of the Son.[3] In Him the Father and the Son are present in the world, carrying on Their gracious work for its salvation.[4]

THE TETRAPOLITAN CONFESSION

Influenced by Capito, Bucer drew up in 1530 the first Reformed Confession, *Confessio Tetrapolitana*, on behalf of Strassburg, Constance, Memmingen, and Landau, four cities of South Germany which had been excluded from any part in the Augsburg Confession on account of their suspected Zwinglianism. Consisting of twenty-three articles, it was presented by its author to the Diet of Augsburg ; and, though it is to all practical purposes a Zwinglian document, its moderation of certain of Zwingli's opinions, especially those regarding the Sacraments, is seen to be part of Bucer's mediating policy. In the course of this Confession far more is said concerning the Person of Christ and the absolute authority of the Scriptures than concerning the Holy Spirit or the Holy Trinity, yet a statement is included to the effect that the Church hitherto has believed that the Father, Son, and Holy Spirit are One (*unum*) in Substance, within which Oneness no distinction, other than that arising purely from the Divine Persons as such, is at all admissible.[5]

[1] Ed 1613
[2] ' Neque enim vel Verbum vel Spiritus Dei aliud est quam Deus ipse, cui nihil accidit, in quo omnia substantia sunt '
[3] Ed 1553, pp 24, 25   [4] *Com on St John's Gospel*   [5] Art 11, ed Niemeyer.

THE REFORMED THEOLOGY OF ZWINGLI

THE CONFESSION OF BASEL

Similar in character is the second Reformed Confession, the *Confession of Basel*, inspired by Oecolampadius and formulated in 1534 by Zwingli's friend and biographer, Oswald Myconius. The first of its twelve articles declares: ' We believe in God the Father, in God the Son, in God the Holy Spirit, the Holy Divine Trinity; three Persons, and one eternal omnipotent God in respect of Essence and Substance; and not three Gods.' The fifth article reads: ' We believe in the holy Christian Church, namely, the Communion of Saints, the congregation of the faithful in the Spirit,'[1] a *spiritual* institution whose members confess the Lordship of Christ, and prove their faith by their works. The Holy Spirit alone, adds the Confession, can raise and sanctify the fallen nature of man.

THE FIRST HELVETIC CONFESSION

The *First Helvetic Confession* (1536), known as the third Reformed Confession, was also the first general Confession of the Swiss Reformed Churches, being the outcome of the considered judgement of delegates elected and sent by them to Basel for the express purpose of composing it. Its twenty-seven articles continue the moderating policy of the Zwinglian theologians, who were anxious that Protestantism should again present a united front to Romanism through their reunion with the Lutherans. Its references to the Holy Spirit are but few. Significantly the first place is given to the postulation of the absolute authority of Scripture as the Rule of Faith: ' Canonical Scripture is the Word of God, delivered by the Holy Spirit,'[2] and, as such, is its own interpreter.[3] ' Concerning God we are of this opinion, that He is One in Substance, threefold in Persons, and omnipotent.'[4] Man's will is free to cooperate with the Holy Spirit in regeneration, and therefore, according to the Zwinglians, is not altogether impotent apart from the Spirit, as the Lutherans believed.[5] The part taken by the Holy Spirit in the Incarnation of our Lord is acknowledged in this Confession (art. xi.) as in the Tetrapolitan.

The early Reformed Church, like the Lutheran, gave an important place to the Redemptional Trinity displayed in the

---

[1] Ed do [2] Art 1 (ed. do) [3] Art 11 [4] Art vi
[5] Art ix —' Homini liberum arbitrium tribuimus, ut qui scientes et volentes agere nos bona et mala experimur

workings of Divine grace, also to the Holy Spirit as operative both in the world of nature and in the human heart. With regard to the use made by the Spirit of the Word and the Sacraments there arose, however, certain differences between the two great Protestant Communions, due mainly to the more practical, or, at least, the less mystical, standpoint of the Zwinglian mind. The Reformed divines thought of the Holy Spirit as working through the written Word which He Himself had inspired and delivered, rather than as working side by side with it as well as through it. For this reason, while Luther pointed to the inward witness of the Spirit as interpreting the Word, Zwingli and his followers pointed to the Word as being its own interpreter. To these, again, baptism was unnecessary to salvation, and the Sacrament of the Lord's Supper primarily a simple commemoration. Grace could, indeed, be received by faith from Christ at His Table, but from Him as present in His Spirit alone, and not also in the elements. The human will, guided by the Spirit, does in fact co-operate with His Will in the work of salvation, which co-operation, after justification, develops into union as the work of sanctification progresses. The Third Person of the Blessed Trinity permeates the Church, while the Church is no mere external or historical organism, but the whole community of spiritual believers.

IV

THE REFORMED THEOLOGY OF CALVIN

UNDER the direction of Calvin the Reformed movement within the Reformation became a progressive force, capturing Protestantism in Switzerland, France, Scotland, and the Netherlands, together with large parts of Germany. In Germany Lutheranism had taken shape in a mould of conservatism, being directed towards a thorough reform of the old system. Calvinism, on the other hand, aimed at an entirely new system.[1] For this reason Protestantism, as seen in Calvin's native country of France, aroused the bitterest hostility on account of its own intolerance, and failed in consequence to usher in any general policy of religious toleration.

JOHN CALVIN

During his early years as a law-student, John Calvin (1509–1564) had come into contact with Humanism at Orleans and at Bourges. On resuming his theological studies after his father's death, he devoted his brilliant gifts to furthering the cause of the Reformation, and in this he figures not so much as a preacher as a divine, his writings being characterized alike by his legal training and the stern setting of his personality. Compelled by the outbreak of persecution to leave France, he fled to Strassburg, publishing two years later, when only twenty-five years of age, his famous *Institutes of the Christian Religion* (Basel, 1536). In this, styled by Lord Acton ' the finest work of Reformation literature,'[2] he sets forth with unmistakable force the teaching of the Church, and especially of the Reformed Churches, with regard to the Person and work of the Holy Spirit. Careful consideration is given to the term ' Person ' as used in reference to the inner Divine Life. ' Since the Essence of God is simple and indivisible, the whole of which

---

[1] 'Calvinism possessed the important faculty of self-government, whilst Lutheranism required to be sustained by the civil power '—Lord Acton, *Lectures on Modern History,* p 155
[2] *Ibid* , p. 131.

He contains within Himself, His character will by no means be improperly or ineptly spoken of as in division or in detachment, but in entire perfection.' God is One, in three Persons, Each of whom is God, who also retain Their proper distinctions. 'Now of these three Subsistences I affirm that Each One, as related to the Others, is distinguished by His individual character (*proprietas*). Here Their relation is clearly portrayed, since, where the mention of " God " is simple and indefinite, no less does this name belong to the Son and to the Spirit than to the Father,' even while it is particularly appropriate to the Father. The Deity of the Spirit is unmistakably exhibited in both Old and New Testaments ; and such ' proof ' passages as are given are reinforced by the consideration of His Divine influence in justification, the uniqueness of the work pointing to the uniqueness of the Being by whom it is performed. That this Being is ' personal ' is shown by the use in baptism of the Threefold Name, in which Person would be combined only with Person ; and between Person and Person there exists distinction, though not division. ' Yet the eternity of the Father is also the eternity of the Son and of the Spirit, for God could never be without His Wisdom and His Virtue ' ; and so the Three Persons exist simultaneously. ' Moreover, such distinction does by no means obscure the most simple unity of God, so that, from this, one may demonstrate that the Son is one God along with the Father, since He co-exists with Him in one Spirit : but that the Spirit is not something different from (*aliud diversum*) the Father and the Son, because He is the Spirit of the Father and the Son. If only the whole Divine Nature is understood to be in each hypostasis, together with this, that to each One adheres His own individual character.' This, adds Calvin, is the orthodox faith concerning the Trinity as taught by Justin, Hilary, and the Fathers, to the present condemnation of Servetus and the anti-trinitarians who assert ' a Divine Person to be nothing else than a visible appearance of the Glory of God.'[1]

The Catechism of the Church of Geneva, composed by Calvin in 1545, contains the following references to the Holy Spirit : ' I perceive that the Spirit of God, while He dwells within our hearts, brings it about that we experience the virtue of Christ. For it is by the illumination of the Holy Spirit that we receive

[1] *Works*, ed 1667–1671 1 13 (vol. IX, pp 24 ff)

with the mind the benefits of Christ ; it is by His persuasion that they are sealed in our hearts. Finally, He alone makes room for them within us. He regenerates us, and is the cause of our being new creatures.' A different line of argument, however, is found in his *Defence of the Orthodox Faith of the Holy Trinity against the Prodigious Errors of Michael Servetus*, published in the year following the burning of Servetus at Geneva. Calvin begins his refutation of the errors of Servetus with a simple statement of the Doctrine of the Trinity from the Western standpoint, which is supported by quotations from Tertullian and Irenaeus. The *Defence* is a lengthy document, consisting largely of extracts from the writings of Servetus, and is therefore unimportant as an example of its author's constructive thought.[1]

Four years later, in 1558, Calvin issued his *Answer to the Questions of Georg Blandrata*. Blandrata, then resident at Geneva, was a physician of some repute who had embraced the Reformation but also had become prominent as a holder of anti-trinitarian opinions. To him Calvin writes : ' When we say that we believe in one God, under the name of God we understand a single and simple Essence in which we comprehend three Persons or hypostases. Therefore as often as the name of God is stated indefinitely, no less do we believe in the Son and in the Holy Spirit than in the Father, . . . and we distinguish between the Persons. . . . That there is but one Essence of the Father, the Son, and the Holy Spirit is certain from the clear testimonies of Scripture.' One such testimony is the command of Christ to baptize into the Threefold Name. Another is the remark of the Apostle Peter to Ananias (Acts v. 3, 4), in which ' Christ Himself and the Holy Spirit are understood no less than the Father.'[2] These arguments, however, did not convince Blandrata of his errors, which he continued to disseminate during the remaining thirty years of his life.

Calvin's *Confession of Faith*, drawn up in 1561, was directed against Valentino Gentilis, another anti-trinitarian Reformer in Geneva.[3] ' We profess,' he declares, ' that God the Father

---

[1] *Ibid*, vol viii, pp 510 f, 530 ff.
[2] *Ibid*, pp 585 ff
[3] Valentino Gentilis, the son of Franciscus Gentilis of Naples, was required by the civil authorities at Geneva to sign an orthodox confession. On his persisting in giving vent to his anti-trinitarianism he was arrested , accordingly Calvin refers to him in the *Confessio Fidei* as ' captivus Genevae propter confessionem veri Dei.' Two years after Calvin's death he was executed for heresy at Berne.

has so begotten from eternity His Word, or Wisdom—which is His only Son Himself, and that the Holy Spirit has so proceeded from Both of Them, that the Essence of the Father, Son, and Holy Spirit is single and simple. And as to the Father being distinct from the Son, and the Holy Spirit from Both, we profess that this obtains in respect of the Persons. So we condemn and detest the error of those who assert that the Father exists simply in respect of His own Essence, and since (as they themselves say) He is the only true God, . .
Jesus Christ and the Holy Spirit would be Gods proceeding from Him ; consequently the unity of the Divine Essence would be divided and separated. On the other hand, since we profess only one God, we acknowledge that whatever of glory and Essence is attributed to His Deity equally becomes the Son and the Holy Spirit, seeing that the subject of our thought is simply God—without any mutual comparison of the Persons. But if the Persons be mutually compared, there should be noted the characteristics of Each, by which They are so distinguished that the Son is not the Father, and the Holy Spirit is not the Son.' The whole Essence of the Godhead, he adds, dwells in Each Person.[1]

Much of Calvin's pneumatology is found in his Commentaries. His comment on John xv. 26 reads : ' Therefore it is Christ who sends the Spirit, but out of the heavenly glory ; so that we know that the Gift is not human, but as a sure earnest (*pignus*) of Divine grace. Whence it is clear how frivolous may have been the subtlety of the Greeks when, on the pretext of these words, they have denied that the Spirit proceeds from the Son. For Christ, as was His wont, here mentions the Father in order that He may raise our eyes to the contemplation of His own Divinity.' The expediency of Christ's departure on account of the promised advent of the Spirit (xvi. 7) draws from the commentator this observation : ' More advantageous by far and more to be desired is the Presence of Christ by which, through the grace and virtue of His Spirit, He offers us enjoyment of Himself, than if He were present with us before our eyes.'[2] The famous interpolation, 1 John v. 7 (A.V.) affords an opportunity for a restatement of the Doctrine

---

[1] *Works*, vol viii , pp 568 ff Also in his *Responsum* (1560) and *Brevis Admonitio* (1563), both *ad Fratres Polonos*, Calvin upholds the unity of God against their belief in three Essences instead of three Persons.
[2] *Ibid* , vi , pp 144 ff

of the Trinity with the accent on the Divine unity, while the commentary on the Epistle to the Romans abounds in references to the work of the Spirit in regeneration. 'The rule of the Spirit,' he declares, 'is the abolition of the flesh.'

THEODORE BEZA

Among those who co-operated with Calvin were Heinrich Bullinger († 1575), Zwingli's successor in his Zurich pastorate and a theologian of repute; Johannes Junius (1545–1602), a Calvinist preacher in Holland who wrote against Socinus; and Theodore Beza (1519–1605), Calvin's close friend and biographer. Like his leader, Beza entered the legal profession, but also became accomplished in the study of the classics, where his Greek learning provided the foundation for his later pre-eminence in New Testament scholarship. Having turned away from the gaiety of his early years, he became in 1559 theological professor at Geneva, succeeding to the control of the Reformed Churches on Calvin's death.

In 1560 he published his *Confession of the Christian Faith*. 'We believe,' he declares, 'that there is one Divine Essence which we call God, not only because a contemplation and survey of natural phenomena exhibits it to us, but much more because Holy Scripture is a witness to us of that truth. . . . Holy Scripture clearly teaches us that in this single Divine Essence three Persons subsist, distinguished indeed from One Another by Their individual characters, namely Father, Son, and Holy Spirit; yet Each of these three Persons is one and the same God, eternal, infinite, and in Himself most perfect. These Persons, moreover, are consubstantial and co-eternal without any confusion of characteristics or relations, likewise without any inferiority or inequality among Themselves.[1] We believe in God the Father, whose Person is neither the Son, nor is He the Holy Spirit, as He who proceeds from the Father and the Son. . . . So we ascribe to the three Persons, Father, Son, and Holy Spirit, Their own distinct characteristics, in such a way that we do not separate either the Son or the Holy Spirit from the Father.[2] We believe that Jesus Christ is . . . one God together with the Father and the Holy Spirit.' The instrumentality of the Holy Spirit in the miraculous Birth is also recorded here as an article of

[1] Chap i (ed 1587)   [2] Chap ii.

faith.¹ Again, 'we believe in the Holy Spirit, who is the Essential Virtue of the Father and the Son, in whom He resides as co-eternal and consubstantial, and from whom He proceeds; so that He is one God along with Them, though a Person distinct from Them Both.' The Holy Spirit is the Creator and Preserver of mankind. He it is who ' by faith alone makes us partakers of Christ' through the Word and the Sacraments.² Beza follows Calvin in his belief concerning the inward witness of the Spirit in the regenerated life; but, strong predestinarian as he was, he strictly limits such witness to the elect, as it were in confirmation of their own election. His open approval of the burning of Servetus cannot in justice be construed as merely a strategic move in support of a friend. Rather was it a deliberate testimony to a genuine zeal for trinitarian orthodoxy, a zeal, however, none the less misguided in view of the horror for which it was responsible.

THE GALLICAN CONFESSION

The year 1561 marks the formal presentation to King Charles IX of the *Gallican Confession*, the Symbol of the Reformed Church of France, which had already been adopted in 1559. Drawn up in forty articles in Latin and in French upon a foundation of Calvin's construction, it follows the line of the ecumenical creeds, and contains an elaboration of predestinarian belief which especially delighted Beza. Article vi. states: ' This Holy Scripture points out that in this sole and simple Divine Essence, which we have confessed, there are three Persons, the Father, the Son, and the Holy Spirit : the Father, the First Cause, the principle and origin of all things ; the Son, His Word and eternal Wisdom ; the Holy Spirit, His Virtue, Power, and Efficacy ; the Son eternally begotten of the Father, the Holy Spirit proceeding eternally from Them Both ; the three Persons not confused, but distinct ; yet not divided, but of one and the same Essence, eternity, power, and equality.'³ The usual Reformed view of the Church as intrinsically a spiritual institution is herein embodied, the Church being described as ' the company of believers,'⁴ whose pastors are all on an equality under only one bishop, namely Jesus Christ.⁵ The Sacraments, which are but two in number, are, together

¹ Chap. iii. ² Chap. iv.
³ *Confessio Fidei Gallicana*, ed. Niemeyer (French form).
⁴ Art xxvii ⁵ Art xxx

THE REFORMED THEOLOGY OF CALVIN 275

with the Word, means of grace to those who partake of them with 'a pure faith.' Through these 'exterior symbols' God operates, incorporating us, by virtue of His Holy Spirit, with the Body of Christ.[1] Thus in baptism we are renewed into sanctity of life by the Spirit of God,[2] while in the sacrament of the Lord's Supper Christ, by virtue of His own mysterious Spirit, nourishes and quickens us as by faith we partake of His Body and His Blood.[3] The latter sacrament, in particular, is regarded as a spiritual symbolism to which the efficacy of the Holy Spirit is attached as from without, and through which that efficacy is supplied in response to living faith.

THE BELGIC CONFESSION

During the same year the *Belgic Confession*, the Symbol of the Reformed Church of the Netherlands, was composed, and, in 1562, presented to King Philip II. Consisting of thirty-seven articles, it was revised by the Dutch theologian Johannes Junius, and finally confirmed by the Synod of Dort in the form here used. 'We believe,' it declares, 'in one God alone, namely, in the Father, the Son, and the Holy Spirit. . . . The Holy Spirit is eternal and essential Power and Virtue proceeding from the Father and the Son. Even so, this distinction has not the effect that God is, as it were, divided into three parts, since Scripture teaches us that the Father, the Son, and the Holy Spirit Each possesses His own hypostasis or subsistence, distinguished by its own characteristics. . . . Meanwhile, however, these Persons are thus distinct, but are not divided, nor confounded, nor intermingled.'[4] Evidences found in the Old and New Testaments in 'fullest' proof of the existence of the Trinity are then adduced, such as Christ's Baptism and His command to baptize into the Threefold Name; and in this connexion the Holy Spirit is pointed to as 'our Sanctifier through His indwelling in our hearts.'[5] 'Moreover,' it continues, 'we believe and confess that the Holy Spirit proceeds from the Father and the Son from eternity, and so has not been made, nor created, nor begotten, but has only been proceeding; who in order is the third Person of the Trinity, of the same Essence, glory, and majesty along with the Father and the Son. Therefore He Himself too is true and eternal God.'[6]

[1] Art xxxiv [2] Art xxxv. [3] Art xxxvi
[4] *Confessio Belgica* (ed do), art viii [5] Art ix [6] Art xi

The work of the Spirit also receives due attention in the Confession. 'We believe that the Holy Spirit incites in our hearts true faith, which embraces Jesus Christ with all His merits. . . . Rightly, then, we affirm with Paul that we are justified by faith alone, or by faith without works.'[1] It is by true faith, through the hearing of the Word of God and the operation of the Holy Spirit, that we are regenerated.[2] Article xxvii. affirms the spiritual nature of the Church universal in much the same words as does the Gallican Confession, adding specifically that all true Christian believers look for salvation in one Jesus Christ, are cleansed by His Blood, and are sanctified and sealed through His Holy Spirit, while Article xxxi. repeats the declaration concerning the equality of all ministers of the Word under Christ as sole bishop. 'The Sacraments are visible signs and symbols of internal and invisible facts, through which (signs and symbols), as through intermedia, God Himself, by virtue of the Holy Spirit, works within us:'[3] so that the Holy Spirit, while responsible for certain inner effects, also operates through those rites in which they are simultaneously symbolized. The document embodies definite belief in baptismal regeneration. In baptism the water is held to symbolize the Blood of Christ which, by the power of the Holy Spirit, regenerates children of wrath into children of God; hence the importance of baptism for infants of believing parents[4] Finally, the Sacrament of the Lord's Supper is regarded as the channel of spiritual efficacy only as it is partaken of in the Spirit by faith.[5]

The Second Helvetic Confession

Much more elaborate is the Second Helvetic Confession. Drawn up in 1564 by Bullinger in thirty chapters for private use, it was sent by him to Frederick III, the Elector-Palatine, who, on transferring his affections from Lutheranism to Calvinism, desired from him a comprehensive statement of faith to prove the apostolical nature of the Reformed beliefs. After its production by the Elector it was soon adopted by the Swiss, who had never been fully satisfied with their first

---

[1] Art xxii The Dort Canons also emphasized the impotence of the will and its consequent inability even to wish to return from depravity to God, apart from the promptings of the Holy Spirit
[2] Art xxiv [3] Art xxxiii [4] Art xxxiv
[5] Art xxxv So the Heidelberg Catechism.

short Confession, and, in later stages, by Scotland, Hungary, France, and the Reformed Churches in general.

At the outset a statement is made concerning the twofold source of Christian knowledge. For the purpose of salvation God chooses to work through man's powers of reason; accordingly He has given to man the written Word as well as His Holy Spirit. But this in no sense belittles the direct influence of the Spirit, through whom God arouses living faith in the hearts of His elect.[1] 'We believe and teach,' continues the Confession, 'that God is One in Essence or Nature, subsisting *per se*, in all respects self-sufficient, invisible, incorporeal, boundless, eternal. . . . In truth we abominate a plurality of Gods. . . . None the less do we believe and teach that this same boundless God, One and undivided, is inseparably and unconfusedly distinguished as Father, Son, and Holy Spirit in this manner, that the Father has from eternity begotten the Son, the Son has been begotten by an inexpressible generation, the Holy Spirit, however, proceeds from Both, and that from eternity, with Both to be adored; so that They are indeed not three Gods, but are three Persons, consubstantial, co-eternal, and co-equal, distinct as to Their hypostases, and One preceding Another in order, yet with no inequality. For as touching Their Nature or Essence They are thus united, inasmuch as They are one God and the Divine Essence is common to the Father, the Son, and the Holy Spirit.' The 'manifest distinction of the Persons' is taught by Scripture in such instances as the presence of the Three at the Baptism of Christ.[2]

The work of the Spirit in salvation is clearly acknowledged without denying some co-operation on the part of the will. 'In regeneration the will is not only moved by the Spirit but is also instructed in the faculties, so that of its own accord it may will and perform the good' (*ut sponte velit et possit bonum*),[3] which is evidence of a desire to reach a compromise in the synergistic controversy. Other evidence of moderation is found in the statement that faith is God's gift not only to the elect but also to all, since God yearns for the salvation of all.[4] For the attainment of salvation, however, outward penance is unnecessary in view of the Sacrifice of Christ, as is auricular

[1] Chap I (first ed 1566), cf chap xviii
[2] Chap iii   [3] Chap ix   [4] Chap x

confession; but what is necessary is inward penitence, that change of heart brought about by the written Word and the Holy Spirit, and received with true faith.[1] Good works will follow, which are the natural outcome of this faith, and which are made possible through the Holy Spirit.[2] Accordingly the true Church consists of 'the saints of every communion who really know the true God in Christ our Saviour, through the Word and the Holy Spirit.'[3] Since, then, the Church is essentially a spiritual institution, it can only have a spiritual Head, even Christ,[4] only a ministry in which there is equality of privilege, only One who can rightly be termed Priest.[5] The Sacraments are defined as Divine ordinances in which God exhibits and renews His benefits toward us, seals His promises, and is Himself present. Through them, therefore, by the operation of His Spirit in our hearts, He strengthens and increases our faith.[6] So baptism is the public seal of our regeneration by the Holy Spirit. 'We all are born in sin's uncleanness and are children of wrath; but God freely cleanses us from our sins by the Blood of His Son, and thereby adopts us as sons, . . . and enriches us with various gifts so that we can live a new life. All these are sealed in baptism, for we are inwardly regenerated, purified, and renewed by God through the Holy Spirit.' Consequently the children of believers should be baptized and thus have given to them the *sign* of the covenant in which they already are.[7] Again, the Sacrament of the Lord's Supper is a reminder and a seal of the great benefits of Christ's redeeming power and love of which by faith we are partakers. It is thus the outward expression of what is invisibly accomplished by the Holy Spirit Himself within the heart. The Body and Blood of Christ are thus spiritually received by faith through the Holy Spirit,[8] whose inward operations in conjunction with faith receive here as elsewhere the first emphasis.

Upon Calvin and his followers devolved the heavy task of defending the trinitarian position against the growing anti-trinitarianism of the time, and from first to last they took their stand on the testimony of Scripture. On one side Calvin routed an enthusiast of the name of Caroli, who had wrongfully accused him of Arian tenets; on the other side he proceeded

[1] Chap xiv   [2] Chap xvi   [3] Chap xvii   [4] Chap xxvii
[5] Chap xviii.   [6] Chap xix   [7] Chap xx   [8] Chap xxi

THE REFORMED THEOLOGY OF CALVIN 279

vigorously against the anti-trinitarians Servetus, Blandrata, and Gentilis, while Junius challenged the heresy of Socinus. The attacks made upon the Doctrine of the Trinity by these heterodox writers came principally from the ' Arian ' quarter ; in consequence, the Calvinist theologians laid the stress upon the Divine Unity. So far is God from being ' divided ' that His *whole* Essence resides in Each of the Persons, a statement which directly implies the full Divinity of the Holy Spirit. Though the name ' God,' when used simply and indefinitely, is peculiarly appropriate to the Father, the Son and the Holy Spirit are God no less than He. The eternal procession of the Spirit from Them Both means, not only that through Him They are present in the world, but also that He is Himself God ; and the uniqueness of His work in creation and justification strengthens this conclusion. Calvin is seen to adopt Zwingli's view of the Bible as an inspired Book of law, together with Luther's belief that the inward witness of the Spirit attests its truth.[1] To him, again, and to his associates, baptism, though not vital to salvation (in view of the fact that some are not predestined to it), is a symbol of the regenerating power of the Spirit as actually effected there and then in the soul. The Sacrament of the Lord's Supper, to those who partake with faith, is a seal of God's redeeming love, experienced in the heart by contact with Christ through the Holy Spirit.[2] Both sacraments are outward signs of inward facts. Through them, by the Holy Spirit, men become one with Christ, and of such members is the true Church composed.

The Reformed Church of Calvin kept to the fore the work of the Spirit in justification and sanctification. Through Him men become new creatures in Christ, with new affections. Through His indwelling justification leads to sanctification, to union with God in Christ. Of his acceptance with God the sinner has assurance, for he perceives it.[3] But Calvin's doctrine of Assurance was overshadowed, and therefore impaired, by his doctrine of predestination, in which Augustinianism is worked out to its bitter conclusion. By making man responsible for his preordained sin, and then by practically

---

[1] Cf. Paterson, *The Rule of Faith*, pp 69-71.
[2] The Calvinists rejected Luther's sacramental theory of the omnipresence of Christ's Body in the elements The elements are but symbols of His presence in His Spirit
[3] Calvin, *Institutes*, III , chap xi , § 16 , and *Commentary on Romans*

limiting the scope of Divine grace in order to prove its sovereignty, Calvin makes possible only one interpretation of Assurance, namely the realization that God has been pleased to elect a particular individual.[1] In his system good works are evidence not so much of faith as of election, seeing that it is in the elect alone that the Holy Spirit stimulates faith. Not until two centuries had passed was this dogma of election forced to relax its grip upon the Reformed Churches.

[1] See H B Workman, *New Hist of Methodism* vol 1, p. 23.

V

THE THEOLOGY OF ENGLISH PROTESTANTISM

UNLIKE the Reformation in Germany or Switzerland, the Reformation in England was essentially secular.[1] Henry VIII was antagonistic to Luther, his motives for reform being of a commercial nature. Elizabeth loved the Renaissance more than the Reformation, her motives for reform being of a political nature. Considerations of self as well as of state, which involved the steering of a middle course between Rome and Geneva, accounted to no small extent for those constant oscillations in belief which marked the English movement. The theology of English Protestantism eventually took a Calvinistic mould,[2] and in the early Independents, with their exaltation of the absolute authority of Scripture, may be discerned most clearly the influence of the great divine of the Reformed Churches.

WILLIAM TYNDALE

It is no exaggeration to say that the publication in 1525 of the New Testament in English is the foundation of English Protestantism. For this that great scholar and writer William Tyndale (1484–1536) is responsible. Concerning the Divinity of the Spirit and His place in the Trinity he wrote little, whether in the prologues to the Books of the New Testament or in his separate works, preferring to emphasize the importance of the Spirit's work in the human heart. Accordingly in the *Prologue upon the Gospell of S. Mathew* he speaks of the unique place held by the Scriptures in human experience. ' For the nature of God's Word is that whosoever read it, or hear it reasoned and disputed before him, it will begin immediately to make him every day better and better, till he be grown into a perfect man in the knowledge of Christ and love of the law of God ; or else make him worse and worse, till he be

---

[1] Cf Acton, *Lectures on Modern History*, pp 141 f
[2] See Seeley, *Growth of British Policy*, vol. 1, pp 65 ff

hardened, that he openly resist the Spirit of God, and then blaspheme.' So does the Spirit attempt to win men through the written Word. But those whom He has won He indwells, for ' John speaketh . . . affirming that we have God Himself dwelling in us.'[1] Moreover, that Tyndale closely links the inward working of the Holy Spirit with justification by faith is evident from the *Prologue upon the Epistle to the Romaines*. In this he writes : ' Such a new heart and lusty courage unto the law ward canst thou never come by of thine own strength and enforcement, but by the operation and working of the Spirit. For the Spirit of God only maketh a man spiritual. . . . Where such a Spirit is not, there remaineth sin. . . . Now is the Spirit none otherwise given than by faith only, in that we believe the promises of God. . . . Given is the Holy Ghost, and His working which He poureth into the hearts of them on whom He hath mercy and whom He favoureth. . . . Right faith is a thing wrought by the Holy Ghost in us, which changeth us, turneth us into a new nature, and begetteth us anew in God. . . . And he [St. Paul] expoundeth more largely what the nature of the flesh, and of the Spirit, is, and how the Spirit cometh by Christ,[2] which Spirit maketh us spiritual.' There could thus be no justification at all apart from the operation of the Spirit, for the faith by which a person is justified is itself a gift of the Spirit. There could be no sanctification apart from the operation of the Spirit, for this gift of faith, after its reception, secures the further Gift of the Spirit Himself, through whose indwelling the justified person now actually becomes spiritual. One conclusion Tyndale draws from this is that there is no spiritual efficacy in any ordinance apart from the operation of the Spirit. When writing in *The Obedience of a Christian Man* on the subject of Confirmation he remarks : ' The Holy Ghost came by preaching of the faith, and miracles were done at the prayer of faith as well, without putting on of the hands. . . . Putting on of the hands was the manner of that [the Jewish] nation.' This is reminiscent of the constant denials on the part of the continental Reformers of bestowal of grace by the sacraments *ex opere operato*, while it indicates the outlook which brought its advocate into

---

[1] *Works*, ed 1573
[2] In his first original work, *A Pathway to the Holy Scripture*, Tyndale alludes to the Holy Spirit as ' the Spirit of Christ,' carefully maintaining the close unity between the Two.

violent collision with the English king and his prelates. To this saintly scholar the deep simplicity of Scriptural truth meant far more than the pretensions of mediaeval ecclesiasticism, things inward far more than things outward. 'How shall we know,' he asks, 'whether we have the Spirit? Alike John and He will say : " If we love one another." '[1]

THE THIRTY-NINE ARTICLES

The Thirty-nine Articles of the Church of England, adopted in their Latin form by Convocation in 1562 and ratified in their English form by Parliament in 1571, are spiritually akin to the Reformed Confessions. Of the Being of the Holy Spirit and His place within the Divine Life they set forth the orthodox Western view. 'There is but one living and true God, everlasting, without body, parts, or passions; of infinite power, wisdom, and goodness. . . . And in unity of this Godhead there be three Persons, of one Substance, power, and eternity; the Father, the Son, and the Holy Ghost.'[2] 'The Holy Ghost, proceeding from the Father and the Son, is of one Substance, majesty, and glory with the Father and the Son, very and eternal God.'[3] These statements follow the testimony of the ecumenical creeds, which rest upon Holy Scripture, which, again, 'containeth all things necessary to salvation.'[4] Apart from the grace of God within man, the will is not free to exercise that faith in response to which alone saving grace can be bestowed and justification pronounced.[5] 'Not every deadly sin willingly committed after baptism is sin against the Holy Ghost, and unpardonable. . . . After we have received the Holy Ghost, we may depart from grace given, and fall into sin, and by the grace of God we may arise again and amend our lives.'[6] This, however, is governed by Article xvii, which plainly preaches predestination. 'Wherefore, they which be endued with so excellent a benefit of God be called according to God's purpose by His Spirit working in due season; they through grace obey the calling; they be justified freely.' So 'the godly consideration of predestination and our election in Christ is full of sweet, pleasant, and unspeakable comfort to godly persons, and such as feel in themselves the working of the Spirit of Christ,

---

[1] *An Exposition upon the First Epistle of S John* (iv 12, 13).
[2] Art i [3] Art v [4] Art vi, viii [5] Art x, xi [6] Art xvi

mortifying the works of the flesh and their earthly members, and drawing up their mind to high and heavenly things.' On the other hand it is admitted that 'curious and carnal persons, lacking the Spirit of Christ,' may well be driven to despair, as having 'continually before their eyes the sentence of God's predestination.' This Article, with its Calvinistic flavour, is a notable indication of the link between Elizabethan Protestantism and the Reformed Churches of the Continent.[1]

On the questions of the Church and the Sacraments these Articles follow the lines adopted in the Reformed Confessions. 'The visible Church of Christ is a congregation of faithful men, in which the pure Word of God is preached, and the sacraments be duly ministered';[2] whose authority, including that of its General Councils, is accordingly subordinate to the authority of the Word.[3] In the two sacraments God works in us invisibly, 'and doth not only quicken, but also strengthen and confirm our faith in Him,' if we receive them by faith.[4] This being so, the sacraments are not rendered ineffectual if the one administering them possesses an evil character.[5] 'Baptism is . . . a sign of regeneration or new birth, whereby, as by an instrument, they that receive baptism rightly are grafted into the Church; the promises of the forgiveness of sin and of our adoption to be the sons of God by the Holy Ghost are visibly signed and sealed.'[6] The Supper of the Lord is partaken of 'only after a heavenly and spiritual manner. And the mean whereby the Body of Christ is received and eaten in the Supper is faith.'[7]

THE SECOND BOOK OF HOMILIES

Due place is given to the Person and work of the Holy Spirit in the *Second Book of Homilies* of the Church of England, issued in 1563. The Whit-Sunday Homily (No. xvi., pt. 1) declares that 'the Holy Ghost is a spiritual and Divine Substance, the third Person in the Deity, distinct from the Father and the Son, and yet proceeding from Them Both.' In the account of Christ's Baptism, for example, 'note three divers and distinct Persons, the Father, the Son, and the Holy Ghost; which all notwithstanding are not three Gods, but one God.' Reference

---

[1] 'The articles of our own church seem totally irreconcilable with the scheme usually denominated Arminian'—Hallam, *Hist of England*, vol 1, pp 400 f
[2] Art xix [3] Art xx, xxi [4] Art xxv [5] Art xxvi
[6] Art xxvii [7] Art xxviii

is also made to the Lord's command to baptize into the Threefold Name, and to His promise of ' another Comforter.' ' These and such other places of the New Testament do so plainly and evidently confirm the distinction of the Holy Ghost from the other Persons in the Trinity that no man can possibly doubt thereof, unless he will blaspheme the everlasting truth of God's Word. As for His proper Nature and Substance, it is altogether one with God the Father and God the Son, that is to say, spiritual, eternal, uncreated, incomprehensible, almighty ; to be short, He is even God and Lord everlasting. Therefore He is called the Spirit of the Father ; therefore He is said to proceed from the Father and the Son ; and therefore He was equally joined with Them in the commission that the Apostles had to baptize all nations.' It is He who inspired the prophets. ' It is He which inwardly worketh the regeneration and new birth of mankind.' ' It is the office of the Holy Ghost to sanctify ; which, the more it is hid from our understanding, the more it ought to move all men to wonder at the secret and mighty workings of God's Holy Spirit which is within us. For it is the Holy Ghost that doth quicken the minds of men, stirring up godly motions in their hearts. Neither doth He think it sufficiently inwardly to work the new birth of man, unless He do also dwell and abide in him. . . . Oh, what comfort is this to the heart of a true Christian, to think that the Holy Ghost dwelleth in him ! . . . He giveth patience and joyfulness of heart, in temptation and affliction, and is therefore worthily called " the Comforter " (John xiv. 16). He doth instruct the hearts of the simple in the knowledge of God and His Word ; therefore He is justly termed " the Spirit of truth " (John xvi. 13).[1] And [according to Bede] where the Holy Ghost doth instruct and teach, there is no delay at all in learning.' His presence in the soul is evidenced by ' the fruit of the Spirit ' (Gal. v. 22, 23). ' Such is the power of the Holy Ghost to regenerate men, as it were to bring them forth anew, so that they shall be nothing like the men that they were before.' Part 2 of the same *Homily* states that ' the Holy Ghost was given, not only to the

---

[1] ' He that keepeth the Word of Christ is promised the love and favour of God, and that he shall be the dwelling-place or temple of the blessed Trinity ' (*Homily on the Scriptures*, pt 1) But ' the more obscure and dark the sayings [of Scripture] be to our understanding, the further let us think ourselves to be from God and His Holy Spirit, who was the Author of them ' (*Another Homily on the Scriptures*).

Apostles, but also to the whole body of Christ's congregation,' adding that the Popes of Rome, as is seen by the behaviour of many of them, have not enjoyed an exclusive possession of this Divine Gift. This inspiration of all believers is alluded to also in the Homily for the Rogation Days (No. xvii., pt 3) : ' In the power of the Holy Ghost resteth all ability to know God and to please Him. It is He that purifieth the mind by His secret working. He enlighteneth the heart, to conceive worthy thoughts of Almighty God. He sitteth in the tongue of man, to stir him to speak His honour. He only ministereth spiritual strength to the powers of the soul and body. And if we have any gift whereby we may profit our neighbour, all is wrought by this one and the selfsame Spirit.'

The theologians of English Protestantism were careful to uphold consistently the Godhead of the Holy Spirit and His personal distinction from the Father and the Son as revealed in Scripture. This was the necessary foundation at once of the new effort to instruct the people of England in spiritual things, and of their gradual awakening to the supremacy of inward authority. Such an awakening was due in no small measure to an increasing esteem for the Bible as an instrument of the Holy Spirit, and therefore as containing spiritual truths which could only be spiritually discerned. It was due also to a growing insistence on the spiritual meaning of the sacraments, and consequently on the inefficacy of the same apart from the operation of the Spirit and the faith of the participant. This movement toward a deeper religious experience was, moreover, greatly furthered by the teaching of the Church concerning the work of the Spirit in the human heart. Every good obtained or dispensed has its origin in the Spirit of God. He it is who bestows that grace which empowers the will to good, also that faith by which a man is justified. He it is who sanctifies the justified, and comforts him in the hour of trial. It is difficult to dismiss the thought that any belief in Assurance which was held by the English Church of the sixteenth century must have been somewhat narrowed by her adherence to the dogma of predestination. The Calvinistic emphasis on the Divine sovereignty which prevailed in that Church gave rise to the conviction that saving faith is bestowed by the Holy Spirit only upon those whom He favours and accordingly predestines, and that those who do not display the fruit of the Spirit are manifestly not so predestined. The fact that this conviction was voiced in the Articles yet not in the Homilies serves only as a reminder of the natural difference, as then recognized, between their respective purposes; it does not dismiss the conviction. But concerning the spiritual nature of the visible Church of Christ the English divines never entertained a doubt, and their clear declarations of this are especially significant as coming during the period of the break with Rome.

VI

LATER LUTHERANS AND THE PHILIPPISTS

ANDREAS OSIANDER

THE interrelations of the later Lutherans and the followers of Melanchthon are marked by controversies associated with the names of Osiander, Major, and Strigel, three theologians who assaulted the strict Lutheran position at various points. Andreas Osiander (1498–1552), the first of three Lutherans to be considered in this chapter, was commendably orthodox on the Doctrine of the Trinity, as his *Commentary on St. John's Gospel* reveals. John xvii. 3, he remarks, 'must not be understood as if the Son and the Holy Spirit are not God in the same essential Godhead; but that the Godhead of the Father which He Himself communicates to Those abiding in the Unity of the Essence—to the Son begotten by Himself, and to the Holy Spirit proceeding from Both—is one and only one, outside of which there cannot be God.' Osiander includes in his trinitarian theology the belief that the whole Godhead resides in Each of the Divine Persons,[1] to which belief the theologians of the Reformation generally subscribed. 'No advantage,' he asserts, 'is gained by the Greeks of the East who depend upon this (i.e. xv. 26) to prove that the Holy Spirit proceeds from the Father alone. For such a thing Christ neither affirms nor hints. Otherwise in exactly the same way everything that is affirmed of the Father should be denied to the Son!'[2] With regard to the gift of the Spirit recorded in xx. 22 he writes: 'At that season Christ conferred upon His Apostles certain gifts of the Holy Spirit, namely a firmer faith as touching His resurrection, and a fuller understanding of Holy Scripture.' He indeed links the work of the Holy Spirit to justification, but his view of justification is utterly unsound, and, in consequence, his estimate of the Spirit's work in relation

---

[1] Cf Rudolf Frederick Grau in his tract *De Andreae Osiandri Doctrina Commentatio* (1860)
[2] On John xv. 26 (*Commentary on the Bible*, ed. 1600).

thereto far from adequate. In expounding Luther's teaching concerning justification he sets forth his own theory of ' essential righteousness,' which proved to be a complete distortion of his leader's opinions. To Osiander, faith is actual righteousness, since it permits Christ to take up His abode within us. Any notion of an imputation of righteousness is erroneous, for we cannot imagine that God would call the unrighteous righteous. If, then, we are called by God righteous, we must, by that call, be constituted righteous. Thus we are not *treated as* righteous by Divine mercy; rather do we actually *become* righteous by virtue of an infusion of the essential righteousness of Christ. Luther and Calvin have therefore been mistaken. So declares Osiander.

No wonder both these men considered him to be a greater danger to Scriptural truth than the Roman Catholics,[1] for so closely did the Reformers join to justification the sanctifying work of the Spirit that his mystical fancies impaired the latter as well as the former. The theory of an infusion of Christ's righteousness into the soul dispenses entirely with any necessity for the indwelling of the Holy Spirit. The Osiandrian conception of justifying faith as making man part of God equally dispenses with any necessity for the Holy Spirit to unite justified man with God. By propounding a doctrine of justification that was fundamentally wrong, Osiander could find no proper place for the Divine Sanctifier. Here was an omission which humanity in its desperate need could never afford, and this should have been immediately and universally realized. Unfortunately no such realization occurred, and for some time to come the disciples of Osiander were centres of discord.

Johann Brenz

Co-operating with Osiander in establishing the Lutheran cause was Johann Brenz (1499–1570), a convert from Catholicism to Lutheranism, whose reforming activity was associated particularly with Würtemberg. His pneumatology is found mainly in his commentaries,[2] in which he is concerned much more with the work of the Spirit than with His Person. In his *Commentary on the Epistle to the Philippians* he is engaged principally in the consideration of the Godhead and the Saviourhood of Jesus Christ, though he makes mention of the oneness

---

[1] See Calvin, *Institutes*, III, chap xi, § 5.   [2] Ed. 1566

of the Divine Essence and of the three distinct hypostases or Persons within the same. In his *Commentary on St. Luke's Gospel* (thirty-first homily on chap. iii.) he refers to the Lord's baptism (iii. 21, 22) as revealing ' the three Persons of the one Divine Essence, the Father, the Son, and the Holy Spirit ; and the authority of the baptism is affirmed since at the baptism the Father is present, together with the Son and the Holy Spirit. This homily, as in the case of nearly all the homilies of this commentary, concludes with the phrase : ' Jesus Christ our Lord, who in all things with the Father and the Holy Spirit is God, for ever to be praised.' Thus, throughout all his exposition of those parts of Pauline theology which exhibit the operations of the Spirit of God in the soul, Brenz was sound on the question of the absolute Deity of the Spirit and His position within the Divine Life. As to this exposition itself, of which his *Commentary on the Epistle to the Romans* is the conspicuous example, it yields nothing which may be regarded as a definite contribution to the development of the doctrine. The work of the Spirit in the heart before and after justification is treated from the typically Lutheran standpoint.

Georg Major

A second controversy arose around Georg Major (1502–1574), a Philippist divine who asserted that good works are necessary to the attainment of salvation. Against the wild attack made upon him by the rigid Lutheran Amsdorf, who, in his desire to emphasize the necessity of faith, spoke disparagingly of good works, Major held his ground, and a perusal of his *Commentaries on the Pauline Epistles* reveals little extravagance on his side. It remained for the Formula of Concord (1577) to establish the truth by a *via media* in which faith was held to be the first essential, and good works its indispensable sign.

In the course of his commentaries both the Person and work of the Holy Spirit are treated at length. God is Father, Son, and Holy Spirit. ' The Father is God, as also the Son is God, as also the Holy Spirit is God, yet there are not three Gods ; but God is one in unity of Essence, though threefold in Persons.'[1] ' We confess,' he continues, ' that the eternal God is one in Essence, and yet distinguished in Persons, as, for

---

[1] *Ep ad Gal* , 1..

instance, the Son is begotten from the Father; for neither is the Father nor the Holy Spirit begotten, . . . yet He is in Essence true God, and one with the Father and the Holy Spirit.'[1] Seeing then that the Son is true God, He and the Father together are the Source of the Holy Spirit, for They Both send Him and, at one and the same time, breathe Him into our hearts.[2] Therefore the Holy Spirit, the third Person of the Godhead proceeding from the Father and the Son, is called not only the Spirit of God but also the Spirit of Christ.[3] Concerning the work of the Spirit, Major insists throughout the commentaries upon His influence on the human will, for He alone can enable it to exercise saving faith and to produce works that are good. The sanctifying operations of the Holy Spirit are expounded particularly in the *Commentary on the Epistle to the Romans*, but the exposition proceeds along familiar lines.

MATTHIAS FLACIUS

With the name of Matthias Flacius (1520–1575) is associated a third controversy, which closely affected the Doctrine of the Holy Spirit. A strict Lutheran, and in consequence a bitter critic of the Leipzig Interim, in which the Philippists had made such generous concessions to Rome, he plunged into all the discussions of his day, thereby arousing the animosity of friends as well as of enemies. His part in the synergistic controversy, which is our present concern, was marked by the vehemence with which he contended for the impotence of the will in salvation, as against the Philippist belief in the power of the will to co-operate with the Holy Spirit when under His influence. His strange conviction that original sin forms an actual part of human nature accounted for his hostile attitude toward synergism, which held to the two efficients in regeneration, and prompted his conclusion that if man is regenerated he must be regenerated by the unaided action of the Holy Spirit. Before the promulgation of these views in connexion with his *Key to Holy Scripture*, Flacius had published his *De Vocabulo Fidei*, in which the Holy Spirit is set forth as 'the Spirit of God,' equal to the Father and the Son, who alone regenerates the heart of man, and in whom man can cry 'Abba, Father.' He it is who guides the soul in spiritual things, consoling it in

[1] *Ep ad Eph*, 1.   [2] *1 Ep. ad Cor*, xv.   [3] *Ep ad Rom*, viii.

trouble, and sanctifying it unto life eternal. Neither in the *Vocabulum* nor in his other works does there occur a detailed exposition of the theology of the Spirit. His *Catalogus testium veritatis*, an 'apology' for the Reformation issued in 1556, contains a brief statement of trinitarian doctrine from the Western standpoint, but with scarcely any comment.

VICTORINUS STRIGEL

In the debate on the relation of the will to the work of the Holy Spirit in salvation Flacius' principal opponent was Victorinus Strigel (1514-1569), who took the Philippist view upholding synergism. This view is advocated especially in his *Commentary on the Psalms*, but also appears in the course of his commentaries on certain Books of the New Testament. On the famous interpolation 1 John v. 7 (A.V.) he comments as follows: 'Although there are therefore three distinct Persons in the Godhead, the eternal Father, the Son who is the λόγος [Word] and εἰκών [Image] of the Eternal Father, and the Holy Spirit, yet there is not a plurality of Divine Essences but only one Essence, Divine and Eternal, common to the three Persons.'[1] With reference to the statement 'All things whatsoever the Father hath are Mine' (John xvi. 15) occurs the remark: 'This sentence making the Son equal to the Father should be carefully noted, and there is no doubt but that His power is equalled, seeing that the Son, being omnipotent, is God by Nature; wherefore He is also consubstantial (ὁμούσιος) with the Father. From this it follows that the Holy Spirit proceeds from Both.' This is indicated by the Lord's breathing of the Holy Spirit upon the disciples (John xx. 22); 'for even as the Son is the Image of God begotten from the Mind of the Father, so the Spirit proceeds from the Will of the Father and the Son as the Love, or Fire and Breath of Love, in which the Father and the Son mutually embrace (*mutuo complectuntur*). Similarly runs the comment on the promise of John the Baptist (Luke iii. 16) : ' " He shall baptize you with the Spirit," who is a substantial Fire or Flame, uniting the Father and the Son, uniting also God and the Church Or " He shall baptize you with the Holy Spirit and with fire," that is, He shall pour out upon you the Holy Spirit in the form of flames. For the term " fire " can be applied

[1] *Commentaries*, ed 1565

either to the Person of the Holy Spirit, or to His manifest outpouring, such as took place on the day of Pentecost and other days.' It is necessary, nevertheless, that there should be no misunderstanding regarding the exact nature of this intimate relation of the Holy Spirit to the other Persons of the Trinity. 'Petrus Lombardus, in his third *Sentence* and fourth *Distinction*, asks whether the Holy Spirit can be spoken of as the Father of Christ, seeing that the text in Matthew says: " That which is begotten in her is of the Holy Spirit " (i. 20). I reply that he alone is spoken of as " father," who transfers his own substance to that which he begets. Therefore, though the Holy Spirit forms the body of the nascent Messiah in the womb of the Virgin, He is in no wise called " Father," because He does not transfer His own Substance.' Concerning, however, the personality of the Holy Spirit, there is no lack of scriptural proof. In John xiv. 16 Jesus promises that the Father will give the disciples ' another Comforter '; and ' when He says " another " He distinguishes this Paraclete from the Father and the Son.' ' The term " Comforter " (*consolator*),' Strigel continues, ' strictly means " Advocate," as in a court of justice. It indicates, therefore, that the Church has continual struggles with the devil and his instruments,[1] and with our own infirmity. So the Holy Spirit is given that He may be an Advocate, assisting us with counsel and comfort, warning us and strengthening us.'

MARTIN CHEMNITZ

Between Flacius on the one side and Strigel on the other came a welcome mediator in the person of Martin Chemnitz (1522-1586), a Philippist theologian who may rightly be termed the Summist of the Reformation. While refusing to yield to the Lutherans his belief in a real co-operation of the will with the Holy Spirit in salvation, he conceded that such co-operation can be effected with the will only in so far as it is spiritualized by the Spirit of God. The will, then, in its natural state cannot so co-operate, and thus for all practical purposes is impotent. That this compromise was but temporary is obvious from succeeding events. It reveals, nevertheless, the importance attached by Chemnitz to the

[1] In a note on Luke xi 20 Strigel observes that, in the opinion of some, Jesus cast out devils by the Holy Spirit: ' Aliqui intelligunt Dei digitum de Spiritu sancto, sicut brachium Domini de Filio intelligitur.'

inward operations of the Spirit as the prime necessity in salvation, even as his decided opposition to the Osiandrist theories reveals the importance attached by him to these same Divine operations in the sanctification of life. His lectures on Melanchthon's *Loci Communes*, delivered at Wittenberg, were expanded later into his *Loci Theologici*, which was published five years after his death, and is the recognized standard of Philippist theology. Here both the Being and the work of the Holy Spirit receive careful systematization. The 'Locus' or Discussion entitled *De Deo in Genere*[1] contains the following table summarizing the Protestant doctrine of God:

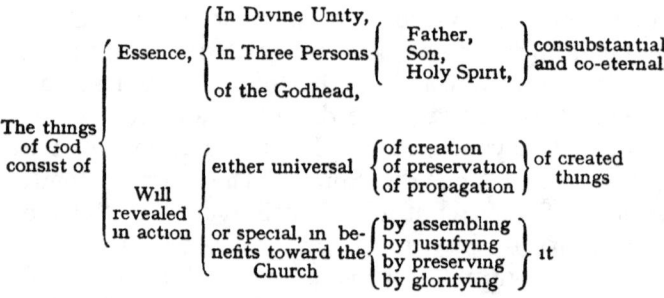

The upper section of this table forms the text of the following 'Locus,' *De Deo in Specie*. In this, firstly, the unity of the Divine Essence is demonstrated from Scripture and from the early Christian writers.[2] Secondly, the Trinity of Divine Persons is upheld as a revelation of Holy Scripture, being indicated by the three Manifestations at Christ's Baptism, the baptismal formula of the threefold Name, and the reference to 'another Paraclete' (John xiv. 16). The doctrine of the Trinity was in no wise 'first fabricated' at the Synods of Nicaea and of Constantinople, but was there simply re-stated.[3] Hence, after bringing together the two truths of the Divine Unity and the Divine Trinity, Chemnitz remarks that 'in God the Divine Nature is common to the Father, the Son, and the Holy Spirit, and the whole Nature is in Each; and yet the Father, the Son, and the Holy Spirit are so distinguished by certain characteristics of Their own that the Father is neither the Son, nor the Son the Father, and the Holy Spirit

---

[1] Chap ii. (ed 1623).   [2] Chap i   [3] Chap ii

LATER LUTHERANS AND THE PHILIPPISTS 295

is neither the Father nor the Son,' &c. This statement regarding the distinct Persons within the Deity naturally leads to a definition of 'person,' which, after long discussion, is given as 'an indivisible substance, intelligent, incommunicable, which is not sustained either in or from another substance.'[1] The basis of this definition is a similar definition of Melanchthon's, but the definition itself appears to overlook the evidence of the relations of source within the Godhead, to which the great Scholastic theologians attached so much importance when treating of Divine Personality. In the following chapter, however, Chemnitz adds that though the operations of the Trinity are divided *ad intra* they are undivided *ad extra*. In every external relation the Persons act together as One.[2]

The 'Locus' *De Persona Spiritus Sancti* presents the reader at the outset with another table, summarizing the Protestant doctrine of the Spirit:

The Holy Spirit is		
	1	The third Person of the Godhead
	2	Not made, nor created, nor begotten, but eternally proceeding from the Father and the Son
	3	He in whom the Father, through the Son, created all things visible and invisible, angels and men, and sustains, preserves, and governs what He has created
	4.	He who was sent by the Father, through the Son, in visible form upon the Apostles, and who is now sent by the Father through the Son also invisibly into the hearts of believers, that He may illumine, convert, and regenerate them

Thus, in Himself, the Holy Spirit is God, a Person, and the subject of the twofold Procession as held in the West; while, in His work, He is the medium both of creative and of saving energy. A mass of quotations from earlier writers supports the truths summarized in the table, and especially the full Divinity of the Holy Spirit. 'If these things,' he concludes, ' which we have so far laid down from the Word of God concerning the Godhead of the Holy Spirit and His consubstantiality with the Father and the Son are true, certain, and unshakable, as undoubtedly they are; and if worship is nothing else than the confession that we ascribe to that Essence, which we address in prayer, those things that are peculiar to God alone, even as they are enumerated in the definition of God so our faith should worship the Holy Spirit in prayer just as the Father and the Son; for, on the contrary, a withholding

---

[1] Chap. iv.   [2] Chap. v.

(*negatio*) from such worship is really a denial (*abnegatio*) that the Holy Spirit is the third Person of the Deity, consubstantial with the Father and the Son.'[1]

Later Lutheran theology, in the wider sense which embraces Philippism, thus held to the Doctrine of the Trinity as handed on by Luther. God is one, though the whole Godhead resides in each Person. No confusion can enter within the Trinity, the truth of the *Filioque* is attested both by Scripture and by reason, and the Holy Spirit, as one of the Divine Persons, has His own recognized function in nature and in grace. On the question of co-operation on the part of the human will with the Spirit in salvation no real agreement took place, for the Formula of Concord, which was to end the controversy, summarily rejected any such co-operation,[2] and, brushing aside the compromise of Chemnitz, confirmed the Lutheran belief in the impotence of the will. Moreover, this belief was about to be assailed again more fiercely than ever by the apostles of Arminianism. But, whatever view prevailed regarding a human response in salvation, there was fundamental agreement as to the first place, in time and in importance, being allotted to the Spirit's operation in the work of salvation as also in that of sanctification. He it is who fortifies the regenerate soul against evil, imparting that personal knowledge of God which alone makes possible a real union between Him and His Church.

---

[1] The Godhead of the Spirit is asserted at length also in his *Examen Concilii Tridentini* (1565–1573), his great ' Apology ' for the Reformation

[2] ' Contra hunc errorem supra demonstratum est, quod facultas applicandi se ad gratiam non ex nostris naturalibus propriis viribus, sed ex sola Spiritus sancti operatione promanet ' (F C.).

VII

EARLY SOCINIANISM

THE most considerable breaking away from the trinitarian position of the Mediaeval Church, known as Socinianism, professed to exalt the functions of reason in theology, and in so doing set out from a purely rationalistic principle. Later Nominalism, the rationalism found within the Church before the Reformation, also exalted the functions of reason, but at the same time recognized its limitations when treating scriptural revelation. While, then, the latter was able to remain within the Church, the former was utterly unable, since it directly collided with her teaching, particularly with that of the Reformers, to whom the Trinity and the personality of the Holy Spirit were truths not only of metaphysics but also of experience. Because the Socinians had no such experience they fell back on reason, forgetting that reason is a faithful servant but a fickle mistress.

In addition to the anti-trinitarians previously referred to as having been dealt with by Calvin (cf. chap. iv.), mention may be made of Ochino († 1565), a brilliant preacher and ex-Romanist who was esteemed by the great Reformer in spite of his doubts. But prominent among the forerunners of Socinianism was the Spanish physician, MICHAEL SERVETUS (1511–1553). Convinced that the Doctrine of the Trinity was an error of the Church, he applied himself to bring Reformation theology to coincide with his own views. This he essayed to do in three works, *De Trinitatis Erroribus* (1531), *Dialogorum de Trinitate Libb. ii.* (1532), and *Christianismi Restitutio* (1553), the last of which he issued anonymously; and it was in the vain attempt to influence Calvin, and through him the Reformed Church of France, that he was ultimately tried and burnt at Geneva at Calvin's instigation. His earlier heresy was concerned more with the Deity and the personality of Christ than with those of the Holy Spirit, but all the Divine Persons soon came under his notice, and the speculative system which he worked out in reference to Them alienated Catholics and Protestants alike. Calvin's *Refutation*[1] of his errors contains a summary of them which is reported for the most part in *oratio obliqua*. In this Servetus is alleged to have declared

'That all who firmly believe in a Trinity in the Essence of God are tritheists, real atheists; and possess a God only divided into three parts (*tripartitum*) and assembled together' (*aggregativum*).[2]

'That those incorporeal beings, distinct in the unity of God, cannot possibly exist, and are an imaginary triad.'[3]

'That Christ Himself is the Son of God inasmuch as He was begotten by God in the womb of the Virgin Mary; and that was not solely by the power of the Holy Spirit, but because God begat Him from His own Substance.'[4]

'That, in times past, Wisdom itself was at once the Word and the Spirit, and, since there was no real distinction, Wisdom itself was the Spirit.'[5]

'That in the Substance of God there are parts and partitions not as in the creatures, but according to a division of dispensation, so that in the partition of Spirit the portion of Each is God.'[6]

'That it is wrong to doubt that both our soul (*anima*) and Christ's Holy Spirit Itself have essentially united to themselves an elementary substance such as the Word has united to Himself; and that created and uncreated things unite in one substance of soul and Spirit.'[7]

'That God is the Father of the Holy Spirit.'[8]

'That no real generation or spiration has ever taken place within God.'[9]

Later in Calvin's *Refutation* occurs a paragraph entitled 'What is the Spirit to Servetus?'[10] 'The Spirit,' so he makes answer, 'is called a certain gentle breathing (*aura*), which is brought forth from the created Word in the creation of the world, not as if He possessed a particular and distinct hypostasis. Now He is said to have been the same as the Word; now He is said to have been the shadow of His Substance which succession of time has made perceptible. His distinction from the

---

[1] Calvin, *Works* (ed 1667–1671), vol viii, pp 523–566
[2] Bk 1 *De Trin*, p 30   [3] *Ibid*, p 29   [4] *Ibid*, pp 11, 12.   [5] Bk. ii, p 66.
[6] Bk iii, p 121; 'eternal self-manifestations,' Fisher, *Hist of Christian Doc*, p 321
[7] Bk. v. pp 181 f   [8] *Ibid*, p 187.   [9] *Ibid.*, p 189.   [10] *Works*, vol viii, p. 566.

EARLY SOCINIANISM

Father, however, is alluded to elsewhere, since the Other [i.e. the Word] exists in the condition of a "mixed creature" (for Deity is unmixed) (*mera*), as, in fact, something from the Essence of God mixed together with created manhood. And, from the Word, God is said to work in us by the Spirit. But from Christ's Ascension He [the Spirit] is said to have existed as a new God, or mode of the Deity.'

In this summary of Calvin's, inconsistency is apparent; indeed, inconsistency and heresy go hand in hand. It appears, however, that the fundamental idea in the mind of Servetus is that God is not simply One in Essence but One in Person, a view which Mohammedan teaching doubtless influenced him to adopt.[1] This one Divine Person has employed various modes of self-manifestation, but this by no means warrants the conception of a Trinity of Divine Persons. To Servetus the Son is not eternal, while the Holy Spirit is neither eternal nor personal. Relationship, in his opinion, certainly exists between God and the Son as well as in some mysterious way with the impersonal Spirit, but it is external, not internal relationship; and relationship between the Spirit and the human race is asserted, but in terminology which is decidedly pantheistic. During his lifetime Servetus stood alone against the growing hostility of all sections of the Church, yet his execution for heresy rightly brought upon Calvin almost universal condemnation, notwithstanding the remarkable fact of Melanchthon's approval.[2]

FAUSTUS SOCINUS

Socinianism proper arose with Laelius (Lelio Francesco Maria Sozzini, 1525-1562) and Faustus Socinus (Fausto Paolo Sozzini, 1539-1604), uncle and nephew, who, being Italians, were imbued with the restless spirit of the Renaissance. Laelius, though a secret disciple of Servetus, sought converse with the Protestant leaders in Germany and Switzerland in the rôle of an earnest seeker after truth, and actually lived for three years under Melanchthon's roof. But Faustus, who had come under his influence, was the real leader of the movement, the very success of which in Poland during the

---
[1] Cf Calvin, *Lib. i de Trin*, p 36 ' Incorpoream Deitatem realiter distinctam, Mahometo causam dedisse negandi Christum '

[2] Gibbon characteristically attributes the burning of Servetus to personal malice on the part of Calvin (*Rome*, vi, p 252n), but of this there is no proof whatever.

years immediately following 1579 accounted for that kingdom's isolation. He was also the theologian of the movement, his literary activity commencing during the year of his uncle's death.

His *Reply* to a pamphlet by a certain Jacobus Wiekus, defending the Deity of the Son and of the Holy Spirit,[1] in which he reserves a few thrusts for Cardinal Bellarmine, illustrates the manner in which, he holds, reason should be applied to scriptural revelation. Most of the *Reply* is devoted to an attempt to prove that the Son is not God and equal to the Father, the line of attack being to produce certain 'trinitarian' texts and then to explain away their orthodox interpretations. In noting, for example, 1 John v. 7 (A.V.), he remarks that the Spirit, as he has shown previously, is simply ' the power and efficacy of God in the earth,' and that, at all events, the text is a spurious addition which is contained neither in the Syriac nor in the most trustworthy of the Greek and Latin versions. In any case, the Three are One only in the sense that ' They unite in one witness.' The Person of the Spirit is considered with especial care in the tenth and last chapter of the book. ' To the Holy Spirit,' he writes, ' I have ascribed those things which are characteristic of the one God, since It is undoubtedly the power and efficacy of God; from which it follows that what the Holy Spirit does God Himself is most justly said to do. It appears, however, that this is not enough to satisfy the mind of our adversaries unless it is precisely stated that the Holy Spirit, or that same power and efficacy of God, is a Person distinct from God Himself. . . . Since the Holy Spirit is the Spirit of God, my reply will be that it is generally established that the spirit of a person cannot be a person distinct from that person whose spirit it is; since also those things are ascribed to the Holy Spirit which are characteristic at once of a person and of God Himself, none the less is it established that nothing else should be understood by the name of " Holy Spirit " than God Himself *by* His Spirit, namely, acting and working by His own power and efficacy. . . . Every one sees that it is impossible for the power and efficacy of any one to be a person distinct from him.' ' I believe,' he concludes, ' that I have sufficiently

---

[1] *Responsio ad Libellum Jacobi Wieki . . . de Divinitate Filii Dei et. Sp. sancti* ed. 1624).

shown that the Holy Spirit is not a person any more than other characteristics or effects of God are persons, since It is nothing else than a certain special power and efficacy of God; ... since, too, no one is unacquainted with the fact that the grace of God is not a person.' His comment on Matt. xxviii. 19, the passage containing the commission to baptize into the threefold Name, reads: 'Though the Father only is Creator, the Son and the Spirit, on the other hand, are creatures; and this connexion of the Creator with creatures in baptism must appear much more endurable (*multo tolerabilior*) than when mention is made simply of baptism into a creature (!).'[1]

A similar line of argument is put forward in the *Defensio Animadversionum*, in which the Holy Spirit is declared to be the energy (*vis*), reason (*ratio*), or efficacy (*efficacia*) of God, and not to be 'an infinite Substance' or 'a distinct Person' within the Godhead. Dealing further with v. 7 (A.V.) in the course of his *Commentary on I. John*, Faustus raises again the question of the uncertain reading, and remarks that, even if there be no uncertainty, the text does not support the notion of a Trinity of Divine Persons. It is doubtful that 'the Word' refers to Christ, but it is beyond all doubt that the Holy Spirit is simply the 'efficacy' of God the Father. Again, he reasons, 'spirit,' 'water,' and 'blood' are not of the same essence; but they are manifestly placed in apposition to the Father, the Word, and the Holy Spirit; therefore the Father, the Word, and the Holy Spirit, as the Three that bear witness in heaven, are not of the same Essence. His *Praelectiones Theologicae* contains comparatively little with regard to the Holy Spirit, being practically confined to the consideration of the Person of Christ and His atoning work, but in his last publication, *De Jesu Christo Servatore* (1598), he returns to the charge with reference to the Trinity as a whole.

[1] At least two *Replies* to this book against Wiekus appeared. Johannes Junius (†1602), the Dutch Reformer, wrote an *Examen Responsionis Fausti Socini ad Librum Jacobi Wieki de Divinitate Filii Dei et Spiritus sancti* (ed 1628), in the seventh *classis* of which he upholds the Godhead of the Spirit (cf 1 Cor xii 11), and the truth that He is *persona distincta* He asserts that, 'by the common consent of the whole of mankind, those things that befit a person are existence, life, the reasoning faculty, intellect, will, an indivisible single substance, subsisting incommunicably But all this pertains to the Holy Spirit Therefore He is a Person' Moreover, 'he who proceeds from another is necessarily distinguished from him from whom he proceeds The Holy Spirit proceeds and is sent, not the Father, the Spirit is sent from the Son, therefore He is distinguished from Him' The usual Scripture proofs follow Paulus Tarnovius (latter half of 16th cent), in the course of his *Examen Responsionis Fausti Socini* (ed. 1625), covers much the same ground as Junius, concluding 'Pater est a nullo, Filius a Patre, Spiritus sanctus ab utroque; consimiliter de attributis statuendum et dicendum est.'

The Racovian Catechism

The Catechism of the Polish Socinians, which was issued at Racow in 1605 on the basis of the writings of Faustus, affords an elaborate statement of their opinions. At the outset the assertion is made that Christians, who openly hold that the Son and the Holy Spirit are Persons in the one Deity as well as the Father, are gravely mistaken, in that they bring forward arguments which disclose a misinterpretation of Scripture. There is in the Divine Essence but one Person, namely the Father. The Holy Spirit is His influence or power. Jesus is a glorified Man, who was begotten by the Father through the Holy Spirit, endowed for His unique work by the Father through the Holy Spirit at His baptism, and exalted by the Father at His resurrection. The mysterious dogma of Three in One must be rejected by reason. ' In Scripture,' continues the Catechism, ' the Holy Spirit is never expressly called God. Because in certain places, indeed, Scripture attributes to It those things which pertain to God, it does not thereby speak as if It were either God or a Person of the Godhead ' (question 80).[1] On the other hand, in Scripture there are things attributed to the Holy Spirit that in no sense pertain to a person. The Spirit is spoken of as something given, poured forth, with which men are empowered, that is increased, distributed in parts, sometimes present and sometimes not, and that may be quenched. The conclusion is that the Holy Spirit is not a person, and this is supported by the fact that, whereas the Holy Spirit may be said to be in God, God may not be said to be in the Holy Spirit (q. 371).[2] Again, since

---

[1] Cf John Owen, *Vindication of the Doctrine of the Trinity* (1669) ' The Socinians, observing that such things are assigned and ascribed unto Him (the Holy Spirit) as that, if they acknowledge Him to be a person, or a substance, they must upon necessity admit Him to be God, though they seemed not at first at all agreed what to think or say concerning Him positively, yet they all concurred peremptorily in denying His personality Hereon, some of them said He was the gospel, which others of them have confuted, some that He was Christ Neither could they agree whether there was one Holy Ghost or more; whether the " Spirit of God " and the " good Spirit of God " and the Holy Spirit be the same or no. In general now they conclude that He is *vis Dei*, or *virtus Dei*, or *efficacia Dei*, no substance, but a quality that may be considered either as being in God, and then they say it is the " Spirit of God "|, or as sanctifying and conforming men unto God, and then they say it is the " Holy Ghost " ' (p 88). On the ' polytheism ' of the Socinians, following logically upon their worshipping Christ, cf *ibid*, p 106

[2] Cf Reginald Heber, *The Personality and Office of the Christian Comforter* (Bampton Lect, 1815) ' Whatever name the scholars of Socinus think fit to bestow on the Comforter promised by our Lord, yet if purity, motion, power, resistance, if doing or suffering be predicated (and predicated they doubtless are) of the Spirit of God in Scripture, they must, I repeat, ascribe those accidents to some real existence, material or spiritual, or else they must maintain that our Saviour and His Apostles have clothed an abstract idea under the form of an allegorical personage ' (pp. 56 f).

there is no such thing as original sin (q. 423), man simply needs to exercise his will in order to turn about from self to God. This he does by believing in the promises contained in the Gospel, thereby receiving the gift of the Holy Spirit, the afflatus of God (q. 369), which will enable him to mortify the deeds of the flesh (q. 421). Side by side with these interior operations of God stand the Scriptures, of which the doctrinal sections, in particular, are due to the direct inspiration of God through His Spirit.[1]

Though championed by such keen debaters as Volkel and Schmalz, two of the compilers of the Catechism, and by Crell, the outstanding Socinian theologian, the new rationalism failed to alter the course of the development of the Doctrine of the Holy Spirit in the Church, while its progress during the seventeenth century roused the Church to defend that Doctrine in face of the denial of the Spirit's Personality and the belittlement of His work. 'Socinianism,' says Harnack, 'was simply a step backwards,' but sweeping back with it people with spiritual needs like unto our own, who knew not what they were missing.

[1] According to Socinian belief, the New Testament practically makes obsolete the Old Testament The *Rac. Catech* refers to the Holy Spirit as ' qui per *apostolos* locutus est ' (q. 345)

VIII

THE COUNTER-REFORMATION

THE Reformation had been primarily the work of individual Reformers; the Counter-Reformation was primarily the undertaking of the Roman Church as a whole. For this reason, her judgements in Council naturally preceded the judgements of individual Counter-Reformers, and present discussion must accordingly observe that precedence.

THE COUNCIL OF TRENT

Rome's attempt to overcome Protestantism by coercion as well as by argument was essentially a revival of the 'relentless orthodoxy' of the Mediaeval Church, a revival which took shape pre-eminently at the Council of Trent. In its interrupted sessions, which stretched from 1545 to 1563, the Romish bishops met from time to time ' to the praise and glory of the undivided Trinity,' but so subservient were they to the wishes of the Pope that their declaration that the Holy Spirit presided over their deliberations was received with scepticism by French politicians, who queried whether the Holy Spirit could be conveyed by courier between Trent and Rome! A Jesuit view that General Councils are not guided by the Holy Spirit unless called and controlled by the Pope might have added to the scepticism. Howbeit, the *decrees* of the Council, which are formal statements of dogma, and its *canons*, which contain condemnations of Protestant opinions, together form the basis of the modern Roman Catholic system.

The decrees[1] reveal adherence to the Apostles' Creed, and confirm the mediaeval developments concerning the Trinity, with marked emphasis on Its indivisible Nature. When, however, the bishops advance from the consideration of the Being of the Holy Spirit to that of His work, they immediately invade the debatable area. They agree that the Scriptures are inspired of the Holy Spirit, but proceed to include in the

[1] *Canones et Decreta Concilii Tridentini* (ed 1571)

THE COUNTER-REFORMATION 305

canon the bulk of the Apocrypha. Tradition is asserted to be equivalent in authority to Scripture, since both were dictated either by Christ or by the Holy Spirit (session iv.). Original sin points to the grace of the Holy Spirit as necessary for salvation, but to this grace as conveyed through the sacrament of baptism, which sacrament, therefore, remits the guilt of original sin. ' Justification is not merely remission of sins, but also sanctification,' the ' efficient cause ' of which is ' the merciful God, who freely cleanses and sanctifies, sealing and anointing with the Holy Spirit.'[1] Justification is thus held to include sanctification because it is itself regarded not as an imputation of righteousness but as an infusion of the same, not as declaring a man just but as actually making him so; and the Holy Spirit is spoken of as the Source of this infusion.[2] Moreover, the third canon on justification declares · ' If any one should say that, without the prevenient inspiration of the Holy Spirit and His help, a man can believe, hope, love, or repent, as he ought, in order that the grace of justification may be granted to him—let him be anathema ! ' It is only in response to the co-operation of the human will with this ' prevenient inspiration ' that infusion of righteousness begins to be possible,[3] and, even so, cannot take effect fully apart from the sacraments, all of which confer grace *ex opere operato*, or through the performance of the act itself (session vii., canon 8).[4] The third canon on the sacrament of penance anathematizes those who deny to the Church the power of remitting sins, given by Christ when He breathed the Holy Spirit upon the disciples (John xx. 22, 23). The fourth canon on the sacrament of Orders reads : ' If any one should say that through holy ordination the Holy Spirit is not given, and accordingly that the bishops say to no purpose, " Receive ye the Holy Spirit " ; or that through it the character is not

---

[1] Session vi (*de justificatione*)

[2] *Ibid*, continuing . ' Quanquam nemo possit esse justus, nisi cui merita passionis Jesu Christi communicantur, id tamen in hac impii justificatione fit, dum eiusdem sanct passionis merito per Spiritum sanctum caritas Dei diffunditur in cordibus eorum qui justificantur, atque ipsis inhaeret, unde in ipsa justificatione cum remissione peccatorum haec omnia simul infusa accipit homo per Jesum Christum, cui inseritur, fidem, spem, et caritatem '

[3] As against the Augustinianism of the Catholic Jansenists

[4] On the phrase *ex opere operato* see Paterson, *Rule of Faith*, pp 248 f , Pope, *Compendium of Christian Theology*, iii , pp 302 f , and Banks, *Manual of Christian Doctrine*, pp 236 f Cf also *Prof Fid Trid* , art iv ' Profiteor quoque septem esse vere et proprie sacramenta novae legis a Jesu Christo Domino nostro instituta, . . illaque gratiam conferre '

impressed; or that he who was once a priest can become a layman back again; let him be anathema!' The Council also decided that, by virtue of the Holy Spirit conferred upon them in ordination, even sinful priests can efficiently exercise the power to remit sins. But with regard to any operations of the Holy Spirit through the seven sacraments of the Roman Church little indeed is mentioned, and, in face of the theory of the efficacy of sacraments *ex opere operato*, the defence that belief in sacramental virtue is not inconsistent with belief in the virtue of the Holy Spirit[1] is hardly convincing. The direct inward working of the Holy Spirit is here lost sight of behind a system, doubt is cast upon assurance of salvation,[2] and the teaching of the Reformers concerning the spiritual nature of the Church is replaced by the doctrine of her visible unity. In the *Professio Fidei Tridentinae*, drawn up in 1564 by order of Pius IV, and summing up in brief the decisions of the Council, there occurs but one reference to the Holy Spirit, namely that found in the Nicene Creed (as enlarged at Constantinople) therein embodied, with the addition of *Filioque*.

THE ROMAN CATECHISM

The standard Catholic Catechism (*Catechismus Romanus*)[3] which, like the Profession of Faith, was composed in accordance with a decree of the Council and issued in 1566, does little more than reiterate certain conclusions of scholastic pneumatology. 'The Apostle,' it affirms, 'did not allow certain Ephesians to remain ignorant of the Person of the Holy Spirit (Acts xix.). . . . Wherefore it must be taught that by the name of 'Holy Spirit' the third Person of the Trinity must be understood. . . . Indeed, in the New Testament we are commanded to be baptized in the Name of the Father, and of the Son, and of the Holy Spirit. . . . Now since the proper name for the bringing forth (*productio*) of the third Person is not laid down, but is called spiration and procession, it follows that the Person also, who is brought forth, lacks a proper name. . . . So the people should be instructed at the outset that the Holy Spirit is God just as the Father and the Son, equal to Them, equally omnipotent and eternal, . . . and of the same Nature along with the Father and the Son. I John

---

[1] *De Confirmatione*, canon 2 [2] Session vi. Cf Paterson, *ibid*, p 306
[3] More fully, *Catechismus ex decreto Concilii Tridentini ad Parochos*.

v. 7 (A.V.) is referred to as authentic evidence for the truth of the Trinity. The term 'Spirit of Christ' clearly points to the truth of the *Filioque*, and since from the words ' whom the Father will send in My Name ' (John xiv. 26) we understand the procession of the Holy Spirit, it is evident that He proceeds from Them Both.' From the will of the Father and the Son, as from one Source, He has been brought forth. All three Persons of the Trinity are held to be the Authors of the Incarnation, but, since the Incarnation was essentially an act of love or grace, it is attributed especially to the Holy Spirit. They all work within the soul for its salvation, the work of the Father and of the Son taking effect through the Holy Spirit as Love ; and justification, by which new life is imparted to the soul, is the Spirit's chief gift. According to the Roman Catechism, since the Church is governed by the Holy Spirit, she cannot err in the faith.

Among the theologians of the Counter-Reformation, who furthered its cause in different countries, appear such notable writers as Canus († 1560) in Spain, Canisius († 1597) in Germany, Andrada in Portugal, Maldonatus and Francis of Sales († 1622) in France, and Bellarmine in Italy. It was DIEGO DE PAIVA DE ANDRADA (1528–1575), a member of the Council of Trent, who provoked Chemnitz to undertake that great work against the Jesuits, the *Examen Concilii Tridentini* ; and in his *Defensio Tridentinae Fidei*, a reply published in 1578, Andrada briefly refers to the work of the Spirit in the course of a discussion on justification. ' That is the efficacy (*virtus*) of the Holy Spirit,' he writes, ' that He pervades every recess of the mind, dispels the clouds of ignorance, subdues by His presence the vileness of the passions, and arouses the bitterest hatred of them.'[1] From Him alone is the gift of ' the discerning of spirits ' to be obtained (1 Cor. xii. 10).

JOHANNES MALDONATUS

Johannes Maldonatus (1533–1583) was a Jesuit of Spanish extraction who made his name at Paris as a theological lecturer. His principal work, *Commentaries on the Four Evangelists*, published posthumously in 1596, affords many careful observations on the various references to the Holy Spirit. He would have it made clear that the Holy Spirit is not the Father of

[1] Ed 1579

Christ, but that the birth of Christ was effected by the Father through the Holy Spirit (Matt. i. 18).[1] On the promise of John the Baptist that Christ should baptize with the Holy Spirit and with fire (iii. 11) he remarks: ' There is no doubt but that by "fire" the Holy Spirit is meant; for the conjunction " and " is here not connecting, but explanatory.' When, again, the Holy Spirit is described as descending as a dove at the Baptism (iii. 16), no real dove descended, but the Holy Spirit in that likeness. The Spirit assumes what expressions he may desire, and in this instance His appearing in the form of a dove was intended to show the love of the Father for the Son.[2] That the same occasion had often been brought forward also as an indication of the Trinity Maldonatus does not overlook. ' All the ancient authors,' he writes, ' and particularly those who argued against the Arians, gave another reason, . . . that it might reveal the mystery of the Trinity—of the Father speaking (iii. 17), of the Son receiving the testimony, and of the Holy Spirit descending in the form of a dove.' Of the sin against the Holy Spirit (xii. 31, 32) the commentator's view may be thus presented: The attitude of mind here referred to is that which perverts not only the dignity of God but also the dignity of man, and does so by calling the operations of the Spirit of God the operations of Beelzebub. This sin is without excuse, for it is done not by ignorance or infirmity but by deliberate intent, and therefore cannot be forgiven. Forgiveness is impossible not simply because God will not forgive; it is impossible from the nature of the case itself. For this is not a matter of words, but of the heart.

The last occasion in the Gospel of St. Matthew that mention is made of the Holy Spirit—in connexion with the use of the Threefold Name in baptism (xxviii. 19)—is dwelt upon at some length. Baptism into, that is, by the authority of, the Name of the Father, and of the Son, and of the Holy Spirit is handed down by tradition as the usage of the Church, for ' all bishops and presbyters who may have baptized otherwise than in the Name of the Father, and of the Son, and of the Holy Spirit are excommunicated.' He agrees that ' the question may naturally be put why Christ wished that baptism

---

[1] *Commentarii in quatuor Evangelistas* (ed Raich, Mayence, 1874)
[2] Commenting on Luke iv 1, Maldonatus observes that Jesus was always full of the Holy Spirit, but this appears more clearly in all His actions after His baptism.

should be administered in this form. Many reasons, however, can be given for this. The first, that He might make known from whom baptism has its efficacy (*vim*), surely from the Father, who sent His own Son that He should die for men ; from the Son, who instituted baptism, sprinkled it, as it were, with blood, and made it fertile, productive, and efficacious ; from the Holy Spirit, who, just as water cleanses (*lavat*) bodies outwardly, Himself cleanses souls inwardly—by sanctifying them. The second, lest those who were being baptized should suppose that they were receiving anything merely human, and should not only part asunder men by saying, " I am of Paul, I am of Apollos " (1 Cor. i. 12), but even, in a measure, God Himself, by saying, " I am of the Father, I am of the Son, I am of the Holy Spirit," as if they were being baptized in the Name of only one Person. The third reason Fulgentius has brought forward, that men might perceive that the same One who had been the Author of their generation is the Author of their regeneration, namely, the Father, the Son, and the Holy Spirit. . . . Consequently, these words, " In the Name of the Father, and of the Son, and of the Holy Spirit," must be referred not only to the word " baptizing," but also to those who baptize. Again,' he resumes, ' from this verse ancient writers have rightly demonstrated the mystery of the Trinity.' The Sabellians declare that the Father, the Son, and the Holy Spirit are only one Person, in that Christ did not say, " Baptizing them in the names, but in the Name of the Father, and of the Son, and of the Holy Spirit." These men Basil repulses, stating that this rather should be inferred from the verse, that there are three Persons, and one Nature ; for, though the Father, Son, and Holy Spirit are called by name as three distinct Persons, yet to Them belongs one Name of Deity, one power. From this verse others have demonstrated against the Arians the Godhead and the equality of the Father, the Son, and the Holy Spirit, and that we are not baptized in the name of any creature.' These words, concludes Maldonatus, signify at least that, though Christ departs, He would rejoin the disciples, since the Holy Spirit was to be sent in His stead to teach them all the truth.

The references to the Holy Spirit in the closing chapters of St. John's Gospel are also fully treated. The promise of ' another Comforter ' (xiv. 16) implies that, while Christ also is a Comforter, the imparting of comfort is a special feature of the work of the Holy Spirit, the eternal Helper of man. Him the world cannot receive (xiv. 17), because it is estranged (*alienus*) from Him, but the disciples will receive Him and be reminded by Him of what they had heard from Jesus (xiv. 26). In xv. 26, as in xiv. 16, reference is made to a Trinity of Divine Persons. From xv. 26 'the argument is established that the Holy Spirit proceeds also from the Son. For, even if He (the Son) does not openly affirm that He proceeds from Himself—lest possibly He should seem to speak more assumingly with reference to Himself, yet, since we know that no Person of the Trinity is said to be sent unless by One from whom He proceeds, we conclude that the Holy Spirit proceeds also from the Son, seeing that He is sent by Him.' Christ's statement that the advent of the Holy Spirit was dependent on His own departure (xvi. 7) means that, whereas it was within the realm of possibility that such an advent could have taken place before that departure, Divine Providence decreed otherwise 'in order that all the three Persons of the Trinity might operate in procuring the salvation of men : the Father, by sending the Son and attracting men to Him ; the Son, by teaching, redeeming, and freeing men ; the Holy Spirit, by perfecting men and enriching them with Divine gifts.' The Holy Spirit would guide the disciples into all the truth they ought to know (xvi. 13), though He would not speak from Himself. ' Therefore, as He is not from Himself but proceeds from the Father and the Son, so He shall speak only what He receives from the Father and the Son in proceeding from Them.'

Regarding Christ's breathing of the Holy Spirit upon the disciples before Pentecost (xx. 22) Maldonatus notes certain opinions which had been previously expressed. Some had said that this was a promise, not a gift ; others that only the grace of the Holy Spirit was given, in preparation for the full bestowal later ; others, again, that this was an anticipation of that full bestowal on purpose to show that the Holy Spirit proceeds from the Son as well as from the Father. These opinions Maldonatus deems unsatisfactory. 'Christ had stated beforehand that, if He Himself did not depart, the Holy Spirit would not come visibly and with all His gifts ; and this is true to fact, for He did not come in this manner before the day of Pentecost. At this point, before He departed, He gave Him to the Apostles, though with a visible sign, yet invisibly, because when He sent them forth into the whole world it was necessary to fortify them with some provision for their journey.' So, while the Holy Spirit was to be given more fully at Pentecost, He was given now to deepen the disciples' love for Christ, and to bestow upon them the power to remit sins in His name as Redeemer. Assuredly He could bestow such power on any members of the Church He chose; and, as assuredly, He would see to it that in this respect Thomas was not placed at a disadvantage by being absent.

ROBERT BELLARMINE

Very different from Maldonatus in mental attitude was Robert Bellarmine (1542–1621), Cardinal and the greatest of Jesuit theologians, with whom this study may fittingly be brought to a conclusion. A keen and powerful controversialist, he devoted his brilliant intellect to the task of furthering the cause of the Counter-Reformation, his lectures on its behalf appearing under the title of *Disputationes de Controversiis Christianae Fidei*. Most of the Disputations are foreign to the present purpose, only the section *On Christ (De Christo,* in vol. i.) containing a full treatment of the doctrines of the Trinity and the Holy Spirit. The Trinity, declares Bellarmine, is an ineffable mystery,[1] and though we cannot comprehend how three Persons can be one Essence we must hold to the truth that They are one Essence, believing what we cannot prove.[2] The third Person is Divine even as the Others, as both Old and New Testaments indicate. Scripture calls Him God, but never a creature. His attributes, therein revealed, are the attributes of God, as also are His operations, particularly His part in the work of justification. His recorded miracles and His government of the Church are further testimonies to His Deity.[3]

The purpose of Book ii. is made clear at the outset. ' Hitherto,' writes the author, ' we have shown that the one true God is not only the Father, but also the Son and the Holy Spirit. Now it is necessary to show that these Three, the Father, the Son, and the Holy Spirit, are truly three hypostases

[1] Bk 1, chap iii, § 12 (ed 1721)   [2] *Ibid*, §13.
[3] *Ibid*, chap xiii Objections to the Deity of the Spirit are disposed of in chap xx, where Bellarmine uses Augustine freely.

(*supposita*), and distinct, but not three Names, or three existences of the reason '; this Bellarmine proceeds to do under five heads, while making no noticeable contribution of his own. On the question of the *Filioque*, too, he resolves himself into a summist of previous teaching. It is true, he admits, that the Latins added *Filioque* to the creed without the consent of the Greeks,[1] and sketches the history of this addition from the time of Theodoret.[2] On the other hand, it is proved from the evidence of Scripture (especially the fourth Gospel and the Pauline Epistles),[3] from the affirmations of the Councils,[4] from the Latin,[5] and even from the Greek Fathers.[6] It is confirmed also by reason. 'Every distinction in God arises from relations of source; but if the Spirit were not to proceed from the Son there would be no relation of source between Them; therefore if the Spirit were not to proceed from the Son He would not be distinguished from the Son. . . . Moreover, if all perfections (*absoluta*) were not common to the three Persons, the three Persons would not be one Essence (*res*). Neither could we defend the elementary Nature (*simplicitas*) of God, nor demonstrate that there is no perfection in one Person that is not in Another. Wherefore it should not be doubted but that it is relation alone which distinguishes the Trinity.' Therefore, from the above reasoning, the Spirit must proceed from the Son. Once more, if the Holy Spirit were not to proceed actively from the Son, generation and spiration would be one mode, and not two; but, in point of fact, they are distinguishable by reason as two modes; therefore the Holy Spirit does proceed actively from the Son.[7] Chapter xxvii., which follows, is devoted to demolishing the Greek arguments against the disputed addition to the creed, and Chapter xxviii. to demonstrating that this addition was properly made. 'To believe,' concludes Bellarmine, 'that the Spirit is not from the Son is, as we have shown, an error against the Scriptures, and therefore must be avoided.'

The theology of the Counter-Reformation, built as it was on

[1] Bk II, chap xx
[2] *Ibid*, chap xxi   For Theodoret's view see Swete, *H Sp in the Ancient Church*, p 269
[3] *Ibid*, chap xxii.   [4] Chap xxiii   [5] Chap xxiv.
[6] Chap xxv   The Greek Fathers cited as supporting the truth of the *Filioque* are . Gregory Thaumaturgus, Gregory of Nyssa, Athanasius, Basil, Gregory Nazianzus, Cyril of Jerusalem, Chrysostom, Epiphanius, Didymus and Cyril of Alexandria, Simeon Metaphrastes, Anastasius, Tharasius, Maximus, and John of Damascus.
[7] Chap xxvi.

that of the Schoolmen, argued from Scripture, reason, and the testimony of earlier authorities, the truths of the Trinity, the *Filioque*, and the Deity and personality of the Spirit. On these subjects it was at one with the teaching of the Reformers, but on all other subjects connected with the Spirit the differences were manifest. To the exaltation of tradition to the level of the Bible, on the plea that both were in equal measure inspired and dictated by the Spirit, the Reformers could never consent; nor could they tolerate a sacramental system, working irrevocably *ex opere operato*, which had the effect of obscuring the operations of the Spirit *through* the sacraments, and, indeed, of limiting in thought those direct operations as a whole. Not that the sanctifying power of the Holy Spirit was not distinctly taught by the Counter-Reformers; but such power, for its effectual working, requires the co-operation of the will, which, as they said, can only become effectual through the medium of the sacraments. Accordingly the Roman view of justification, as an infusion of righteousness dependent on the sacramental medium, gave little encouragement to the doctrine of Assurance, founded, as this must be, on a conception of salvation which is freely bestowed in response to faith alone, as apart from anything suggestive of merit. Thus the Roman idea of the Church of Christ was a visible organization kept from erring by the guidance of the Spirit, to the rejection of the idea of the Invisible Church as consisting of all those who have passed through an inward experience of salvation. Counter-Reformation theology was therefore an attempt, in a measure successful, to revive, and even to intensify, the externality of mediaevalism. But a new day had already dawned at the Reformation, a day in which the emphasis would pass gradually from the external to the internal, from the work of the Holy Spirit through ecclesiastical mediation to His work as immediate and as shedding abroad the love of God directly in the heart of man.

PART V

SUMMARY OF THE DOCTRINE OF THE HOLY SPIRIT IN THE MEDIAEVAL CHURCH

  I. THE GODHEAD OF THE SPIRIT
 II. THE RELATION OF THE HOLY SPIRIT TO THE FATHER AND THE SON
III. THE PERSONAL LIFE OF THE SPIRIT
 IV. THE WORK OF THE SPIRIT IN CREATION
  V. THE WORK OF THE SPIRIT IN INSPIRATION
 VI. THE WORK OF THE SPIRIT IN THE INCARNATION
VII. THE MISSION OF THE SPIRIT
VIII. THE WORK OF THE SPIRIT IN THE SACRAMENTS
 IX. THE WORK OF THE SPIRIT IN JUSTIFICATION AND SANCTIFICATION
  X. THE WITNESS OF THE SPIRIT

'The Holy Spirit qualifieth us to be the sons of God by His effectual grace, and assureth us that we are so by His comfortable testimony .. We should thus mind the Blessed Spirit of God and be suitably affected towards Him.'—ISAAC BARROW.

'The sufferings and merits of Christ, as they are sufficient to do away the sins of the whole world, so they are only effectual to those that are regenerate by the Holy Ghost, who breatheth where He will of free grace'—FRANCIS BACON.

I

THE GODHEAD OF THE SPIRIT

THROUGHOUT the centuries herein surveyed, with the exception of the tenth, the Mediaeval Church has gradually placed Pneumatology on a level with Christology, thus developing the process already begun in the age of the Fathers. Its earliest writers follow the lead of their predecessors in asserting that the Holy Spirit is neither a temporal creation of the Son, as the Arians affirmed, nor less than the Father and the Son, as the Donatists affirmed. Both East and West unite in upholding His Deity and His co-eternity with the Father and the Son within the Godhead, the Three being One (*unum*) in ' an unchangeable simple Essence,' One therefore in every Divine operation. Mention of His mission from the Son, or of His being the Spirit of the Son, was regarded as implying no inferiority in any sense. Though sent by the Father and the Son, He is stated to be sent of His own accord, while the Anti-Adoptionists actually argue from His own acknowledged Divinity to the Divinity of the Son! Again, though the word ' God,' when used indefinitely, is, as Alcuin and Calvin point out, especially appropriate to the Father, the Holy Spirit is nevertheless ' perfect God,' and is Holy Spirit in respect of His own Nature.[1] From Isidore to Bellarmine the Church bears consistent witness to the Holy Spirit's equality to the Father and the Son, equality in respect not of relation but of unity of Essence ; and this witness, as in the case of the ancient writers, is based upon the revealed truth of both Old and New Testaments. Testimony to this Divine equality was greatly in evidence by the time of pre-scholastic days. Before the entrance of Anselm and his successors the Holy Spirit was said to proceed equally from the Father and the Son and therefore to be Divine, since only God can proceed

---

[1] Alcuin, *ep* 161 : 'Deus natura est Deus, et Filius natura est Filius, et Spiritus sanctus natura est Spiritus sanctus ' So also Nicolas of Cusa

from God.[1] If He is the Love and the Unity of the Father and the Son, He must Himself be God even as They. Prayer is thus rightly addressed to the Holy Spirit alone, just as to the Father alone, or to the Son alone, while worship of the Father or the Son is also worship of the Holy Spirit.

At the hands of the Schoolmen, these statements received both addition and elaboration. Roscellin, with his tritheistic tendencies, believes in the equality of the Persons as the equality of three parts of a whole, and not of three wholes. But the Church would have none of any conception of equality arising from any suggestion of partition. Absolute equality in relation to the Divine Persons means that any Two are not *together* greater than a Third. Accordingly, in the Trinity, the Holy Spirit is not less than both the Father and the Son, even as in the analogy of mind, knowledge, and love, love is not less than both mind and knowledge. The *whole* Godhead resides in *Each*, All act in the acts of *Each*, no other conclusion being consistent with revelation.

Doctrinal development is indebted to Aquinas for the most valuable contribution to thought on this particular subject. Not only does the substance of the above appear in his writings, but also further proof that the Holy Spirit is fully God (*plenus Deus*). The unforgivable nature of sin against Him, the fact that members of Christ are His temples, His operations in creation and in searching the deep things of God, His speaking through the prophets, His dispensing of gifts according to His own judgement, His close connexion with the Father and the Son at the Baptism of Jesus and in the baptismal commission, all these are unmistakable signs of His Deity. Moreover, contends Aquinas, since the spirit of man is essential to man, the Spirit of God is of the same Essence as God. Inequality would divide the Essence of God, which is impossible. To these considerations Bellarmine adds the Holy Spirit's government of the Church, so plainly recorded in the Acts of the Apostles. Aquinas proceeds to anticipate the Reformers by emphasizing the Divine Nature of the Holy Spirit on account of the Divine character of His work in the soul. Sanctification is a function peculiar to God, as also is adoption

---

[1] The *Filioque* and the Spirit's Godhead were regarded by the Westerns as mutually supporting, cf Hildefonsus, *Ann de Cognit Bap* (c 55) ' Spiritus sanctus ideo praedicatur Deus, quia ex Patre Filioque procedit, et substantiam eorum habet ' So also Aquinas, Galatinus, Erasmus, the Belgic Confession, and the Anglican Homilies.

into God's family. The Reformers follow by asserting the same in reference to justification, and to all the operations of the Spirit in the individual, which are so vividly portrayed in the New Testament. Can one creature sanctify another? Can one creature adopt another into Divine sonship? Can one creature take so important a part in the justification of another in the sight of God? Since, then, these operations must be Divine operations, and are stated to be operations peculiar to the Holy Spirit, the full Divinity of the Holy Spirit is established beyond question. The same position is occupied by Mysticism, whose designation of the Holy Spirit as Love and as the One in whom union with God is attainable, can be based only upon His Godhead; for how could such a union be possible through a creaturely medium? The conclusion of the Mediaeval Church is, therefore, that the Holy Spirit is 'very and eternal God,' or, in the words of St. Bernard, 'The Holy Spirit is God Himself.'

II

THE RELATION OF THE HOLY SPIRIT TO THE FATHER AND THE SON

THE Mediaeval Church accepted without question the conclusion of the Fathers that God is not 'a vast and unrelieved monotony of existence,' but that within the Divine Life there are three co-eternal, co-equal, and personal Subsistences, Father, Son, and Holy Spirit. This truth is unexplainable by the finite intellect, for it is primarily a matter of revelation, not of demonstration. While, however, it cannot be intellectually comprehended, it can be intellectually conceived, if not by logic, by faith based on ratiocination ; so that the mystery of the Trinity is an article of faith because reason can draw no other inference from Scripture.[1] There are in God three 'Persons' who cannot be merged into one Person. Reason supports this by an argument from effect to cause, the effect being the three principal Divine operations of creation, redemption, and salvation. Unity does not imply confusion, and among the Persons there exists the one precedence and the one means of distinction indicated by the terms 'begetting,' 'begotten,' 'proceeding.' God eternally and unchangeably knows Himself as Son, and loves Himself as Holy Spirit (Aquinas). Since God is Love, Love demands plurality for Its self-expression ; accordingly there must be plurality in God, and such a plurality as this which is revealed. Revelation gives no encouragement to the thought that Each of the Persons is successively God, or, on the other hand, to the modalism of Erigena or of Gilbert. The Divine Essence is not one Person, for in this case one Person would beget Himself, be begotten from Himself, and proceed from Himself, which is absurd. Nor do we speak of the Divine Essence as begetting Itself, being begotten from Itself, and proceeding from Itself, which is confusing ; for the Essence *is* the Trinity,

---

[1] On the spurious 1 John v 7 (A V), so often adduced, there is an excellent note by Westcott in his *Epp of St John*, pp 202 ff.

RELATION TO THE FATHER AND THE SON 321

and is, at the same time, wholly contained in *each* Person. The safe course is to keep to the language of the Church, which, while it cannot avoid mystery, certainly avoids difficulty.

Again, the term ' generation ' is used with reference to the Son, and the term ' procession ' with reference to the Holy Spirit. The Son is said to proceed by nature or by understanding, and the Holy Spirit by will or by love, so that, in the human conception, that is, in theological development, the former procession precedes the latter, since nothing can be loved until it has first been conceived in the mind.[1] But such precedence exists only in the conception. Valuable as is the psychological analogy for purposes of illustration, it can never be exact (Nicolas of Cusa), and these two functions themselves cannot but be simultaneous in spite of analogical suggestions to the contrary (Durandus). Yet, simultaneous as they are, they must be distinguished in thought, if not by comprehension, for the sake, again, of avoiding confusion. The Western divines assert that they differ in point of source, generation being from One, procession from Two. They were able, however, to show the necessity for distinction apart from any entering-in of the *Filioque*, for if the Holy Spirit be begotten there are two Sons in the Trinity, if He be unbegotten there are two Fathers in the Trinity ; hence He must be regarded only as proceeding. Moreover, as He proceeds He unites the Trinity as the Bond of the eternity of the Father and the equality of the Son, as the mutual Love of Them Both, or as the common Life of the Three[2] ; so that no one Person can be conceived apart from the Others.

For this reason, the ' properties ' which compose the various analogies of the Divine Triunity are intended to be particular rather than exclusive, as portraying a distinction of specific attributes which exists only in thought. As such, these analogies vary considerably in value. Indeed, Durandus, together with the Scholastic critics, resembles the Fathers in discouraging the use of the analogy on the ground that neither Divine Infinity nor the Trinity revealed therein has any

---

[1] Illingworth, *Personality, Human and Divine* (1894), p 73 ' It is under the more fundamental psychological analogy that we find the doctrine of the Trinity slowly defined, with the natural consequence that the conception of the Word is completed sooner than that of the Spirit, since a personal object is easier to imagine than a personal relation '

[2] In this connexion the Spirit constantly figures as *communio, connexio, nexus, copula*, &c

real likeness in the realm of the finite. On the other hand, theologians such as Bonaventura and Reuchlin argue in support of employing the analogical method, since it strongly suggests Divine facts even though it cannot fully explain them ; and similar views may be credited to the mass of Latin writers who were content to have recourse to the same method without argument. Of the above variations in value these writers themselves were assuredly quite conscious. That many of their analogies could only be of the nature of pure illustration required no expert mind to perceive, so it may safely be assumed that this, and only this, was the purpose of their using them. Analogies of this character are drawn from nature (sun, sun's beams, heat ; fountain, river, sea), created substance in general (matter, form, their unity ; power, form, motion), the Divine attributes (unity, truth, goodness ; might, wisdom, favour), and geometry (cf. Bacon and Nicolas of Cusa). But the example of Augustine led to the employment, by Schoolman and Reformer alike, of a certain form of analogy more than any other, a form which he and his successors in the West held to be not only an illustration but a definite indication of the Holy Trinity. Man is made in the image of God (Gen. i. 26), therefore an examination of the inner nature of the one will reveal indications of the inner Nature of the Other. Thus in the human mind there is the seat of mental activity, or memory, there is knowledge or understanding, and there is volition or love. Again, we can discern absolute wisdom, wisdom proceeding from the absolute, and love ; or mind, reason, and impulse. In all these analogies the particular, rather than the exclusive aspect of the ' properties ' is retained, being demanded by the unity of God as, indeed, by the unity of man. It is significant that the anti-Scholastic Mystics, who consistently emphasize the Divine Unity, are fond of employing the analogical method to increase this emphasis. But even the indications of the human analogy are never put forward as proofs.

Toward the close of the mediaeval period the existence of a Trinity in God as revealed in Scripture is also seen to be revealed in the experience of salvation. The Reformers are at one with the later Schoolmen in speaking of the Father as adopting man through the Son by the indwelling of the Holy Spirit. Calvin undertakes his vigorous defence of the Doctrine of the Trinity against anti-trinitarian heresies not for the sake of metaphysics or of bare orthodoxy, but for the sake of the Christian doctrine of salvation which, he perceives, these heresies impair. Maldonatus, the Counter-Reformer, gives as the reason for the Holy Spirit's delaying His coming till after Christ's departure the Divine intention that the whole Trinity should operate for man's salvation.[1] It is pointed out by Dr. Swete that 'the worship of the Trinity was a fact in the religious life of Christians before it was a dogma of the Church,'[2] but during the greater part of the Middle Ages the Church appears to be obsessed by the latter rather than the former. It remained for the Reformers to rediscover the Trinity in the hallowed experience of God enjoyed by the believing soul, and thereby to combine the testimonies of internal and external revelation.

If, however, God is not 'one simple Nature,' the Christian Doctrine of the Trinity is at once discredited. This doctrine does not destroy the Unity of the Divine Substance, for It *is* the Divine Substance. From the earliest days of the Mediaeval Church the unity of God is constantly asserted, the inseparable procession of the Holy Spirit only serving to bring into relief the *tota Trinitas* as *unus Deus*, since He unites into One (*in unum*) the Father and the Son. Seeing that the Trinity is the Absolute, and the Absolute is not multipliable, the Trinity is One in will and operation, and acts directly as One in (i.) creation, where the oneness of the universe reflects the oneness of the First Cause; (ii.) the world of men; and (iii.) the human heart. This was a truth which in the early days of Bede received necessary emphasis in face of Mohammedan satire; and in order to uphold the Divine unity, threatened later by Adoptionism, the Anti-Adoptionists affirm that incorrectness of view regarding one Person entails incorrectness of view regarding the Others. Granted the unity of God, reason, *per se*, will grasp the impossibility of either inequality or division. Conversely, since equality is the cause of unity, the unity of God is not disturbed by being tripersonal. Though each Person is the first principle, the three Persons together are also the first principle, and the very perfection of Their unity ministers to a Divine oneness

---

[1] See Pope, *Compendium of Christian Theology*, ii , pp 276, 393, the revelation of the Trinity being bound up with the revelation of redemption
[2] *The Holy Spirit in the Ancient Church*, p 159

which is 'sole yet not solitary.' Is it not possible, then, to see in Jesus the character of both His Father and His Spirit?

The Scholastic age, throughout the development of trinitarian teaching, conserved the unity of the Deity as fundamental. Such unity, it declares, is the necessary basis of philosophic thought; and since Scripture teaches that God is three Persons, the unity of the Deity is not the unity of one Person but of one Being, not *ipse* but *ipsum*, not *unus* but *unum*. This consideration in no wise impairs the unity, for each Person is present in Each, the whole Trinity operates in Each, the relation of the Divine Substance to Each is the same, and any two Persons together are in no wise greater than a Third. The Persons are not *res separatae*, for Each is *alius*, not *aliud*. The Holy Spirit is not separate from the Son, for understanding and will are essentially one. In fact, the distinctions revealed within God are not numerical but essential. 'I love; I am lovable; I am the union arising out of the love wherewith I love myself; yet I am one.' 'I think; I consider; I determine; yet I am one.' Accordingly the baptismal commission reads, not 'into the names,' but 'into the *Name*' of the Father, and of the Son, and of the Holy Spirit (Matt. xxviii. 19). Hence in God, who is Infinite Unity, there is neither number, nor inequality, nor otherness (*alteritas*). Rather, reason the later Schoolmen, do we find in Him unity, equality, and their bond. But unity is the Absolute, and must be eternal, equality precedes inequality and otherness, so must be eternal, while the bond of unity and equality must also be eternal. Therefore the three Persons thus indicated are One, and, not only so, but the highest Unity can only be understood as threefold. The Unity *is* the Trinity, as well as the Trinity the Unity.[1]

On the vexed question of the source of the Spirit's procession there is much debate and, indeed, definite development. During the pre-Scholastic period in the West some uncertainty is apparent concerning the correctness of the twofold procession which had previously received the imprimatur of the Latin Fathers. Erigena will have none of it, and even Bede seems none too confident. In Spain, however, it is quoted by the Anti-Adoptionists against the Adoptionists with a

[1] Cf. Illingworth, *ibid*, pp 69 f

view to elevating the Son, and from the eleventh century it goes forth with the official approval of the papacy. The *Filioque* itself is admitted to be a mystery, yet the Western divines declare that the pronouncements of the Church must be accepted, based as they are on revealed truth and the implications of trinitarian analogies. The Holy Spirit proceeds from the Father and the Son as love proceeds from memory and understanding. But the impossibility of employing these terms exclusively means that *each* Person may be typified by the three terms *together*, in which case the Son stands for more than simply understanding. If, then, the position of the Son is more than medial, the Holy Spirit must proceed also from Him. Thus the Father and the Son, separately and unitedly, are the Source of all the Divine Love, the above argument being merely the analogical version of John xvi. 15, ' All things whatsoever the Father hath are Mine.' Accordingly, while the mass of Western theologians agree that the Father is the ultimate Source of the Spirit's procession, they decline to follow Augustine in saying that this procession originates *principally* from the Father. From earliest mediaeval times it is the perfect equality of the procession from the Father and the Son that is unfailingly stressed,[1] perfect equality in that the procession is wholly from the Father and wholly from the Son, beside being inseparably, eternally, and simultaneously from Them as from one Source. The more the Church gives thought to the *Filioque*, the more does she regard it as safeguarding both the Divine unity and the personal distinctions. That what it involves cannot suit a triad of different, or even separate, beings is always abundantly clear. Not, however, till Aquinas treats the subject is it equally clear that the *Filioque* serves the latter purpose. Filiation and procession could not of themselves indicate the presence of two Persons, for the processions of understanding and will can take place in a single person. Again, a single person may be said to differ from himself according to his varying characteristics, as witness the colloquialism, ' He is a different man,' or ' He is not himself.' But the distinctions within God can only be distinctions of

---

[1] So Alcuin, *De Fide S Trin* , 1 11 · ' Spiritus sanctus hoc habet proprium, quod ex Patre et Filio aequaliter procedit ; et est amborum Spiritus, eiusdemque substantiae et aeternitatis cum Patre et Filio . . Et haec tria unum . . . et hoc unum tres '

source. Therefore, in order that the Spirit may be conceived as a Person distinct from the Son, He must of necessity proceed from the Son. So when He is referred to in Scripture as 'the Spirit of the Son,' this is clearly the meaning of the reference, for the very authority with which the Son sends the Spirit is such as could only be attached to source.

Within the limits of the mediaeval period the Greek contributors are comparatively few. In regard to the Spirit's procession the Eastern Church refused to go beyond the words of Scripture or the Greek Fathers. Indeed, she had a rooted objection to any form of doctrinal development, and also considered herself somewhat above arguing with Latins! Those of her theologians who allow themselves to be drawn into controversy stand by the position of John of Damascus that the Holy Spirit proceeds *from* the Father *through* the Son. In their opinion, the words of our Lord as recorded in John xv. 26 can mean nothing else. Procession from the Father and the Son is contrary to Scripture, which never asserts two 'Causes' of the Holy Spirit; and the Western attempt to evade the difficulty by stating that the Father and the Son are one Source of the Spirit is a turning aside to Sabellianism. Moreover, they add, procession from the Son means procession from the humanity of the Son, which is absurd.

The Church of the West proved quite capable of defending her own conclusions. John xv. 26 does not say 'from the Father *only*;' it simply marks the distinction between the Father and the Son, and so involves no contradiction of the *Filioque* (Alcuin). Nowhere, in fact, does Christ even hint that the procession of the Spirit is from the Father alone. Again, the Greeks assert that since the *Filioque* does not form part of the Apostles' Creed it is denied by the spirit of that Creed. On the contrary, inasmuch as it is not expressly denied in this symbol, it cannot be contrary to its spirit, and Bonaventura presses once more the 'argument from silence' in affirming that the early Greek Fathers never denied the Spirit's procession from the Son as well as from the Father. The Latins concede that the addition of *Filioque* to the ecumenical creeds was somewhat arbitrary as having been made without the consent of the Greeks, but, so far from appearing apologetic, they insist on the entire correctness of the addition. It is implied by the truths of Scripture which are held alike by East and West,[1] and demonstrated by the Councils, by Greek as by Latin Fathers,[2] and by reason. As to what the Greeks say concerning the absurdity of the Spirit's procession from the Son's humanity, their opponents repudiate the notion,[3] and assert rather that the procession must be from the Son as perfect God, since there are no degrees of Godhead. If the Greeks were to think less of the Son as ' the Word made flesh ' and more of Him as the eternal Son of God, of one Substance with the Father, their difficulty in respect of His being a Source of the Spirit's procession would be diminished considerably. Let one deny that the Son is a Source of the Spirit, and one may just as well deny to the Son other things which are ascribed to the Father, with little heed to the truth of John xvi. 15.

Gibbon condemns the *Filioque* dispute as a ' superfluous research,'[4] and it may readily be allowed that the academic savour of much of the long debate lends colour to this criticism. But to suppose that the dispute itself was superfluous as being concerned with non-essentials is to misread the facts. The Western Church realized that to uphold the closest connexion between the Son and the Spirit was vital—not so much to the cause of dogmatic precision as to the cause of the gospel in the world. Whereas the Greeks regard the Spirit as an external Breath, the Latins regard Him as an inner Love (Bonaventura). It is on the ground of the redeeming work of the Son that He carries forward His sanctifying work.[5] By proceeding from the Son He wholly reveals the Son, and in such a way as to keep before men the mighty truth that Jesus Christ is still present among them by His Spirit.[6] Those

---

[1] For the *Filioque* as a ' fair inference ' see Harnack, *Hist. of Dogma*, iv , p 128 ; Beet, *Manual of Theology*, p 121 ; Swete, *The Holy Spirit in the N T* , p 304 ; and Pope, *Compendium of Chr Theol* , 1 p 266

[2] Bp Pearson (*Exposition of the Creed*) states that, under differing forms of speech, the Greek and Latin Fathers before the time of Theodoret were in practical agreement regarding the truth of the twofold procession.

[3] According to Wyclif, the very silence of Christ on the matter of the twofold procession teaches that the Holy Spirit does not proceed from the Son in respect of His manhood It was after the Resurrection that Christ breathed the Spirit upon the disciples, and it was from heaven that He sent the Pentecostal Gift.

[4] *Rome*, vi p 524

[5] Cf Swete, *Holy Spirit in N T* , pp 204 ff

[6] Cf W H T Gairdner, *World Missionary Conference Reports*, iv p. 153 : ' The Holy Ghost must be represented always as in vital and essential connexion with the Incarnate One, that He must not be preached as simply another Person of the Trinity, as the Spirit of God (simply), proceeding from the Father ; but that the *spirit*, if not the letter, of the *Filioque* version must be ever and always preached . . . that to us, at least, dispensationally, the Spirit of God is the Spirit of Jesus '

Christians of whom Wessel speaks, who had accustomed themselves to refer to the Trinity under the simple name of Jesus, had manifestly made this truth their own, even though their thinking was grossly incorrect. And wheresoever this truth lives in experience the power of the Redeemer goes forth. But this is the very truth which was missed by the East. To quote Dr. Smeaton: 'So calamitous have been the results of denying the essential relation of the Spirit as the Spirit of the Son that we cannot fail to perceive that the Spirit was largely dissevered from the Son in the whole Eastern theology, and the Greek Church has become much of a fossil in consequence. It has been untouched by any reformation and by any revival such as has revived again and again the Church of the West.'[1]

[1] In a lecture on 'The Procession of the Holy Spirit,' delivered at Edinburgh, 1882.

III

THE PERSONAL LIFE OF THE SPIRIT

SABELLIAN and Arian attacks had strengthened the conviction that the Holy Spirit is a Person in the Godhead, and this conviction was strengthened still further in the course of succeeding centuries. Gilbert cites with evident disapproval the theory of Macedonius that the Spirit is merely the Deity of the Father and the Son, or the manifestation of the one God. Caution is given that the word 'Spirit' should not be allowed to mislead. It signifies neither a created impulse, nor 'an incorporeal nothing' such as the Divine energy. Nor does it signify an accidental perfection of the human mind, inasmuch as the Holy Spirit, as a distinct Self, is the voluntary cause of all its perfections. Within the Godhead there are relations, and relation implies personality; so that the Father, Son, and Holy Spirit, being distinguished by relations of source, are distinguished by that by which Each is constituted in personal Being (*esse personalis*). Admittedly, the simple fact that the Father, Son, and Holy Spirit are three distinct Realities does not of itself necessitate personality. Distinction, which is implied by procession, cannot alone imply personality, for the former is essentially negative, the latter essentially positive. But it is the *eternity* of the distinction in question which rules out negation and points accordingly to the existence in God of a positive Character or 'Person.'[1] It is possible also that the mutuality of the love of the Father and the Son—Augustine's *condilectio*—does not of itself necessitate personality, yet there occurs the conception of the mutual love of the two Persons as demanding a third Person for its highest and most complete expression. So the Holy Spirit is regarded as a Person existing *per se*, even as the Father or the Son. Seeing, then, that God is One, and that the Holy Spirit is both numbered with and equal to the

[1] In contrast to the temporal distinction of 'character' which is afforded by the *persona* or actor's mask. The term 'person' was the best available. Albertus Magnus is content to use it because 'what a person is is common to the Three'

Father and the Son, who are acknowledged Persons, the Holy Spirit also must be a Person, if only that the perfect oneness of God may be preserved. This being the case, He possesses an identity which He cannot lose.

To this the written Word bears testimony. No trinity of attributes is upheld by Scripture, but rather a Trinity of Persons to which reference is made in the account of Christ's Baptism and in the baptismal formula. The Spirit of God is He who moved upon the waters at the creation, and who is portrayed in the New Testament as a subsistent Person, proceeding from the Father, receiving from the Son, and acting by His own will in nature and in grace. He is the 'other Paraclete,'[1] as personal therefore as the Son; and any refusal to accept His 'personality' carries with it the refusal to accept the personality of the Son in whose stead He came. He is One against whom sin may be committed, One to whom prayer may be made. He is the 'Life of souls,' working within them for their spiritual growth. The Book of Acts shows Him to be not *agitatio* but *agitator*, and St. Paul speaks of Him as the Giver of every good gift (1 Cor. xii. 4 ff). In short, whereas those things that pertain to a person are existence, life, the reasoning faculty, intellect, will, and 'an indivisible simple substance subsisting incommunicably,' (Melanchthon, Junius, Chemnitz, &c.), and whereas these very things are seen to pertain to the Holy Spirit, it may reasonably be inferred that the Holy Spirit is a Person.

The Mediaeval Church, however, is careful to insist that such an inference in no sense counteracts or impairs the absolute oneness of God. On the contrary, the unity of the Divine Life is regarded as being enhanced by Its being tri-personal.[2] Clearly, then, the term 'person' must receive different interpretations as it is used of perfect God or imperfect man. For general purposes it is defined as 'an indivisible nature of rational substance,' or, as Aquinas prefers, 'an indivisible substance of rational nature,' or again, as Melanchthon prefers, 'an indivisible, intelligent, and incommunicable substance'; yet in the Trinity there are not three rational substances. Moreover, the addition to Melanchthon's definition made by Chemnitz—'which is not sustained either in or from another substance'—cannot hold good of the Persons

[1] Cf Swete, *Holy Spirit in N.T*, Note D.   [2] See the previous chapter.

of the Trinity, for it cuts right across all that the Schoolmen write concerning relations of source in God which alone account to the reason for such internal distinctions. When Durandus refers to a person as that which is subject to the intention of mind (*res intentioni subjecta*), and consequently as deriving from both substance and relation, he does not hesitate to assert that the three Divine Persons are not three Objects in themselves but three Objects of relation, there being a real distinction between the Persons but not between Their attributes.[1] It is manifest, then, that human numeration does not enter here. 'Three horses are not one animal' (Lombardus), but the three Persons are one Essence. Even three men of one nature are separate; on the other hand, within the Godhead Two are not greater than One, and Three are not greater than Two, for All are in Each. Triunity differs from triplicity in that both the natures *and* the relations that are in the Divine Persons are the Persons Themselves, so that the eternal and essential relations of paternity, filiation, and procession *are* the Father, Son, and Holy Spirit respectively. Hence within the Godhead there is no otherness, since Each, while Another (*alius*), is not something else (*aliquid*). 'The Persons,' remarks Nicolas of Cusa, 'are not Persons save in a state of union.'

The theologians of this period keep always to the fore the truth that the existence of personal distinctions in the Deity is supremely a matter of revelation and not of reason. To certain questionings which naturally occur the finite mind can never offer a complete answer. But the finite mind knows from experience, as taught by Scripture, that God the Holy Ghost is present everywhere personally (*personaliter*), and that the fullness of His personal Life as exerted in the midst of mankind is indicated most surely by the character of his saving operations in the soul. This history vindicates, for the Church has gained or lost in spiritual force as she has upheld passionately or lukewarmly the Doctrine of the 'personality' of the Spirit.

---

[1] Cf Paterson, *Rule of Faith*, pp 216 f

IV

THE WORK OF THE SPIRIT IN CREATION

NOTHING outside of God is or exists *per se* or *sui causa*. Everything requires a Cause exterior to and greater than itself. Thus it is necessary that there should be a 'first and most simple Cause,' and to this Cause is given the name of 'God.' Since, then, the one Divine Principle and Framer (*artifex*) of all things is revealed as Father, Son, and Holy Spirit, the external activity of the Three in creation is one and the same, inasmuch as the Father created all by the Son while the Holy Spirit co-operated with Them Both; and since Each of the Three is God the whole Trinity operated, and still operates invisibly, as the matter, form, and unity of created substance. Indeed, each single created substance, by virtue of its possessing these three qualities, points to the triune Nature of its Maker, which, again, is indicated by the triad of fruitfulness, bringing forth, and love displayed in His creative energy. It is the triune Nature of God which accounts for the three main classes of creatures in the universe, the spiritual as embracing the angels, the corporeal as embracing vegetables, animals, and the elements, and that which is both spiritual and corporeal as embracing man. Such at least is the theory propounded by Nicolas of Cusa. But this and similar theories apart, Scripture and reason together support the verdict of the Early Church that there is but one creative energy of the three Persons. What One does All do; therefore there is complete unity of action on the part of the Three in the creation, preservation, and government of the universe.[1] The Trinity is its Maintainer, Sufficiency, and End, the Father creating and perfecting it through the Son with or in the Holy Spirit.

While the Triunity of God presupposes the participation of the three Divine Persons in creation, the Church taught

---

[1] Hildefonsus, *Ann de Cognit Bap*, 4 · ' Haec tota Trinitas unus Deus fecit omnia . . . omnia creavit, omnia continet, omnia gubernat '

that the Holy Spirit in particular is the Person through whom this participation becomes effective.[1] He is energizing Life (*vita spiritalis*), the very Principle of Life (*principium vitae*). There could be no emanation of creating life from God but for the emanation or procession of the Holy Spirit. And since He proceeds by way of love, He is the Origin not merely of all motion, but of ' the created spirit of the universe ' which unifies the creation in love. As in the Father there abides all possibility, and in the Son all action, so all unifying and harmonizing motion abides in the Holy Spirit. As such He is the Cause of the development of the material things He has made, completing the creative work of the Son by the power of His own love (Capito). Having voluntarily brought all into being, He is in all and over all, God in whom all co-inheres.[2] But the function of perfecting nature is itself incomplete until it is extended to the perfecting of human nature, to the conveying of the Divine goodness from the Creator-Spirit to the hearts of those whom He has fashioned in the Divine Image. He is ' the Lord and Giver of life,' of the life of the soul (*anima*, ψυχή) as well as of the life of the body (*vita*, ζωή). How wrong, then, to imagine that He is in any sense responsible for the creation of evil ! The devil and his angels were originally good when He created them. It was of their own accord that they ever became evil.

[1] Lombardus interjects that the Holy Spirit has not existed as an Origin in eternity, as have the Father and the Son as His Source; but that He appeared as an Origin in time at the creation of the universe.
[2] Hildefonsus, *Ep* 15 : ' A quo omnia, per quem omnia, in quo omnia '

V

THE WORK OF THE SPIRIT IN INSPIRATION

EVERY truth spoken is from the Spirit of Truth, that is, the Spirit of the Son who is the Truth; thus He teaches all truth infallibly. That His teaching of truth is found in Scripture, which is therefore inspired by Him with a view to the redemption of the race, is a fact which the Mediaeval Church received without demur. Her earlier writers recognize that the Holy Spirit in the written Word speaks to man what He hears from the Father and the Son pertaining to salvation and the guidance of the Church, and her later writers, particularly Calvin, emphasize accordingly the doctrinal unity of both Old and New Testaments. Upon this acknowledged basis of scriptural authority the various controversies concerning inspiration arose. In this subject the Schoolmen, headed by Aquinas, manifest a keener interest than do the Reformers, though, indeed, the space allotted to it in their writings is comparatively small. Granted that the Spirit infallibly teaches truth, do no obstacles originate from the fallibility of His human instruments? Granted that the holy men of Scripture spake as they were filled with the grace of the Spirit, how much of the human element found place in their speech? Account must be taken of the frail and fleshly channels through which the Spirit's messages were from time to time delivered. No one knows the Mind of God save he to whom God by His Spirit reveals Himself, and the measure of such revelation increases as does man's ability to receive it. Hence, as the prophets learned more of the Mind of God, so were their words inspired to a greater degree; even so, the varied character of their interpretations of the Divine Mind, consequent on the varied character of their own minds, would tend to enlarge the human element in the words themselves.[1] So reasoned the Schoolmen, and, to a certain extent, the

---

[1] That Abelard was right in urging similar considerations with regard to the Apostles the Church gravely doubted.

Reformers. Thus belief in verbal inspiration, held so tenaciously by the Fathers, recedes into the background and is not again forced to the front till the seventeenth century. In face, therefore, of these opinions, it does not altogether follow, as the Anglican Homilies assert, that, since Scripture was given by the Holy Spirit for our instruction, the more obscure its sayings appear to our understanding the further are we ourselves from their Divine Author. At the same time, when the Homilies declare that he derives most profit from Scripture who himself is most inspired by the Spirit, they express at least the conviction that the Bible, as an ordered whole, is uniquely the inspired Word of God, whose eternal truths are applied by the Spirit to the simple and the learned alike, for their redemption and sanctification.

The Reformation brought into evidence considerable divergence of view on the question of interpretation. To the Reformers the written Word was the principal instrument of the Spirit in all matters of faith. In Luther's judgement its interpretation is guided by the Spirit through His inward witness in the soul; in Zwingli's judgement, by the Spirit apart from any inward witness. But to both Lutheran and Reformed Churches, which together regarded the Spirit as bestowed upon the whole body of believers as upon a universal priesthood, the Interpreter is that same Spirit acting directly within or upon the individual mind. On the other hand, Tridentine Catholicism so conceived of the Spirit's government of the Church as to declare not only that the Church herself, in this case Pope or Council, is the interpreter of Scripture, but also that the tradition of the Church possesses an authority equal to that of Scripture itself. From such assumptions liberal-minded men turned away with impatience.

At no stage, however, in the history of the Mediaeval Church was the consideration of the work of the Spirit in inspiration confined to anything written. In all ages He has been present as the 'fountain of wisdom' to vouchsafe His perfect guidance to mankind corporately and individually. As a mighty flood (*flumen*) He is being poured out upon human life, in particular upon the Church, so that in all her decisions she may be able to say, 'It seemed good to the Holy Ghost and to us' (Acts xv. 28). As such, adds Lombardus, He also flows into the minds of the faithful in response to faith, making them teachable and then delivering to them His teaching. So Nicolas of Cusa speaks of Him as the supreme Teacher of knowledge, the Bestower of intellectual gifts and perfections, the Medium of Divine comfort, the Inspirer of holy desires and right choices, sent into the reasoning faculty of the mind. That He is all this, he declares, experience testifies. While voicing agreement, Bernard affirms that beside inspiring the mind the Spirit imparts life to the soul, teaching and training it to love God ; and it was the belief of the Schoolmen in general that, in so doing, He employs the written Word because He chooses to work partly through man's powers of reason. In Tyndale's view, the fact that the reading of Scripture actually makes some people better and others worse is but a testimony to its uniqueness as an instrument of the Holy Spirit.

VI

THE WORK OF THE SPIRIT IN THE INCARNATION

THE Mediaeval Church followed the Fathers in believing that the Holy Spirit imparted to the prophets the news of the forthcoming Advent, and in the fullness of time joined the Father in sending into the world the Word in the flesh. The more, however, the Triunity of God and its implications came to be discussed, the more the position came to be upheld that in the Incarnation of the Son the whole Trinity participated, though the part taken by the Son was, in the nature of things, different from that taken either by the Father or the Holy Spirit. Herein is a mystery which probably accounted for Wessel's report that people were frequently using the word 'Jesus' when they really had in mind the whole Trinity. Such a mistake, of course, had its own dangers. Thus in Roscellin's opinion the unity of the Trinity was being over-emphasized to such a degree as to necessitate the incarnation of the Father and the Holy Spirit along with the Son, and in order to avoid this conclusion he took refuge in practical tritheism. But the Church unhesitatingly condemned this expedient of avoiding one wrong by fleeing to another. Rather is it the very unity of the Godhead that conserves the Incarnation of the Son, for if the Holy Spirit had also become incarnate there would have been the unthinkable result of two Sons in the Trinity. Anselm puts this forward convincingly, and receives Abelard's support. And if, in this case, it is affirmed (as it is by Gilbert) that the whole Divine Nature did not become incarnate, the answer of the Church is that the whole Deity did become incarnate, but in the Person of the Son alone.

> That fullness of the Deity,
> He died for all mankind

While, then, the work of the three Persons is necessarily inseparable, it is to the Holy Spirit that Scripture ascribes the function of the Conception. The Word become flesh is the most perfect example of the Spirit's creatorship. In no sense does this imply that the Spirit is the Father of the Word; for though He formed the nascent Body of the Messiah He did not transfer His own Substance to the nascent Body. Moreover, He could hardly be the Father of the One from whom He proceeds, and even were He so represented there would follow the other unthinkable result of two Fathers in the Trinity. It was through the Spirit that the one Father exerted His own function and power of Fatherhood. The sinlessness of Jesus, again, was regarded in certain quarters as being due to the action of the Holy Spirit, Gerhohus asserting that Jesus was 'conceived and sanctified' by Him, and Huss that by His descent upon Mary, whereby she was cleansed from all sin, the flesh of Jesus was preserved from moral defilement. And, though the Holy Spirit came openly after the departure of the Lord's bodily presence, He secretly accompanied Him during all the days of His earthly ministry.

The distinction must be clearly maintained between the visible manifestations of the Son and of the Spirit. The Son united to Himself human nature, the Spirit being the Cause of the absolute union in Him of the two natures; thus He may rightly be spoken of as less than the Father in respect of that united nature, though in respect of that alone. The Spirit, however, did not unite to Himself the nature of any perceptible form by which He was manifested.[1] The dove which appeared at Christ's Baptism was no real dove, but simply the likeness adopted by the Spirit to show the love of the Father for the Son. The visibility of the Spirit's mission was due in every instance to His assumption of the form without the nature.

---

[1] Aquinas states that while both the Son and the Spirit were sent visibly, the Son as the Author of sanctification and the Spirit as the Evidence of sanctification, the Spirit did not, like the Son, assume into one Personality the forms in which He visibly came.

VII

THE MISSION OF THE SPIRIT

LONG before the Scholastic Age the distinction of eternal and temporal had been maintained between the procession and the mission of the Spirit respectively. Further distinctions, however, were brought in by the Schoolmen, who pronounced that procession may itself be eternal or temporal, and mission visible or invisible. Eternal procession is applied by them to the timeless emanation of the Holy Spirit from the Father and the Son, temporal procession to His emanation from the Father and the Son toward created objects. Visible mission is applied to those spectacular manifestations of the Holy Spirit recounted in Scripture, invisible mission to His continuous effusion upon mankind. Temporal procession and invisible mission are thus one and the same function.

The early Church declared that the mission of the Spirit implies no separation from the Father and the Son who send Him, nor any inferiority to Them in the Godhead. To the Mediaeval Church, always emphatic concerning the Divine Unity, these declarations were axiomatic. The one invisible God is present everywhere, and not more here than there, but wholly (*totus*) in every place. It is the presence of the Entire Trinity, not simply the revelation of the Father and the Son, which is conveyed by the mission of the Spirit. By it the three Persons in undivided action are in the world, seeking to enter man's heart and striving unceasingly for his salvation.[1] Accordingly, it is not as the mission of ministering spirits, but as the imparting of a 'natural substance,' the Energy of God Himself. The Spirit is sent by the Father and the Son equally, as from one Source,[2] to enlighten and inspire humanity, so His mission has attached to it the authority of the Father and the Son. At the same time it is entirely voluntary, for a

---

[1] Inge, *Christian Mysticism*, p 49 'The purpose of the Incarnation was to reveal the Father . The purpose of the mission of the Comforter was to reveal the Son'

[2] Though adhering to the *Filioque*, Lombardus prefers to speak of the Spirit's mission as taking effect *from* the Father *through* the Son

Divine Person is said to be 'sent' only inasmuch as He has His source in another Divine Person, and it must not be forgotten that the Spirit is in all respects equal to Those who send Him. The perfect unity of will and of operation that exists in the Trinity serves but to demonstrate the voluntary aspect of His mission. How vain, then, are the imaginings of those who consider that the mission of the Holy Spirit can be directed by the authority of any prophetic or ecclesiastical office!

The scope of this blessed mission is unlimited. The Spirit is present with 'rational creatures' of all kinds, good and evil, and through Him the perfect will of God is everywhere effected. Since He proceeds by way of gift, and not by way of nature, as does the Son, He, as the Origin of infinite Love, controls the creation and guides it forward to a state of perfection. To this end His mission has a peculiarly spiritual import. While His Omnipresence increases the sum of good in the world at large, it is only in so far as the gospel is embraced that the highest good can be attained, and no man can say that Jesus is Lord save in the Holy Spirit. It is in response to the gift of *Him* that men return through repentance from sin to grace. For this reason the Father and the Son send to men the Holy Spirit, that by His mission, which is itself a going forth of the Love of Them Both, they may become lovers of God. So to the Mystics the Spirit is the immanent Love of God, the one Reality, illumining and drawing mankind up into Himself as its true End. In short, the final purpose of His mission is the sanctification of the race, for, though holiness is unattainable by mere human effort, it begins to exist in the soul in which love is diffused by reason of His admission. In varied ways, such as through preaching and intercession, He can be imparted to the soul, and when He is imparted He brings comfort by affording a firm belief in God, fulfilling the office of Advocate by counselling, warning, and strengthening. The regenerating and sanctifying purposes of His mission as directed to each individual believer are emphasized especially by the Reformers.

While, however, the Holy Spirit is outpoured upon the whole race for its salvation, it is the Church which is the principal channel of His outpouring. This is evident from the Acts of the Apostles, in which those who were filled with the Holy

Spirit were filled as with a Holy Fire, and burned with wondrous enthusiasm and spiritual power. Fire is here a symbol of perfect love (*ignis consummatae caritatis*), so that when we speak of God as a consuming Fire (*ignis consumens*) we are reminded that in Him only perfect Love exists. As this Fire of Love, or as a fertilizing River, the Spirit of God is still being outpoured upon the Church, and, in asserting that He permeates all things in general and the Church in particular, the Reformers join hands with the Fathers. But these and similar statements led to a new necessity for defining terms. What is the Church? What is the essential nature of a Church? The answer of the Roman Catholics was that the Church is a visible organism, governed unerringly by the Holy Spirit, and possessing the power of remitting sins by virtue of His first bestowment upon the disciples by Christ (John xx. 22, 23). The Church is therefore held to signify the priesthood,[1] including priests of evil life, so that in the Church as such office takes precedence of character. To the Reformers, however, this answer is by no means the answer of the New Testament Rather does the Church consist of all those who really know God in Christ through the written Word and the inward teaching of the Spirit, who have been cleansed by the Blood of Christ and sanctified by the power of the selfsame Spirit. The Church is thus essentially spiritual and not official, internal and not organic. Her being governed by the Holy Spirit rests upon the fact that she is also justified and glorified by Him, insomuch that it is fundamentally necessary to the existence of a true Church that He should dwell in the hearts of her members. This being understood, the Church is described as ' the congregation of the faithful in the Spirit ' in which the Word is preached and the sacraments are administered. Both Erasmus and Strigel declare that the Holy Spirit knits together Christ and His Church just as He knits together the Trinity ; even so, such a union cannot be preserved without consistent effort on His part to increase the spirituality which the Church possesses.

The question as to the difference between the abovementioned Easter gift of the Holy Spirit and His Pentecostal gift commands the attention of several theologians. His

[1] But see Swete, *Holy Spirit in the N T*, pp 307 ff , where the gathering of disciples mentioned in John xx is declared to be representative of the *whole* Church, ' and not of the Apostles only and their successors in the ministry of the Church '

bestowment recorded in John xx. is held to indicate that He is the Spirit of the Son, and is put forward by the Anti-Adoptionists as proof of the pre-existence of the Son. Alcuin, with his fondness for allegorical exegesis, suggests the unusual distinction that by the Easter gift the disciples were to be divinely aided to love their neighbours, by the Pentecostal gift they were to be divinely aided to love God. It is generally agreed, however, that the former gift was essentially preliminary to the latter.[1] The Holy Spirit had always been influencing the world of men, but never had He been fully given; not even on the Resurrection Day was He fully given, else there would have been no urgency for the second bestowment at Pentecost. A number of Roman Catholic authorities refer to this preliminary gift as simply the power or charism of remitting sins, with which Christ has for ever endowed the Church; and to this Maldonatus adds a deepened love for Christ which such a gift would cause, whereby the disciples would be fortified for their missionary journeys. The Reformers, on the other hand, appear to attach little importance to this particular charism, and refer rather to two preparatory gifts of the Spirit which they consider were then conferred, namely, a firmer faith in the Resurrection and a fuller understanding of the Scriptures. Of the various views Ruysbroek's is the clearest. In his judgement Christ gave the Holy Spirit to the disciples (i.) before His death, for physical miracles, since their love for Him was then physical; (ii.) after His Resurrection, for the spiritual functions of baptism, remission of sins, and the teaching of the truth, since their spiritual love for Him was becoming greater than their physical love; (iii.) after the Ascension, that they might accomplish Divine achievements and also themselves become one with God. To this end they received at Pentecost not only the Person of the Holy Spirit but also the whole Trinity. In fuller measure than ever before, God came down to win human hearts to Himself.

---

[1] Cf Swete, *ibid*, pp 165 ff

VIII

THE WORK OF THE SPIRIT IN THE SACRAMENTS

THE Sacraments are one of many ways in which the Holy Spirit is given to the believer. The Divine Gift is not restricted to any human medium. God alone can give Himself, and only then in answer to the prayerful attitude of the heart. But, in so expressing himself, Leidradus gave utterance to an exceptional view. 'The third and fourth centuries tended to make the sacraments the only channel of the Holy Spirit,'[1] and this tendency becomes more and more marked in succeeding centuries, only that the Schoolmen prefer to speak of the grace of Christ, rather than the Holy Spirit, as being sacramentally imparted. If it was true in the case of the Ancient Church that to magnify the sacraments was to magnify the Holy Spirit,[2] it was fast becoming true that to magnify the sacraments was to magnify the priesthood; for while the Church of the Scholastic Age said much concerning them she had little to say concerning Him in relation thereto. The idea of their conferring grace *ex opere operato*, an idea which became prominent in that age, accounts for this to no small extent as being naturally independent of the *spiritual* attitude of both priest and communicant. Against any such notion the Reformers rose in revolt, denying that the sacraments of themselves either justify or sanctify. The Lutherans at least, who regarded the sacraments as essential to the spiritual life, would not question for one moment the belief of the Mystics that these are necessary to spiritual growth and to union with God, inasmuch as to them, as to all the Reformers, the Spirit of God is always present in the sacraments, renewing His benefits and sealing His promises. Tyndale does not hesitate to declare that the operation of the Holy Spirit is vital to the spiritual effectiveness of any ordinance. Yet, though the Reformers were careful to exalt the Holy Spirit in

---

[1] Dr Swete, in conversation at Cambridge, June 15, 1911
[2] Do, *Holy Spirit in the Ancient Church*, p 399

the sacraments, they saw no benefit whatever in them apart from faith. True, the sacraments are enjoined by God, and the promise of grace is attached to them; but grace is conferred not *per ceremoniam* but to those only who exercise faith, and through this very exercise faith is itself increased by the operation of the Holy Spirit in the soul (2nd Helv. Conf.). They are immediate symbols of internal facts directly caused by Him (Belg. Conf.), and through which He works; and that they are considered such is apparent from the striking manner in which the Reformers associated them with the preaching of the Word. On the question of their spiritual potency the English Church recognized the necessity alike of the Holy Spirit's work and of the exercise of faith, and for this very reason concluded that the sacraments are not rendered ineffective should the person administering them possess an evil character. The same conclusion was reached by the Catholic Church, but along her own line of argument, namely, that the sacraments are effective *ex opere operato*. It is significant that Durandus upholds this conclusion on the plea that it is the Holy Spirit, and not the priest, who bestows every sacramental grace.

Augustine had declared that in baptism the Holy Spirit forgives sins in response to faith, and the immediate successors of the Fathers concurred. In their opinion, the New Birth accompanies baptism, through which rite a person is brought into a filial relationship with God as his Father and the Church as his mother. Yet none other than the Holy Spirit is the source of forgiveness and grace. Bede and Alcuin make it clear that sins are cleansed away *in* baptism, not *by* baptism but by the grace of the Spirit operating through it. Scholasticism lays down that since baptism confers forgiveness and sanctification it is therefore necessary to salvation, though in certain specified cases intention may serve in place of the actual rite; and the Council of Trent follows with the assertion that in baptism the grace of the Holy Spirit remits the guilt of original sin. Luther and Calvin agree in regarding the Holy Spirit as the source of spiritual efficacy in this sacrament, and faith as the necessary response to His gifts; while the water symbolizes the Blood of Christ which by the Spirit's power changes children of wrath into children of God. They agree also in stipulating that faith is equally necessary after baptism, in order that the spiritual endowments therein received may be maintained and developed. But they differ on the question as to whether baptism is essential to salvation. Luther holds that it is essential, Calvin that it is not ; in other words, the former accepts baptismal regeneration, the latter rejects it. To Luther baptism secures adoption through Christ and regeneration through His Spirit, seeing that it is through baptism and the Holy Spirit that men must be born anew (John iii. 5). It is an ordinance which must be administered to children in order that, by virtue of the faith of their sponsors, the promise of salvation may apply also to them. To Calvin, however, baptism is not vital to salvation, since certain people, in his opinion, are not predestined to salvation ; neither, then, can it be vital to the salvation of those who are so predestined. In this he agrees with Zwingli, yet he is not content with Zwingli's position that baptism is simply a sign of Christian witness and of adoption into God's family. He believes that in it we are renewed by the Holy Spirit unto sanctification of life, and that, accordingly, it is the outward sign and seal of inward regeneration. Whereas the Ancient Church affirmed that it is by this sacrament that men are made partakers of the Divine Nature, the Mediaeval Church prefers to ascribe this particular description to an effect of the Lord's Supper. But this is merely a matter of phraseology.

Ever since Radbertus propounded the dogma of transubstantiation the Sacrament of the Lord's Supper was a constant theme of debate, and in the sixteenth century was the principal subject of controversy.[1] Radbertus announced transubstantiation as a work of the Holy Spirit, nevertheless such a theory cannot from its very content allow much scope to the work of the Holy Spirit in the Eucharist, for its commitment to the real presence of Christ's Body from the moment of the consecration of the elements serves only to obscure Christ's real presence by His Spirit. Almost as strong a statement can be made with reference to Luther's theory of consubstantiation, in which there takes place a mysterious union of the bread and the wine with the Body and Blood of Christ, which are spiritually received as such by the mouth (*manducatio oralis*). Reformed teaching, on the other hand, did not hesitate to uphold an intimate connexion between the Holy

[1] Hallam, *Hist of England*, vol 1, pp 89 f

Spirit and the Lord's Supper,[1] which meant the outward expression of what is inwardly accomplished by Him in the heart ; for it is a seal of the redeeming love of Christ in His Body and Blood, of which we partake by faith. Zwingli, while regarding this sacrament as primarily commemorative, agrees that by faith grace can be received therein from Christ through the Holy Spirit. But here, again, he is too external for Calvin. To the latter the Holy Spirit is present at the Lord's Supper as the Medium of Divine grace. This grace, though not essentially different from that obtainable at any other ordinance, is that by which He incorporates the communicant with Christ, inasmuch as He dwells both in Christ and in him. Through Him, then, believers are sharers in the glorified Body of Christ, the elements being symbols of Christ's Person. Even so, Christ's Body does not exist everywhere, as Luther supposed, though His Person is certainly omnipresent through His Spirit. On the human side faith is regarded by all the Reformers as essential to the reception of spiritual benefits at the Lord's Table. Only as we partake of the elements by faith does Christ quicken us through His Spirit, and so make us partakers of His Life. Hence, in the only two sacraments recognized as such by Catholics and Protestants alike,[2] the Holy Spirit continues to be set forth, in varying degrees but none the less definitely, as the Source of grace and the Giver of every perfect gift.

---

[1] See Pope, *Compendium of Christian Theology*, vol III, p 303

[2] The Catholic Church regarded the Gift of the Spirit by imposition of hands, whether in Confirmation or Ordination, as a divine and not a human gift Alcuin speaks of those who received remission of sins in baptism as receiving the Holy Spirit by means of episcopal confirmation immediately following, and the purpose of this Gift by manual imposition was that He might supply strength whereby Christ might be confessed before the world In this way the Roman sacrament of Confirmation was held to resemble Pentecost To the Reformers, however, such a sacrament has no divine mandate Bucer does not deny that the Holy Spirit is given at Confirmation, howbeit he declares that this bestowment is not sacramental but evangelical, while Tyndale asserts that it is effected not by the laying-on of hands but by faith In Ordination, according to the Catholic Church, the power of the Holy Spirit is received for the varied functions of the priesthood, especially that of offering the Sacrifice in the Church Also, the Holy Spirit is given in this way finally, so that an evil-living priest still possesses the power of remitting sins in virtue of his office, and, in any case, a priest can never again become a layman (Council of Trent) Luther, taking his stand on the New Testament, refused to recognize any sacrament of Orders responsible for erecting a barrier of such essential distinction between clergy and laity Melanchthon, with some support from Bucer, conceded a sacramental character to Ordination in so far as the rite concerns the ministry of the Word ! But, to the Reformers generally, Ordination is the laying-on of hands by those who *recognize* the Holy Spirit's call to the ordinand, together with the presence of His gifts whereby the call can be effectually answered Their insistence on the universal priesthood of believers did not imply an overlooking of Divine vocation to, or of Divine assistance in, the ministerial office, but simply an acknowledgement of order without Orders

IX

THE WORK OF THE SPIRIT IN JUSTIFICATION AND SANCTIFICATION

ALCUIN, the first theologian of the Mediaeval Church to emphasize the saving work of the indwelling Spirit, speaks of it as in reality the work of the whole Trinity, and in so doing he was to receive the support of later writers, especially Nicolas of Cusa and Maldonatus.[1] Such a view follows naturally upon the truths of the Divine Unity and the Redemptional Trinity, so that when the Holy Spirit is inbreathed by the Father and the Son unto sanctification the Father and the Son are Themselves introduced into the soul. Adoption as God's sons, forgiveness, inward cleansing, are functions of the Deity through the Spirit, and adopted sons, possessing a new joy in God, henceforth do the will of the Father from the motive of love. Nevertheless it is the Holy Spirit in particular who is regarded by both East and West as the Source of sanctification. He is 'the Spirit of sanctification,' 'the Life of souls.' He it is who quickens man to an increase of good works, who implants that motive of love which mortifies the earthward tendencies of his nature, whose regenerating and sanctifying power ensures victory over evil spirits, and imparts love for an enemy, moral purity, and, in short, a new life. And 'those whom the Holy Spirit arrests He unexpectedly makes spiritual.' In company with the Fathers, Faber cannot but mention the surprising character of the triumphs of His grace (John iii. 8).

The regenerating work of the Spirit is, therefore, essential to salvation, for He is the Cause of the New Birth. He is also the Cause of that faith by which man is justified. Yet neither Schoolmen nor Mystics were eager to employ in this connexion the word 'faith,' which to them possessed above all an intellectual significance; on the other hand they preferred to represent the necessary human response by 'love,' a term

[1] See Pope, *ibid*, III pp. 5 f, 14

of which the 'faith' of the Reformers is a probable synonym. If, then, love is at the bottom of intellectual assent, nothing else than love is required in order that saving grace may be supplied. Accordingly Ruysbroek remarks that the Holy Spirit brings together the Father, the Son, and the saints in a delightful unity, for He demands nothing from us but love. But, to mediaeval churchmen, love is peculiarly associated with the Holy Spirit; therefore it must be the Holy Spirit who, in turn, is peculiarly associated with the supply of saving grace. So Aquinas argues that, since the Holy Spirit proceeds from the Father and the Son by way of the love wherewith God loves Himself, it is the special function of the Holy Spirit to make men lovers of God. The love by which God is in us and we in God is due to the mediation of the Holy Spirit. Bernard is another notable exponent of the same view. Further, the different ways of interpreting 'faith' foreshadow different ways of interpreting justification. In the opinion of the Schoolmen and Mystics, justification includes both forgiveness and sanctification. By dwelling within the soul the Spirit justifies those whom He has called (Bernard). Justification is thus a process including repentance, adoration, filial reflection, and sanctifying love (Nicolas of Cusa), and is in due course explained by the Council of Trent as an infusion of righteousness. In this inclusive sense it is declared to be the Spirit's chief gift, granted through the medium of the sacraments. The Reformers, on the contrary, insist that it is no process, but rather a definite act of Divine pardon in which the righteousness of God is not infused but imputed. They consider that the notion of an infusion of righteousness discourages appropriation of Christ's merits, beside overlooking the inward action of the Spirit. It is sanctification which is the process, dependent on this act of imputation.[1] While justification and sanctification are clearly distinguished in the theology of the Reformers, their close connexion is as clearly maintained, for both the imputation of righteousness and the purifying process ensuing are equally operations of the Spirit. It is on the ground of the redeeming work of the Son that the Spirit carries forward the work of sanctification in the justified soul, and follows the gift of faith with the gift

---

[1] Bernard's language is similar, when he refers to the indwelling of the Spirit as the necessary complement to the Sacrifice of the Cross, adding 'Neither is of benefit without the other'

of Himself[1]; yet Lutheran teaching does not hesitate to give warning that the Holy Spirit may depart from the justified if they show no desire for sanctification, though He may graciously return if they once more show such desire. So the *Apology for the Augsburg Confession* declares justification by faith to be the necessary beginning of the new life of love, which again is dependent primarily on the regenerating power of the Holy Spirit. Tridentine theology, on the other hand, with its adherence to the meritorious nature of good works, asserts that the new life of love is based not on faith alone in Christ as Saviour, but on faith as itself a work which is prompted by love; hence the provision for expiation of sin after baptism and the *ex opere operato* view of the sacraments, which have been prominent in the Roman Church ever since the later Schoolmen exalted human merit at the expense of the Spirit's operations. While, however, anti-scholastic Mysticism emphasizes union with God with little mention of imputed righteousness, its soteriology resembles that of the Reformation far more than terminological differences might lead one to imagine. Mystic theology was a protest not so much against the Pauline doctrine of justification as against the sacramentarian sacerdotalism of the Mediaeval Church. Ruysbroek bears testimony that sin has to be conquered, spiritual growth has to be real, the standard of human affection has to be raised, before the greatest gifts of the Holy Spirit can be obtained or union with God reached. In effect this differs little, if at all, from Calvin's judgement that sanctification is union with God in Christ. 'It is enough to say,' writes Dr. Pope, ' that in the long series of the purest and most saintly mystical writers the love which seemed to displace faith as the condition of acceptance was in reality no other than faith itself in its self-renouncing and Christ-embracing character.'[2] The Reformers were more careful to add that faith must be proved by works.

The teaching of Luther concerning justification revived the subject of the relation of the will to the operation of the

[1] Again, the language of Nicolas of Cusa is similar when he asserts the Holy Spirit to be the Cause of Divine adoption, effecting perfection of life in the heart, so that man may ascend through perfection more nearly to the Divine likeness So also Durandus.
[2] *Ibid*, ii, p 428 The rigid ecclesiasticism against which the Mystics revolted is plainly set forth in the writings of Biel and Nicolas of Cusa There is a wide gulf between it and the statement of Luther that by faith alone and the Holy Spirit we are made partakers of Christ through the Word and the Sacraments

Holy Spirit. Nicolas of Cusa had already stated that the Son, through the mediation of the Holy Spirit, attracts the rational soul by the diffusion within it of Divine love, and the Council of Trent affirmed accordingly that the will co-operates with the 'prevenient inspiration' of the Holy Spirit. On the other hand, Luther's Augustinian conception of the sovereignty of grace would allow of no other view of faith than a personal venture on the love of God in Christ brought about entirely by the inner working of the Spirit, unaided by any human concurrence, so that when the origin of faith is explored man's will is seen to be impotent and the Holy Spirit the *sole* Cause of salvation. From this conclusion Melanchthon broke away and propounded the theory of synergism, namely, that in the work of conversion the Holy Spirit is assisted by a free response on the part of the will; even so, the Holy Spirit is regarded as the Cause of the exercise of faith in the first instance, since He alone can create new affections. With this second view, as against Luther's, the Reformed Churches revealed their sympathy,[1] though in course of time they began to limit the operation of saving faith to the elect,[2] succeeding also in influencing the English Church in a like direction.[3] It was, however, within the Lutheran community especially that the controversy of monergism *versus* synergism continued to be waged and Chemnitz brought forward his somewhat ingenious effort at reconciliation. But his compromise, to the effect that the will co-operates with the Holy Spirit only in so far as it has lost its natural state on becoming spiritualized by Him, was put forward to no purpose, and the *Formula of Concord* was more truhfully a Formula of victory on the part of Lutheran opinion over the Semi-Pelagian bias of the Philippists.[4]

---

[1] Zwingli The Holy Spirit influences man to the exercise of saving faith and then dwells within him to unite him to God *Conf Helv* 1 Man's will is free to co-operate with the Holy Spirit in regeneration.

[2] Calvin The Holy Spirit gives faith to the elect, who can thereby be justified *Conf Belg* The Holy Spirit incites in our hearts true faith whereby we lay hold of Christ and His merits, and are regenerated *Conf Helv* 11 Through the Holy Spirit God arouses living faith in the hearts of His elect The Holy Spirit not only moves the will but also instructs its faculties, so that it may will the good of its own accord

[3] Tyndale · Justification depends on the Holy Spirit, for saving faith is His gift to those whom He favours *xxxix Artt* . The grace of God enables the will to exercise that faith which receives saving grace ; but this refers to the will of the predestined

[4] As against the *Formula of Concord* Arminianism asserted a real co-operation of the natural will, influenced by the Spirit's prevenient grace (cf Episcopius, *Remonstrant Conf*, xvii) Dr Pope (*ibid*, ii, p 390) notes that Methodist teaching upheld the same position on the ground that the state of nature is also a state of preliminary grace on account of the merits of Christ

WORK OF THE SPIRIT IN JUSTIFICATION 351

The Spirit's work of sanctification, which also is conditional (secondarily but vitally) on the human will, figures prominently in the teaching of the Reformers just as in the teaching of the Schoolmen. The Holy Spirit resembles purifying Fire or fertilizing Water. As the Finger of God He casts out devils and fights on man's behalf against all the forces of evil. By His indwelling He brings to the soul a deep knowledge of the Father, causes it to experience the virtue of the Son, and imparts joy to it whether in affliction or temptation. He dispels ignorance and subdues the passions. Carnal excitement is abolished under His rule, while even the best of human affections are transcended by His love. In brief, His regenerating power is that by which men are absolutely remade, and by which they possess on earth the first instalment of the life of heaven. What, then, *could* be the sin against the Holy Spirit but that of self-despair or obstinacy in view of the wonders of Divine mercy?

X

THE WITNESS OF THE SPIRIT

THROUGHOUT the centuries covered by the mediaeval period the doctrine of assurance of personal salvation, with Rom. viii. 16 as its scriptural basis, gradually gained in the world of religious thought. Its progress, however, was slow in the nature of the case, inasmuch as it was opposed by the very spirit of mediaevalism. The discouragement with which Gregory the Great met certain inquiries concerning the possibility of Assurance[1] is reflected in scholastic theology and again in the proceedings of the Council of Trent, which condemned any such notion of direct saving witness from the Holy Spirit to the individual. The Romanist conceptions of salvation by merit, sacramental grace, and probation could lead to no other conclusion. Among the pre-Reformation Reformers, whose theology knew no such accretions, the condemnation of Assurance—this time as a mystical theory—was equally strong,[2] and nearly as strong among the Reformers themselves.[3] The *Augsburg Confession* speaks of the Christian as believing that he is received into grace, but belief and assurance are by no means identical, and in his later years Luther gave his support to the former while withholding it from the latter. Calvin affirmed not only an inward witness of the Spirit attesting scriptural truth, but also a personal perception of reconciliation to God on the ground of accepting this truth; and he expressed all confidence in the regenerating work of the Spirit as experienced in his own life. But in Calvin's system this can mean no more than a realization that God has been pleased to elect a particular person.

---

[1] The account of the correspondence between the Empress Gregoria's lady of the bedchamber and the Pope is recorded by Dr. Workman, *New Hist of Methodism*, 1, p 21, and by Harnack, *Hist of Dogma*, v p 271n

[2] The fact that the Hussites, with their strong Calvinistic tendencies, emerged from the Counter-Reformation to become the Assurance-preaching Moravians of Wesley's day can be satisfactorily accounted for only by the increasing vitality of their own spiritual experience and a sane perception of its implications

[3] See Workman, *ibid*, pp 22 ff

THE WITNESS OF THE SPIRIT 353

Doubtless this is Assurance, but an Assurance so narrowed by predestination as to bear little resemblance to the Assurance afterwards preached by the Wesleys.[1] The same naturally holds good of the teaching of Beza. Thus there is ample justification for the remark of Auguste Sabatier that, with the Reformers, the 'Witness of the Spirit' was not *saving* witness so much as a witness in respect of moral judgement.[2] True it is that the doctrine finds a place in the *Homilies* of the Church of England, a fact which Wesley, in the First Part of his *Farther Appeal to Men of Reason and Religion*, makes clear by means of extracts. Yet it is extremely doubtful whether the English Church of 1563, with its Calvinistic temperament, believed whole-heartedly in Assurance as the privilege of *all* persons, and therefore it is a moot point how far this doctrine was expressed by the letter of the *Homilies* and not by their spirit. The *Homilies* are recommended in the thirty-fifth of the *Thirty-Nine Articles*, the seventeenth of which distinctly advocates predestination,[3] so it is a fair inference that, in actuality, the *Homilies* were enshrouded with a Calvinistic cloak, which was little in evidence inasmuch as homiletic literature is always broader than creedal, and that the later outcry against Wesley's doctrine of Assurance arose from his snatching off that cloak. This might well have been an instance of difference not so much between creed and practice as between creed and creed.

Mysticism in emphasizing experience emphasized an Assurance of its own. Let the personality but become a spiritual unity and the Divine Unity is discovered within as well as without. In striving to follow Christ one can be certain of the presence of the Holy Spirit in the soul (Tauler). Such an Assurance, however, was the product of an unbalanced subjectivism which overlooked the fact that religion is a matter not only of feeling but also of reason.[4] That Wesley, at least, acknowledged no contribution to this doctrine on the part of

---

[1] Pope, *ibid*, iii, p 124 · 'The doctrine of Assurance, taught by what may be called the Calvinistic system . . . makes assurance a special privilege of the few, who through much discipline attain it as a gift of God'

[2] *The Religions of Authority and the Religion of the Spirit*, ii, chap iv

[3] Those who feel within themselves the working of the Holy Spirit know that they are predestined to salvation, and experience comfort in so knowing And those who lack the Holy Spirit may well be driven to despair, 'having continually before their eyes the sentence of God's predestination' Cf also Hallam, *Hist. of England*, 1, p 401

[4] See Inge, *Christian Mysticism*, pp 18, 21.

the Mystics is patent from his writings. ' It is by God's peculiar blessing upon [the Methodists] in searching the Scriptures, confirmed by the experience of His children, that this great evangelical truth has been recovered, which had been for many years wellnigh lost and forgotten.'[1] As this truth is maintained, so will experience be developed side by side with doctrine, and the Church of modern days be empowered by the Holy Spirit mightily to proclaim the whole message of the gospel, which is the only hope of the present age and of ages yet unborn.

[1] Wesley, *Sermons*, Vol I, serm xi. (1767).

INDICES

I. INDEX OF SCRIPTURE REFERENCES.
II. INDEX OF GREEK AND LATIN WORDS.
III. INDEX OF PERSONS.
IV. INDEX OF SUBJECTS.

I

GENESIS:
- 1 1, 2 .. 138
- 1 2 .. 93 f, 158, 211, 264, 330
- 1 26 .. 46, 257, 322

LEVITICUS:
- xxii 9 .. 156

JOB:
- xxxiii 4 .. 156

PSALMS
- civ 30 .. 158

ISAIAH
- ix 6, 7 .. 152
- xlviii 16 . 152
- lxi 1, 2 .. 152

ST MATTHEW
- 1 18 .. 308
- 1 20 .. 293
- iii 11 .. 308
- iii 16, 17 . 257, 275, 277, 294, 308, 330
- x 20 .. 156
- xi 27 .. 156, 160
- xii 31, 32 .. 308
- xxviii 19 .. 155, 157, 212, 257, 271, 275, 294, 301, 308, 324, 330

ST MARK.
- ix 3–7 .. 143*n*

ST LUKE.
- iii 16 .. 292
- iii 21, 22 . 290
- iv 1, 3 .. 160, 308*n*
- iv 18, 19 .. 152, 161
- v 39 .. 237
- xi 20 .. 293*n*

ST JOHN:
- 1 1 . 143*n*
- iii 5 .. 345
- iii 8 .. 347
- iii 31–34 .. 143
- iv 24 .. 185
- x 30, 38 .. 167
- xiv 16 . 255, 257, 285, 293 f, 309 f, 330
- xiv 17 .. 310
- xiv. 23 .. 168*n*
- xiv. 26 .. 307, 310
- xv 26 .. 44, 144 f, 151, 155, 157, 160, 180, 228, 233, 238, 272, 288, 310, 326
- xvi 7 .. 45, 272, 310
- xvi 8 . 238
- xvi 12, 13 . 25, 180, 285, 310
- xvi 14, 15 .. 44, 157, 161, 180, 238
- xvi. 15 .. 41, 180 f, 292, 325, 327

ST. JOHN:
- xvi 28 .. 130
- xvii 3 .. 160, 288
- xx 22 .. 30, 33, 45, 145, 189, 238, 288, 292, 305, 310, 341 f

ACTS:
- 1 16 .. 156
- ii 2 .. 264
- ii 4 .. 219, 257
- v 3, 4, 9 .. 156, 258, 271
- xiii 2, 4 .. 157
- xv. 28 .. 157, 335
- xix 2 .. 306

ROMANS:
- 1. 7 .. 160
- v 5 .. 157
- viii 9 .. 143, 160, 291
- viii 16 .. 352

I CORINTHIANS
- i 12 .. 309
- ii 4 .. 259
- ii 10, 11 .. 156
- iii 16 .. 156
- vi 11 .. 156
- vi 15 .. 155
- vi 19 .. 155
- viii. 6 .. 160
- xii 4–11 .. 156, 257, 330
- xii 6, 7 .. 144*n*
- xii 8 .. 157
- xii 10 .. 307
- xii 11 .. 301*n*

II CORINTHIANS
- iii 17 .. 158
- iv 4 .. 192
- iv 16 .. 211
- vi 16 .. 156
- xiii 14 .. 157

GALATIANS:
- iv 6 .. 143, 160
- v 22, 23 .. 285

EPHESIANS:
- iii 16 .. 211

COLOSSIANS.
- 1 15 .. 192

II THESSALONIANS:
- ii 13 .. 156

HEBREWS:
- xi 1 .. 109

II PETER:
- 1 21 .. 156

I JOHN:
- iv 12, 13 .. 283
- v 7 (A.V.) .. 155, 157, 165, 181, 244*n*,272, 292, 300 f, 306 f, 320*n*

II

αἴτιον, αἴτιος, 54, 144n
ἀκτίς, 224

εἰκών, 256, 292
ἐκπορεύειν, 224n

ζωή, 333

ἴδια, 224

καυστικόν, 224

λόγος, 224 f, 256, 292

μοναρχία, 29

νοῦς, 225

ὁμοουσία, 111
ὁμοούσιος, 57n, 254, 292
οὐσία, 25, 98 f, 254, 262

πηγὴ τῆς σοφίας, 143n
πνεῦμα, 225
πνοή, 224
προιέναι, 144n
πῦρ, 224

συνάναρχοι, 225

τριάς, 225n

ὑπόστασις, 254

φυσικὴ ὕπαρξις, 144
φῶς, 224
φωτιστικόν, 224

χάρισμα, 145
χορηγεῖσθαι, 144n

ψυχή, 224, 333

---

absoluta, 183
actio, 101
actus, 110n, 211
aequalitas, 116n, 204
aequaliter, 43, 325n
aeternae, aeterni, 103, 132
agere, 207n
aggregativus, 298
agitator, agitatio, 254 f, 257, 330
alienus, 85
aliquid, 100, 331
alius, aliud, 93, 99, 118 f, 123, 149, 207 f, 270, 324, 331
alteritas, 98 ff, 200, 324
amor, 84, 111, 138, 148, 150, 159n, 185, 203n, 212, — debitus, 138 ; —gratuitus, 138, — mutuus, 167, 216 ; — permixtus, 138 ; — reciprocus, 216 ; — unitivus, 167
ardens, 59
artifex, 118, 332
assignatio, 111
assimilatio, 160n
auctor, 100n, 152

baptizare, 260n
benevolentia, 230
bonitas, 138

caritas, 44, 150, 158n, 305n, 341
causa, 117, 211, 231n

chrisma, 200n
circumscriptibilis, 116
coaequalis, 57n
coaeternus, 57n
cogitatio, 254 f
cognitio, 155
communio, 190n
communitas, 58, 201
compago, 117 f
complacentia, 221
compositio, compositum, 118, 183, 235
concordia, 130
condilectio, 133 f, 138, 148, 329
connectere, connexio, 50, 200 f, 204, 209
consolator, 293
consubstantialis, 57n
contracte, contractio, 203
copulate, 203
corpus, corporalis, 59, 185

deitas, 96
digitus, 293n
diligere, dilectio, 44, 138, 150, 185, 196
discretio, 201
distinctio, 155, 186n
diversus, 92, 270
divinitas, 65, 98, 100, 103, 116n, 160n, 264n
do, donum, 113n, 116n, 192n, 209n

INDICES 359

efficacia, 301 f
ens, entitas, 206
essentia, 39n, 75n, 83n, 97 f, 114, 116, 149, 186n
essentialis, 158n

factor, 101
fecundatus, fecunditas, 137, 191
filatio, 161, 190n
filius adoptivus, 31 ff
flumen, 110n, 335
forma, 98, 117

generari, generatio, 147, 178n, 185n
genitus, 37, 57n, 94n, 113n
genus, 114
germanitas innascibilis, 133

homousia, homousion, 52, 149
hypostasis, 115n

iditas, identitas, 201
imago, 185, 199n, 204
inaestimabilis, 26
indeterminans, 92
indicium, 168
indifferentia, 98, 100n
indivisio, 201
ineffabilis, 61
ingenitus, 37, 57n, 116n, 219
innascibilis, innascibilitas, 138, 164n, 190n
inspirabilis, 138
insufflans, 33
intellectus, 117, 158, 162 f, 206
intelligentia, 24, 84, 138, 148 f, 194
intelligere, intelligibilis, 201, 206
intentio, 190, 331
interius, 163
intrinsecus, 156
ipse, ipsum, 73 f, 324

largitio, 42
lumen, 29

magnitudo, 29
majus, 46, 57n
manus impositio, 42
media, 133
memoria, 24, 84, 138, 149, 194
mens, 24,111,138,148, 150, 163n, 255
mensura, 139n
meritoria, 188
minus, 46, 57n
motus, 209
mysterium, 59

nasci, natus, 26, 107, 113n, 192n
natura, 39n, 43n, 57n, 110n, 148, 165n, 178, 185 f, 201n, 221
naturaliter, 149, 177, 192

nectere, nexus, 118, 167, 187, 196 f, 203 ff, 206
nomen, 57
notitia, 111, 138 f, 148, 150
numen, 110n
numerus, 139n

opus, 72
ordo, 186n
organum, 264

pariter, 86, 92
partus, 211
paternitas, 161, 190n
patronus, 266
per insufflationem, 44
perficere, 65n
perfluvio, 216
permixtio, 38
persona, 74n, 94n, 107 ff, 114, 116, 141, 152 f, 163, 165n, 168n, 190, 256, 264 f, 301n, 329n
personalis, personaliter, 37, 329, 331
pignus, 272
plenus Deus, 47n, 50, 99, 318
pluralitas, 23n, 100n, 205
pluraliter, 72
plures, 92, 94n
plus, 109
pondus, 139n
pontifex, 42
possibilitas, 211
posterius, 46, 57n
potestates, 38
principalitas, 101, 134
principaliter, principalius, 140, 188
principium, 29, 36, 43, 52, 54, 75n, 100 f, 115, 135, 140, 144, 151 f, 158, 161, 165, 178 f, 186 f, 201n, 229, 333
prius, 46, 57n, 140
procedere, processio, 30n, 57n, 94, 107, 130, 158n, 168n, 190n, 207n, 325n
producere, productio, 147, 184, 186n, 187n, 191, 196n, 306
propagatio, 158
proprietas, 37 f, 62, 84, 92 f, 94n, 96, 99, 115n, 117, 133, 149, 179 f, 187, 190n, 270
proprium, 92, 94 f, 110n, 130, 165, 325n

ratio, 301
relatio, 99 f, 165n
res, 90, 92, 102, 122 f, 158, 190, 198, 214n, 229, 232, 312, 331
res relativae, 190
res separatae, 85, 324

sanctus, 139n

scientia, 159
sensus, 241
signum, 179
similitudo, 164
simplex, simplicitas, 93 f, 97, 201, 265n, 312
simul, 75, 100, 133
singularis, singularitas, 97, 204 f
solus, 29, 97, 100
species, 114, 190
spirare, spiratio, 161, 186n, 190n, 221
spiritus veritatis, 56n
status, 135
sua sponte, 44
substantia, 39n, 43n, 74n, 83n, 101, 132n, 141, 204n, 266n, 318n
substantialis, 103
substantialiter, 37, 65, 97, 100 f
summa res, 122 f
suppositum, 163, 179, 312

terminus, 188n
totus, totum, 61, 84, 150, 180, 339
trinitas, 47n, 83n, 103, 109, 115, 132n, 199 f, 201n, 323, 332n

trinus, 177, 183, 211, 235
tripartitus, 298
triplex, triplicitas, 47n, 115, 165
triunus, 202

unguentum, 235
unigenitus, 57n, 116n
unio, unire, 201n, 204, 212
unitas, 46, 57n, 83n, 100n, 138, 201, 204, 212
unitrinus, 202
unum, 57, 84, 101, 106, 119, 136, 181, 197, 200, 218, 237, 266, 317, 323 f, 325n

verbum corporale, 148
veritas, 73, 138
virtus, 159, 183, 302n, 307; — spirativa, 181
vis, 301 f, 309, — spirativa, 187n
vita spiritalis, 93, 333
vivificus, 52
vocabulum, 102
voluntas, 24, 138 f, 148 f, 158, 162 ff, 178, 185, 192, 194, 212n, 259n

III

Abelard, 72, 80, 82, 89, 91 ff, 100, 109 f, 125, 127, 334*n*, 337
Acton, Lord, 146, 244, 258*n*, 269, 281*n*
Adrian, 33
Aeneas, 55
Agobard, 38
d'Ailly, Pierre, 193, 195 f, 198 f, 227, 230
Alanus Magnus, 116 ff
Albertus Magnus, 82, 146*n*, 149 ff, 154, 169, 329*n*
Alcuin, 16, 23, 35, 37, 39, 42 ff, 55, 57, 59, 65, 75, 317, 325 f, 342, 344, 346 f
Alexander of Hales, 81, 137, 147 ff
Amalric of Bena, 126
Ambrose, 57 f, 198
Amsdorf, 290
Andrada, 307
Anne of Bohemia, 229
Anselm, 21, 71, 73, 75, 79 f, 83 ff, 89, 91, 95, 105, 146, 337
Anthony of Padua, 126
Antoninus, 181*n*
Aquinas, Thomas, 17, 82, 146 f, 154 ff, 177 ff, 193, 195, 237, 318, 320, 325, 330, 334, 338*n*, 348
Argyropulos, 241
Aristotle, 81, 146, 154, 177, 210, 214, 249, 252
Arius, 24, 159, 236
Athanasius, 166, 187*n*, 192
Augustine, 14 f, 24 f, 30, 54, 56 f, 60, 64, 74, 82, 106, 113, 115, 133 f, 138, 146*n*, 150, 152, 166, 202, 227, 252, 311*n*, 322, 325, 344

Bacon, Roger, 14, 18, 176 f, 202, 322
Banks, Dr J S, 52*n*, 305*n*
Basil, 309
Beatus, 25, 33 ff
Bede, 28 ff, 45, 324, 344
Beet, Dr J A, 156*n*, 327*n*
Bellarmine, 246*n*, 300, 307, 311 f, 318
Benedict VIII, 69 f
Benedict of Aniane, 36, 38 f, 56, 86
Berengarius, 71 ff, 79
Bernard of Clairvaux, 16, 72, 80, 89, 95 f, 110, 125 ff, 135, 217, 336, 348
Bethune-Baker, Dr, 11*n*
Beza, Theodore, 273 f, 353

Biel, Gabriel, 173, 182, 191 ff, 349*n*
Binius, 96*n*
Blandrata, 271, 279
Blemmydes, 143, 145
Boehme, 222
Boethius' (pseudo-), 96 f, 100, 141
Bonaventura, 125, 137 ff, 146, 154, 177, 322, 326 f
Boniface VIII, 240
Bradwardine, 181*n*, 227
Brenz, 17, 289 f
Bryce, Lord, 48, 68, 246*n*, 249
Bucer, Martin, 265 f, 346*n*
Bugenhagen, 17, 257 f
Bullinger, 273, 276
Buridanus, 182

Caerularius, 54
Calvin, 17, 250, 269 ff, 278 ff, 297 ff 317, 322, 334, 344 f, 350*n*, 352
Canisius, 307
Canus, 307
Capito, 264 f, 333
Carlstadt, 252
Caroli, 278
Charlemagne, 28, 35, 38, 42, 45, 48, 51, 55
Charles V, 258, 262
Charles IX, 274
Charles the Bald, 63
Charles Martel, 29
Chemnitz, Martin, 293 ff, 307, 330, 350
Clement IV, 176
Colet, John, 175, 241 ff
Colonna, 169*n*
Contarini, 255*n*
Cranmer, 265
Crell, 303
Cruciger, Kaspar, 256 f
Cyril of Alexandria, 151
Cyril of Jerusalem, 30*n*, 189*n*

Didymus, 58
Dionysius, (pseudo-), 65
Duns Scotus, 173, 177 ff, 181 f, 192 f
Durandus, 49*n*, 123, 173, 181 ff, 193, 195, 321, 331, 344, 349*n*

Eckhart, 67, 141, 195, 212, 214 ff, 220
Elipandus, 31 ff, 36 f, 49
Elizabeth, Queen, 281
Elten, Gerhard, 233 f

Episcopius, 226n, 350n
Erasmus, 241, 244 f, 250, 341
Erdmann, Prof J E , 28, 64, 96n, 108, 111, 116, 148n, 178n, 182, 199 f, 203 f, 219n
Erigena, Scotus, 63 ff, 68, 70, 79, 82 f, 200, 324
Estius, 191n
Etherius, 32 ff
Eugenius IV (Condulmieri), 200n

Faber, Jacobus, 237 f, 242, 347
Felix of Urgel, 32 f, 35 ff, 49
Fisher, Dr G P , 12n, 21n, 81n, 96n, 102
Fisher, John, 243
Flacius, Matthias, 291 f
Francis of Assisi, 126, 137
Francis of Sales, 307
Frederick III, 276
Fulgentius, 309

Gairdner, W H T , 327n
Galatinus, 193
Gardner, A , 65n
Gaskoin, C J B , 46n
Gennadius II (Scholarios), 17, 193, 224 f
Gentilis, Valentino, 271, 279
Gerhohus, 116n, 338
Gerson, John, 125, 182n, 195 ff, 198 f, 227
Gibbon, 48n, 50, 54n, 127n, 142n, 144, 299n, 327
Gilbert of Poitiers, 89, 96 ff, 108, 141, 212n, 329, 337
Goethe, 81
Gottschalk, 60, 63
Gratian, 110
Grau, Rudolf F , 288n
Green, J R , 227n, 243n
Gregory I (the Great), 16, 23, 49n, 352
Gregory VII, 71, 79
Gregory of Nazianzus, 14n
Guitmund, 73 ff

Hallam, Dr Henry, 284n, 345n, 353n
Hare, Julius Charles, 17n, 69n
Harnack, A , 15 f, 49n, 55, 59, 64n, 69, 82n, 96n, 125, 146n, 154, 249, 253, 303, 327n, 352n
Heber, Bp Reginald, 302n
Henry II, 70n
Henry VIII, 281
Hieronymus, 58
Hilary, 113, 151n
Hildebert, 105 ff, 130
Hildefonsus, 25 ff, 47, 318n, 332 f
Hincmar, 55, 60 ff, 86

Homer, 244
Hugh of St Victor, 105, 110, 129 ff
Huss, John, 17, 174, 229 ff

Ignatius, 21
Illingworth, J R , 321n
Inge, Dean W. R , 14n, 66 f, 125, 139n, 174n, 214 f, 250, 339n, 353n
Innocent III, 79, 110, 121, 124
Isidore, 23 ff, 35, 47, 50

Joachim of Floris, 116, 121 ff, 126, 135 ff
John VIII, 62
John of Damascus, 15 f, 51 f, 142, 166, 226, 326
John of Salisbury, 110n
John of Wesel, 17, 233 f
Junius, Johannes, 273, 275, 279, 301n, 330

Kűnneth, Johannes T , 89 f

Lanfranc, 70 ff, 89
Lascaris, 144 f
Leander, 24
Leidradus, 36 ff, 343
Leo III, 39, 48 ff, 52 f, 223
Leo the Isaurian, 51
Lessing, 12n
Lombardus, Petrus, 13, 81, 105, 109 ff, 121 ff, 129, 135, 147, 184, 232, 293, 331, 333n, 335, 339n
Lullus, Raimundus, 169n
Luther, 15, 234, 239, 243 f, 246, 249 f, 252 ff, 257 ff, 262 ff, 268, 279, 296, 335, 344 ff, 350, 532
Lychetus, 178n

Macedonius, 97, 159, 256, 329
Mahomet, 23, 79n, 299n
Major, Georg, 288, 290 f
Maldonatus, 307 ff, 323, 342, 347
Marsilius of Inghen, 182
Melanchthon, 242, 249 f, 253 ff, 257 ff, 265, 299, 330, 346n, 350
Migetius, 31
Milman, Dean H H , 28n
Moberly, Prof R C , 12, 14n
More, Sir Thomas, 241, 243 f
Myconius, 267

Nicephorus, 52
Nicholas I, 53 f
Nicholas V, 240
Nicholas of Menthone, 143
Nicolas of Clémanges, 198 f
Nicolas of Cusa, 23n, 195n, 199 ff, 255, 321 f, 331 f, 336, 347 ff
Nicolas of Lyra, 180 f, 208
Nitzsch, 17, 69n

Occam, William of, 173, 178n, 181 ff, 227
Ochino, 297
Oecolampadius, 263 f, 267
Origen, 11n, 225n
Osiander, Andreas, 288 f
Owen, John, 302n

Palaeologus I, John, 223
Palaeologus II, John, 223, 225
Palaeologus, Michael, 142
Paterson, Prof W P, 12n, 82n, 134n, 279n, 305n, 331n
Paul of Samosata, 256
Paulinus of Aquileia, 35 f
Pearson, Bp, 49n, 62, 327n
Petrarch, 240
Philip II, 275
Photinus, 256
Photius, 52 ff, 55, 61
Picavet, F, 90n
Pius II, 241n
Pius IV, 306
Plato, 81, 177, 240 f, 244
Pope, Dr W. B, 82, 127n, 214n, 305n, 323n, 327n, 346 f, 349 f, 353n
Porphyry, 177
Pullus, Robertus, 105 ff, 110, 114

Radbertus, 55, 58 ff, 63, 71 f, 345
Ratramnus, 55, 73
Raymond of Sabunde, 199
Reuchlin, 241 f, 253, 322
Richard of St Victor, 129, 131 ff, 148
Rienzi, 240
Roscellin, 85, 89 ff, 103, 127, 318, 337
Rupert of Cologne, 141n
Ruysbroek, 214, 218 ff, 342, 348 f

Sabatier, Auguste, 12, 250n, 353
Sabellius, 57, 236
Saulnier, F, 90n

Savonarola, 235 ff, 240, 242
Schaff, Prof Philip, 16
Schmalz, 303
Schwenkfeld, 250
Seeley, Sir J R, 281n
Servetus, 17, 270 f, 274, 279, 297 ff
Smeaton, Dr, 328
Socinus, Faustus, 16 f, 273, 279, 299 ff
Socinus, Laelius, 299
Soto, Dominicus, 191n
Sprenger, 233n
Strigel, Victorinus, 288, 292 f, 341
Suso, 214 ff
Swete, Prof H B, 11, 13n, 21n, 24 f, 49n, 52n, 54, 151n, 187n, 215n, 323, 327n, 341n, 343

Tarnovius, 301n
Tauler, 141, 214 f, 217 f, 353
Theodoret, 312, 327n
Theodulf of Orleans, 23, 55 ff, 59
Theophylact, 143 ff
Trevor, Canon G, 124n
Tyndale, 17, 243, 281 f, 336, 343, 346n, 350n

Urban V, 223

Valla, Laurentius, 246n
Volkel, 303

Wagenmann, 182
Waldenses, the, 227
Wendelin, 191n
Wesley, John, 353 f
Wessel, John, 234 f, 242, 328, 337
Wiekus, 300 f
William of Champeaux, 91, 127, 129
William of Normandy, 71
Workman, Dr H B, 280n, 352n
Wyclif, John, 174, 227 ff, 327n

Zwingli, 17, 249 f, 262 ff, 268, 279, 335, 345 f, 350n

IV

Adoptionist discussion, the, 31 ff, 323–4
Alombrados, the, 250
Anabaptists, the, 250
Analogy, method of, in discussion of the Trinity, 14; used by Augustine, 15, in Isidore, 24; denied by Johannes Scotus Erigena, 64–5, use of, by Guitmund, 74; by Abelard, 94; criticized by Gilbert, 99, used by Alexander of Hales, 148, by Albertus Magnus, 149; criticized by Durandus, 184, used by Nicolas of Cusa, 202; by Erasmus, 245; its value, 321–2
Aristotelianism, 81, 149, 154, 210, 214, 215
Articles, the Thirty-nine, 283–4
Assurance, 218, 279–80, 286, 306, 313, 352–4
Augustinianism, 15, 54, 56, 57, 94, 124, 133, 279

Baptism, Christian, and the new birth, 27, 257, 276, 344–5
Baptism and the Trinity, 30, 37, 42, 45, 308–9
Birth of Jesus, the, and the Spirit, 36, 308, 337 f
Bond, the Holy Spirit the, 50, 61, 118–9, 187, 196, 197, 200, 204, 215, 216

Calvinism, 269 ff
Carlovingian Renaissance, the, 21 ff, 28, 31 ff, 63 ff
Catechisms. the Genevan, 270–1; the Racovian, 302–3, the Roman, 306–7
Christ, the Birth of, and the Spirit, 36, 308 See *Incarnation, Jesus*
Church, the, and the Spirit, 136–7, 264, 278, 284, 307, 341
Co-equality and co-eternity of the Spirit, 32, 38–9, 40, 46, 50, 65, 114, 131, 132, 134, 148, 317
Conceptualism of Abelard, the, 91
Confession: the trinitarian, of Albertus Magnus, 150; of Gennadius, 224; the orthodox, of the Eastern Church, 226, the Augsburg, 258 ff; the Tetrapolitan, 266; the Basel, 267, the First Helvetic, 267–8; Calvin's, 271; Beza's, 273–4; the Gallican, 274; the Belgic, 275–6; the Second Helvetic, 276 ff
Confirmation, 243, 346*n*. See also *Imposition of Hands*
Consubstantiality of the Spirit, 32, 34, 42, 43–4, 58, 97, 105, 131, 133, 254
Controversies in Protestantism, 288 ff
Council, guidance of the Spirit in a, 199, 204
Councils, of Basel, 204; of Constantinople, 53; of Constance, 230; of Ferrara and Florence, 223, of Frankfort, 51, the Lateran (Fourth), 121–4, 127, 135, of Nicaea (Second), 51, 234; of Rheims, 96, 103, of Toledo (Third), 51
Creative principle, the Spirit as, 134, 158, 209, 332–3
Creed of Constantinople, the, 41, 53

Deity of the Spirit, the, 34, 39, 75, 93, 155–7, 317–9
Descent of the Spirit, 59 See also *Gift of the Spirit, Mission*
Dispensations, the theory of, in Joachim of Floris, 135
Dominicans, the, 149 ff, 215, 217, 235 See also under *Albertus Magnus* and *Thomas Aquinas*
Dove, use of the figure of the, 59, 338

Eastern Church, the, 15, 51 ff, 122, 142 ff, 223 ff, 326
Effect of the Spirit on man, the, 159, 160 See also *Justification, Love, Sanctification, Work of the Spirit*
Election, 280
English Protestantism, the theology of, 281 ff
Eucharist, the See *Sacraments*
Evolution in the doctrine, 13 See Part V
Experimental side of religion, the, 83, 158–9, 175, 198, 208, 209, 251, 253, 322–3

Filioque Clause· 14 ff; in Isidore, 24, in Bede, 30; progress of

INDICES 365

controversy, 41 ff ; condemned in Eastern Church, 51 ff , in Theodulf, 57 , used in the West, 62 , why appropriated by the Schoolmen, 70 ; in Abelard, 93, in Hildebert, 106–7 , in Robertus Pullus, 109 ; in Petrus Lombardus, 112–3 ; adopted by Fourth Lateran Council, 122 ; in Hugh of St Victor, 130 ; truth of, presupposed by the fact that the Spirit is the Bond, 130 , in the Eastern Church, 142 ff ; in Thomas Aquinas, 161 ff ; in Durandus, 186 , in Nicolas of Cusa, 201 ; in Gennadius, 224–6 ; in Johann von Wesel, 233 ; defended by Bellarmine, 312 , surrendered by the Old Catholics, 226 , meaning of the controversy, 327–8
Franciscan Theology. See under *Alexander of Hales, Bonaventura, Duns Scotus*

Gifts of the Spirit, 136, 145
Gift of the Spirit to the disciples, in John xx , 45, 95, 288, 311–2, 341–2, at Pentecost, see *Pentecost*
Godhead of the Spirit, the, 317–9. See *Deity*

Hands, the laying on of. See *Imposition of Hands*
Heresy Johannes Scotus Erigena accused of, 63 ff , in Berengarius, 73 ; in Roscellin, 89 ff ; in Abelard, 91 ff , in Gilbert, 96 ff ; of Joachim, 121, 135 ff , of Servetus, 297 ff , of Socinus, 299
Homilies, Second Book of, 284 ff
Humanism, 174, 240 ff ; influence on the Reformation divines, 249, 254, 262, 263, 269, 273

Iconoclastic controversy, 51
Illuminati, the, 250
Illumination by the Spirit, 210. See *Truth*
Immanence of the Spirit, taught by Hildefonsus, 26 , by Gerson, 197 ; by Eckhart, 215 ; by Ruysbroek, 219
Imposition of Hands, and the Gift of the Spirit, 38, 42, 136, 266, 346*n*
Incarnation, the, and the Spirit, 25, 307, 337–8 , whole Trinity engaged in, 26–7, 121
Indwelling of the Spirit in the soul, 197, 218, 221, 256, 259, 263, 275, 282, 285, 322

Inspiration, work of the Spirit in, 136, 198–9, 217, 265–6, 267–8, 334 ff. See also *Scriptures*

Jesus : the fact of Jesus the basis of the doctrine of the Trinity, 327–8 See also *Christ, Incarnation*
Justification, and the Spirit, 207, 208, 260–1, 263, 270, 279, 282, 305, 347 ff

Love for God, cultivated in man by the Spirit, 159, 196, 340, 348
Love of God, the Spirit the, 18, 94, 106, 118, 119, 129, 138, 139, 159, 178, 215, 218 See *Bond*
Lutheranism, 252 ff, 288 ff

Mathematical analogies, 176, 202
Mission of the Spirit , in Theodulf, 57–8 , in Anselm, 87 , in Richard of St Victor, 134 ; in Theophylact, 144 , in Thomas Aquinas, 168 , in Durandus, 189 ; Summary, 339–342
Modalism, charged against Abelard, 91, 96 , tendency to, in Gilbert, 104
Mohammedanism, spread of, 28–9 ; influence of, 31, 299 , examined by Nicolas of Cusa, 211 See also 256
Moral effect of the Spirit, 59, 136, 207, 220, 243
Mysticism, in Johannes Scotus Erigena, 65–67 , Scholastic, 80–1, 125 ff, 137, 141 , in Gerson, 196 ; German, 173–4, 212, 214 ff ; testimony of, to Deity of the Spirit, 319

Neoplatonism, in Johannes Scotus Erigena, 63 ff
Nicaea, Second Council of, 51, 234
Nominalism, 80 ff, 89 ff, 177, 181 ff, 191 ff, 252

Omnipotence of the Spirit, 34
Omnipresence of the Spirit, 115–6, 264, 340

Pentecost, the meaning of, 45, 218, 301–11, 342
Personality of the Spirit, 17, 34, 92, 152, 157, 164–5, 190, 254–5, 257 ; denied by Servetus, 298–9 ; by Socinus, 300–1 , by the Polish Socinians, 302–3 ; Summary, 329–31
Philippist theology, 253 ff, 290, 292 ff

Predestination, in Beza and the Gallican Confession, 274; in Calvin, 279; in the Thirty-nine Articles, 283-4, 286

Procession, the, of the Spirit (see also *Filioque Clause*): In Isidore, 25; in Elipandus, 32; in Hincmar, 62; in Anselm, 86; in Abelard, 92, in Hildebert, 106-7, in Petrus Lombardus, 112-3, in Bernard, 128, in Hugh, 133, in Richard of St Victor, 130; in Bonaventura, 139-40, in Alexander of Hales, 147, in Albertus Magnus, 150-2, in Durandus, 186 ff, in Huss, 231; Summary of the development of the doctrine, 324 ff; meaning of the controversy, 327-8

Procession of the Spirit, distinguished from the generation of the Son, 27, 36, 178, 232, 257, 321

Quaternity in God, charge brought against Petrus Lombardus of teaching, 116, 122-4, 135; impossible, 132-3

Rationalists, the Scholastic, 89 ff
Realism, and Nominalism, 80 ff, Realism of Gilbert of Poitiers, 96 ff, 103-4
Reality of Evil, denied in Johannes Scotus Erigena, 65
Reformation theology, 15, 16, 17, 249, 252 ff
Regeneration, and the Spirit, 209, 258, 260, 271, 276, 347-9
Renaissance, the, 174, 235, 249 See also *Humanism*
Renaissance, the Carlovingian, 21 ff, 28, 31 ff, 63 ff

Sabellianism, opposed by Bede, 28; tendency towards in Realism, 82; Roscellin liable to charge of, 90
Sacraments, the, 243, 257, 259, 263, 268, 274-5, 276, 278-9, 284, 305-6, 343-6
Sanctification and the Spirit, 36, 155-6, 208, 213, 255, 265-6, 279, 282, 285, 296, 305, 340, 347-51

Saxon Theology, embodied in Bede, 28
Scholasticism, 21, 68 ff, 79 ff, height of, 146 ff
Scriptures, the, inspired by the Spirit, 136, 198-9, 217, 265-6, 267, 268, 334 ff; place in human experience, 281-2; reliance on, 41, 144-5, 155 ff, 238, 250
Socinianism, 16, 297-303
'Spiration,' 161, 164, 168, 181, 192, 193
Summists, the, 108 ff, 119-20
Synergist controversy, the, 255, 291 ff, 351

Tradition, respect for, in Alcuin, 42; the Spirit speaks through, 217; exaltation of, in the Roman Church, 305, 313
Trinity, analogies of the, 14, 106. See *Analogy*. For general treatment of the subject see *Filioque, Unity, Procession, Bond*, etc; and pp 320 ff
Trinity, in relation to the Incarnation, 26 121
Tritheism, tendency towards, in Nominalism, 82, 89-90
Truth, the Spirit the teacher of, 73, 180, 210, 334

Unity of God, stress on, 26, 28, 34, 39, 65, 68, 72, 75, 84, 97, 111, 130, 131, 147, 203, 323

Victorine Theology, the, 137 See *Hugh* and *Richard of St Victor*

Will of God, the, the source of the Spirit, 192
Will of man, the, and the Spirit, 291, 292, 293, 349-51. See *Synergist controversy, Augustinianism*
Witness of the Spirit, the, 352-4. See also *Assurance*
Work of the Holy Spirit, the, 17, 119, 158-9, 207, 213, 276, 282, 307. See also *Justification, Regeneration*, and *Sanctification*

Zwinglianism, 262 ff

www.ingramcontent.com/pod-product-compliance
Lightning Source LLC
Chambersburg PA
CBHW071226230426
43668CB00011B/1326